Run Rabbit Run

The Life, The Legend, and The Legacy

of Edna "Rabbit" Murray

"The Kissing Bandit"

as told by her Granddaughter

PAM PADEN TIPPET

Table Of Contents

Players List

Family:

Nicholas Drew (N. D.) "Charles" Stanley – Edna Stanley's father

Louie Nettie "Lou" Rosadell Stanley (nee Waddell) –
   Edna Stanley's mother

Dora Vinita "Doris" Stanley – Edna Stanley's sister

Kenneth Farrell – Doris' (nee Stanley) first husband

---- Mott Clinton "'Little' Mott" Farrell
   son of Kenneth and Doris Farrell

Earl G. Simpson – Doris' (nee Stanley) second husband

Emory Connell – Doris' (nee Stanley) third husband

Earl Stuchlik – Doris' (nee Stanley) fourth husband

James B. "Jay" McCormick – Doris' (nee Stanley) fifth husband

Fred Stanley – Edna Stanley's brother

Lucille Stanley – wife of Fred Stanley

Gloyd Augusta "Ginney" Stanley – Edna Stanley's brother

Jewel Stanley (nee Sullivan) – wife of Gloyd "Ginney" Stanley

---- William James "Bill" Stanley
   son of Gloyd "Ginney" and Jewel Stanley

Harry Clinton Stanley – Edna Stanley's brother

Mary "Sybil" Stanley – wife of Harry Clinton Stanley

Family (continued):

Martha "Edna" Murray (nee Stanley)

---- (aka "Rabbit" and "The Kissing Bandit")

George Taylor Paden – Edna's (nee Stanley) first husband

---- Preston LeRoy Paden – son of George and Edna Paden

---- Naomi Bell Paden (nee Keith) – wife of Preston LeRoy Paden

---- Pamela Lou Paden – daughter of Preston and Naomi Paden

Walter Price – Edna's (nee Stanley) second husband

"Diamond Joe" Sullivan – Edna's (nee Stanley) third husband

Jack Murray – Edna's (nee Stanley) fourth husband

Carl Memmott – Edna's (nee Stanley) fifth husband

Henry "Hank" Potter – Edna's (nee Stanley) sixth husband

Mott Stanley – Edna Stanley's brother

Helen Stanley (nee Hemphill) – wife of Mott Stanley

Barker-Karpis Gang Members:

George Barker – Arizona Donnie Clark "Kate" Barker's husband

Arizona Donnie Clark "Kate" Barker – (aka "Mother" and "Ma")

---- Arthur "Doc" Barker – son of George and "Kate" Barker

---- Fred "Freddie" Barker – son of George and "Kate" Barker

William Bryan (Byron) Bolton – (aka Monty Carter)

Wynona Burdette – girlfriend of Harry Campbell

Harry "Buddy" Campbell

Earl Christman

Volney Everett "Curly" Davis – Edna's sweetheart

Dolores Delaney – girlfriend of Alvin Karpis

Jess Doyle – Doris' sweetheart

Myrtle Eaton – girlfriend of William "Bill" Weaver

Helen Ferguson – girlfriend of Earl Christman

Russell "Rusty" Gibson – (aka Roy "Slim" Gray)

Clara Fisher Gibson – wife of Russell Gibson

Fred Goetz – (aka "Shotgun" George Zeigler)

Irene Goetz (nee Dorsey) – girlfriend/wife of Fred Goetz

Eddie Green

Bessie Green – wife of Eddie Green

Paula Harmon – girlfriend of Freddie Barker

William J. "Willie" Harrison

Barker-Karpis Gang Members (continued):

Alvin "Slim" Karpis – (aka "Ray" Karpis and "Creepy" Karpis)

Vivian Mathis – girlfriend of Verne Miller

Verne Miller

Joseph "Doc" Moran

Frank "Jelly" Nash

Frances Nash (nee Luce) – girlfriend/wife of Frank "Jelly" Nash

Harry "Dutch" Sawyer

Gladys Sawyer – wife of Harry Sawyer

William "Bill" Weaver – (alias for Phoenix Donald)

James J. Wilson – nephew of Doctor Joseph "Doc" Moran

Introduction

Written for my daughter, Stacy Tonette Tippet Carver, and for my Grandson, Chase Charles Carver, this story is true, in all respects, to the best of my ability to tell it.

It's been a long time coming, for me to be able to publicly discuss the details of my daddy's family; especially his mother — and my grandma, Martha Edna Stanley — better known as Edna Murray.

I've always known about Edna, from as far back as I can remember. She never made any bones about her actions. In fact, she usually spoke of them in a rather proud and reminiscing way. She told me why she was called "The Kissing Bandit," and how she broke out of prison so many times that she was given the nickname of "Rabbit." I guess she told me just about everything she ever did. Some of it stuck with me forever and some of it went in one ear and out the other. That's the way it was.

Ever since the movie about Bonnie (Parker) & Clyde (Barrow) premiered in 1967, I had thought that Grandma Edna's story would make a good book or movie. But who was I to air the family laundry, and what would people think about my family? But there comes a point in life when it becomes evident that everyone is responsible for their own actions, and not those of their relatives. If I decided to tell the secrets that Grandma Edna told me, I think she would be proud.

Now when it comes to my daddy, Preston LeRoy Paden — that's a whole different story. I was daddy's little girl. But don't get me wrong. Daddy never tried to cover up anything as far as I can tell, when I remember back. In fact, maybe he did tell me everything there was to know about him. Kids kind of remember the best things — the best — you know. And so it was with daddy and me. I knew he was an ornery little kid in Cardin, Oklahoma, growing up in the badlands of an uncivilized part of the country. I knew his grandpa, who raised him, made him be tough, and would have kicked his butt if he ever heard of him backing away from a fight. I knew he had gone to jail for fighting, and later for hauling liquor during Prohibition. I knew he had run with his mother's notorious Barker-Karpis Gang during the "Gangster Era," but so what? He didn't do anything that bad — not my daddy.

The biggest shock of my life came after I had decided to write grandma's story and was doing research on the Internet. Someone said, "Edna Murray had a son, Preston, who was sentenced to life in prison for the murder of a Night Marshal." I was so horrified. I said under my breath, "You are so full of crap — you don't know what the hell you are talking about." I was in shock for about a week. I did some more research. It was true. Although my daddy did not fire the shot, he was part of a group of four intoxicated hoodlums who were not even doing a good job of robbing a safe, when a Night Marshal came upon the scene and was fatally wounded. You never know what "diggin' up bones" is going to reveal.

For so many reasons, I feel obligated to pass on the stories I know, so that my daughter and grandson will know the true history of my Grandma Edna and her family — their family — to the best of my knowledge.

Much of my story about Grandma Edna and her family comes from my memories as a child, when I would listen to her tell me so many of the exciting stories in her life. I can't always remember what I had for breakfast in the morning, but I remember parts of my childhood like it was yesterday.

I have an even greater respect for authors than before, because I now know, without a doubt, how difficult it can be to relate these true and deep-rooted personal thoughts to their readers.

I actually started writing this book about Grandma Edna back in 1979. We were living just outside of Aberdeen, Scotland, while my husband, Casey, was working offshore. Our daughter was in school all day, with what there was of it. The sun didn't come up until about 10:30 a.m., and was down again by 3:30 p.m. Not only that, it rained horizontally every day with winds that would chill you to the bone. Out of boredom, and without any resources for verifying my research, I started writing in a huge journal. It was at least 26 years later when I dragged out that old journal. I surprised myself when I compared what I had written, off the top of my head, to the research that I was gathering. My memory had been amazingly accurate. Therefore, I do trust much of what I can remember from childhood.

It has been one of my goals to prove to myself that my memory has served me well and that I am telling this story as truthfully — and as accurately — as it can be told. When stories that Edna, herself, told to various newspapers or magazines signal red flags for me, I know that she was sugar-coating the truth in order to protect someone else. I am privileged in that respect, because quite often I have heard the real story from the one who lived it. Grandma Edna pretty much told it straight when talking to her family in later years. She never seemed to have any remorse for her past and reminisced about it until the end of her life. I know. I am her granddaughter and I was there to listen.

Pam Paden Tippet

Prologue

Edna didn't know how much more she could take. She was sick — and she was exhausted. The doctor had told her she was in need of an operation, and that she might have cancer, but he needed her medical history from her previous doctor. Medical history — what a joke, she thought! When you're on the lam, you can't have any kind of history — or even your own name, a home, or anything else to call your own.

Every inch of this damned bumpy back road they were on was making her feel as if whatever was left of her female organs — what hadn't been eaten up with disease — was falling out. Edna thought she must surely have gonorrhea. Why wouldn't she, what with Volney Davis running around with other women behind her back as he had so often done? And where the hell was he, anyway? And what was she supposed to do with him just "up and disappearing" like that? He had to have been arrested — why else would he not have come back to their apartment in Kansas City? And Doris, her little sister — she was supposed to be "the smart one" in the family. What the hell was she trying to pull when she shot that woman? This was surely going to be the end for all of them. Edna just had a "gut feeling" that the end was near. They would either be gunned down by the G-men — or captured — and she would be returned to prison for the fourth time. She wasn't sure she could survive being locked up again since she wasn't as young as she had been the many times before, and her health had also deteriorated in the meantime.

Jess Doyle had a worried look on his face as he tried to dodge the potholes in the road that had been carved by winter's weather. He most certainly hadn't wanted to leave Doris behind in the Kansas City Jail. He was crazy in love with her — hell, all the guys that Doris had been with were in love with her! Edna wished Volney loved her as much as Jess loved Doris. "Rabbit," Jess said to Edna, "you got your pistol with ya, don't cha?" "Yeah Jess, I got it," Edna answered. She wondered why he asked, but then again, she knew — all too well — why. They were headed to the home of her brother, Harry Stanley, in Pittsburg, Kansas. It hadn't been safe hanging around in Kansas City since the town was crawling with G-men who knew the gang was there. With Doris — and probably Volney too — under arrest, Jess Doyle and Edna were next in line. They just needed a place to lie low and rest up for a while. The last thing Edna wanted was to have a shoot-out with Hoover's boys, but if the situation arose, she would have "Jess' back" until her dying breath. They both knew their day was coming soon — it was just a matter of time.

Chapter 01: Grandma Edna's Wardrobe Trunk

"Mama," I squealed, "Grandma's trunk is here." My mama, Naomi Paden, grumbled something under her breath that I thought might have included a curse word as she reached for her purse to pay the delivery charges on Grandma Edna's trunk. I was real proud of myself, for it was I who had spotted the big truck rolling up in front of our apartment building in Sapulpa, Oklahoma, and ran up to the truck to investigate its purpose for being there. And it was I who, when asked if I knew where the Preston Paden residence was, answered, "Yes sir, just follow me," directing them up the steep flight of stairs and down the long, dimly lit hall to the apartment at the very end that was ours. It was the early part of July in 1954, and I was anxiously waiting to become 8 years old in August. Small framed and thin, wearing long, dishwater-blonde braids, with rather large brown eyes and ears that stuck out farther than I wished they did, I was fidgeting with excitement as mama paid the delivery men. "When is grandma getting here, I asked her. "I didn't even know she was on her way, Pammy," my mama answered, in a tone that let me know that she wasn't as pleased as I was about grandma's visit. Running into our tiny living room where my daddy was lying on the couch, holding a mask over his face and breathing air from his oxygen tank, I started quizzing him about grandma's arrival. "I don't know for sure, Pammy Lou. I guess we will find out when she gets here." That's always the way it was with Grandma Edna. Not only was her arrival time a mystery, there also seemed to be a lot of things about her that I wasn't supposed to know about or even hear about.

I ran back to my room in our tiny two-bedroom apartment to admire grandma's trunk once the delivery men brought it in. There was always something about that trunk that fascinated me. I had never seen another like it. Grandma called it a "wardrobe" trunk. I had remembered that from the last time I had seen it. It was gray, stood on one end, and the top opened up to reveal a mirror and small dressing table with compartments for hairbrushes, combs, makeup, hairpins, and so on. When the main part of the trunk opened out, it revealed a closet on the left side with hangers for hang-up clothes, and a chest of drawers on the right side with five big drawers for folded clothes. I thought it probably also held lots of secrets. My mama, obviously, had different thoughts about it. I can still remember some of her comments about it being sprawled out in the middle of the room, and was in everybody's way. Grandma Edna did have a unique way of making herself feel at home. But I enjoyed her visits, and thought she was funny — especially after she had consumed a few beers and became talkative. You just never knew what she might say.

The very first memory I have of grandma's trunk was the summer of 1952, when she came to visit us in Sapulpa, Oklahoma. Daddy was still able to work and drive at that time. We had a Chevy Coupe that I believe was a 1947 model. I remember that it was on a day in August — hot and humid — when daddy, along with mama and I, drove to the Tulsa, Oklahoma, airport to pick up grandma. Daddy's health was beginning to fail even to the point that I could detect it. He was starting to struggle with each breath, lifting his shoulders a little in order to assist himself when he would inhale. Even light physical exertion would cause him to have to use his nebulizer, a funny-looking thing with a plug that, when removed, left a hole for putting in his medication, called asthmanefrin. It had a hose with a bulb on the end that he pumped, in order to create a mist of medication from the front of it. He would breathe in the mist through his mouth. This was a crude version of today's inhaler. I always hated it when he had to use that thing. For one reason, I was afraid that my daddy couldn't get his breath, or was in pain, or might even die. And for another, I was a little embarrassed when people would stare at us in public when he was using it. But, other than having lost a little weight, daddy was still pretty much like I had always known him to be. He had always been slender, and was actually about 5'7" or 5'8" in height, even though he thought that he was 5'9" tall. He always kept himself impeccably dressed, with his hair neatly combed, his face clean-shaven, and all around, he was always very nicely groomed. His eyes were a dark gray, and his hair, a lighter shade of brown. He had a proud and distinctive Cherokee Indian shape to his nose, and a Cheshire grin that made you wonder what he was up to. He had always taken the time to listen to me. He always found time to tell me things that he

Pammy Lou sitting at the lumber yard across from our apartment building at 313½ E. Hobson, Sapulpa, Oklahoma.

believed to be important for me to know, and I was always daddy's little girl."

Mama was sitting in the front seat with daddy. Other than work, he hardly ever went any place without mama. They

were a team, like "bread and butter" or "peanut butter and jelly."
Mama, too, had her share of health problems, but she never complained. Mama was a pretty lady — very slender — standing
5'6" which was considered rather tall for a lady back then. She
had brown hair that seemed to turn red when in the sunshine.
Her eyes were dark brown. She also had a somewhat distinctive
Cherokee Indian shape to her nose from her father's side of her
family and, although her lips were rather thin, she had a beautiful
smile with pearly white teeth. I always thought my mama was a
very beautiful woman.

Upon our arrival at the airport, I will never forget how
grandma looked. Having started her journey from her home in
San Francisco, California, where the weather had been considerably cooler, Grandma Edna stepped off the plane in Tulsa, —
"dressed to the nines" — as she walked onto a steaming airport
runway that was, as I recall, 107 degrees that day. Not very tall,
standing about 5'1½" or so, and not heavy at all — maybe 120
pounds, but a little plump in the rear section — grandma was
wearing a light blue suit — baby blue seemed to be her favorite
color — with a creamy chiffon blouse tied at the neck into a big
bow. She was wearing nylon stockings and beige wedge sandals.
She often wore open-toed shoes. I remember that because she
had ugly toenails that were really thick, and I think enclosed-toe
shoes hurt her toes. To top it all off, atop her reddish-brown hair
sat a little baby blue hat that had a net on it. I don't think I had
ever seen a hat quite like that before — not in Sapulpa, Oklahoma,
for sure — and especially not during a heat wave. The next thing
that happened I will never forget. Grandma started swearing,
"My God, I'm gonna have a damn heatstroke. I should have
known better than to come to Oklahoma in goddamn August.

4

Just how hot is it, anyway? What's the damn temperature here? I can't believe people live in this (weather). You have to be crazy. Let me get some of these clothes off before I die. Hell, it was cool when I left 'Frisco!"

"Just where did you think you were going, mom? You knew it would be like this in August, didn't you," daddy asked, with a grin on his face. I still hadn't been able to close my mouth since it fell open when I first saw her. My mama was getting a laugh out of the whole ordeal as she sat in the front seat of the car in her pedal pushers and sleeveless blouse with her hair tied up off her neck with a little polka dot scarf. Grandma Edna had gotten into the back seat with me, yelling at daddy to "Get this hot son of a bitch moving and get some air in here before I die. I'm not used to this shit." I was dodging elbows and garments as my grandma threw off her blue hat, took off her suit jacket, untied her big bow and unbuttoned several buttons on her blouse before rolling up her sleeves as far as they would go. Next, she pulled up her skirt, grabbed the top of one of her nylons and started rolling it — garter and all — all the way down to her ankle, before pulling the whole stocking off and placing her bare foot into her high wedge heel sandal. Then the other stocking came off, followed by more complaining and swearing. Searching around on the floorboard for something, she came up with her smashed hat from under her jacket, and started fanning herself while yelling at daddy, "Preston, stop at the first damn place you see where I can get a cold beer." And that's how I remember the arrival of grandma's trunk. That wouldn't be last time I would see it.

Chapter 02: N. D. "Charles" Stanley's Daughters

Martha Edna Stanley was grandma's given name. Born in the Flint Hills, at Diamond Creek, Chase County, Kansas, about four miles due west of Cottonwood Falls, she was named after her maternal grandmother, Martha Edna Bragg Waddell. Called "Edna" by her family, she had three older brothers and was also preceded by four siblings that didn't survive infancy. Her parents, Nicholas Drew Stanley and his wife, Louie Nettie, were farmers at the time of Edna's birth, on May 26, 1898.

Mr. Stanley, nicknamed "Charles," — having completed two years of college — was quite knowledgeable for a man of his day. He had a good head for business. He was also very close-minded, and was regarded as a stubborn man that few ever dared to cross.

Ten years younger than her husband, Louie Nettie was a hard-working, spunky, good-natured, and loving lady. She was 18 years old and working as a housekeeper when she and Charles married in Wayne County, Indiana, in 1886.

During their early years of marriage, Charles and Louie farmed in the Diamond Creek, Chase County, Kansas area. By 1910 they were living in Narcissa, Oklahoma, a tiny community in Ottawa County, Oklahoma, and they eventually settled in the small town of Cardin, Oklahoma.

Charles owned and operated a water route to the mining camps surrounding Cardin. His sons assisted him with the water route that was the only one in the area. For additional income, he purchased a number of shanties that he rented out to the miners.

My great grandpa "Charles" Stanley passed away before I was born, but I remember visiting my great grandma, Louie, in the modest, neatly kept home that they had shared in Cardin, Oklahoma. It was a small, yellow frame house that was one block north and two blocks east of the city hall.

Edna wasn't exactly averse to work, but she had her own plans of doing something other than the boring chores of helping around the house. As she grew older, she yearned for excitement and became increasingly resentful of her father's rules. She knew she was a cute little thing and had no trouble wrapping the boys around her finger. Her father didn't want her gallivanting around with older boys, and Edna seemed to get her greatest pleasures from defying him. Even worse, Edna's influence was starting to rub off on her sister — only two years younger — Dora Vinita, who was following closely in Edna's footsteps.

Born on July 20, 1900, at Diamond Creek, Chase County, Kansas, Dora Vinita Stanley was the ninth child born to Charles and Louie Stanley. With dark hair and big eyes, she was quick to catch on — and had a quick temper. Dora was definitely her father's daughter. Being the baby of the family for about four years, she wasn't exactly pleased with sharing her limelight with little brother, Gloyd Augusta Stanley — called "Ginney" — who was born on December 17, 1904. The nickname came from his contagious laugh that his father said sounded "… like a damned old guinea."

Dora, not unlike Edna, had visions of bigger and better things. And, as time would tell, these gals would run a close race of "Big Time" and "Big Trouble" in their lives.

Chapter 03: George & Edna Paden

Edna's father, Nicholas Drew "Charles" Stanley, although part Cherokee Indian himself, was known to say, "The only good Indian is a dead Indian." My daddy, Preston Paden, told me of his grandfather's comment on several occasions. Although my daddy appeared to laugh it off, it bothered him, and he resented his grandpa for making that comment.

It would be safe to say that one of my Grandma Edna's biggest attractions to my daddy's father was that he was, in part, a Native American Indian. This would have been the ultimate defiance of her father's wishes. By the time Edna was 17 years old, she had already married George Taylor Paden — a Cherokee Indian from Welch, Oklahoma — and had given birth to their son, Preston LeRoy Paden, and shortly later, she had taken George to court for desertion. They were married in Carthage, Missouri, in 1915, but it is doubtful that they ever lived together as man and wife. Why did George desert her? Maybe it was because she flirted with every man she ever saw — maybe it was due to the fact that his father-in-law would rather he be dead — or maybe, it was because she didn't bake cookies. All that is on record is that on January 3, 1916, a week after my daddy's birth — December 27, 1915 — Judge E. M. Probasco ordered George Paden, age 21, to pay a fine of $50 to his 17 year old wife, and to give her $2.50 per week thereafter, which was a considerable sum of money at that time. They eventually divorced a year later, on January 2, 1917.

Forced from the warmth of his mother's womb into the shocking chill of the room, slapped on his wet behind, and gasping for his first breath of air, little Preston LeRoy Paden entered screaming, into this cruel world. He just became one of the 100 million United States citizens living here at the time.

Ushered in by Doctor J. C. Jacobs, M. D., at 5:00 a.m. on December 27, 1915, in the small northeastern Oklahoma town of Miami, Preston was born to Martha Edna Stanley Paden, 17 years of age; and George Taylor Paden, 21 years of age.

Oklahoma had been a state for only 8 years, and was far from being civilized. The whole country was a mix of new technology and older ideals and customs. The Ford Motor Company had just rolled out its 1,000,000th automobile off the assembly line; the charter for the new Ku Klux Klan had just been accepted by the Superior Court in Fulton County Georgia; and practically the entire world was involved in, or about to be involved in, the war to end all wars, World War I. It was anybody's guess now as to what the future would bring.

Little Preston's mother, Edna, as everyone called her, had already ended her relationship with Preston's father even before she bore their child. George Paden was a Cherokee Indian farmer from Welch, Oklahoma, and most likely, he didn't anticipate fathering Edna's child in the first place. George and Edna in all likelihood, probably never lived together as man and wife. If they lived together at all, it was not for a very long period of time, as evidenced by the fact that Edna was living at home with her father and mother, in Cardin, Oklahoma, when she gave birth to her son. Except for a short period of time when Edna moved out on her own and took her son with her, Preston grew up in the home of his Grandma and Grandpa Stanley in Cardin, Oklahoma.

A couple of years after Preston's birth, his Aunt Doris, Edna's sister, gave birth to her son, Mott. "Little" was attached to his name in order to not confuse him with Edna's and Doris' older brother, Mott, whom he was named after. "Little" Mott also spent most of his childhood living with his grandparents, so Preston and "Little" Mott grew up together almost as brothers. Preston, being the older of the two, always felt responsible for taking care of "Little" Mott.

When, as a child, asking about my grandpa, George Paden, my parents told me who he was and where he lived, and I was satisfied with that. It wasn't until after I had reached adulthood that I chose to look him up. While I was running for the office of County Clerk for Labette County, Kansas, I was campaigning in the town of Chetopa and I knocked on the door of the retirement apartment where George and his wife, Frances, resided. I presumed that he had retired from his former position as a professional barber, since he had owned and operated a barbershop for most of his life.

After I introduced myself to him, I told Mr. Paden that I believed that he was my grandfather, and I could see right off the bat that my daddy resembled him considerably. He immediately began to deny that he had ever known an Edna Stanley, denied that he ever had a son named Preston Paden, and insisted I must have him confused with someone else. Yet he invited me inside, and seemed to welcome the visit. As I told my story as to why I believed him to be my grandfather, he would often look at his wife and shake his head — "No." But he was curious as to what had become of my Grandma Edna, and what my daddy was doing.

I visited with George and Frances for a while. She, too, had some questions for me. We then all exchanged information about our children and families. I told them that my daddy had died when I was 10 years old, and that my mother died on the same date 7 years later — and that I had just recently found out that Grandma Edna had died a few years after my mother died. I think I was feeling guilty that I had not contacted Grandma Edna for a long time prior to her death and that was maybe part of the reason why I wanted to look up my grandfather. I wasn't really surprised that he didn't want to admit to being married to grandma. I had heard that the one time that my daddy had looked him up, Grandpa George gave my daddy the cold shoulder. That was actually after I was born, when I was about 3 or 4 years old. I was in my late twenties when I heard about it from one of my daddy's confidants. We were in his place of business, celebrating my class reunion — my daddy's name came up, and my daddy's confidant told me how he remembered the time that my daddy went to see his father, and his father didn't want to have anything to do with him. I was saddened to hear that.

I was starting to feel uncomfortable, realizing now that my presence hadn't been welcomed with open arms, and possibly I had opened up a can of worms that George Paden was going to have to explain to Frances. I excused myself, and just couldn't help but say, "It was nice to meet you, Mr. Paden. Maybe I will find a grandpa that will claim me some day."

I left and after I got into my car, just as I reached for the ignition, George came running from his house and up to my car. I rolled down the window and he stuck his head in, and with big tears in his eyes — and I'll always remember this — he said, "I'm the guy you're looking for — I was married to your grandma."

I wasn't sure why it was so painful for him to admit that, and I felt pity in my heart for him. I said, "Well, don't cry, it's okay."

He was probably still a little bit in shock at the revelation of his previously never-before-seen granddaughter. He went on to tell me that he and Edna were young and things just didn't work out for them. He indicated that the only reason they ever got married was because she was expecting a baby. And I think he said that they never lived together. He didn't say anything bad about her, but he said that the last he had heard of her, she had taken off with some outlaw named "Murray." I said, "Yes, that would be grandma." He said that Frances knew all about Edna, but I don't think their children did at that time. We talked for a bit longer and he asked me to come back and bring my husband and daughter and visit him and his wife. I said I would, but I never did. I guess I always thought there would be plenty of time for that.

My Grandfather, George Taylor Paden, was born in Indian Territory on November 1, 1894 — and passed away on December 8, 1983, at the Chetopa Nursing Home in Chetopa, Kansas. He is buried in the Oak Hill Cemetery, also in Chetopa, Kansas.

After George Paden had died, I spoke with one of George's sons, who was daddy's half-brother, and found him to be a very likable fellow. George raised a nice family and it is understandable why he would want to get on with his life, and stay clear of Edna. I still, to this day, do not know where I stand on the issue of how George dealt with daddy. With a gangster moll for a mom — and a grandpa who believed that "The only good Indian is a dead Indian" — this child lived in an environment that might have posed some serious danger for George. But growing up not knowing, or even seeing, his father, was harder on my daddy than he would ever let on. In addition, he had been told by his mother that his father had deserted them — and by his grandpa, that his father was no good.

Chapter 04: Husbands Two, Three — And More

A short time after divorcing George Paden, Martha Edna Stanley Paden married Walter Price, who was said to be a farmer, that is, when he wasn't into certain questionable activities in, and near, Cardin, Oklahoma. This marriage, too, didn't last long, as records indicate that they were divorced by 1920, which would indicate that Edna was twice married and divorced by the age of 22.

Edna's true heartthrob, the one man she could never stay away from or get over, was Volney Davis. Unable to find work in Cardin, Edna went to Sapulpa, Oklahoma, where she had some friends. Being in the heart of the oil fields, Sapulpa was booming at the time. Wages were good and finding a job was easy. Edna had been working for about a year as a waitress at the Imperial Café, 9 North Main Street, when she first met Volney Davis in 1921. He introduced himself to her as Freddie Jackson, and she immediately started calling him "Curly," because of his thick head of curly hair. He put the "charm offensive" on Edna from the start and they soon became sweethearts. They were a good-looking couple that turned heads everywhere they went. Both had a mischievous and daring nature and they seemed to feed off the energy of each other. Edna was attractive and petite, with small, firm breasts, and a nice well-rounded behind. Volney was handsome, with curly chestnut brown hair, and a big grin that showed off his pearly whites. At the time, Edna was 23 years old and Volney was only 19 years old — still just a kid. According to Edna, the first time she knew his real name was when police officers came to her apartment and asked him who he was. When Volney told them that his name was Freddie Jackson, she was informed by the police that she was mistaken, and that he was, in fact, Volney Davis. Edna continued to call him "Curly Jackson" for the rest of her years, probably just to aggravate him as much as anything else. According to Edna, it was only after their courtship was in full bloom, and she had fallen in love with him, that she found out he was wanted by the law. By that time, she didn't care what he had done in the past. She would be loving him always, no matter what he had done. Edna continued seeing Volney, knowing he was on the lam, and in so doing, put herself in continuous jeopardy of the law. Actually, it was just that element of danger that made the act of being with him all the more exciting.

Volney Davis – 17 years old "Courtesy of Bob Winter"

Once, when they were out for a ride, the police caught sight of them. Seeing that they were being followed, Volney pushed the accelerator to the floorboards. He knew if he didn't shake the police, he was doomed to be spending the rest of his life in prison. Edna said the car nearly shook to pieces, bouncing along the road at breakneck speeds. Finally they ditched the police, who, according to Edna, didn't have the nerve to drive like Volney did. After Volney dropped her off a few blocks from her apartment, she spent a sleepless night with her heart pounding from an adrenaline rush.

Still feeling a little nervous and shaky the next morning at work, she nearly had a stroke when she saw Volney walk in the front door of the café. To make matters worse, there was a

16

plainclothes policeman sitting right in front of her at the counter having coffee. "Hello, honey," Volney said to her. "How are you feeling today?" For a second, Edna couldn't even get her mouth to utter a sound. Then, seeing that the plainclothes officer was staring at Volney and obviously recognized him, she screamed out, "He's a copper. Run." And like a flash, Volney ran out through the door and into the crowded street. The officer had his gun drawn, but couldn't fire into the crowd of people. That was another lucky break for Volney. Edna said, "The copper was so irritated with me that he convinced my boss to fire me." She didn't even care that it meant the loss of her job. Edna was with Volney again that night.

Volney Davis grew up in a large and — what he considered — a loving family. He was born on January 29, 1902, in the Cherokee Nation portion of Indian Territory, in the area that became Tahlequah, Oklahoma. His father, Rodney E. Davis, and his mother, Amanda S. Davis, who was about ten years younger than Rodney, had five other children, all girls. Volney's sisters were Mildred, Bertha, Ruby, Irene and Beulah. Beulah suffered from mental problems and, after she married, was eventually committed to the Oklahoma Hospital for the Insane at Vinita, Oklahoma.

The family moved to Tulsa, Oklahoma, close to an area that has been referred to as the "Cradle of Crime." Hanging out with the hoodlums of the "Central Park Gang," Volney was befriended by the likes of Harry Campbell and Freddie and Arthur "Doc" Barker, the sons of Kate and George Barker. Volney spent so much time with the Barkers that Kate considered him one of her boys, and Volney called her "mother," just as her own sons did. The first time that Volney spent any time behind bars was on February 5, 1919, right after his 17th birthday, when he was charged with grand larceny and he was turned over to the Tulsa County Jail. The Tulsa World Newspaper carried a story on September 20th of that year, stating that "… Volney Davis, the youth who has a long record of arrests, and who has escaped from both the county and the city jail on numerous occasions, entered pleas of guilty to two grand larceny charges in district court yesterday, and was sentenced to 3 years in prison. Davis pled guilty to robbing the Turk Brothers Shoe Store of $50 worth of shoes on December 27th of last year, and also of stealing automobile casings from the Chestnut & Smith Gasoline Company in Tulsa on August 31st of this year. Davis had escaped from the county jail in July, was captured on the east side of the city a month later, and made an attempt to escape from the officers two weeks ago, while being brought from the county jail to court for his preliminary hearing."

On September 28, 1919, he was sent to the Oklahoma State Penitentiary in McAlester, Oklahoma. He was given an early release on June 28, 1921. Then, less than two months after his parole, on August 26, a night watchman by the name of Thomas J. Sherrill was shot to death by burglars attempting to steal the payroll money at the construction site of St. John's Hospital in Tulsa. Volney was later convicted of this crime, as was Doc Barker, but not before being involved in a shoot-out with police officers in Okmulgee, Oklahoma, on January 8, 1922. This gun battle resulted in the deaths of Captain Homer Spaulding and Barker Gang associate, Jimmy Sexton. Although Detective Mark Lairmore and Patrolman M. E. Spence wounded and captured suspects Ed Lansing and Harry Thompson (alias Frank Hadley), other members of the gang, including Volney Davis, escaped.

On February 10, 1922, Doc Barker was convicted of the Sherrill murder and sentenced to life in the Oklahoma State

Penitentiary. Volney was captured and held in the Tulsa County Jail for almost a year. Then, on February 3, 1923, Volney Davis was also convicted of Sherrill's murder — and he, too, was sentenced to life in prison at the Oklahoma State Penitentiary.

Edna said she visited Volney in the Tulsa County Jail every week for a year before his sentencing. After he went to prison, Edna moved to Kansas City, Missouri, where she joined her sister, Doris. She once wrote, in a story about herself for a detective magazine, that after she arrived in Kansas City, she moved in with a girlfriend and they worked in a candy factory. This "girlfriend" of Edna was, in reality, her sister, Doris. But Edna knew that Doris would have been very upset if she had mentioned her sister in the story.

Edna's next husband was "Diamond Joe" Sullivan. He was a jewel thief among his other talents, and had recently lived in Kansas City, Missouri. Joe was born in New York in 1890 or 1891, with parents named "Mr. W. and Mrs. Lillian W. Steinhoff." He was brought up in the Catholic religion, and had completed two years of college.

"Diamond Joe" had been arrested in Wichita, Kansas, on January 28, 1918, on a conspiracy charge, and released on bond. On May 28, 1918, he was convicted of grand larceny in Kearny County, Kansas, for an attempted post office robbery in Pierceville, Kansas, on January 27, 1918. He was sent to the Kansas State Penitentiary at Lansing, Kansas, as Joe Sullivan, inmate number 6276. After his sentencing on September 27, 1918, for the conspiracy charge, he was held at Lansing, Kansas, until April 15, 1919, at which time he was moved to the U. S. Federal Penitentiary in Leavenworth, Kansas. He served his sentence at Leavenworth, as Joe Steinhoff, inmate number 13831, until his minimum term expired. He was then released on May 13, 1922.

19

At the time he was received at Leavenworth, Joe stated that his father was no longer living, he didn't know where his mother was, and he had a wife named Mrs. Dorothy Steinhoff, whose residence he did not know, and he had no children. He was 28 years old, and in case of illness or death, there was nobody that he wished to be notified. He stated that his last address was in St. Louis, Missouri.

Joe Sullivan's criminal activities began as far back as September 29, 1916, when he was charged with larceny in Rockford, Illinois. That charge was eventually reduced to disorderly conduct and he was fined $300 plus court costs.

Even while he was out on bond for the post office robbery, Joe was a busy man. A Kearny County, Kansas, newspaper article mentioned that "… Joe Steinhoff (aliases of Joe Simmons and Joe Sullivan) who was tried at the last term of court for the burglary of the O'Loughlin Store, and whose trial resulted in a hung jury — upon learning that he could not gain his liberty by giving bond, and upon being informed that he would be immediately arrested for the burglary of the Deerfield Garage if released on bond, concluded he might just as well plead guilty."

On Friday, May 24, 1918, the County Attorney, E. R. Thorpe, secured the presence of Judge Downer, and Mr. Sullivan subsequently pled guilty to grand larceny and was sentenced to not more than 5 years in the state penitentiary. Sheriff Houser escorted him to Lansing on train No. 12 the following Monday evening. Mr. Sullivan and his female traveling companion, Velma Champagne, were both under indictment in the federal court at Wichita, for a post office robbery. Sullivan, who was known to be a safe-blower and a highwayman, was also wanted at Great Bend, Newton, and Wichita, Kansas, as well as in St. Louis, Missouri.

Author's note:

This record of Joe Sullivan is where government agents came up with the false notion that Edna Murray had an alias of Velma Champagne. But Edna Murray did not know Joe Sullivan in 1918, so this was a different woman than Edna Murray.

Edna once claimed that she and Joe were married in Los Angeles, California, in 1923, after a two month courtship. This is possible, yet doubtful. But if true, the marriage ended when "Diamond Joe" Sullivan was electrocuted in Little Rock, Arkansas, on April 18, 1924, for the murder of two policemen in Little Rock.

Shortly before "Diamond Joe" Sullivan's electrocution, Edna took up with a man named Jack Murray. It is doubtful that they were legally married, but she took his name, and she

Dora Vinita "Doris" Stanley – circa 1916 "Courtesy of Bill Stanley"

went by the name of Edna Murray throughout her criminal career.

Edna's little sister, Dora Vinita, or "Doris," wasn't far behind Edna when it came to husbands and relationships. At the age of 15, Dora Vinita Stanley of Cardin, Oklahoma, stating her age as 18, married Kenneth M. Farrell,

22, also of Cardin, Oklahoma, in June of 1916. Dora gave birth to Preston's cousin, Mott Clinton Farrell. The child was born on April 19, 1918, and was named after Dora and Edna's older brothers, Mott and Harry Clinton.

This marriage didn't last long, because on August 8, 1918, in Miami, Oklahoma, Dora Stanley of Picher, Oklahoma, and Earl G. Simpson, of Webb City, Missouri, (who was given an Honorable Medical Discharge from the U. S. Army) — along with another couple — awakened Judge Lampkin in Miami, Oklahoma, at 10:00 p.m. to perform a double wedding ceremony.

This marriage also ended quickly because by January 13, 1920, Edna Price, age 22 and divorced, her son Preston Paden, age 4, as well as Dora Farrell, age 20, and her son, Mott Farrell, age 1 year and 9 months, all were residing together in Cardin, Oklahoma.

Dora, as Doris V. Stanley, and Emory Bernard Connell were married on January 3, 1923, in Harrison County, Mississippi. Doris was 22 years old at the time. Emory and his brother, Max — born to a respectable family in Chippewa Falls, Wisconsin — were as wild as the March winds and were already expert criminals when Doris first met them. Emory Connell was in cahoots with "Diamond Joe" Sullivan, and convicted on the same murder charge as he was, of two policemen in Little Rock, Arkansas.

Chapter 05: The Twenties Roared

Throughout the era known as the Roaring Twenties, my father, Preston, and his cousin, "Little" Mott, were raised by their grandmother, Louie Nettie — known better as "Louie" or simply, as "Lou" — and by their grandfather, Nicholas Drew "Charles" Stanley. When questioning their mothers' whereabouts, their Grandma Louie would tell them that their mothers were working as "models" in New York. For both boys, this explained why their mothers were so seldom around, and it also accounted for the expensive little suits and hats that their mothers sent home for them to wear. It was certain that no other little boys of their ages could be seen in Cardin, Oklahoma, walking around in such fashionable attire.

Dressed up – Little Preston L. Paden, about 10 years old, had no idea what the future would hold for him.

Preston and "Little" Mott grew up just as if they were brothers, my cousin Mott told me not so long ago. My daddy felt so deeply that "Little" Mott was figuratively his own brother, that he always referred to him as being my (Pammy Lou's) "Uncle" Mott.

After World War I ended, everyone tried to return to a normal life, but life had become quite different and it changed for everyone. The American soldiers had fought in foreign lands and the girls became part of the workforce. They weren't willing to return to the old rules, the old roles, and the former moral attitudes of the past. Thus, the younger generation no longer abided by their parents' sets of customs and values.

The girls rebelled by changing everything that defined a woman's femininity. They cut their hair in bobs and Dutch Boy haircuts, wrapped their chests to make themselves appear flat-chested, threw away their corsets, and lowered their waistlines down to their hips. Their hems rose up and their stockings were rolled down. They made themselves up with cosmetics, such as rouge, eyeliner, and lipstick — something that had been pre-viously done by only "loose women." Then they started the habits of smoking and drinking in public — luxuries that had formerly been reserved for men only. Added to that, were the outrageous dances, such as the Charleston and the Shimmy. But the absolute ultimate in female rebellion was the availability of Henry Ford's automobile, in which they not only rode in, but also drove, and, at times, climbed into the back seat for extra-curricular activities!

I don't recall the particulars, but Grandma Edna once told me, at a time when my mama wasn't around, that she and "Diamond Joe" once robbed a house safe that had a magnificent long flapper string of genuine pearls in it. I can't remember what else they took, but she told me she was saving it for me when I turned 18. I wasn't particularly impressed at the pros-pect of someday owning a stolen string of pearls; yet, I always wondered where it was hidden for so long a time — and, alas, I never did see it.

"Diamond Joe" Sullivan, Edna, Doris, and Emory Connell "Courtesy of the Collection of Debbie Moss"

At times, when school was out, Edna and Dora — who was then going by the name of Doris — would go home to Cardin and take their sons on a vacation for a few weeks. On one of these occasions, Edna and "Diamond Joe" Sullivan, and Edna's son, Preston — along with Doris and Emory Connell, and Doris' son, "Little" Mott — went to Hot Springs, Arkansas, where they rented a house. At the time, Preston was about 7 years old, and "Little" Mott was about 5 years old.

The vacation was to include business, as usual, for Emory and "Diamond Joe." Many people of questionable character came and went during this vacation. Edna and Doris tried to keep their sons from hearing too much, so they often sent them outside to play. Most of the men's business took place either in Hot Springs or in Little Rock, and sometimes they were gone for two or three days at a time before returning to the cottage. Nothing seemed out of the ordinary, until one evening when the girls picked up a newspaper — and saw mug shots of Emory and "Diamond Joe" on the front page.

It seemed that Emory and "Diamond Joe" had gone to the home of one Arthur "Rube" Waddell, a colored operator of the S

& S Taxi Company, located at 1005 Chester Street, in Little Rock. "Rube" operated as a "fence" for hot merchandise they had stolen, and he especially dealt in jewels. At 7:40 a.m., on July 24, 1923, Detective Sgt. Luther C. Hay and Detective Sgt. George W. Moore were investigating a complaint concerning an alleged dice game and other illegal activities taking place at this address. A lady had phoned in a complaint that there was a whiskey party and a dice game going on in her neighbor's house again. Officers had been watching Waddell's home for quite some time and knew him to be bootlegging and dealing in stolen goods, but, thus far, had not been able to prove it. As the officers were entering the house, they were shot without warning by Emory Connell (alias Arthur C. Lange), and by Joe Sullivan (alias Joe Shaw). Sgt. Moore was shot three times in the head and sank to the floor, fatally wounded. Sgt. Hay was hit by six shots, but somehow managed to get off four or five of his own after he hit the floor. One of his shots shattered a bone in Connell's left leg just as he was fleeing out of the same door that Sullivan had just gone through. "Rube" Waddell jumped through a window and took off as soon as the shooting began. Two colored women, who were also in the home, ran out of the house and down the street to a neighbor's house. Seeing that Connell was unable to run, Sullivan — with a pistol in each hand — went back and carried him to their car that was parked at the curb. The ringing of the pistol shots had alerted the neighborhood and a crowd quickly gathered near the house. Joe told the crowd that he was a police officer as he was helping Emory into the car. He then drove off, leaving one officer dead and the other still alive, yet mortally wounded.

By the time it was discovered who was who, and that the crowd had been fooled, Connell and Sullivan were long gone.

Sgt. Luther C. Hay was taken to the city hospital where he died two days later.

"Rube" Waddell told his story to police officers later at the police headquarters. He claimed to have known "Diamond Joe" as a bartender in Kansas City, and that Joe and Connell had been to his house before. He also said that the two men had called and informed him that they had a diamond to sell. Waddell went on to say that they had arrived at his home shortly after 7:00 a.m. that morning, with a diamond that they were trying to sell for $500. Shortly after that, the officers arrived and the shooting began.

Emory Connell was in extreme pain and "Diamond Joe" made him feel as comfortable as possible by leaving him in the woods with two pistols while he went for medical supplies. He knew he was taking a big chance — and sure enough — he was quickly spotted and captured by a newly formed posse. Knowing that Emory was going to die shortly if he didn't receive prompt medical treatment, "Diamond Joe" told the posse where they could find him. There, in the thick woods, they found Emory, with a gun in each of his hands. He didn't dare shoot since he was in so much pain that he was happy to see them in order to receive emergency medical treatment.

Chapter 06: The Vacation Comes To A Halt

Emory Connell and "Diamond Joe" Sullivan were taken to the prison at Little Rock, Arkansas, for safekeeping. Meanwhile, Edna and Doris were at a complete loss as to what to do next. Doris believed they should just sit tight, and wait to hear something. She figured that the boys' attorney would be contacting them soon. And sure enough, that's what happened. Two days after the boys were captured, a lawyer called the two sisters, asking them to come to Little Rock. When they arrived at his office, he informed Doris that her husband, Emory Connell, made it quite clear that he did not want her coming to the prison. So Edna proceeded on to the Little Rock Prison with the attorney, while Doris stayed behind. Edna was arrested the minute she arrived at the prison warden's office. Then the lawyer returned to his office and informed Doris that her sister had been arrested. Doris left the office immediately and got a ride out of Little Rock before the police could apprehend her.

The authorities were convinced that Edna was Emory Connell's wife, and nothing she could say would convince them otherwise. They mentioned 7 or 8 murders that Emory was responsible for, and wanted information from his wife. Edna was getting a real grilling because she couldn't convince them that she was Joe Sullivan's wife, and not Emory Connell's wife. They roughed her up pretty good, and fired questions at her, left and right. Edna wasn't one to be easily intimidated, but she was getting a bit desperate, when she suddenly remembered her ring. She took the ring off, and inscribed inside was the message — "From Joe to Edna." At this point, the police started believing her and finally let her go. Edna was satisfied that her ring had saved her from additional abuse, and perhaps, many days in jail.

Although Edna was happy to be released in Little Rock, she didn't know where to turn next. It was for sure that she was being followed, because the police were expecting her to lead them to her sister, Doris, who was the real Mrs. Emory Connell. Edna mingled through the crowd downtown, dodging in and out of various places, and finally, when she was sure that she didn't have someone tailing her, she hopped into a cab and went to the next little town about twenty miles from Little Rock. From there, she caught a train to Hot Springs, Arkansas.

The next morning, Edna left Hot Springs, accompanied by her son and nephew, and went home to Cardin, Oklahoma, to her parent's home.

Doris, on the other hand, headed down to New Orleans, where, according to Edna, Doris got into some trouble with Melvin Stofer, Arthur Clay (aka Buzz Clark), and George Owens (aka Tom Morgan). They had stolen an automobile in Little Rock and then went on a robbery spree down in Louisiana.

After leaving Preston and "Little" Mott with their Grandma and Grandpa Stanley, Edna headed back to Kansas City, where she stayed with a woman by the name of Margaret Clinger, who had a flat at 8th and Tracy Street. While there, she received $2,000 from "Diamond Joe's" mother for use in retaining an attorney for his upcoming trial in Little Rock.

Chapter 07: Doris Languishes In Jail

For months, Emory Connell, his brother, and other members of the gang had been waging a campaign of robbery and bloodshed in Louisiana and Mississippi. The stealing of automobiles, the robbing of post offices and the waylaying of pedestrians constituted their chief pursuits. George Owens, Melvin Stofer, and Arthur Clay were said to be members of the Connell Gang. Stofer, who was well-known to New Orleans Police, along with the two other men, and Doris, were transported from Pearl River to New Orleans, as they disembarked from a ferry at Chef Menteur, Louisiana.

Doris Stanley – circa 1923 "Courtesy of the Collection of Rick Mattix"

On August 11, 1923, Doris (now known as Mrs. Emory Connell), Melvin Stofer, George Owens (an ex-convict from Oklahoma), and Arthur Clay, would have been on their way to Little Rock had federal court convened that day. Doris Connell and Arthur Clay, — whose only known claim to fame was "… given my tools and 15 minutes, I can fix any automobile so that no one can identify it," were both charged with stealing a Cadillac in Little Rock, Arkansas. Stofer and Owens were charged by federal officials for being accessories to the same crime. Doris Connell and Arthur Clay were each under $10,000 bonds, while the other two were each under bonds of $5,000.

Doris made the only effort to make bond. This failed, however, because U. S. Commissioner Arthur H. Browne ruled that he could only accept a real estate bond on property against which there was no mortgage. Consequently, Doris stayed in jail in New Orleans along with her comrades in crime.

According to the authorities, Doris became more despondent as the time drew near when she would have to return to Little Rock. Clay and the others didn't want her returning there, either. According to New Orleans police, the men feared that Doris' composure would falter and she would eventually break down and confess to the various crimes in which she and the five suspects, including her husband and Joe Sullivan, took part in, before they were arrested for the slaying of the two police officers in Little Rock. Owens, Stofer, and Clay worried needlessly if they thought Doris would be the one to break.

It was expected that when federal court met again the following week, a removal order would be asked to return the four to Little Rock. Although Doris insisted that she would fight extradition, prosecutors said they had enough evidence to force her removal at once.

Doris Connell, George Owens, Melvin Stofer, and Arthur Clay were held for a while awaiting trial. As of October 1, 1923, the four were being held in the Clinton, Louisiana, Parish jail, which was the parish seat of East Feliciana Parish, Louisiana. It was early on the morning of September 30th when the four accused were acquitted in Clinton, Louisiana, of charges of robbing the West & Bridges Store in Norwood, Louisiana, when money, liberty bonds, and war savings stamps totaling $20,000 disappeared.

As soon as the jury heard the evidence against the four and returned its verdict, H. C. Mosley and John J. Hessler, Deputy U. S. Marshals, took the four into custody on the charge of having stolen a Cadillac automobile in Little Rock in July, shortly after Emory Connell had killed two detectives there.

George Owens was also wanted by Oklahoma authorities for violating his parole from the Oklahoma State Penitentiary. However, federal officials said they would hold him until the Little Rock charge was disposed of.

The four were returned to Little Rock for the purpose of being brought up on charges regarding the theft of a Cadillac Touring Car the previous July, which belonged to Louis Michael of 1302 Cumberland Street in Little Rock, Arkansas.

The automobile was stolen from a garage in the rear of the Michael home after the lock had been hacked off the garage door. It was later recovered and returned to Mr. Michael upon the arrest of Doris and the three men.

Arthur Clay pleaded guilty to the auto theft charges, saying that he alone was responsible. He was sentenced to 2 years at the U. S. Federal Penitentiary in Leavenworth, Kansas. George Owens was returned to the Oklahoma State Penitentiary. Melvin Stofer was cleared of all charges and set free, and — according to officials — Doris Connell continued on to Chicago.

Doris, though never becoming as notorious as her older sister, Edna, was far from being an innocent woman. In fact, it was she who was the instigator of many crimes.

Chapter 08: Life At "The Walls"
(The Arkansas State Penitentiary)

The Old Military Prison, and Arkansas State Penitentiary, located on the present site of the State Capitol. The stone wall was built by Alexander George, the Lessee, in 1855. Below the wall was a rail fence.

The Arkansas State Penitentiary, known as "The Walls," opened its doors in 1910. It was located just southwest of Little Rock, Arkansas, and stood at the site where the State Capitol Building was later constructed. When Governor Junius M. Futrell closed "The Walls" in 1933, the inmates were moved to either the Cummins Farm or the Tucker Farm. The death chamber was moved to the Tucker Farm at that time.

Edna later spoke of visiting "Diamond Joe" while he was in the death cell at the Arkansas State Penitentiary. This was a visit that she would not soon forget. When arrested, "Diamond Joe" weighed 180 pounds. After one month in the death cell, he was just a shadow of his former self. He had not yet been convicted, but knew his chances of beating this rap were no better than a "snowball's chance in hell." He was surprised to see Edna there, but didn't have much to say and he ended the visit by asking her not to come back. She assumed that he didn't want her to see him in his current physical condition — a man broken under the strain. As Edna was leaving, the warden asked her, "Mrs. Sullivan, would you like to see the electric chair?" Caught a little off guard, she asked, "The electric chair? Where is it?" Without giving much thought to what she was about to witness, she followed the warden, and not 20 feet from "Diamond Joe's" cell door — there it was, covered with a black oilcloth, awaiting a date with "Diamond Joe." It was a wonder he had not lost even more weight, and Edna was at a loss to find words to say anything. Just looking at that chair would make anybody sick, just as she was starting to feel. She was sick to her stomach, and was thinking that she also felt faint. "Take me the hell outta here," she said to the warden. "Would you like to see Connell while you're here? He's over in the hospital, the warden added." Edna said she would like to see him. When she went into Emory's room, he was on a cot, playing cards with a colored trustee. Emory's left leg was now reduced to a bandaged stub, yet he didn't seem too concerned. He joked and laughed with Edna as if everything was just fine. She could only tolerate being there for a few minutes, and then she said that she had to leave.

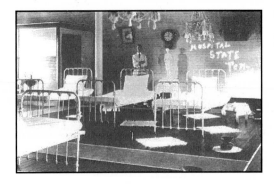

"The Walls" Hospital – 1924

"The Walls" – Mess Hall, Hospital, and Barracks on Roosevelt Rd., Little Rock, Ark.

On their way across the exercise yard to his office, the warden commented to Edna, "I'll be glad when I can turn the juice on that fellow, Connell." When Edna asked why, he told her, "He is a dangerous man — and the most cunning man I have ever seen." He went on to tell her how Emory had written a note for the trustee to mail to his wife. Instead, the trustee turned it over to the warden. The note contained diagrams of the prison as well as descriptions of escape plans that Doris was to deliver to Emory's friends on the outside. The warden thought he had put a stop to Emory's plans, but he just didn't know Emory.

"The Walls" State Penitentiary, Little Rock, Ark., Front Gate

Chapter 09: The Escape From The Arkansas State Penitentiary

Although Emory Connell and "Diamond Joe" Sullivan were represented by two of Little Rock's best attorneys when they went on trial for their lives, they still lost. The evidence against them was just too strong, and they were both sentenced to death in the electric chair. They appealed to the Supreme Court, but again their request to reduce the sentence was denied. They knew then that they were destined to die so they figured that they had nothing to lose. They then began planning what came to be known as the most daring prison break in the history of Arkansas, which was mainly engineered by Emory Connell, even though he had been fitted with an artificial leg and couldn't get around very well. This was the same man that the warden had insisted was "… the most cunning man he had ever known." Emory used a razor blade wired to a stick to carve a wooden gun, using the toilet seat in his cell. He stained it with his medication, cascara, and burned a hole in the muzzle with a heated rod. Tinfoil was stuck in place with chewing gum, and it looked real enough to fool anyone. Connell also arranged for friends to toss a package containing real guns over the prison wall during the night. Another convicted murderer, Eulos Sullivan (no relation to Joe Sullivan), was also in the death house with Emory and Joe. It was reported that as the warden, Hamp Martin, and two trustees were delivering breakfast on the morning of February 1, 1924, Connell fooled them with his wooden gun, which looked very realistic in the dim light of his cell. After the warden unlocked the cells, Joe ran out and picked up the package containing the real guns. Now they were in business!

Wooden gun thought, by prison officials, to have been carved by Emory Connell.

Emory had two guns and Joe Sullivan and Eulos Sullivan each had one. Next came the tough part. They had to get across the exercise yard to the garage, where the warden kept his car. Keeping their guns out of sight while the warden was walking right in front of them, they easily made it to the garage. Then with the warden sitting behind the wheel of his car, Emory was crouched down on the floorboard in the front of the car with a gun focused on the warden, and both Sullivan men were down low in the back seat. The warden knew that if he made a wrong move, Emory would shoot him right there on the spot. All three of these men had killed before, all three had been sentenced to death, and one more murder wouldn't have made a nickel's worth of difference to them.

The warden's car rolled out of the garage and through the big gates as the warden gave his usual wave to the guard. Emory, Joe, and Eulos were free again. They pushed the warden out of the car a few miles down the road, and Connell then took the wheel and proceeded to drive like a wild man. They knew the alarm would be issued soon, and they needed to get far away, as fast as possible. They abandoned the car, stole a boat, and paddled down the Arkansas River after it got dark. The fugitives hid out in the woods, and traveled only at night. It was extremely cold, and Emory's leg was starting to throb and ache very badly where his stump was rubbing against his artificial leg.

One night in their camp, while Emory was cleaning his gun, it went off accidentally, hitting Joe in the shoulder. Shortly thereafter, Joe's arm became paralyzed and he started to run a high fever. He declared himself done for, and told the other two to go on without him. The others then dragged him into a barn and continued on by themselves.

Meanwhile, as Emory and Eulos were hiding in the woods, crouched under a fallen treetop, the posse had passed by without even noticing them. Then, inexplicitly, the two fugitives started blasting away at the posse. During this gun battle, both Emory Connell and Eulos Sullivan were killed. Emory and Eulos may have beaten the chair, but they didn't beat their fate. Their days were over.

Officers later found "Diamond Joe" still lying in the barn, unconscious. He was then taken back to the prison hospital, where they patched him up sufficiently from the gunshot wound, just in time for him to meet his next adversary — that adversary being the electric chair.

Burl C. Rotenberry, Chief of Police of Little Rock, had printed up 5,000 circulars bearing pictures and descriptions of Connell and the two Sullivans — intending to send them all over the country. They were instead returned to the printer with instructions to convert them into scratch pads.

Joe Sullivan   Eulos Sullivan   Emory Connell

"Diamond Joe" Sullivan – Eulos Sullivan – Emory Connell "Courtesy of the Collection of Debbie Moss"

The Prison Board was embarrassed by the stories on the front pages of the papers, describing how Warden Hamp Martin was duped with a wooden gun that was carved from Emory Connell's death cell toilet seat. Consequently, Warden Martin and his night gateman, Sam Taylor, were discharged from their duties at the State Penitentiary. Dee Horton, who had been in charge of the state convict farm at Tucker, Arkansas, was temporarily placed in charge of "The Walls."

The story of the "whittled gun" became a jailhouse legend.

A decade later, the notorious bank robber, John Dillinger, escaped from the Lake County Jail in Crown Point, Indiana, while awaiting trial for the murder of a police officer. On the morning of March 3, 1934, Dillinger, likewise, fooled his guards with a fake gun and convinced the guards to open his cell. He and another inmate locked up the guards, grabbed some machine guns, and fled the jail with a deputy as a hostage. Once they made their way to a nearby garage, they proceeded to steal Sheriff Lillian Holly's brand new Ford V-8 automobile. The fugitives then fled across the Indiana state line into Illinois, which turned out to be their fatal mistake, since the act of transporting a stolen vehicle across a state line had been deemed to be a federal offense and, needless to say, got the full attention of the FBI — attention that Dillinger was not anticipating, and certainly did not need.

Making headlines – John Dillinger is shown here "chumming" with officials.

Chapter 10: Life Goes On ... As Edna "Murray"

With the remaining money from what "Diamond Joe's" mother had sent her to pay for his legal defense, Edna bought furniture and rented an 8 room flat at 1126 East 15th Street in Kansas City, Missouri. In addition to renting out 4 rooms, she augmented her income through the sale of home-brew. While there, she met Jack Murray, whose real last name, she suspected, might be Ely, since that was the last name of his mother. He had been incarcerated at the U. S. Federal Penitentiary in Leavenworth, Kansas, for white slavery — otherwise known as prostitution. He was later paroled on March 30, 1920, and shortly thereafter, he was arrested in Kansas City for sending narcotics through the mail to his buddies who were still incarcerated. His parole was immediately revoked and he was returned to Leavenworth to serve additional time. Later, after his release from Leavenworth in June of 1922, Murray was arrested at 116 East 16th Street for having narcotics in his possession. Then, in late 1924, he was arrested several more times with Edna, but they were never charged with any crime. According to other police reports, Murray was also wanted in Joplin, Missouri, for jumping bond.

Years later, Edna recalled that about a month after she met Jack and began running around with him, he went to work driving a taxi for the Yellow Cab Company. "But," Edna claimed, "… the police kept raiding my place after finding I was 'Diamond Joe' Sullivan's wife, so I turned the place over (sublet) to a man and his wife and got $450 for my furniture."

After Doris' release from the parish prison in Louisiana, and barely squeaking out of the auto theft charge, she joined Edna in Kansas City. The two sisters rented a small flat where Jack Murray also stayed when he wasn't staying with his mother, Mrs. Ely, who managed the Drapery Department at the Emery, Bird & Thayer Dry Goods Company in Kansas City.

Jack and Edna decided that they would take a train trip to Los Angeles, California, since Jack had tuberculosis and his doctor recommended that he go there for his health. They rented an apartment on Monroe Street, where Doris joined them shortly thereafter. Edna recalled that while they were there, she (Edna) was arrested by Los Angeles detectives on a charge of selling mortgaged property, because a friend of Doris' — Daisy O'Neill — had sold the furniture she left in the flat on 15th Street in Kansas City. According to Edna, "It was all just a misunderstanding." Edna spent three days in jail before the charges were dropped.

Edna Murray spent 3 days in jail while in Los Angeles, Calif. "Courtesy of the Collection of Debbie Moss"

Also, while in California, they read about Emory Connell having been killed, following his escape from the death cell in Little Rock. Shortly thereafter, Doris boarded a train for Chippewa Falls, Wisconsin, where Emory's body was taken for burial. She wanted to speak with Max Connell, Emory's brother, regarding some clothes and other possessions that she had left in storage.

The residents of Chippewa Falls were saddened by what the Connell family was going through, and many letters were sent to the local newspaper. An example of how they expressed their collective sympathy for the tragedy follows:

"Emory Connell, the desperado who was killed near Redfield, Arkansas, on February 5, 1924, in a gun battle with a posse after he and Joe and John Eulos Sullivan had escaped from the death cells of the Arkansas Penitentiary, was of excellent parentage," it was declared in a letter from C. L. Muggah, a druggist at Chippewa Falls, Wisconsin, Connell's former home. *"His father being a mail carrier of the city and his mother being a fine woman, they sure have had their cross to bear, and their suffering has shown on them both. Emory has a brother who is of a similar type, but the other two children are very fine young people. It seems strange that from two such fine people these boys should spring. Out of respect for his parents, there was quite a large funeral."*

About a week after Doris left for Wisconsin, Jack and Edna bought a Buick touring car in Los Angeles, and drove back to Kansas City. They first rented a place at the Bliss Apartments, around 10th Street for a couple of weeks. Then they moved to 1114 Troost Street, where they purchased the furnishings that were already there, for about $450 down, and $50 a month. At this new location, they sold home-brew downstairs and rented kitchenette apartments upstairs. Jack and Earl Stuchlik, a buddy of Jack's, ran crap and poker games in the back. Doris returned from Wisconsin and lived with them.

It was at this address that Edna began to live under the name of Edna Murray. Business was booming for several months before the police raids ensued. Edna later remembered that they were always being "… annoyed by the coppers (sic) … because they knew all about her late husband, 'Diamond Joe' Sullivan, and acted as if all of her friends were criminals." After several police raids on the Troost Street rooming house, it was starting to cost them more money to keep out of jail than they were making through their illegal activities.

Doris sold the furnishings from the rooming house for about $250 to a second hand furniture dealer. She and Earl Stuchlik had formed a close relationship, so they moved into an apartment together on Broadway Street. Doris worked at the nearby Croft Café on 12th Street, where she sold bootlegged whiskey out of the back of the store. Around this same time, Jack and Edna rented an apartment in the 2700 or 2800 block of Harrison Street.

Chapter 11: Waiting In The Death Cell

A contemporary newspaper article published on Sunday, April 13, 1924, reported the news that Joe Sullivan was scheduled to die in the electric chair on the following Friday for his part in the murders of Detective Sergeants George W. Moore and Luther C. Hay. The article went on to state that Joe Sullivan was not the "same man" who initially had been confined to a death cell, along with his former partner in crime, Emory B. Connell. Since Connell's death on February 5th, Sullivan had lost all confidence and desire to speak with reporters.

The Arkansas Gazette reported:

"Yesterday, the condemned man told reporters in a polite way, 'nothin' doin,' as far as an interview was concerned. 'If I die on Friday morning, I'll just die,' he said, 'but, I'll not talk any more for the public. If I have to go, I'll walk to the chair like a man, because that's all there is to it. Just walk.' When asked if he thought he had a chance to 'beat the chair,' Sullivan answered, 'I don't think so. The Governor has the case now, and if he doesn't interfere, I will have to die.'

"Warden Evans said Sullivan was 'bearing up well.' He had recovered from his gunshot wound to his shoulder received accidentally from his partner, Connell, during their last escape. He had also put on some weight. Warden Evans said the condemned man finds amusement in 'kidding' three Negroes in the adjoining death cell, and at times, frightens them considerably. Sullivan tells the Negroes that he, Connell, and Eulos Sullivan will return as ghosts after his death, and each Friday night will come and sit

on the Negroes' cots. The superstitious Negroes take much stock in Sullivan's threats and immediately fall into fervent prayer."

After eight months of incarceration, Joe Sullivan still stuck to his story that he was present at the shooting on Chester Street, in Little Rock, on the night of July 24, 1923, but he did not take part in the shooting. Yes, he helped his partner escape, and carried him to the car, but he did not shoot anyone. He stated that he met Emory Connell only about six weeks before they got into this trouble in Little Rock. He further stated that the meeting took place only because he had married Emory Connell's wife's sister, Edna. He said he had nobody to blame but himself, and he should have steered away from Connell from the start.

Joe Sullivan went on to say that walking to the electric chair and taking his dose couldn't be any worse than the mental anguish of waiting in the death cell. He said that if a man who has been sentenced to death tells you he isn't worried, and that being cooped up doesn't bother him, you can bet that he is lying. Joe also said that the one consolation he has over most people is that he knows **when** he is going to die, and that being the case, he can better be prepared to meet his Savior than he would otherwise have been.

Warden Evans spoke of the doctor changing Joe's dressing for him for the last time before he walks to the electric chair. Joe said he had been changing the dressing himself, but since he would be getting it wet while taking his last bath, it might be better for the doctor to change the dressing at that time. A faint smile crept over his face, and he said, "It's all useless. I won't be using it anymore." His right arm was still in a sling, having never completely healed because the bone had been shattered. Unlike his athletic appearance when he was first arrested, Joe Sullivan was now a pale and sick looking skeleton of a man. His hair had thinned out and he had a partially bald spot on the back of his head from lying down so much. While being measured for his funeral robe — a new suit, shirt, and necktie — Sullivan told Warden Evans that it would not be necessary to give him a new shirt, since he had one that would be "… plenty good enough."

On April 18, 1924, "Diamond Joe" Sullivan took his last seat, when he was put to death in the electric chair for murder. Joe stated that he didn't care what they did with his body after he was dead. Unbeknownst to him, his mother had already made arrangements to have his body returned to Kansas City for burial. Edna admitted that she didn't grieve much over "Diamond Joe," and didn't really miss him. "Besides," she said, "he was 12 years older than me."

Author's note:

At the time of "Diamond Joe" Sullivan's death, his age was listed at 34 years old in the prison personnel files, and Edna was just one month shy of her 26th birthday. Therefore, the age difference between the two was closer to 8 years than the 12 years she stated.

"Diamond Joe" Sullivan took his last seat in "Old Sparky." "Courtesy of the Collection of Debbie Moss"

Chapter 12: "Diamond Joe's" Last Interview

Immediately after the recapture of Joe Sullivan at Redfield, Arkansas, on February 5, 1924, Detective Captain James A. Pitcock, and several other officials, obtained a statement from Sullivan that revealed, for the first time, the "inside story" of the escape plots. Sullivan told his story only after the promise that it would not be published until after his death. Sullivan died at the Arkansas State Penitentiary — known as "The Walls" — on the morning of April 18, 1924, and his statement was printed in the Arkansas Democrat Newspaper on that very day.

Throughout his lengthy statement, Sullivan gave his partner, Emory B. Connell, all the credit for making the plans and enlisting outside assistance.

The following is the news article from the Arkansas Democrat Newspaper on April 18, 1924:

"Sullivan said that after he and Connell had been convicted and imprisoned at "The Walls" on September 22, 1923, they were confined with John Eulos Sullivan, Oklahoma desperado, who participated in three escape plots with them, and who was killed with Connell by a posse near Redfield, Arkansas, the same day that Sullivan was retaken.

"Connell immediately began laying plans for a getaway. According to Sullivan, he (Connell) always thought he knew better than anyone else. Sullivan said that early in November, Connell received a coded letter from someone and he informed his cellmates that they were to receive visitors soon. 'He knew who they would be and what it meant,' Sullivan said, in speaking

of Connell. At that time, Doris Connell, his wife, was in jail at New Orleans, and he thought the visitors would be friends of his (Connell's) sister, also named Doris, who lived in Chicago.

"'Shortly after that, on a Sunday, visitors were admitted to the prison. Connell's friends came — a man and a woman. He recognized them, and as they were about to pass the outside windows of our cell, Emory "blew" them a note.'

"Sullivan said Emory had cut a small hole in the window screen, and placing a bit of tinfoil with the note, was able to "blow" the message some distance. Sullivan said Connell's confederates took turns in dropping their handkerchiefs near the notes and picking both up at the same time. 'It was in this manner that Connell informed his confederates of what he needed, and how he wanted the plans carried out,' Sullivan said. 'I don't know the exact words Connell wrote in his notes,' Sullivan said, 'but he told them everything he wanted them to know in the notes. He (Connell) thought he was smarter than anyone else. He wrote them to fix up a can of Prince Albert smoking tobacco, and place some briars on the inside. He was always bumming someone for Prince Albert tobacco.'

"By "briars" Sullivan had meant hack saws. Connell's plans were well laid (out) as shown by the fact that he continuously asked for Prince Albert tobacco, and then gave his confederates instructions to "fix" a can of the same brand. Sullivan said the can was well "made." The internal revenue stamp had been removed and the saws were placed on the inside. The stamp was replaced and no one could detect that it had been removed.

"'Who was the man who came to see Emory?' Sullivan was asked. 'His name was Frank Howard,' Sullivan said, 'and he

was about 22 to 24 years old, and dressed like a jelly bean.' Sullivan said that he didn't know the name of the woman except that they called her Patsy. He said she was a "good looking" woman and he thought they had come from Chicago. 'Howard is a daylight man there,' Sullivan continued. By "daylight man," Sullivan meant that he (Howard) robbed in the daytime, such as payroll bandits (did).

"Sullivan said Howard and the woman visited the prison four or five times at irregular times, sometimes on visiting days and sometimes on weekdays.

" 'What does Doris Connell, sister of Emory, do in Chicago?' Sullivan was asked. 'She's a dancing teacher,' he replied. 'Was she ever here?' he was asked. 'Not that I know of,' Sullivan answered.

" 'Several days after our friends reached Little Rock,' Sullivan said, 'they talked with Emory at his cell door, and during that conversation, Emory asked for a can of Prince Albert. Howard gave him the "fixed" can. After Howard and Patsy left us, Emory opened the can and found four big briars and three small ones. They were doubled up in the can.'

" 'Tell about sawing the bars of the death cell on the night of November 12th, when Connell succeeded in getting into the prison yard,' Sullivan was urged.

" 'We got some tar soap and started to work. The briars got to breaking. This hampered us much and the escape was put off a week. Howard visited Connell on November 5th and Emory told him of our hard luck. He also told Howard of the postponement of the escape. The next week Howard returned and signaled to us that everything was all right for the next Saturday night which was on November 12th.'

"The trio experienced trouble again after sawing the bars of two windows. Connell was the only one who could squeeze through the opening, but he was caught the following morning on top of a water tank inside the prison yard.

"Sullivan said, 'Something went wrong on the outside. Connell had planned to find some "rods" (guns) lowered over the "Walls" and with these weapons to make a flight for liberty. It appeared that the confederates misunderstood their instructions on this point. After Connell left the cell that night, he hobbled about on his crutches, and marks on the ground showed that he walked back and forth near the wall, apparently looking for the rods. Finding that the guns had not been delivered, Connell then made a rope with a hook attached and attempted to scale the wall, but failed. Daylight sent him up on the water tower where he was found several hours later.'

"Sullivan also said that Howard and a man named Charles McGhee attempted to steal a Marmon automobile belonging to Ed Hurley, 1868 Gaines Street and, when foiled, stole a Cadillac owned by L. E. Whitmore. Howard and McGhee left the Cadillac near the southwest wall of the prison on the night of the planned escape. The two left Little Rock immediately after the delivery of the automobile.

"Sullivan said Connell owned equity in an apartment house in Chicago that he paid for with Liberty bonds. He also said Connell and Howard were "tangled up" in several daylight robberies in Chicago.

"The proprietor of a North Little Rock pawnshop gave the police a statement in which he told of selling two men the weapons used on February 1st, by the trio in making the daring escape.

It was on January 25th, that the two men entered the pawnshop and rented a pair of field glasses. On January 30th, they returned and bought a .44 caliber rifle. The cartridges for the rifle were bought from a Little Rock sporting goods house. They also asked for a new .45 caliber revolver, and the pawnbroker ordered one from the Bush Caldwell Company in Little Rock, and sold it to the pair. The next day they returned and wanted to buy two .38 caliber pistols. Not having those in stock, the pawnbroker lost that sale. One of the confederates left the store and returned in a short time with two pistols wrapped in a newspaper. He showed them to his partner, and when his partner passed judgment on them, they left. That was on the afternoon of January 31st, the day before the last, and successful, escape.

"Sullivan told the officers he was certain that Howard had a man assistant in Little Rock but he didn't know his name. He said they were the two men who hoisted the ladder to the south wall on the night of January 31st, and lowered the board on which the rifle and two revolvers, used in the escape, were fastened. They had built the ladder themselves. It consisted of four sections. The timber was new and void of knots making it very strong and durable. The sections were fastened together by heavy bolts and the ladder was varnished to make it almost invisible after dark.

"Connell had carried out the plans in the last escape as he had with Howard and Patsy, except that McGhee was with Howard. 'He continued to "blow notes" from the death cell window,' Sullivan said. 'Our friends walked behind the convict that was showing them through and picked up Emory's notes. In fact, in all three of his escapes, he got messages to his confederates in the same manner,' he said.

"Sullivan said, 'Connell was the brains, and had no out-side help on the night of January 20th, when he attempted to dig through the wall of his cell.' Several days after this attempt failed, Connell dropped on his cot and said: 'If I don't get out of here soon I will be nuts. I can't stand it much longer.'

"Sullivan said Eulos Sullivan, whose sentence at that time had been affirmed by the Supreme Court, also was anxious to get out.

"'We got to sitting up at night time and talking and planning how to make the break,' Sullivan said. 'It was during one of these talks that the wooden pistol idea was decided on.'

"'What were you going to do if Warden Martin resisted?' was asked. 'There was always a supposition that Martin might not go. I was going to make a flight of it.'

"'How did Howard and McGhee know when to deliver the guns?'

"'We gave them notice a week ahead of time so we could be ready. They visited us on the Wednesday, preceding the Friday we escaped.'

"Sullivan said he didn't know whether the Dickinson Brick Yard Plant was set on fire on the eve of the escape as a signal that the guns had been delivered or not.

"Sullivan then was asked how they knew the guns had been placed outside the prison wall. 'Slick Austin told us just where the rods were Thursday afternoon, the day before the escape. Connell told Austin he wanted him to look behind the stockade building on the following morning, and see if a package was on the ground,' Sullivan said. 'Austin appeared at their window on the morning of the escape and said, 'Jesus Christ, it **is** here!' Austin, at the same time, held his hands pointed down to the ground, which Sullivan said was some sort of a signal.

"'Emory had a long talk with Austin at the window then,' Sullivan said. 'I did not hear what was being said, but Emory told us after Austin left that the time (for the escape) had arrived.'

"Sullivan said they had figured Martin would be alone with the unarmed guard and the Negro trustee who carried their meals to them, but instead, two (additional) strangers walked to the cells with him. 'We did not know who they were,' Sullivan said. 'But they didn't act like anybody (we knew). Connell was given his breakfast and when the door of the cell occupied by the Sullivans was opened, Connell shouted, **"Let's go!"'**

"'Eulos held the wooden pistol on Martin and forced him against a wall. I don't know what the other men did as I ran for the guns outside,' Sullivan said.

"The Austin referred to by Sullivan was Louis Austin, held at the penitentiary for Canadian officers who wanted him on a bank robbery charge. At the time of the interview with Joe Sullivan, Austin had been extradited to Canada.

"Sullivan was then asked to tell how he was shot, by Connell, during their brief flight. 'He was always fooling with a pistol and pointing it at Eulos or me, or was taking one apart,' Sullivan replied. 'I was about 8 feet away from him, lying down in some weeds. He was sitting down and playing with his pistol. I had my chin rested on my hand when the gun went off. He cussed and I looked at him. If the shot had been 6 inches higher, I would have been killed there,' he said.

"'Connell said he was getting too nervous and acted as if he was sorry.'

"'Do you think he did it on purpose?'

"'Well, he is dead now and I want to give the Devil his due. I don't know why he would want to do it. I was still leading him and it was not helping myself a damn bit.'

"The next question asked Sullivan was, 'How long did it take you to make the wooden pistol?'

"'We were a week making it. Emory jimmied his all up, and we wouldn't let him have anything to do with the one Eulos and I made.'

"'Did you have anything to eat after you made your escape?'

"'We saw an old farmer and told him a funny story one day. He got us some biscuits and some butter and a gallon of butter-milk. I ate two biscuits.'

"Sullivan was asked if anyone connected with the prison had anything to do with the escape plots, to which he replied in the negative, adding that Connell, Eulos, and he were the only ones besides the confederates of Connell's (involved).

"'Was O'Keith going out with you?'

"'No, Captain, we would not risk our lives with a punk.' ("Punk" was the terminology used by criminals for someone who was no good).

"At the time of the release of Joe Sullivan's interview, O'Keith had been convicted of the murder of a Kansas prison guard and was serving a sentence at Tucker.

"The condemned man said they took $45 from Warden Martin before leaving, as that was the amount they had entrusted him

with, upon entering prison. He said they gave him back the remainder of his money.

"Sullivan said Connell and his wife, and he and Mrs. Sullivan, rented a furnished house in Hot Springs just before the killing of detectives Moore and Hay. The house was located near 175 Ramble Street, he said. He said he and Connell came to Little Rock by train on July 22nd, and remained there only a short time between trains, (before) leaving for Pine Bluff. There they stole two Ford cars and came to Little Rock the following day. The killings occurred shortly after they arrived in Little Rock. Sullivan said Connell obtained the diamond ring they were selling to Waddell from a dealer in New Orleans, paying for it with Liberty bonds, when the officers entered. Joe Sullivan said Connell's main headquarters was in New Orleans. While they were in Hot Springs, three of Connell's friends were there, who were arrested some time later in New Orleans with Connell's wife. They were Melvin Stofer, Arthur Clay (aka Buzz Clark), and another man whose name he could not remember. George Owens (aka Tom Morgan), was the man whose name Sullivan had forgotten.

"Sullivan said that Buzz was the one who stole the Cadillac belonging to Louis Michael in Little Rock, and drove it to Louisiana.

"'Did you and Emory have a "plant" anywhere?' was asked. (A plant in criminal parlance is a cache of stolen goods).

"'No Sir! We were together only a short time. I met him a little before the killing of John Lund, an Oklahoma police officer.'

"'Do you know whether Connell killed Lund?'

"'I don't know for sure, but I always thought he did. I was in the city at the time but was not with him,' Sullivan replied.

"Sullivan said Connell never "pulled a job" in Kansas City or St. Louis. He also said Connell's brother, Dr. Max Connell, "is not steady." 'Max is first here and then there, stealing $15 or a silk shirt,' he said.

"Efforts to return Howard and McGhee to Little Rock, for aiding and abetting a criminal's escape, were abandoned when Sullivan positively refused to identify them as the ones who aided them. Without his corroboration, officers could not prove the charges.

"'I'd be a helluva guy if I stuck them,' Sullivan remarked. 'NO! I won't do it. Not after they helped us like they did.'

"A second statement made by Sullivan, on February 25th, gave additional information but none that would be of any value to the officers. Sullivan again gave vent to his feelings regarding Connell by referring to him as a '... "rattle-brain," subject to "brain storms" ...'

"Sullivan told Capt. Pitcock that he and Eulos used the picture of a .22 Colt automatic pistol as a pattern in making the wooden pistol.

"The condemned man was asked who the man was who accompanied Connell to Little Rock several years ago when Detective Sergeant Wilson was knocked off (in) an automobile while attempting to arrest them.

"'His first name was Johnnie,' Sullivan said. 'That's all I know. He went up for killing a man in Okmulgee, Oklahoma. I never saw him but I heard him talk about him.'

"Sullivan said he never "pulled a job" in Arkansas except the final one at Pine Bluff. There, he and Connell entered a house, *stole some silverware and drove away in two Ford cars and had planned to drive back north. 'Connell had a crazy idea to start with, when we came to Hot Springs. It wasn't a bank but pretty near the same thing. He wanted to get the Bolz Jewelry Store.'*

"*Sullivan said Connell had planned to "rob the boxes" at night and that just the two of them were to stage the robbery.*

"*'What did you do?' (he) was asked.*

"*'I took a lot of it and told him no. He had hop dreams at times, I thought. He had dreams that would make a hop-head ashamed of himself. He took everything for granted. He was a great fellow for reading things and trying to pull the same thing.'*

"*Sullivan said Connell "pulled" most of his work in the south, adding, 'he raised a lot of hell down in Mississippi.'*

"*The condemned man said Connell was most likely the man who killed Patrolman John Lund at Sapulpa, Oklahoma, and that he (Sullivan) had been arrested for the crime. He proved his alibi and was released. Sullivan said he was in bed suffering with a wound to his foot at the time Lund was killed. He said he received the shot accidentally while he and his dad were hunting.*

"*'How many were you with Connell at the time of the Lund shooting?' was asked of Sullivan.*

"*'Only one, but Emory done all the shooting. I would rather not say who was with him.' And he didn't say.*

"*'Wasn't Emory always quick to shoot?'*

"*'Yes, Sir,' replied Sullivan. 'Ordinarily he was a fine fellow, but the minute anything started, he wasn't human. In an argument between friends, the first thing, he would have his gun out. He was a crack shot. I am considered a pretty good shot, but he*

*could take a .45 automatic pistol and shoot as well as I could
with a rifle.'*

"*During a lull in the conversation, Sullivan voluntarily said,
'In my dealings with the Little Rock police, I found more truth
and honor. There wasn't an officer that got on the stand and
swore a lie, but that preacher sure did. If Hay would have lived,
I'd never gone to the chair. I'm positive Hay never said they
were officers as they entered the Waddell home.'*

"*Sullivan said he went to Waddell's house several days before
the shooting and got a half pint of whiskey. He said he first met
Connell at Pawhuska, Oklahoma, where he (Sullivan) was in jail
for bank robbery.*

"*'What bank robbery was that?' was asked.*

"*'The Bank of Grainola, Oklahoma,' (The Grainola State
Bank), was the reply.*

"*'What did they do with you?'*

"*'I was guilty, but they didn't identify me. They identified
one of my partners, Dick Osborne. He was killed a little later in
Missouri, by his own gang, while they were "kicking in a jug."
He was killed by mistake.' (By "kicking in a jug," Sullivan was
referring to robbing a bank)."*

Chapter 13: Whiskey "Runs" From New Orleans

Picher, Oklahoma, a tiny little mining town in Ottawa County, in the northeast corner of Oklahoma, was home to the richest lead and zinc mining fields in the world. During the 1920s, more money was made in Ottawa County than all of the other counties combined in the whole state. Starting from bare prairie land, the community sprang up almost overnight.

The boom town of Cardin, Oklahoma, was first known as Tar River, and sprang up just as fast as Picher. It was just a hop, skip, and a jump from Picher and consisted mainly of miner's shanties and rooming houses. Some of the more notable mines that operated in Cardin were the Dorothy, the Rialto, the Bill, the Goldenrod, the John Beaver, and the Croesus.

The towns of Picher and Cardin, after several years of modernization, improved from barren and treeless shanty towns at the turn of the century, to much more civilized communities by, and during, the decade of the 1920s.

Edna took Jack Murray home to Cardin and they later decided to settle nearby in Picher, Oklahoma. A short time later, they bought a 50% interest in the DeLuxe Barber Shop on Second Street. It turned out to be a good "front" for their bootlegging activities in the whiskey trade. They lived at the nearby Vernon Hotel when they weren't transporting liquor between New Orleans, Louisiana, and Kansas City, Missouri. This was during the Prohibition Era, and a lot of folks were making a lot of money in this manner. They paid $32 a case for the liquor in New Orleans, and then sold it for $100 a case in Kansas City on these trips. Since they could accommodate 20 cases of liquor in one car, they could accumulate a gross profit of over $1,300 per trip, before expenses. Sometimes, when Edna would drive a coupe, and Jack would drive a roadster, their combined gross profit for the trip could top $2,000. This arrangement was working out so well, that Doris and her new beau, Earl Stuchlik, decided to get in on the action, and soon, they too were also making whiskey runs from New Orleans to Kansas City.

Dora Vinita "Doris" Stanley & Martha Edna Stanley Murray "Courtesy of Bill Stanley"

According to Edna, they always stayed at the Mandeville Hotel in Mandeville, Louisiana, before driving to Kansas City. Boarding the ferry at the Helena Crossing into Arkansas was a bit risky, but usually after making it through that phase of the trip, they were home free.

1-16-1920, the day before the 18th amendment was to take effect, liquor stores across the nation put out their signs for "Last Call for Alcohol." A vast and unstoppable illegal trade was born on January 17, 1920 – "Bootlegging" during prohibition.

Once, when Edna was with Jack, they were stopped by the sheriff in a small town in Arkansas. Upon a search of their vehicle, the sheriff discovered the hidden whiskey. Jack talked to the sheriff for a while and, it turned out that for $100, plus the confiscation of the whiskey, Jack and Edna could continue to be on their way. Another time, in the fall of 1924, they were in the vicinity of Clarksville, Arkansas, when Jack was arrested with a full carload of liquor in his vehicle. Edna was walking out of a nearby store at the time, and managed to avoid arrest by walking away when she saw what was happening. She then proceeded to hop on a train headed for Joplin, Missouri, where they had rented a house on West 4th Street the previous month.

On or about October 6, 1924, both couples, along with two other men, were arrested in New Orleans. Realizing that Doris was the widow of Emory Connell, that story occupied the newspapers for days. New Orleans police and U. S. Department of Justice agents grilled the six prisoners who were being held in the parish prison, all believed to be members of the notorious "Connell Gang," whose former leader was slain after a long series of crimes. The newspaper accounts went on to incorrectly speculate that Doris Connell was Emory's sister, as well as his successor as leader of the gang. Meanwhile, Mrs. Jack (Edna) Murray, along with Jack Murray, Gus Nichols, Earl Stuchlik, and Jess M. Grutcher made up the rest of the gang.

The police reported to the newspapers that Doris had been married to Emory Connell before he and a pal named Sullivan were sentenced to death in Little Rock, for the slaying of two detectives. The police further related to the newspapers how Connell staged a spectacular escape a few days before the execution, but was later killed by a posse in a shoot-out.

Edna got a chuckle out of the fact that they had Sullivan's widow in there too, right under their noses, and missed their chance at a **REALLY** big story.

The papers further stated that authorities in New Orleans and in other cities planned to question them as alleged suspects in a number of crimes. It was said that at least two of the six prisoners being held had connections to the infamous Starr Gang of Oklahoma outlaws, which had broken up recently when their leaders were killed by posses and deputy sheriffs.

Unable to come up with any concrete evidence against the so-called "Connell Gang," the New Orleans police released them after several days.

Earl Charles Stuchlik – Doris Stanley's 4th husband "Courtesy of Robert Winter"

Whether she did so legally or not, Doris changed her last name to "Stuchlik," and she and Earl, along with Edna and Jack Murray, shared an apartment near 35th and Broadway, in Kansas City. Edna later recalled that Jack was sick throughout this time period due to his addiction to morphine. It wasn't until then that she learned he had been using morphine for quite some time, stating that he used it "… on account of his tuber-culosis." By this time, she almost always went with him on the whiskey "runs" from New Orleans because he would tire so easily and he couldn't make the long round trip by himself. But Jack didn't know how much more bad luck was in store for him.

Chapter 14: Happy New Year, 1925

By the end of the year, 1924, Edna still had not stopped thinking about Volney Davis, who had now been in prison for about four years. During this time, she did not fail to send him candy and gifts every Christmas. This year Doris helped her fix up a nice box of gifts for him, and Volney, in return, sent the gals a nice note thanking them for their thoughts and generosity. It was only a few days later that Edna and Doris, upon reading the newspaper, discovered that Volney and several other prisoners had made a desperate break over the walls and escaped from the Oklahoma State Penitentiary on January 8, 1925. Edna received a telegram the day after the escape, asking her for money to travel to Kansas City. She knew he would do the same for her. Besides, just the thought of being able to see him again was all the hope she needed. Doris wired the money to Volney, where he was currently lying low in Texas — somewhere along the Red River. About two days later, he showed up at their apartment in Kansas City.

It had to have been a bit awkward for Edna, having her husband, her former lover, and herself — plus her sister and brother-in-law — all living together in such close quarters. Edna suggested they get Volney one of the little sleeping rooms down the hall, so Doris rented a room for him. The wheels in Edna's head were turning now, and Volney had no doubt whatsoever what she was up to. Doris and Earl were "on to her" too, but they couldn't really blame her. After all, Volney was Edna's one true love, and they probably would still have been together had he not gone to prison. Edna's husband, Jack, was in a delusional state most the time, anyway, either from the liquor or the morphine he consumed daily. It was all he could do to get any relief from the horrible choking cough, caused by his tuberculosis.

Edna and Volney enjoyed their time together for a little over a week, with Doris keeping them fed well in order for them to keep up their strength. Nobody had yet come up with any ideas as to what Volney was going to do next. One day, Edna went into town to pick up a few things, and in her new and renewed state of euphoria and again being love-struck, she was observed by a police officer who became suspicious of her activities.

Arriving back at the apartment, Edna chatted with Doris, Earl, Jack, and Volney as she unpacked her grocery sacks. She had been inside the apartment for only a few minutes, when there was a knock on the door. Upon opening it, three police officers abruptly entered. Volney took one look at them. His adrenaline kicked in and his first instinct was to run for it. He made a quick dash for the door and ran down the hallway, looking for his first real chance for escape — found it — and proceeded to jump out of a second story window. The instant he hit the ground, two more police officers were quick to attack him, and commenced to beat him severely about the head. After a few more well placed kicks to the head and a few more night sticks to the midsection, they hauled him back upstairs to the apartment.

Of course, Volney wrongly assumed that the police were after him, and he therefore thought that someone had tipped the police off, concerning his whereabouts. Edna knew better, but Volney was unable to stick around long enough to find out. The only thing that the police were looking for was whiskey, but that fact was of no help to Volney at this point.

As a result of that raid, which occurred on January 21, 1925, all five occupants went to jail. Doris arranged bail for everyone except Volney, which she could not do since he was going back to prison in McAlester, Oklahoma, to face his punishment for his latest escape, and to resume his life sentence for murder.

Shortly thereafter, in mid-February, Jack and Edna Murray rented their own apartment on Jefferson Street. Life was now somewhat normal, as if there was ever anything approaching normalcy in Edna's life. She believed that once the police found Volney at their place, the police were determined to arrest her and Jack on one charge or another. Frequently arrested for anything that had happened in, or around, the city, they would often be held over for investigation, only to be later released for lack of evidence. The Kansas City Chief of Detectives told Jack Murray that he knew he was a thief, and he was going to send him to the penitentiary.

"But, I'm not a thief, I'm a bootlegger," Jack told him. "If you weren't a thief, you couldn't be her husband," the Chief responded, pointing to Edna. "All she knows is thieves, like Joe Sullivan and Volney Davis." That statement hit too close to home, which made Edna come completely unglued, and she launched into a tirade of cursing. That put the frosting on the cake as far as the Chief was concerned. If he didn't like her before, the Chief, for sure, certainly didn't like her now.

Edna realized, only later, that she had acted foolishly with this outburst of temper.

Author's note:

This is an important turning point in the story. At this point, Edna has realized that she has been identified as an independent entity, and as a person marked for the police to use to identify criminals and criminality.

Chapter 15: The Origin Of Edna's Nickname: "The Kissing Bandit"

Edna and Jack Murray were still in the business of transporting liquor from New Orleans to Kansas City, when, on one of these visits they had an intermediate stop in Joplin, Missouri, to deliver 12 of the 20 cases of whiskey to the home of one of their clients. During this transaction, Jack was arrested by the local police, and his car was confiscated along with all 20 cases of liquor inside. Edna had evaded capture and was able to pay for his bond the next day, and then they continued on their way to Kansas City to regroup.

It seemed that times were getting harder, even for bootleggers. Edna and Jack were having a rough go of it as of late, especially since Jack's lung condition was getting worse by the day, and both he and Edna had bad habits and addictions that were getting all the more difficult to financially support.

Probably half lit on "hooch" herself, and accompanied by someone with possibly a morphine addiction, Edna and Jack Murray robbed a clergyman in Kansas City who was also a collector for the Independence Avenue Cash Market. Edna drove the car while they kidnapped Reverend H. H. Southward and robbed him of his valuables and shoes.

Witnesses later reported that Edna seemed to be in charge of the abduction. They described her as having a blonde bobbed hairdo and she approached Reverend Southward with a smile on her face, in the alley near the Commerce Trust Bank, asking, "Where are you going, cutie?"

Reverend Southward then turned around to find out that he was facing the "business end" of a revolver just before his coat was wrapped around his head and he was unceremoniously deposited into the bandit's car. Edna drove the car, described as a Dodge Touring model. She smiled and waved at several traffic policemen when they would give her the signal to proceed. She even asked one officer what would be the best road to Dodson Avenue, in Kansas City.

After taking the clergyman's cash — $112 — plus $83 in checks, Edna asked the reverend if he would like a kiss, as her idea of a type of consolation for this crime. The clergyman later said that he turned her down. Even though the incident gained her the nickname of "The Kissing Bandit," that refusal of her offer had to be a bit deflating to her ego.

Then on April 6, 1925, Edna and Jack were driving in their Buick Roadster automobile, with Edna at the wheel, when they were pulled over and arrested at 18th & Oak Streets, in Kansas City. The arresting officers were J. Ed Joy and E. R. Surface, who were working out of the Motor Theft Bureau.

"The Chief (of Police) wants to see you," one of the officers said. Jack and Edna gave their address as 13th and Lydia Avenue. Once they arrived at the police station, they were booked for investigation like so many times before, and then promptly thrown in the "slammer." The next day, Jack and Edna were taken through a police lineup. Afterwards, one of the detectives came in and said, "Well, Edna, that's a tough break." Feigning innocence, Edna blinked her eyes and asked, "Well, what do you mean, detective?" The detective responded by saying, "You and Jack have been identified for highway robbery."

74

Jack and Edna played their act out for all it was worth, pretending not to have a clue as to what the detective was talking about. Finally, realizing that she was convincing no one — and it was getting way past "toddy" time without having yet had a drink — Edna, befittingly, threw another one of her screaming tantrums. The police officers just pushed her back in her cell and shut the door. She then proceeded to call the Kansas City Police Chief every foul name she could think of. Later, she said that after that arrest, she and Jack got blamed for everything, despite her persistence that they had been framed for this particular incident.

The judge set each of their bail at $10,000. Jack said he didn't want to waste money getting bond, and he would prefer to just sit in jail. Not so, for Edna. She wanted to get out of there and she needed a drink, pronto! She called upon Doris to promptly arrange for her bail.

The trial was first set for July, 1925, but was later postponed and rescheduled for 2 months later, in September. Edna's lawyer told her not to worry since he had five witnesses lined up for her defense.

Charged with armed robbery in the first degree, Jack and Edna Murray were each sentenced on October 1, 1925, to 25 years in the Missouri State Penitentiary at Jefferson City, Missouri. Edna left the courtroom screaming, "I've been framed!"

Edna Murray was confined to the Missouri Women's State Penitentiary to begin her 25 year sentence on December 3, 1925, shortly before Christmas. The newspapers across the country were filled with stories about "The Kissing Bandit."

Jack Murray (Edna's 4th husband) and Edna Murray (with the Missouri State Penitentiary Building in the background). "Courtesy of the Collection of Debbie Moss"

Chapter 16: Conditions At
The Missouri State Penitentiary

On March 26, 1876, Carrie Katherine "Kate" Richards, the third of five children, was born to Kansas homesteaders Andrew and Lucy Richards. Growing up in Ottawa County, Kate Richards absorbed her parents' devout Campbellite faith. As she came of age, she became involved with a variety of philanthropic organizations. Kate had hoped to become a minister or missionary, but women were not allowed to join the clergy. So after graduating from high school, she moved to Pawnee City, Nebraska, where she earned her teaching certificate. She taught elementary school for a short time while, and at the same time, she also began her journalistic career by contributing articles to a populist newspaper in Burchard, Nebraska.

After becoming disenchanted with teaching, Kate then moved to Kansas City where her father worked as a machinist. She initially worked for her father as a clerical assistant, while he taught her to persevere in a male-dominated line of work. Kate later filled a position as a machinist's apprentice where she was harassed by the men who didn't believe she should be doing a man's job, and was subsequently given the worst tasks in hopes that she might quit. Ultimately, Kate became one of the first women to have a membership in the International Association of Machinists. Her growing interest in industrial unionism caused her to reject organized religion when she discovered that affluent congregation members were violating workers' rights, employing children, and renting properties to be used for brothels.

Kate Richards was attending the Cigar Makers International Union Ball in Kansas City when she listened to 65 year-old Mary Harris Jones speak about dedicating her life to labor activism. From that moment on, Kate immersed herself in socialist teachings. She joined the Socialist Party of America in 1901 and attended the International School of Social Economy in Girard, Kansas. While in Girard, she met and fell in love with Frank P. O'Hare. They married on January 1, 1902, spending their honeymoon traveling and promoting socialism in Missouri and Kansas.

Kate Richards O'Hare traveled the country and delivered countless speeches from 1904 through much of the 1920s. She had a natural charm and was a national sensation by the time she was only 30 years old. Her physical appearance added to her impact as she accentuated her long slender frame and red hair by dressing in flaming red dresses.

On July 17, 1917, Kate gave a speech to a crowd in Bowman, North Dakota. Justice Department officials, who had been following and observing the O'Hares for some time, seized upon this opportunity, and arrested Kate on July 29th, and indicted her for "… willfully obstructing the enlistment and recruiting services of the United States." Although Kate's version of what she had said was in no way illegal, she was nevertheless convicted under the Espionage Act, which had only been enacted into law one month earlier, on June 15, 1917.

Kate Richards was later sentenced on April 15, 1919, to 5 years in prison at the Missouri State Penitentiary in Jefferson City.

On May 30, 1920, Kate Richards O'Hare was pardoned by President Warren G. Harding, responding to pressure from a nationwide campaign of progressives and socialists to free her.

Kate Richards O'Hare (assigned federal prison number 21669), from the first day of her 14 month incarceration, vowed that she would devote the remainder of her life to remedying the abuses of the prison system. She documented her time spent in prison and filed a report to the government after her release. The following was taken from her almost 200 page document that was released to the public on June 29, 1925:

"The Prison" — *"The state penitentiary at Jefferson City, Missouri, has enjoyed the distinction of being the largest prison in the United States, if not in the world. The females' wing, which, at the time I was there, was about 15 years old. It was constructed of stone and concrete with tile and cement floors, heavily barred but plentiful windows, and a fairly modern but woefully dilapidated heating system.*

"The cell house, which is the living quarters of the women prisoners, is a long building with a cage of cells in the center, four cells high and two deep, facing in opposite directions. The cells are seven feet wide, eight (feet) deep, and seven (feet) high. The ceiling, back, and sidewalls of each cell are of solid steel, the floor of cement, and front of steel bars. Each cell is supplied with a toilet and a lavatory with running cold water. At the time I was there each woman had her own cell, and considerable latitude was given the women in furnishing and decorating their cells, at their own expense. Each cell was supplied with a steel bunk fastened to the wall; two bags of straw, one for a mattress and the other for a pillow; a crude kitchen table; a stool or chair, usually in the last stages of decrepitude; and a broom and dustpan. Each woman is given, when she is "dressed in," three

coarse brown muslin sheets, two pillowcases, two brown wash towels, and two coarse and very dirty blankets of most questionable antecedents. The women were required, under severe penalty, to keep their cells as clean and tidy as was possible in their dilapidated condition. Thursday evening after work hours was cleaning time, and each woman was required to remove everything from her cell and clean and scrub it.

"At the time I entered, the wing was very dirty and, in most essentials, shabby and unsanitary. Every crack and crevice of the cell house was full of vermin of every known sort, which no amount of scrubbing on the part of the women could permanently dislodge.

"The dining room was light and airy. At the time I entered, the walls were streaked with grime and the ceiling covered with an unbelievably heavy coat of fly specks. The dining room was not screened, and 15 years' accumulation of well preserved flyspecks was an astounding thing to behold. My first prison meal is, of course, a vivid memory. I found the dining room filled with long wooden benches like the old-fashioned school desks, each seating eight women. The white women occupied one side of the room and the colored women the other. The dishes were of rusty, battered tin ware, the knives and forks of cast iron, and, for some incomprehensible reason, the spoons were non-existent. If a woman wished to use a spoon, she was compelled to buy it with her own money and carry it about in the one pocket she possessed, along with her pocket handkerchief and other movable property.

"The first thing that struck me was the dead, rancid odor, the typical institution smell, much intensified. It was the concentrated

odor of dead air, venerable hash, ancient stews, senile "wienies," and cabbage soup, mingled with the musty odor of decaying wood saturated with rancid grease and homemade soap.

"The benches and tables were very old, having done service for more than half a century. Many generations of prisoners had scrubbed them; they creaked and groaned with the infirmities of age, and every crack and crevice was inhabited with old and well-established cockroach families. They were very hungry roaches, who insisted on sharing our meals with us; so we ate with one hand and picked roaches out of our food with the other. I was not adept at one-handed eating and could not develop a taste for roaches to garnish my food. I made enough fuss about the matter to induce the management to have the dining room cleaned and painted, and to provide tables, chairs, white tablecloths, and real dishes. The dining room is now quite civilized, except for the missing spoons.

"Few of the older prison buildings are so well supplied with windows as the females' wing of the Missouri State Penitentiary, but for the most part the windows are quite useless. Fifteen years' accumulation of dirt was fairly efficient in shutting out light and sunshine, and where it was not entirely satisfactory, the windows had been painted over with gray paint — to prevent the women flirting with the men on the other side of the wall, the matron said. Many of the windows were nailed shut, and the dread of fresh air so common to all ignorant people, kept the others tightly closed except in the very hot weather. The absolute control of the ventilation of the cell house was in the hands of a Negro stool pigeon whose fanatical fear of night air kept us in a state of semi-suffocation both winter and summer.

81

"Rats, flies, and cockroaches, not to mention other vermin unmentionable in polite society, were plagues of our prison life. The rats were perhaps the worst of all. They overran the place in swarms, scampered over the dining tables, nibbled our bread, played in our dishes, crept into bed with us, chewed up our shoes, and carried off everything not nailed down or hung far above their reach. I have not the instinctive fear of rats and mice that many women have, but for weeks I spent sleepless nights routing them out of my bed and chasing them out of my cell. Not until my young son visited the prison and had the ingenuity to think of covering the front bars with screen wire, did I ever know a night's rest.

"The most robust and buxom cockroaches I have ever known were ever-present and fought with the rats for the food which we were permitted to buy. There were no screens, and the flies swarmed about the cell house in clouds. One of the most terrible things which I had to endure was that (of) an Indian woman in the last stages of syphilis, her body covered with open lesions and dripping pus, occupied the cell directly below me. Her open sores were never properly dressed, the stench was frightful, and the flies swarmed over her and then awakened us in the morning by crawling over our faces. The effect of these unnecessary pests upon human nerves can readily be imagined. The sleepless nights caused by them were a very large factor in the punishments administered for "bad work" and failure to make "the task."

"The bathing facilities gave me my first real introduction to prison horrors. At the time I entered there were two old, cracked, rusty bathtubs in the bathroom and one in the unfurnished

hospital room. Naturally, among women so largely recruited from the underworld, venereal disease was very common. There was no effort to segregate the clean women from the infected, and on bathing night, which came once a week, we all used the same tubs.

"On my first bathing night, as I awaited my turn to bathe, an Indian woman by the name of Alice Cox stepped out of the bathroom, and I was ordered to use the tub which she had just vacated.

"As Alice stepped out of the bathroom she was one of the most terrible creatures I have ever seen. From her throat to her feet she was one mass of open sores dripping pus. I have seen her with her clothes so stiff with dried pus that they rattled when she walked, and I have seen live maggots working out of the filthy bandages about her neck.

"Alice had used the bathtub, and I was ordered to use it also. I asked the matron if it was necessary that I use the same tub that Alice had used, and she said it was. I then asked who cleaned the tub, and she replied that Alice was too ill and that I was to do it. I then asked what disinfectants were used. "Disinfectants!" she snarled; 'whatdaya mean?'

"'I mean what prophylactic measures do you use to keep the clean women from becoming infected with venereal disease?' I replied.

"She screeched: 'Hell, we ain't got none of them high-falutin' things here. This ain't no swell hotel --- this is the pen!'

"I protested: 'But Miss Smith, you know what disease Alice has, you know how communicable it is, you know that if I use that

tub I may become infected. You know I am a married woman with a husband and four children. You know I travel a great deal and sleep in Pullman cars and use public facilities. Does the United States Department of Justice expect me to become infected with syphilis and go back to civilized life and infect others who are certainly innocent of wrong-doing?'

"Sputtering and snarling with rage, the matron cried: 'I don't know a thing about that, and care a damn sight less. You are a convict; this is what there is here for you to use. Now get ter Hell outta here and take yer bath!'

"'But I refuse. To do so would be a social crime!' I replied.

"Shrieking and cursing, the matron told me that I would bathe in the infected tub or she would send me to the "black hole" and "break" me. I knew she had the power and temperament to do it. She had broken Minnie Eddy in the black hole a few weeks previous — and Minnie had been carried out in a pine box. So I stepped into the bathroom and turned on the taps — but I did not bathe.

"That night I got a letter out "underground" to my husband. He reproduced the letter and sent it to a thousand influential people. It was published in newspapers and magazines, and a storm of protest arose all over the country. In less than three weeks we had shower baths installed in the females' wing of the prison, and that horror was abated.

"I was able to rout the common bathtub, but I was never able to prevent the diseased women from handling the food. The women who were too ill to work in the shop were used in the dining room. I think all of them were tubercular and syphilitic. I have seen the food which the women were forced to eat handled *by women with pus oozing from open sores on their arms and dripping into the dishes, and it was a common sight to see our food sprayed with tuberculosis germs from the lips of coughing convicts.*

"The great majority of the women prisoners were in sore need of hospitalization; yet no hospital facilities were provided. Regardless of how serious or how contagious the illness that might develop, the women were kept locked in their cells when ill. When the females' wing was built, a fairly good hospital room was provided; but the years have come and gone, and no warden or prison board has ever thought it worthwhile to equip this room, and it was used only for solitary confinement and punishment. Five hundred dollars intelligently expended would equip the room reasonably well and provide the facilities demanded by common decency. The women convicts have produced hundreds of thousands of dollars' worth of wealth in the prison workshop, but not a penny of it has been expended in furnishing a hospital to give civilized care to the women when they have been physically wrecked by the driven labor of the contract shop. Having been seriously ill twice while in prison, I know by actual experience how bad these conditions are. On one occasion I suffered a heat prostration because of the unbearable heat and bad ventilation in the workshop. I was thrown into my cell at two o'clock in the afternoon; and the trustee was ordered by the matron to give all the women notice that no one was to come near my cell, and that if anyone gave me a drink of water, both she and I would go to the black hole. The matron later told the warden that she had given this order because she believed that I was stalling to avoid work, though I had never made the slightest protest against doing the work assigned me. In fever and torturing thirst I lay unattended

from two in the afternoon until the women came in from the yard at six-thirty in the evening. The women told me later that I was quite delirious and begged for water, but no attention was given me until the prisoners started a mutiny. This forced the matron to call the warden. He insisted that I receive medical attention, which no doubt saved my life; but the women were brutally punished for their part in the matter.

"A very large percentage of the women suffered from tuberculosis — just how large I cannot say, for no survey has ever been made. The doctor ordered a special diet for the "tuberculars," but it was never provided. Of the women convicts who served with me, every one whom I have been able to keep in touch with since release is now suffering from tuberculosis or has died from it. The black hole, under-feeding, overwork, polluted air, fear, and punishment reduce the physical resistance of the women until they are easy prey for the ever-present germs, and I feel that very few indeed escape it.

"The average number of inmates of the women's wing was about one hundred, one-third Federal prisoners, and two-thirds State (prisoners). So far as I could determine, about seventy to eighty percent were subnormal mentally and physically; they were practically all neurotic and emotionally unstable and hag-ridden by social grudges that made them markedly psychopathic. There are no facilities for separating the sane from the insane, the feeble-minded, and psychopathic. In fact, no one seemed to have the slightest idea that it should be done.

"On that never-to-be-forgotten first day that looms so large in every prisoner's memory, after the ordeal of being "dressed in," I waited for my first meal with the women who have come to

mean more to me than any other associates I have ever known. With the women who cleaned the halls and worked in the prison laundry, and with those too ill to work, I lined up in a narrow hall and watched these modern chattel slaves march from the workshop to the dining room to eat their coarse and scanty prison fare.

"It was a tragic tale which that line of weary, toil-stained women told as they shuffled by — a challenge to our civilization, an indictment of our social system. There were women there scarred by the marks of toil, marred by the curse of poverty, and broken by the sordid struggle for existence. There were young girls there marked by the stamp of vice before the childish roundness of cheek and chin had settled into the hard lines of degraded womanhood. There were old women, some burned out by vice, and some bent with honest labor and childbearing. There were cripples and degenerates, consumptives and epileptics, dements and sex perverts, morons and high-grade imbeciles, and a very few who, under ordinary conditions, would be classed as normal.

"Because of the publicity aroused by the famous bathtub letter, which I smuggled out, the management gave eighty-six women the Wassermann Test one day. Fifty-eight gave positive reactions on the first test. No other examinations for diseases were given.

"Prison Food" — *"The prison breakfast consisted of corn syrup, bread, hash and a dark liquid, by courtesy, called coffee. The menu was very rarely varied, and monotony was one of its worst faults. The bread was usually very good, the syrup seemed wholesome, but the hash was uneatable. Judging from* its appearance — for I could never muster the courage to taste it — all manner of garbage went into the hash kettle. It was always stale, often rancid, and I have often watched the women who were forced to eat it, remove a nicely stewed maggot from its mysterious depths. Twice a week, oatmeal was served for breakfast, and in the winter months it was a godsend, for it was the only eatable food served hot. But as warm weather approached, so did the oatmeal worms; and as they were very husky specimens, large and hairy, they had a tendency to stick in our throats, and we found it necessary to abstain from this one warm breakfast dish.

"Lunch consisted of beef stew, a vegetable, bread, and water. Now and then "wienies" and mutton stew were served instead of beef stew, and on a few occasions we had liver and onions. The beef stew was usually fairly good, the "wienies" of very poor quality and always more or less tainted, and the mutton stew was rank beyond expression.

"Supper consisted of bread and corn syrup, sometimes a stewed fruit, always well seasoned with worms, (and) on rare occasions, pea soup, and the so-called coffee. A very small portion of skimmed milk was also served each day, sometimes at breakfast and sometimes at supper. The rich milk from the prison's herd of Jersey cows stopped downstairs in the matron's apartment. Every bit of cream was skimmed off and churned into butter by women convicts who told me that the butter was sold by the matron for her "private profit." The women (prisoners) received only the skimmed milk. No butterfat, and not a grain of sugar, was provided in the diet.

"In the fourteen months which I served in prison, the diet never varied and disgust at its monotony added to its unpalatableness.

Our food was prepared by men convicts, who, of course, were harried, unpaid, sullen workers, probably all in as bad condition from venereal diseases as the women who worked in the dining room. The kitchen in the men's wing was something like three blocks from our dining room. Our food was cooked early in the day and sent over as soon as prepared, and usually our dinners arrived about nine-thirty or ten o'clock in the morning and stood uncovered in the shop until stone cold and covered with shop dust, lint, and ravellings

"The only way to live in approximate comfort with the human being is to feed the brute. The average person who has lived a fairly normal life has no conception of what it means to be always hungry, hungry for days and weeks and years, and never to know the well being that comes from being well fed. It was not until I went to prison that I knew what constant and long continued hunger meant. It was not until I experienced it that I realized its mental, physical, and spiritual effects. And I was far more fortunate than most prisoners. I had money to buy what I wanted, and friends and comrades all over the country sent me luxuries of every sort. But I was never able to achieve a balanced ration. My civilized stomach was always affronted by cold food. And the sights and sounds and smells of prison never lost their disastrous effect on appetite and digestion.

"Prison Clothing" — *"When I was "dressed in," all of my own clothing was taken from me, and I was supplied with two each of drawers, chemises, and night gowns, made of the stiffest, coarsest, most raspy sort of brown muslin. I had never seen this "opossum skin" muslin (as it is called in the South) used for*

89

garments — only for awnings or tent flies. It was unbearably hot in summer and just as unbearably cold in winter, and it was so stiff and heavy that with only two garments, one laundered each week, a decent degree of bodily cleanliness was impossible. Our work dresses were made of what down South is called "nigger (sic) hickory shirting," a material now used for rough work blouses. It was "logwood" blue when new, but soon faded to a nondescript gray and shrank from washing until it was thick and stiff as a board. They were made long and wide to allow for shrinkage, and they fitted us like a circus tent draped about the center pole. Our Sunday dresses were made of a fair quality of blue gingham of the vintage of 1910, and they were really not obnoxious. We were supplied with one pair of cheap convict-made shoes that no ordinary human foot could endure, and one pair of cheap cotton stockings a year. Stockings were a source of a great deal of friction and caused many punishments to be inflicted. When a woman was "dressed in" she was given six pairs of stockings. She put on one and went to the shop to work; and the stool pigeon who carried the key to the cells stole the other five, which were again issued to a new prisoner. An eternal squabble went on over this practice.

"The convicts who worked in the laundry used wood tubs and washboards and wrung our circus tent chemises and dresses by hand. Only half enough soap was supplied to wash our clothing properly, and the garments soon assumed the appearance of badly cared for scrub cloths. No effort was made to separate the clothing of the clean women from those of the women infected with tuberculosis and venereal diseases. They were all washed together without sufficient soap and hot water and with no disinfectants, and naturally they came back to us reeking with disease germs.

"Prison Education" — *"While all education that might be helpful and possibly curative was relentlessly shut out, education in the ways of vice and crime and degeneracy flourished. I found learning the prison argot more interesting than any high school teacher ever made Latin. My vocabulary of profanity is rich and varied, and I am sure that I know a greater variety of cuss words, and more dynamic combinations of them, than any student of philology in the country. I also know the best methods of "raising a bill," "fixing a check," "passing the queer," (sic) and "frisking the molls." I have all the latest ideas in shoplifting; I know what to use in the way of knockout drops, and how to use it. A thorough education in sex perversions is part of the educational system of most prisoners, and for the most part the under keepers and the stool pigeons are very efficient teachers.*

"Task and Punishment" — *"In the studies which I was able to make of the small portion of our criminal population which lands in prison, I found the prison officials and their methods quite as interesting as the prisoners, and perhaps more dangerous to society.*

"The Missouri State Penitentiary, at the time I was there, was under the management of the State Board of Control, composed of William R. Painter, J. Kelly Poole, and Henry Andrae. This prison was not only a great penal institution, but it was also a great industrial plant which, during the year I was there, employed 2,600 inmates. The businessmen of Jefferson City advertised $7,000,000 annual sales of manufactured products, substantially all of which were wholly or partly manufactured in the prison. The state received $1,087,663 for this labor.

"It is one of the tragic comedies of our political system that this great industrial plant, transacting such an enormous business, and this penal institution, having the power of life and death over thousands of human beings, should be placed in the hands and under the unsupervised control of laymen; a country editor, a mule buyer, and a livery stable keeper.

"It is but natural that an institution managed by a mule buyer and a livery stable keeper, with its main objective to make the largest possible profit for a politician contractor, should give its inmates about the same care as mules in a livery stable. All these men were blissfully ignorant of penology, criminology, and psychology. I remarked to one of them one day that, if the young brute overseer who had charge of the women were replaced by an older man who knew something of production efficiency methods and human psychology, things would go more smoothly. He stared at me blankly and said: "I don't reckin' we need any of them new-fangled things here. A good hickory club and 'the hole' will fix 'em." I am quite sure that that fairly typical prison official had not a glimmer of understanding of the words used or of their application to his duties. He did not know whether I was suggesting a new brand of religion, a breakfast food, or a corn cure.

"I had fourteen months in which to endure "the task" system myself and to study it in relation to other women. I found that the task had been placed at the extreme limit of the strongest and most expert woman's skill and endurance. That meant that the majority of the women never could make the task regularly and were always at the mercy of this overseer. His theory was that a woman, if driven hard enough and treated brutally enough, would "pull the task," so he drove and bullied, cursed *and blackguarded, harried and punished, until the women made the task, or were utterly wrecked by the punishments inflicted. I could never decide whether it was chance or a well-thought-out plan that made the task consume a woman's life in the average length of a prison sentence. It was in reality the effect of the task system. The average length of time served is about two years, and the amount of labor demanded was just about enough to wear a woman out physically and send her back to society fit only for the human scrap-heap. The long-term women were put into the shop for about two years; then, when the physical break came, they were transferred to lighter work in the dining room or some other maintenance labor, and the newly received women took their places at the machines.*

"In theory the working day was nine hours, but very few of the women could make the task in that time, and the majority of them were forced to take work to their cells to finish. Most of the women spent one to two hours each day, after being locked into their cells, turning collars or snipping thread ends from suspenders.

"The lightest punishment for failure to make the task was to be sent to the cell after work hours, being deprived of letters, recreation, and all communication with other inmates. If this did not bring the required amount of product, the convict was sent to the cell on Saturday at noon, sometimes without dinner, fed on two very tiny slices of bread and water, and denied all privileges until Monday morning. If the task was still not forthcoming, the woman was put in "the hole."

"While in "the hole" the women were given two very thin slices of bread, about two by four inches in size, each day, and

about half a teacup full of water. This was the only food and drink permitted, and if any of the other convicts were detected giving additional food or water to a woman in "the hole," they were severely punished. The women were kept in "the hole" from two to fifteen days. That is, fifteen days was the limit of punishment administered while I was in prison, but before my advent there had been no limit, so the older inmates told me.

"The first cell which I occupied was directly across the narrow corridor from "the hole," and I was an eye witness to certain instances of brutality. A young colored girl, quite plainly demented, threw a pail of hot water on another woman who she thought was tormenting her. One of the male guards, whom the women called "The Gorilla," beat the cowering, pleading dement with his maul-like fists as she staggered down the corridor; then the handcuffs were placed on her wrist, passed through the bars in the blind cell doors, and snapped on the other wrist. The bridle, a sort of gag, which I never had opportunity to examine closely, was placed in her mouth to prevent her screaming, and she stayed there ringed and bridled from early in the afternoon until about nine at night. She was taken down just before the lights were out for the night, and so far as I know was not hung up again. She, however, spent fifteen days in "the hole;" then she was kept locked in her cell, absolutely without outdoor exercise or any privileges except during the hours spent in the shop, for three months. In other instances I heard the blows and the cries and pleadings of inmates, while they were being beaten by guards and matrons; but I did not see these brutalities, because they were out of my range of vision.

"It is a stark, ugly fact that homosexuality exists in every prison and must ever be one of the sinister facts of our penal system. In the Missouri State Penitentiary it is, next to "the task," the dominating feature of prison life and a regular source of revenue to favored stool pigeons. There seems to be considerable ground for the commonly accepted belief of the prison inmates that much of its graft and profits may percolate upward to the under officials. The Negress (sic) trustee or stool pigeon, who had absolute control of the women's cell building and all its inmates from six in the evening until six in the morning, handled the details of pandering to the homosexual vices so rampant in the prison, and there was a regular scale of charges for permitting the inmates to indulge. The charge for the use of a pervert was usually fifty cents, and the charge for having the cell door left open at night by the stool pigeon was one dollar. In fact, homosexuality was not only permitted by this trustee, but indulgence was actively fostered by this colored murderess, and, in cases of young, helpless, and unprotected women, actually demanded and enforced.

"Because this stool pigeon had sole charge of the cell house and of the lives of the women at night; because her word was always and unquestionably accepted without investigation by the matrons; because she, in fact, held the power of life and death over us, by being able to secure endless punishments in the blind cell; she could and did compel indulgence in this vice in order that its profits might be secured.

"Another concession held by this Negress (sic) was that of the sale of tobacco. Among the women of the underworld

95

as well as among those of the upper crust, cigarette smoking is almost universal. The prison rules forbid cigarettes, but their use is general. It was an open secret that this rule was not to be enforced as long as the women secured their cigarettes from the proper source, which, of course, was the stool pigeon. No one in constant contact with the women, as the matrons were, could possibly be ignorant of the fact that ninety per cent of the women smoked; the yellow-stained fingers and the smoke-laden air of the cell house loudly proclaimed it, and no punishments were ever administered during my time for smoking. But the most terrible punishments were administered for securing tobacco on which the stool pigeon did not secure her profits. For instance, Dora Campbell, a federal prisoner from Mississippi, convicted of harboring a deserter from the U.S. Army, was sent to "the hole" while ill, stayed there for a number of days — in fact, until some of the women secretly complained to the prison physician — and was taken out with a well-advanced case of pneumonia from which she never entirely recovered while in prison. Dora Campbell had secured a sack of tobacco without purchasing it from the trustee. The trustee's profits would have turned the most patriotic war profiteer green with envy. The stool pigeon received for a ten-cent sack of Bull Durham, two dollars; for a book of cigarette papers, fifty cents; and matches she retailed at "three for a dime."

"This same stool pigeon had complete control of all the women who were ill; and, since many of them were federal prisoners convicted under the Harrison Drug Act (first enacted in 1914), — (actually named "The Harrison Narcotics Tax Act") — and, of course, drug addicts, (by definition), the punishments

which she was permitted to inflict makes one doubt our claim to being a civilized nation. When drug addicts enter Jefferson City, absolutely all drugs are taken from them and they are left to "kick off the habit," as they say, without treatment or assistance. Naturally, their sufferings are frightful, and quite as naturally, they are noisy and troublesome. The stool pigeon uses any method she sees fit to quiet and subdue these half-demented creatures undergoing the most frightful tortures because of the sudden cessation of their accustomed narcotics.

"One instance stands out with glaring vividness in my memory. Pearl Hall, an elderly drug addict who had used narcotics for more than twenty years, was sent up from Little Rock, Arkansas. She was in very bad physical condition, and when all narcotics were taken from her, she moaned and raved continually. The stool pigeon and another convict quite as brutal, dunked the poor insane old creature in a bathtub filled with ice water until she was too weak to make further outcry. She was then thrown in her cell in her wet clothing, and lay there moaning and raving until, a few days later, pneumonia ended her tortures.

"In all the fourteen months I spent in prison I never heard an inmate addressed courteously; never heard one single kind, encouraging, or helpful word from the petty officials with whom we were in constant contact. One of my most horrible memories is that of the voices of our keepers. They never spoke to us as normal human beings speak; they either snarled at us, cursed us, or screeched at us, and those snarling, rasping hateful voices still haunt my dreams."

Author's note:

After her divorce from Francis O'Hare in 1928, Kate married Charles Cunningham, a San Francisco lawyer, and went to live in California. She remained active in progressive politics and as Assistant Director of the California Department of Penology (1939-1940), she reformed the state's prison system. Following an active life, including attending sessions of California Governor Earl Warren's State Crime Commission, Kate passed away on January 10, 1948, of a sudden heart attack.

Chapter 17: Edna Murray's First Escape — May 2, 1927

Life among the rats and roaches of prison apparently didn't set too well with Edna, who had bigger and better things in mind. By the time she put her plans into action, she had only served a small fraction of her 25 year sentence. After her escape on May 2, 1927, she was on the lam with no particular place to go. It was a lonely and frightening experience, even for someone as daring as Edna. Her son, Preston, was still with her parents in Cardin, Oklahoma, but as much as she wanted to see them, she couldn't take the risk of returning to her home. She knew that would be the first place that the federal boys would look for her.

Edna proceeded to zigzag across Kansas, doing whatever it took to keep on the move. She visited her cousin, Ralph Cressman, and his family, in Emporia, Kansas. Ralph's mother, Zella, and Edna's mother, Louie Nettie, were sisters. Edna was treated decently at the Cressman's home, but they made it known to her that they wouldn't welcome a return visit. Next, Edna went to Parkerville, Kansas, a tiny town of about 125 inhabitants, located on a branch line of the Missouri-Kansas-Texas (M. K. & T.) Railroad Line.

Another one of Lou Stanley's sisters, Neal, and her husband, Henry Taylor, lived on a farm just about a quarter of a mile north of town. They, too, had heard of "The Kissing Bandit" and gave Edna the cold shoulder.

Upon her arrival at Junction City, Kansas, Edna found herself in a more appreciative atmosphere when she ran into some of the boys from the Ft. Riley, Kansas, Army Base. She hung around there as long as she dared, and picked up a few bucks, before heading out of town.

Hitchhiking down the road, Edna found herself in her old neighborhood of Marion, Kansas. The town hadn't changed a great deal, but she had been gone too long to know where to find any of her former acquaintances. She continued on in a southeasterly direction, to the town of Florence, Kansas. There, her brother, Fred, lived when he wasn't working in the oil fields, or drying out in the local jail after being arrested for intoxication. Since the local officials kept a close watch on Fred, Edna decided to cut her trip short.

Edna then made her way west to the town of Hill City, Kansas, where her sister, Doris, and her husband, Earl, were currently residing. Earl's dad also lived in Hill City. At the time of Edna's visit, Doris' son, "Little" Mott, and Edna's son, Preston, just happened to be visiting with them. This was one of very few opportunities during this time in which Edna could visit with Preston since she was currently on the lam. It was also, coincidentally, during this time period that the bank in Hill City was robbed. Officials were never able to figure out who pulled off that job, since no one thought it possible that any local townspeople would even think of robbing a bank in their own town. Maybe that was the idea behind this robbery.

Edna's next destination was for the town of Sapulpa, Oklahoma, where her baby brother, Ginney, and his family lived. Edna still had contacts there and she knew that a gal could always turn a trick, if she so desired, when she checked into the Carlton Hotel. It's quite likely that she may even have run into Alvin Karpis, squiring Carol Hamilton about town. Carol had worked as a prostitute out of the Carlton Hotel right after her release from the Colorado State Penitentiary in Canon City, Colorado, on October 2, 1929. She was Alvin Karpis' girlfriend for a while, having previously been the moll of Herman Barker, one of Ma Barker's boys. Alvin Karpis would later help form the Barker-Karpis Gang.

Edna eventually made her way back up to the more familiar and friendly locale of Kansas City where she knew her way around quite well, and, after that, she found her way to Chicago. It was there in Chicago, on September 10, 1931, that Edna was arrested during a raid on a bar on the north side of Chicago, near the 2200 block of N. Sedgwick Street (Sedgwick Street & Webster Avenue) — only about a block or so away from the location of the infamous St. Valentine's Day Massacre (2122 N. Clark Street), which had occurred in 1929.

In reminiscing about the raid on the bar, Edna once said, "Had it not been for them taking my fingerprints, I think I could have gotten away free." At the time of Edna's recapture in Chicago, she was in a pitiful physical condition. Her addiction to alcohol, coupled with the possible beginnings of a drug habit had "… brought her down, way down, about as low as she could go." Her capture in the Chicago raid was, in reality, a godsend that, in all probability, saved her life.

Chapter 18: Edna Murray: The Triple Escape Queen

Warden Leslie Rudolph designated "Farm Number 1" as the Women's Division of the Missouri State Penitentiary in Jefferson City, Missouri, while he was warden there in 1926.

Farm 1, Women's Prison, Jefferson City, Mo. "Courtesy of the Collection of Debbie Moss"

Edna Murray was one of the prisoners in the first group of approx-imately 50 women moved there from the main penitentiary. Previously, there had been nothing, really, to stop Edna from just walking away, as she did on May 2, 1927, until she was later arrested during a raid in Chicago, Illinois, on September 10, 1931.

Shortly after this raid, during a routine fingerprinting proce-dure, Edna's true identity was discovered, and she was immedi-ately returned to the Missouri State Penitentiary. To her surprise, she was placed in an individual cell in a new cell house that had been built during her absence. Edna was in such poor physi-cal condition from the use and abuse of alcohol and drugs that Warden Rudolph and his wife, who helped run "Farm Number 1," felt sorry for her. It was customary to give those placed in the cell house only bread and water, but they gave Edna good food and an occasional cigarette. She wasn't allowed any illegal drugs, of course, but they did give her sedatives and what they called sleep-ing potions from time to time in order to settle her nerves.

Upon her return to the penitentiary, Edna was placed in solitary confinement for 30 days, and she said that this confinement only made her condition all the worse. She further stated that she "… hated prison officials, the laws, and anyone who had anything to do with her being in prison." She wouldn't talk much and she was already planning for her next escape.

Edna Murray – not happy to be back in the pen

After giving her promise to Warden Rudolph that she would no longer try to escape, she was allowed to return to the main dormitory of the prison. Shortly thereafter, Edna broke that promise, when, on November 4, 1931, she and two other women climbed over the fence and escaped from the farm — a fence that also had been constructed during her absence after her first escape. The penitentiary guards and local law enforcement came up empty-handed during their search for Edna and the girls, but a prison trustee and his bloodhounds fared better. All three women were captured early the next morning before they even had a chance to get out of Jefferson City. One of the women became sick and was duly removed from the obligatory punishment of solitary confinement, but the other two women, including Edna, were not as fortunate.

Warden Rudolph talked to Edna after her return about her having given him her word that she would not try to escape. She calmly admitted that her word was no longer any good, and although she didn't seem to resent being recaptured, she also didn't seem to harbor any ill feelings toward him, according to Warden Rudolph.

Edna was once again behind bars, back in the cell house. This time she occupied a cell on the south side, directly across from Irene McCann.

Irene McCann was about to become another chapter in Edna's life. She had her own history, as is explained in the following excerpts from newspapers of that period:

Carthage, Missouri
December 14, 1930
OFFICER KILLED WHEN MAN AND GIRL RAID JAIL

"A hat and a woman's shoe heel were the only clues officers had to go on after a young man and woman had shot and killed 50 year old E. O. Bray, (a) jailer at the Jasper County, (Missouri), Jail. A four state search was being conducted as officers covered the converging sections of Missouri, Kansas, Oklahoma and Arkansas. It was said that the slayer and his woman companion escaped in a small coupe bearing Kansas license tags. The pair had asked to see Bill Daggett of Joplin, Missouri, who had been released on Friday, after questioning in a petty larceny case. As Bray, acting jailer, turned to look at the jail record, the man seized Bray's revolver. He then shot three times, two bullets piercing Bray's heart. The slayer and the woman seized Bray's keys, unlocked one door and raced upstairs, where seven women were confined. However, after rattling the corridor door there a moment, the couple fled. The woman's lost heel proved to be the couple's downfall. After seeing a woman wearing a shoe with a missing heel, and learning of the clues left behind at the jail in Carthage, the Chief of Police in Chelsea, Oklahoma, arrested the couple. They were Albert McCann and his wife Irene McCann

who had been on a mission to release Albert's friend, Raymond Jackson, from the jail."

Carthage, Missouri
April 26, 1931

"Death by hanging is the penalty Albert McCann, 18-year-old Joplin slayer must pay for the December 14th murder of E. O. Bray, Carthage, (Missouri), jailer. 'We, the jury, find the defendant guilty of first degree murder and assess his penalty as death,' Judge Davis read. McCann, who sat with bowed head and folded hands, closed his eyes and seemed to flinch as he heard the death sentence read.

"There was a moment of silence as members of the family sat apparently dazed by the verdict. Then Mrs. Willard McCann, mother of the condemned youth, who had been with her son during the entire trial, collapsed in her chair and had to be carried out. Members of the audience were visibly affected as Mrs. McCann screamed, 'My son, my son!'

"McCann was led from the courtroom almost immediately after the verdict had been read. His stoic composure broke for the first time when his sister, Mabel McCann, went into the sheriff's office and threw her arms around his (Albert's) neck to comfort him. Shortly afterward, (Albert) McCann was allowed to go into the law library and see his mother, who had been placed on one of the long tables there following her collapse. His mother sobbed, 'Albert, Albert,' as her son put his arms around her. 'Don't cry mother, don't worry about me. I'll be all right,' McCann told his mother, and sobs wracked his body as he tried to console his grief-stricken mother. He was then led away to the county jail at Carthage, Missouri.

106

"The defense had tried to prove that Albert McCann suffered from insanity, exhibiting abnormal childhood temper tantrums, and that he had inherited insanity from his family. The jury was instructed not to consider the insanity of uncles and aunts of McCann unless it had been proved that insanity is hereditary in the family, and that the type of insanity from which the relatives suffered was (of) the same species as that with which the defendant was afflicted.

"The murder of E. O. Bray climaxed the brief, but eventful, career of crime for Albert McCann. At the beginning of the trial, family members told how Albert, as a school boy, would steal money from his home, as well as other articles, and even stole his grandmother's motor car.

"His confession after his capture told how he and his associates had embarked upon a career of banditry which led to the robbery of a number of places in the district, including two Joplin, (Missouri), drug stores. The climax in that career came in Kansas City, Kansas, when McCann and a friend, Paul Hindman, attempted to hold up a drug store. The druggist, R. S. Pinegar, was killed and Hindman was fatally injured. McCann, accompanied by his wife and Mrs. Peggy Moss, fled from Kansas City, and from then on he was a hunted criminal.

"It was while hiding in Oklahoma City that McCann said he and his wife conceived the plan of liberating Raymond Jackson, (a) convicted highway robber, from the county jail at Carthage. After the two arrived in Carthage on the morning of Sunday, December 14, (1930), Mrs. McCann went to the jail to "get the lay of the land." She returned with her husband, and that was when McCann pulled the gun from the jailer's holster and shot him."

WIFE OF McCANN WEEPS AT JAIL

"Irene appeared grief-stricken when told of the fate of her husband, who had been sentenced to death by hanging by a circuit court jury. Her court appointed attorney, Clifford Casey, said, after an interview with her, she was "broken up" when she received the news of her husband's conviction. Lou Drane, county jailer, told Mrs. McCann of the jury's verdict. He said she wept but made no comment.

"Irene McCann, herself awaiting a court date, had been confined to the county jail since she and her husband had been arrested the previous December. She had stated after her arrest that she was a native of Alabama. She said she had met McCann in Springfield, Missouri, when she was a waitress there and she and McCann married in Columbus, Kansas. She was with him in Kansas City when he attempted the drug store hold-up that ended in a shoot-out, killing Hindman and R. S. Pinegar, (the) druggist. They had been on the lam ever since. She had said that she felt sorry for the boy. (Meaning Albert McCann, who was only 18 years old)."

Carthage, Missouri
May 20, 1931
JURY DEADLOCKED IN MURDER TRIAL OF IRENE McCANN

"A circuit court jury, in whose hands rested the fate of Irene McCann, was locked up for the night. Judge Grant Emerson, at 10:00 p.m., had instructed the deputy sheriff in charge of the jury to take them to a hotel.

"The state had asked that the death penalty be imposed, but the highlight of the day had been when Irene McCann had taken the stand in her own defense.

"*Irene took the stand and told a story of how she had been beaten, intimidated, and kept in constant fear for her life by her husband during the brief period they lived together the previous fall and winter.*

"*She said when she went to the jail, with Albert, she thought they were going so that Albert could see a friend, not effect a jail delivery. She denied knowing Raymond Jackson and denied the state's allegation that she had a revolver when they went to the jail and that she fired a shot hitting her husband in the leg. She stated that she had closed her eyes during most of the shooting and that she did not know how many shots were fired.*

"*Irene admitted that she removed the jail keys from Bray's body after he had fallen to the floor, but she did so because her husband told her to and because she feared him.*

"*She accompanied him and remained with him, she testified, only because he kept her constantly within his sight and because she was afraid he would kill her if she attempted to leave him.*

"*It was an unhappy life she led after she wed McCann at Columbus, Kansas, on the previous November 7th, she testified. She wept as she told the jury that many times McCann beat her, and she detailed two occasions upon which, she said, he attempted to shoot her during a drunken rage. Once, she said, she saved herself by striking his arm so that when the revolver that was aimed at her discharged, the bullet went wild. There were many other times, she said, too numerous to detail.*

"*When she and Albert left Tulsa, Oklahoma, the day before the Bray killing, she said he told her they were going to Joplin so he could see his mother. On the way to Carthage, he began drinking and taking drugs. He became quarrelsome and abusive, and instead of going to his mother's house, they drove out on a road she believed was near Lamar, and spent the night. Sunday morning, he told her he was going to the jail to visit his friend. When they stopped the car about a block and a half from the jail, she testified, he ordered her to go to the jail and see if Bill Daggett was there. She did, she said, and returned to tell him that Daggett was not there. He called her a liar, she testified, and said they would go back to the jail. She accompanied him, and after asking for Daggett again, she said, McCann grabbed the jailer's gun and in a scuffle that followed, the jailer was slain.*

"Irene said that she started to accompany McCann up the jail stairs, but he suddenly changed his mind, grabbed her by the arm, and said, 'Come on, I can't do it, let's go.' They then fled out of the jail and drove away.

"She said her purse was in the car when she went to the jail the second time, and she did not carry a revolver. (Albert) McCann was wounded in the scuffle with the officer. In (Albert) McCann's statement, introduced into evidence in his trial, he accused his wife of having shot him in the leg during the scuffle when the jailer was killed.

"Irene told of how, after the shooting, they stopped at Chelsea, Oklahoma, where she obtained some bandages for his leg, and later removed the bullet and dressed the wound at a tourist camp.

"Her story was that she was an unwilling companion of McCann, on his reckless career of banditry throughout the Midwest, but that he compelled her to remain with him.

"In opening her testimony, Irene said she met McCann in a boarding house in Springfield, Missouri, where she had worked the previous fall. She said he appeared to be a pleasant young

man. He courted her over a period of five to seven weeks, calling at the boarding house and eating his meals there. He told her he was a salesman, working for his father, who owned a prosperous business in Joplin. He took her (to) many places, and treated her with the utmost respect. Finally, she said, she learned to love him and when he proposed marriage, she accepted and they were married in Columbus, Kansas, on November 7, 1930. Up to that time, she did not know that he was an outlaw, a highwayman, and a fugitive.

"They lived happily for only one short week, she said, and at Tulsa, Oklahoma, where they went on their honeymoon, he began drinking and became abusive. From then on, he cursed, abused, and threatened her. Only on one occasion was she ever out of his sight, she said. At Independence, Kansas, he kicked her out of his motor car, but he returned and made her get back in with him, threatening to kill her if she didn't. Once, she really thought he would kill her, when he said he was tired of living and he was going to kill her, and then himself.

"Irene McCann said the only time she ever carried a gun was when Albert gave her a small revolver and told her to keep it. That was about two weeks before their capture. She said that she had never fired it and had never fired a gun in her life.

"Irene said she was born near Birmingham, Alabama, and her father died when she was seven years old. Her mother was attending her trial.

"During cross examination, the state attempted to show that Irene had not only kept company with Albert McCann in the Springfield boarding house, but she had also lived there with a highwayman named Jesse D. Biggs."

111

Carthage, Missouri
May 21, 1931
IRENE McCANN GIVEN TEN YEAR SENTENCE

"She received the verdict with a smile. 'I was lucky,' Irene said. 'Although I told the truth on the witness stand, I think that under the circumstances the jury was kind to me and I thank them.'

"A ten year sentence was meted out to Irene, said to be 19 years old, when a jury of (the) circuit court convicted her of second degree murder in the slaying of E. O. Bray, county jailer at Carthage, Missouri. It was the lightest punishment that could be assessed under the instructions of the court. Albert McCann, her husband, had been sentenced to be hanged for his part in the slaying. One would imagine that Irene had feared she may be given the same sentence.

"Albert McCann was advised at the county jail of his wife's verdict by jailer Lou Drane. Albert's response was, 'Is that so?' He then turned away.

"Irene McCann would be taken, along with other prisoners who had been given prison sentences during that court term, probably within two weeks, to Jefferson City, Missouri."

November 10, 1931
LEAVES NOTE BEFORE ESCAPING

"Less than a week after Edna Murray's second escape, Irene McCann escaped from the Women's state prison.

"Leaving a note saying she was going to prove her husband's innocence, Irene had escaped, only to be captured on a bridge near Jefferson City, the next day. Mr. D. B. Julian, a member of

the prison board, had seen her there, and picked her up. Later, the Supreme Court granted Albert McCann a new trial, at which (time) he received a 50 year sentence.

Warden Leslie Rudolph wants Edna Murray captured and returned to the Penitentiary. "Courtesy of Michael Webb"

"Interviewed the day her husband received the 50 year sentence, Mrs. McCann said she was "very happy" he had escaped the death penalty and she would not attempt to escape again."

Jefferson City, Missouri
December 13, 1932
TWO WOMEN CONVICTS SAW WAY OUT OF CELL AND FLEE DURING NIGHT

"Edna Murray and Irene McCann effected their next escapes, those being Irene's second, and Edna's third, by sawing the bars of their individual cells so that they could enter the main corridor. From there, they sawed the bars of a rear window that they escaped from. Edna had gotten four hacksaw blades smuggled inside. She was asked many times how she acquired those hacksaw blades. That was one of the few secrets that Edna never would reveal. It took Edna and Irene six weeks to saw through those bars. At the time of their escape, no matron was on duty in the evenings in the cell house, and only one guard was on duty to patrol the yard and the immediate vicinity of the cell house. The guard said that he never could figure out how or when the two got the saws.

113

Far left is a portion of Edna Murray's manuscript detailing the escape from the cell house. For six weeks, she and Irene McCann (right) worked on the bars of their cells to win their way to freedom. This was Edna "Rabbit" Murray's third escape from the prison.

"After their escape, Warden Rudolf, along with other guards from the penitentiary, tracked their footprints in the snow to the Rackers Filling Station not far away. Officials said that the tracks indicated that a man had met them. At the station, officials were told by Otto Rackers that two men had shown up there and one had called a taxi. When the two women arrived, they left in the taxi. The taxicab driver who answered the call told officials the two women disappeared into a side street after leaving his machine in downtown Jefferson City. There, the trail was lost.

"The cell building from which the women escaped had only recently been completed. It had been constructed especially to house incorrigible women inmates. The Warden said it had been used very sparingly for punishment of the more unruly prisoners."

Edna made the headlines again: "Missouri's Most Notorious Woman Prison Breaker" and the "The Triple Escape Queen," but her nickname among her friends would always be "Rabbit."

Warden Rudolph said Edna Murray was a model prisoner, and that she always did whatever work was required of her. He also stated that she never complained nor talked back to those who were in charge of her. He said that she got along well with the other women prisoners and that her only fault was the fact she could not resist the temptation to escape whenever the opportunity arose.

A columnist once wrote, after interviewing Irene at the Women's Division of the Missouri State Penitentiary, "Irene has lived hard and dangerously. At the age of 17, Irene ran away from her husband of three years and eventually hooked up with Albert McCann, a new beau and partner in crime. They traveled across Oklahoma, Kansas, and Missouri, sticking up filling stations and drugstores, '... enough to keep us in the money' she once said."

Irene McCann told a United Press reporter in an interview at the women's prison farm, "... I guess I wasn't big enough to tell the truth at the trial. Albert will walk right up there and let them hang him before he will say a word."

In another interview with a reporter from the Jefferson City Post-Tribune, Irene said she had fired a pistol while Albert McCann and the jailer fought. A wild shot hit Albert in the leg, but two rounds struck the jailer.

It was reported that Irene's first escape from the prison occurred when she had faked an appendicitis attack. She then escaped from the hospital leaving the note saying she was "... going out to get the evidence which will free Albert, because there was no one else to help him."

Irene McCann was the first to return, thirteen months after she and Edna escaped from the Women's Division of the Missouri State Penitentiary. It was said that, "stinking of gin, in January of 1934, Irene turned herself in at Chicago." Irene had become too ill to care for herself, and needed medical attention. Evidently her illness could not be cured, as she was paroled to her mother's care in January of 1936. Irene's mother, Mrs. Claud (Gladys) Davis, of Little Sioux, Iowa, presumably cared for Irene until she died, at the young age of 25.

Albert McCann never received a parole, and died while still in prison, according to a family member.

Irene McCann regretted the life that had put her name in the headlines, and consequently put her behind bars. She wrote letters to her sister, telling of her regrets and her wish that she could be free. "I have not lived my life the right way. I would give anything in the world to be out there with you," Irene wrote.

There were many similarities between Edna and Irene. Both being attractive women, Edna was a tiny bit taller and they weighed almost the same. Both married young, left home at an early age, didn't stay married long, and then took up with outlaws that were even younger than themselves. Both gave testimonies in court, claiming to be victims of circumstances, and weren't responsible for what their men had gotten them into. But in reality, both women were willing to try most anything to escape the confinement of a cell. And upon returning to prison, both were ill, reeking of alcohol and both were in extremely pitiful condition.

Edna Murray and Irene McCann – Women's Prison Farm 1 is in the background. "Courtesy of the Collection of Debbie Moss"

Chapter 19: Preston's And "Little" Mott's
Early Years In Cardin

Grandpa "Charles" Stanley expected the boys to be "tough," and didn't put up with any "sissified crap," as he called it. His philosophy was, "You never back down. You can get your ass kicked all over town, but you never back down." My daddy, Preston (Paden), really didn't like to fight. He was just a little guy — but if grandpa ever heard of him backing down from a fight, he would have gotten his little butt tanned with a strap.

"Little" Mott Farrell and his cousin, Preston Paden (with the broken arm – probably from fighting)

Once daddy told me about a kid that was bigger than he was, and how he always wanted to pick a fight with daddy over something stupid. One day, the bully followed my daddy all the way home from school, trying to start a fight. It was a nasty day outside in Cardin, Oklahoma, that day, and the streets were muddy. Daddy got almost to the yard of Grandpa and Grandma Stanley's home, when this ornery kid started yelling out, "Chicken! Preston is a Chicken!" Little did the bully know that that was the "straw that broke the camel's back." If Grandpa Stanley did not hear a response to the bully's insult, he would surely take a strap to Preston's rear end! Preston also knew that this bully couldn't hurt him "… near as much …" as his grandpa could, and would. So Preston threw down his books on the driest piece of ground he could spot along the muddy road, took off his coat and hat and placed them on his books, doubled up his little fists and said, "Show me what you got!" Well, the bully showed him what he had all right — and what the bully had, turned out to be "not good enough." They fought and wrestled and rolled around in the mud for a good 15 to 20 minutes. Grandpa Stanley even came out on the porch to see the brawl. This made my daddy even more determined not to get his butt kicked any more than he already had. Luckily, he got in a good punch and hit that big bully right square in the nose. Blood started "… squirtin' and he must have thought that he was gonna die, 'cause he started hollerin' and cryin' and went runnin' for home." Poor little Preston was so worn out he could barely walk, but he picked up his books and clothes and dragged himself into the house. He said his grandpa was "real proud," but little Preston was "… lickin' his wounds for quite some time."

Daddy's cousin, "Little" Mott, related the story to me once that Grandpa Stanley had purchased a set of boxing gloves for them, and taught them how to fight. Mott said that in the beginning, daddy would beat him up pretty good. However, as they grew older, Mott became a husky boy, and one time he "… clobbered daddy a good one." He said that my daddy, Preston, wouldn't box with him anymore, after that. Daddy's cousin, "Little" Mott, thought that was pretty funny. He said my daddy wasn't a dummy!

As best I can, I'll try to relate another occasion that my daddy told me about. He and his cousin Mott went fishing down at the "strip pits" one day. All the mining areas in that part of the country — northeast Oklahoma, southeast Kansas, and southwest

Missouri — have strip pits that are the result of what is left from the many years of coal and zinc mining. They fill up with water, and like a pond, over time, become good fishing holes. Daddy and "Little" Mott were sitting there, minding their own business, "… catching them a big stringer of fish …" for Grandma Louie to fry up. Then, out of nowhere, comes "the town bully." This bully was particularly strange, to say the least. For starters, he was just plain mean. He was so mean that most kids started running and crying whenever they saw him coming in their direction. From what I recall about daddy telling me about this bully, he must have been a child molester as well, and the whole community was afraid of him even being around their children. It's even quite possible that he had hurt some kids pretty badly. But one thing was for sure, and that was that daddy didn't want him anywhere around his little cousin or himself.

The way I remember my daddy telling me the story, the bully walked up to daddy — and, towering over him, informed him of his intentions by stating, "I'm takin' them fishes." Daddy responded by saying, "Those fish belong to Mott and me, and we are keepin' 'em." Of course, daddy was shaking in his shoes, but he knew what his grandpa would do if he heard that this bully got away with stealing their fish. So the bully then walked over to "Little" Mott — he assumed that he was my daddy's brother — and said, "Gimme them fishes or y'all's lil' brother is gonna die!," and he then proceeded to start choking "Little" Mott with his bare hands. But he wasn't a very smart bully, because he made the mistake of turning his back to Preston. Fearful and afraid, Preston then picked up a big rock, smashed it over the bully's head, and literally split the bully's head wide open. Now what?! Scared out of his wits, Preston stared at the bully, lying there on the rocks with his head split open and blood gushing out, and he knew the bully was dead. "We're in trouble now!" he told "Little" Mott. "But he was gonna kill me, Preston," Mott said. "I know, I know," Preston told him, "but that ain't gonna keep us outta trouble. We gotta hide him, and **nobody** can ever know that we did this — **nobody**." They then proceeded to fill the dead bully's trousers with large rocks from around the pit; tied a big rock to his neck with bits of their fishing line, just for good measure; and then rolled him off into the strip pit. Even at their young age — times being as they were in that not-yet-so-civilized part of the country — the boys knew not to brag of their feat, and their story was never repeated until many years later. Needless to say, the bully was never seen again, and apparently, never missed.

I have always wondered why daddy told me that story. Perhaps it was to make a point that such action is sometimes necessary when faced with a life and death situation. Maybe he just needed to get it off his chest, or maybe he shared this with me so that I would have a better understanding of what life was like growing up in Cardin.

Oklahoma had been a state for only a short while at the time that my daddy was born, and in most ways, it was still wide open Indian Territory. It was not exactly what you would call "civilized" for quite some time to come, and folks just knew that they had to "fend for themselves," at times.

Chapter 20: The Great Depression

The Dow Jones Industrial Average hit a high point of 381.17 on September 3, 1929. Then, in late October, the stock market began a monumental nose dive, losing over 89% of its value over the next three years — before bottoming out at 41.22 in July of 1932.

The Great Depression had begun with a bang!

History would later show that the Dow Jones Industrial Average didn't fully recover to its previous 1929 high point for another 25 years — on November 23, 1954.

The Great Depression brought "… a different time and a different way of life …" for the vast majority of Americans. That's the way daddy's cousin, "Little" Mott explained it to me. After "The Roaring Twenties" — a prosperous era of abundant jobs and new freedoms that had never before been known — came another new, and unwelcome, decade of sacrifice and abject poverty for many.

At the height of the Great Depression, more than 250,000 teenagers were living on the roads in America, crisscrossing the country by illegally hopping freight trains. My father-in-law, David C. Tippet, related to me that he rode from town to town on the rails, looking for work and working for meals. He recalled a two year stretch when he didn't have one thin dime in his pockets. He was lucky though, because he didn't have a wife or children to support. He told me that he saw many starving families on his journeys, and it was a heart-breaking experience for him.

My mama told me about living on a small farm with her parents and eight siblings along Highway 7, in a mining area known as Stippville, in southeast Kansas. They had a cow, and they had a garden. For months on end, they had potato soup every night for supper, seasoned with butter, but they didn't have the luxury of having any salt. But as poor as they were, my mama said her mother would never turn down a hungry person. Many a time, a vagabond would knock on their door, and Grandma Keith would stir up something to feed him. Mama said that when the strangers would leave after being fed, all the kids would peek out the front window and see if he left his "mark" on the front gatepost. Supposedly, the vagabonds and hobos had a secret code or mark that they left to inform others that they could get a handout at the coded locations.

It was certainly understandable why thievery became such a common practice in that era. Just imagine looking into the hungry eyes of your babies, and not having food for their little mouths!

The Depression was a long, hard, and sad time. It was no wonder why people like "Pretty Boy" Floyd — who robbed banks and burned mortgage papers — would be elevated to the status of a hero in the eyes of the poor and struggling. However, doing such things, though regarded as heroic, started a regrettable snowball effect. To many, it became acceptable to rob and steal. The lowliest of outlaws and gangsters started to be looked upon as heroes and saviors by the nation's poor and embittered.

Charles Arthur Floyd – in his younger days

My daddy's cousin, "Little" Mott, always said daddy was a hard worker, and very intelligent. If there was a job that was offered, daddy would find it. Mott also told me that my daddy found employment with the Works Progress Administration (WPA), (created in May of 1935). What little income he made was the only income for Grandma Stanley, "Little" Mott, and himself for quite a period of time. At other times, there were simply no jobs available. It was not unusual for the unemployment rate to hit 70% in some parts of the country. Children didn't always understand what was happening, but they knew something was wrong, something was terribly wrong! Fathers came home with news of layoffs, while mothers struggled to make a few days' food last all week. Illnesses went untreated. Worn out clothes were seldom replaced.

Optimism did not come easily for our country when the Depression grabbed hold of it in the early months of 1930, and held its ugly grip for the decade. The children who lived through those years never forgot what it was like, and the experiences they endured shaped their lives forever. The joys and heartaches of growing up during the 1930s stayed with them over the decades, as they fought a World War, built their careers, and raised families of their own. Many of them went on to do great things in times of war as well as in times of peace. Many lived quiet lives of grace and dignity, and many continued to battle adversity throughout their adult lives. The experiences they endured during the Great Depression were instrumental in making them who they became.

"Little" Mott was sharp, and a good scholar. He liked school, was athletic, and was the captain of his high school football team. During this period of time, his only goals were to further his education and to play sports.

On the other hand, his cousin (my daddy), Preston, had inherited the inquisitive nature of wanderlust. He was bored with the small-town life of Cardin, and he wanted to travel, to see the world, and to be somebody. Besides, he was older now, and it had become evident to him what his mother and Aunt Doris (as well as their associates) were doing for a living. It didn't take much convincing for him to get Volney Davis and Jess Doyle to put him to work. After all, he was a smart young man and was a good and responsible person. And Preston was also "family," to boot!

These were all the prerequisites for endearing oneself to a reckless journey and this was the beginning of Preston's career on the wrong side of the law.

Chapter 21: The Kansas City Massacre &
Its Aftermath

On November 3, 1932, Volney Davis was temporarily released from the Oklahoma State Penitentiary under a "Leave of Absence" (LOA) policy which was to be effective through July 1, 1933. This temporary release was accomplished because Oklahoma was a state known to grant such LOAs if a prisoner had both the appropriate funds and an attorney who knew the system well enough to be able to affect his client's temporary release from the penitentiary. According to Edna, it was Arthur "Doc" Barker who was instrumental in procuring this LOA for Volney.

Arthur "Doc" Barker

In January of 1933, a few weeks after Edna's third escape from prison, she received a letter from Volney, through her sister, Doris. Shortly before this, Doris had split up with Earl Stuchlik and moved from Hill City, Kansas, to Kansas City. Most likely, this separation was due to Earl's conviction for passing counterfeit $20 bills in both Russell and Topeka, Kansas, and his incarceration in the Shawnee County Jail. Edna was able to send a letter back to Volney by giving it to Doc Barker, who was also in Kansas City at the time.

According to Edna, Doc Barker found out where she was living through a man who knew Doris. Then, in March of 1933, Edna received another letter from Volney, postmarked from Chicago.

Shortly thereafter, Edna and Doris received a visit from Volney Davis, Doc Barker, and Jess Doyle. Years later, Edna recalled that, "Doris and Jess immediately fell in love with each other."

Jess Doyle "Courtesy of the Collection of Rick Mattix"

"Together again" – Thanks to Doc Barker, Edna and Volney are reunited. "Courtesy of the Collection of Debbie Moss"

The day after their reunion, Volney gave Edna and Doris instructions to drive to Maywood, Illinois, and stay at Jess' place on Fifth Avenue, near Roosevelt Road. The boys made a stop at Neosho, Missouri, to visit Doc's father on their way to meet them. They arrived in Maywood a few days after Edna and Doris did, and the four of them lived, under the respective aliases of Mr. And Mrs. E. A. Conley, and Mr. And Mrs. V. E. Davis. After a few weeks, Edna and Volney rented their own apartment at 609 E. 2nd Street — in the same apartment that had been previously occupied by Verne Miller and his girl-friend, Vivian Mathis.

Vivian Mathis & Daughter Betty "Courtesy of the Collection of Rick Mattix"

It was about this time that Edna and Volney, along with Doris and Jess, began to frequent Louie Cernocky's Roadhouse in Fox River Grove, Illinois. It was here that Edna was introduced for the first time to Kate "Ma" Barker; Eddie and Bessie Green; Freddie Barker and Paula Harmon; Alvin "Slim" Karpis and his girlfriend, Dolores Delaney; Frank "Jelly" Nash and his soon-to-be wife, Frances; Verne Miller and Vivian Mathis; Earl Christman and his girlfriend, Helen Ferguson; and Capone gangster, Louis "Doc" Stacci.

Frank "Jelly" Nash

Fred "Freddie" Barker

Alvin "Slim" Karpis

Dolores Delaney

Once, Edna met a young, blond-haired fellow that she was introduced to as "Jimmy." Jimmy seemed like a bashful boy, didn't have much to say, and did very little drinking. Edna asked Volney what a young kid like that was doing hanging around with Freddie Barker and the gang. Volney got a big laugh out of that. He told Edna that "Jimmy" was married and had kids of his own. "He's a lamster on a life sentence," Volney told her. Then he told her that the man referred to as "Jimmy," was, in reality, Lester Gillis, alias "Baby Face" Nelson.

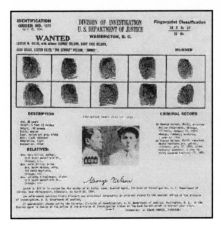

Lester Joseph Gillis (aka George "Baby Face" Nelson) escaped from the Joliet State Penitentiary, in Joliet, Illinois, on Feb 17, 1932.

These were Volney's friends, and Edna got to know them quickly. In fact, most all of them lived in the same apartment building as Volney and Edna, in Maywood, Illinois. Fred Barker and Alvin Karpis were both wanted for murder. Frank Nash was an escapee from Leavenworth. Edna recalled Nash as appearing to be much older than the others — looking to be over 60 years old — but he was actually only in his mid-forties. Earl Christman was also an escaped convict. These men were all red hot according to Volney. Edna had never seen a machine gun before, but soon saw that Freddie Barker, Alvin Karpis, and Frank Nash each kept one close by.

In early April of 1933, Volney told Edna, "You better go to Chicago, honey, just for a while. I'm staying here 'cause we're gonna be busy." As Edna related many years later — "… that word, **'busy'** — meant that the gang had planned a job and was ready to go into action. Whenever their money ran low, they would go out and crack a bank or pull some other job. Maybe some of them would get killed, or more likely some police officer or payroll guard would be rubbed out. But that was all in the game."

Taking Jess' car, Edna drove back to Jess' and Doris' apartment in Maywood. It was about 10 days before Edna and Doris heard from the boys again. When they arrived, it was in Volney's new car, with Illinois license plates. A couple of days later, Edna and Volney headed back to Kansas City. Volney did not discuss the job the gang had pulled, and Edna didn't ask. But on the way back to Kansas City he told her, "Honey, Earl (Christman) took a bullet while entering the get-away car. He's probably dead by now."

The next day, when they arrived in Kansas City, they went to Verne Miller's home at 6612 Edgevale Road. Upon their arrival, they found out that Earl Christman had, in fact, died the day before. According to Edna, the boys had taken him out and buried him. Verne's girlfriend, Vivian, and Doc Barker and Freddie Barker were all sitting around talking as if nothing had happened. The thing that bothered Edna was that "… outlaws would bury their own dead, without any headstone or flowers or any kind words. If an outlaw was hot, they didn't want the law, or even his own family, to know that he had been killed." Edna was afraid that she would end up that way, herself — or perhaps, she worried about being buried in "potter's field," — a term for a place of burial of unknown and indigent people. Having a proper final resting place in a nice cemetery was very important for her.

It was only later that she learned that the job the gang had pulled was the robbery of the First National Bank at Fairbury, Nebraska, for a reported $151,350. This occurred on April 4,

1933, and was committed by Doc Barker, Freddie Barker, Alvin Karpis, Frank Nash, Eddie Green, Jess Doyle, Volney Davis, and Earl Christman.

Eddie Green – Barker-Karpis Gang member

A day or so after the robbery, Freddie Barker, feeling flush and having no moll to spend it on, asked Vi Mathis to phone Paula "Fat-Witted" Harmon in Joplin, Missouri, and ask her to come and join him. She was the widow of Charlie Harmon, who was killed in the robbery of the Kraft State Bank in Menomonie, Wisconsin, on October 20, 1931.

After a trip to Tulsa to visit Volney's sister for a few days, Edna and Volney went back to Maywood and rented another apartment.

The gang had plenty of money again, and it was one continuous round of parties. Edna enjoyed every minute of it; that was what she lived for. In fact, according to Edna, "… outlaws didn't save up for a rainy day, they bought their fun — and lots of it — while they still could." The nightclub where the gang hung out was about 35 miles from Maywood. Frank Nash, better known as "Jelly" to his friends, had lived there for several months with his girlfriend, Frances Luce, prior to their recent marriage in Hot Springs, Arkansas. Volney and Edna would drive out there almost every day, and would always find some of the gang there. Generally, they were all drunk — or were soon to be drunk — and they spent their money very freely. "Jelly" Nash was always the life of the party when the gang spent their evenings drinking, and dancing, and talking.

Mother Barker would often be there too. Although Edna never saw her drink, she was often accompanied by two of her sons, Doc and Freddie. It seemed strange to Edna that a mother would be involved in a gang with her own sons. Mother (or "Kate" to some) Barker could find no wrong in her sons actions and had protected them and stood up for them all their lives — every time they got into trouble — and raised all kinds of hell with anyone who found fault in them. It was she who schooled the boys on how to get out of scrapes with the law from the time they were very young. Edna always claimed that the FBI gave Kate a lot of credit for being the real brains of the Barker-Karpis Gang. Although that wasn't the case, she did play a big role in their criminal upbringing by instilling in her boys, from an early age, that it was all right for them to break the law, just as long as they didn't get caught. Edna would always remember Mother Barker's eyes. The only way she could describe them was to say that they "… stabbed right through a person."

Kate Barker didn't particularly like any of her sons' female friends. Karpis claimed she didn't want any female competition and wanted to be the only woman in her sons' lives. J. Edgar Hoover referred to Kate as a "jealous old battle-axe."

Author's note:

J. Edgar Hoover didn't like Kate Barker, and apparently he didn't like women in general.

Courtney Ryley Cooper was J. Edgar Hoover's literary voice during the 1930s. In Mr. Cooper's 1937 book "Here's to Crime," he wrote a chapter about various gangster molls entitled "HUSSIES IN HIDING."

Not only did Mr. Cooper obviously lack the needed skills of a competent fact-checker, he also had a very wild and untamed imagination that was the cause for many inaccurate and unsubstantiated accusations.

In his writing about Edna Murray, Mr. Cooper, from his first paragraph, shows that he has not done his research. He misstates what Edna's parents did for a living and he incorrectly states how many siblings she had. Mr. Cooper states that the male members of the family apparently kept within the law, but the female members of the family were gun molls.

He states this misconstruction to be factual.

Mr. Cooper was obsessed with telling what a horrendous mother Edna Murray was. He wrote, in part, "… *If they feed their children, if they dress them well, even with crooked money, if they are vociferous about their affection, then nothing else matters. They may parade murderers before them; they may plan robberies, even indulge in sexual intercourse, in the same room with a child old enough to know what is going on, and these are excusable.*"

In addition, Mr. Cooper, again, in referring to Edna Murray, said, "*… she was cohabiting with a robber known as Diamond Joe. Their home was a perfect nest of criminality; crooks of all sorts hung out there. And to that home, Edna Murray brought, with great delight, her baby boy.*" Edna's baby boy, Preston, was 7 years old when she was living with "Diamond Joe" Sullivan, and although he and his cousin, "Little" Mott Farrell visited their mothers; they did not live with them. They actually lived with their grandparents as they always had.

Mr. Cooper went on to say, "... *Edna Murray protested her continued love for Volney Davis. But she slept with a man named Jack Murray, a hold-up artist, with whom she finally went into the highways as a co-worker. Her son was living with her when she was caught by the police and sent to prison on a twenty-five year sentence as a highway robber. 'The Kissing Bandit,' they called her. Edna Murray, with a show of the theatrical, always offered a victim a kiss after she had held him up at the point of a revolver and taken every cent he possessed."* Well, it's not exactly correct to say that Jack Murray was much of a hold-up artist, since the only time he ever held up anyone, he got caught, and his reward was a 25-year prison sentence. Edna's son was living with his grandparents at the time, as he always had. And Edna didn't ALWAYS offer kisses – that was just a onetime occurrence.

Mr. Cooper continued, "... *The woman went to (the) Missouri Penitentiary. She escaped. In this regard, it is always well to remember J. Edgar Hoover's admonition to those who believe that prison escapes come about magically.*

A person cannot escape from prison except through malfeasance or nonfeasance in office."

After a while, "Jelly" Nash told the gang that the club was getting too hot, and he and his new bride, Frances, decided that they would return to the friendlier confines of Hot Springs, Arkansas — the location of their recent marriage. Edna was disappointed that they left since "Jelly" and Frances were two of her favorite people.

Frank Nash was arrested shortly later, on June 16, 1933, in a cigar store in Hot Springs. He was handcuffed and escorted via automobile to the train station at Ft. Smith, Arkansas, by U. S. Bureau of Investigation agents Francis Joseph "Joe" Lackey and Frank Smith, along with Otto Reed, Chief of Police, of McAlester, Oklahoma. The law enforcement officers knew that Nash was a desperate (and soon to be) "lifer," with friends who would stop at nothing to free him. His wife, Frances, and a bookie friend of hers, Dick Galatas, flew from Hot Springs, Arkansas, to Joplin, Missouri, to meet with a friend of the gang, Herb Farmer, who ran an underworld hideout at his place in Joplin. Farmer then telephoned Frank Nash's friend, Verne Miller, in Kansas City.

The three law enforcement officers drove to the train station in Ft. Smith via Little Rock with their prisoner in tow, and arrived well ahead of time for the arrival of the 8:30 p.m. train — an overnight trip to Kansas City.

Upon their arrival at Union Station in Kansas City, Missouri, the following morning, June 17, 1933, at 7:15 a.m., they remained inside the train for a short time for security purposes. Then the trio of law enforcement officers and their prisoner were joined by Reed Vetterli, Special Agent in Charge, from the U. S. Bureau of Investigation's Kansas City office; Raymond J. Caffrey, Special

Agent, also from the U. S. Bureau of Investigation's Kansas City office; William "Red" Grooms, a detective from the Kansas City Police Department; and Frank Hermanson, also a detective from the Kansas City Police Department.

On this hot and sunny Saturday morning, less than 24 hours after Frank Nash was captured and arrested in Hot Springs, this group of seven law enforcement officers was in the process of escorting Frank Nash out of Union Station and into one of the two empty cars awaiting them just outside the building. The law enforcement officers planned to return Frank Nash, within the hour, to the U. S. Federal Penitentiary in Leavenworth, Kansas.

Frank "Jelly" Nash "Courtesy of the Collection of Rick Mattix"

Charles "Pretty Boy" Floyd and Verne Miller were also at Union Station in Kansas City that morning to free Nash — not to shoot him or anyone else. The two counted on the element of surprise and heavy firepower to successfully attain their goal. This plan was scrapped when Special Agent Joseph Lackey panicked while struggling with Otto Reed's shotgun. The gun fired, striking their prisoner, Frank Nash, and forced Verne Miller and "Pretty Boy" Floyd to return fire.

Booking photos from the Pueblo, Colorado, Police Department show Depression-era Charles Floyd in a jacket, vest and bow tie. He was arrested on May 9, 1929, in the company of three women and one man in a rooming house at 322½ N. Union Ave. The five were charged with vagrancy — Floyd had come to town, officials said, in hopes of starting a new career as a pimp. He was given a fine and sentenced to a week in the City Jail. After serving his sentence, Floyd was escorted to the city limits and released, on the condition of his promise never to return to Pueblo, Colorado, ever again.

It is the general consensus, after much study and review by professional researchers that the Kansas City Massacre occurred because of one man's mishandling of a shotgun. The model 1897 Winchester pump — in this case loaded with ball bearings — was handed from Chief of Police, Otto Reed, to the backseat agent, Joe Lackey, who was unfamiliar with this gun, mainly because this particular model had the unique feature of firing automatically if the shooter had his finger gripping the trigger when he pumped in the first round. The hammer, in this case, automatically fell on the newly loaded cartridge, thereby striking Nash in the head, as indicated by the glass on the front cowling of the car. To further complicate matters, the agent also seemed to have hit some officers outside of the car with this "friendly fire."

In this flawed plan, it seemed as if Miller and Floyd wrongly assumed that the law enforcement officers would take one look at the two machine guns, raise their hands in the air, and let Nash escape. Verne Miller and "Pretty Boy" Floyd did not plan for agent Lackey's ill-timed response from the back seat.

Kansas City Massacre--June 17, 1933

Minutes after the Kansas City Massacre

The final tally for this ill-conceived and poorly carried out attempt to free Frank Nash was as follows (alphabetically):

Raymond J. Caffrey, Special Agent, U. S. Bureau of Investigation, Killed

William J. "Red" Grooms, Detective, Kansas City Police Department, Killed

Frank E. Hermanson, Detective, Kansas City Police Department, Killed

Francis Joseph "Joe" Lackey, Special Agent, U. S. Bureau of Investigation, Injured

Frank "Jelly" Nash, Prisoner, Killed

Otto Reed, Chief of Police, McAlester, Oklahoma, Killed

Frank Smith, Special Agent, U. S. Bureau of Investigation, Uninjured

Reed Vetterli, Special Agent in Charge, U. S. Bureau of Investigation, Injured

It has been wrongly theorized by some that Adam Richetti accompanied Miller and Floyd, and he was, in fact, later convicted of participating in the massacre, and was subsequently put to death in the gas chamber of the Missouri State Penitentiary at Jefferson City, Missouri, on October 7, 1938.

Volney Davis and Edna Murray first learned of the massacre from reading about it in the newspapers the following day, June 18, 1933. Volney was understandably quite nervous and very shook-up over this incident. He immediately drove to Oak Park to Mother Barker's apartment and showed her the paper, stating, "Verne Miller did that." In response, Mother Barker said, "He (Verne Miller) murdered that poor old man (Frank Nash)." Kate was never a big fan of Verne Miller.

That night, all Volney and Edna could talk about was the massacre. Volney seemed extremely worried. "That shooting is sure gonna turn the heat on, Rabbit," he told her, and he was correct.

Federal law enforcement officers had been killed. The gang was no longer dodging just county or state police, but now, federal agents as well. It was a bad break and this meant that things were going to get a lot tougher for them from then on. There wasn't an outlaw in the country who didn't know what it meant to have the feds on their trail. Volney had plenty of reasons for concern.

The next day, around noon, while Edna and Volney were sitting in their second floor apartment which faced the street, they suddenly heard a car horn honking, just outside their apartment. Edna went to the window and saw a man getting out of his car, looking up at her. It was Verne Miller. "Is Curly there?" Verne asked. "Yes," Edna replied, uncertain whether or not she was

138

doing the right thing. "Whatcha say, boy? All right?" Verne hollered upstairs to Volney when he saw him in the window. Volney shook his head yes, and Verne asked him to come downstairs for a minute. Volney went downstairs to speak with Verne as Edna carefully watched through the window. She stared in disbelief as she saw Volney walk to the garage they rented across the street, and proceed to drive their car out of the garage in order to make room for Verne's car. She knew that this meant that Verne Miller would be staying with them for a while. Edna immediately fixed herself another drink and told Preston, who was visiting them at the time, to high-tail it over to Aunt Doris' place, and to stay there until she came after him.

Verne walked through their front door, carrying a Gladstone bag, which he dropped on the floor, and then he collapsed on their davenport in a state of exhaustion. "I'm all in," he said. "(I) had a tough time getting out of Kansas City. Ya got any iodine?" he asked. Edna brought him some iodine, and Volney bandaged Verne's finger. One little nick on the finger was all the damage that Verne had received in the shoot-out. Edna fixed dinner while Verne talked about the massacre.

"There were only two of us, but we made them think there had to be more," Verne said, — "myself and 'Pretty Boy' Floyd." The newspapers had reported that five or six killers took part in the massacre. Their plan was to take Frank Nash away from the officers who were in the process of returning him to Leavenworth. But once they arrived at Union Station, there was a change in plans. "'Pretty Boy' and I drove to the station and parked our car," Verne said. "Floyd went into the station and struck up a conversation with a cute little gal at the information desk. He was keeping an eye out for Nash and the coppers. When he saw them coming, he walked outside and gave me the high sign. I was standing by the car with my 'chopper' (machine gun) covered up on the running board. I walked past Nash and the coppers. Nash was cuffed to one of them. He saw me but he didn't bat an eye. I brushed his arm and said in a low voice, 'Here I am old man.' Then, I stepped back to my car, grabbed my 'chopper' and yelled, 'Get 'em Up! Up! Up! quick!' One of the coppers started shootin' and I knew somethin' had gone haywire. There was nothin' else to do but try and rub out everyone in and around the copper cars. I let 'em have it. 'Pretty Boy' was standin' near our car, so he grabbed his 'chopper' and started sprayin' 'em too when I started shootin.' In seconds, we had 'em all cut down. They were layin' in the street. 'Pretty Boy' jumped in our car, with me right behind him, and drove straight out to my house. 'Pretty Boy' was all right, I got hit in the finger. We hung around till dark, when one of his friends came out and took him away. I left for Chicago, and here I am. I hated that the old man got killed, but there was nothin' else I could do. 'Pretty Boy's' a bulldog. He can take it on his own, all right."

Verne's girlfriend, Vi, arrived at Volney's and Edna's apartment the day after Verne arrived, and they stayed there for several more days. Verne was pretty much in a state of panic the whole time. He and Floyd were the hottest men in the country, and he knew they would hang, if caught. He told Edna that he had spoken with Frances Nash on the telephone the night before the massacre, and told her he would do all he could for her husband. "She'll put the finger on me, for sure" he said. Verne then flew to New York, and Vi drove there by car. According to Edna, she never saw either one of them again.

Volney was highly upset over the fact that Verne had come to their apartment in the first place. "I don't know why that son-of-a-bitch would come here, as 'hot' as he is now," he said. "Besides, I never made a dime (on any job) with him in my life."

Edna could never quite understand Verne Miller. She knew he used to be a police officer (sworn in on March 29, 1919, in Huron, South Dakota), and later, a sheriff (originally elected County Sheriff of Beadle County, South Dakota, in the November, 1920, election), and may have had other positions in law enforcement. He always seemed too well-mannered to be part of the gang. He never cursed or yelled, like most of the other men did. He was polite towards women, and was never disrespectful to his girl-friend, Vi. The story Edna heard was that Verne needed money for his wife's (Mildred (nee Brown)) doctor bills (while he was in his position as county sheriff). Knowing of no other way to amass a large amount of money, he stole it (about $6,000). On April 3, 1923, he pled guilty to extortion and was fined $5,200 and sentenced to a "Two to Ten year term" in the South Dakota State Penitentiary in Sioux Falls, South Dakota. He was released after having served only 18 months of his sentence. The way that he felt he had been treated by the police after he was arrested for this offense, led him to lose respect for all law enforcement personnel.

Author's note:

"Pretty Boy" Floyd did "take it" later on, about 16 months later on. On October 20, 1934, while travel-ing with Adam Richetti and the Baird sisters (Juanita and Rose), from Buffalo, New York, to the Cookson Hills of Oklahoma, they had a slight car accident in the

very early morning hours which necessitated that the car be repaired before continuing on. It was decided that the Baird sisters would bring the car in for repairs while Floyd and Richetti kept out of sight for a while. However, Richetti and Floyd were spotted and questioned by local authorities that same morning, which in turn began a sequence of events that ultimately resulted in Richetti's capture that day, followed by Floyd's death two days later.

While in hiding for over 48 hours, Floyd stopped at a farm for something to eat just outside of East Liverpool, Ohio. He was running from behind a corncrib when some G-men gunned him down on the afternoon of October 22, 1934.

The Kansas City Massacre (KCM) wasn't the only notorious crime occurring in June of 1933. Two days prior to the KCM, William A. Hamm, a wealthy St. Paul brewer, was kidnapped. Edna distinctly remembered the night of the Hamm kidnapping, which occurred on June 15, 1933. As she recalled, earlier, on June 12th, Volney left their Maywood, Illinois, apartment and drove his recently purchased Chevrolet to Neosho, Missouri, to visit with his folks. He also needed to make some sort of arrangements concerning his "Leave of Absence" which was due to expire on July 1, 1933. He returned to Maywood on the very day that Hamm was kidnapped in St. Paul. Years later, Edna distinctly stated that Volney picked her up from the beauty shop that was located on 50th Avenue in Maywood on the afternoon of the kidnapping. Preston, who had accompanied Volney from Neosho, was with him at that time. Later, Edna recalled discussing the publicity surrounding the Kansas City Massacre, with Volney telling her that he was glad that he could prove where he was at the time it occurred. Volney made similar statements to her after reading the accounts of the Hamm kidnapping in the newspapers.

Around the first of July, Edna and Volney moved to the Eleanor-Manor Apartments at 7157 S. Cyril Parkway, in Chicago. They didn't live there for very long, but while they were there, Doris and Jess went back home to Cardin, Oklahoma, to visit with her family. Also, about this same time, Volney borrowed $500 from Freddie Barker so he could purchase a new Ford coupe. This wasn't the first time he had borrowed money from Freddie or Doc, since Volney was broke most of the time. It wasn't easy for a convicted murderer to remain out of prison for very long on a "Leave of Absence" if he had no means of financially supporting himself.

Around the middle of July, Freddie Barker and his girlfriend, Paula, rented a cottage on Long Lake, which is located north of Chicago, in Lake County, Illinois. Aware of the fact that Volney and Edna had no money, Freddie invited them to come and live with them in the cottage. Paula later antagonized Edna by telling her that Volney was cheating on her with a girl that lived on the lake. Besides that, she liked to rub it in that Edna and Volney were living off Freddie, and that they didn't have any money of their own. Edna couldn't help but put in her own two cents, and therefore, she and Paula had a few heated arguments. Because of her dislike for Paula, Edna didn't want to stay there at Long Lake any longer, but at the time, she had no other choice. Not long before they left Long Lake, Alvin Karpis paid Freddie and Volney a visit. Edna thought a job was in the works, but Volney never told her as much.

Around the first of September, Edna, Volney, Fred, and Paula left Long Lake. Volney and Edna drove their new Ford coupe directly to Minneapolis. Freddie and Paula traveled in their own car. Their purpose in going there, at this time, was to locate Doris and Jess, who were on a fishing trip on a lake, some distance from Minneapolis. Doris had previously told Edna that if she needed to find them, they could be reached through Harry Sawyer. But, when Edna and Volney reached St. Paul and contacted Harry Sawyer, he said that he hadn't heard from them and was unaware of their whereabouts. They found out later, though, that Sawyer was lying and that he actually did know where they were, but wasn't currently on speaking terms with Jess. It seemed that none of the boys wanted Jess to be with Doris because she was too outspoken, and knew too much of Jess' business. But Jess was in love with Doris and wanted to keep her at his side.

Harry Sawyer "Courtesy of the Collection of Rick Mattix"

Since they were not able to locate Doris, Edna and Volney then decided to drive back down to Cardin, Oklahoma, to see her parents. Edna was unaware of how ill her father had become, and when they reached Pittsburg, Kansas, where her brother Harry lived, she was informed by Harry's father-in-law that Harry had gone to Cardin for the funeral of his father, who had passed away a mere four days earlier. They waited for Harry and his wife, Sybil, to return to Pittsburg, and Edna spent the night with them while Volney visited his folks in Neosho, Missouri.

When Volney returned from visiting his parents, he and Edna left for Chicago, where they rented an apartment near 65th Street and Dorchester Avenue. While living there, Edna and Volney had another one of their many quarrels over his chasing around with other women. Their relationship was further strained due to the fact that they were still living off of money borrowed from Freddie Barker, so Edna decided to pack up and leave. She traveled alone to Minneapolis, where she finally located Doris and Jess, and stayed with them for a while. Volney followed Edna there a few days later where they reconciled, and rented an apartment together on Lyndale Avenue, near Lake Street. After being there for only a couple of weeks — and nearly broke — Volney suggested that they drive out to Reno, Nevada, where he could borrow some more money. He knew that the boys were in Reno at the time, and not long after arriving there, Doc Barker helped them find an apartment.

While in Reno, Edna met Harry Campbell and his girl-friend, Wynona Burdette. They also met up with Freddie and Paula; along with Alvin Karpis and his girlfriend, Delores Delaney; who had all been living in Reno for a while, prior to Volney and Edna's arrival. Volney borrowed more money from Freddie Barker and took Edna to the Bank Club, a pretentious gambling establishment, where he showed her around.

Harry Campbell

Every night was a continuous round of nightclubs, parties, and drinking. Doc Barker gambled heavily and lost a lot of money. This angered Freddie, and they had some very heated arguments over his gambling activities. One night, when they had all gone to Carson City — like so many times before — Doc and Volney both had too much to drink, and became embroiled in an argument with some fellow in the tavern. It ended up in a free-for-all fight that attracted a lot of attention. The gang then decided it was time, once again, to move on.

Pretty Wynona Burdette "Courtesy of the Collection of Rick Mattix"

Around December 1, 1933, after hearing that Verne Miller had been found murdered in Detroit a few days previously — on November 29th — Volney and Edna left Reno and headed back to St. Paul, Minnesota.

Verne Miller "Courtesy of the Collection of Rick Mattix"

Everyone had arranged to meet at a tourist camp in Salt Lake City, Utah, on the way to St. Paul. After one night there, their next stop was Cheyenne,

Wyoming. Edna later recalled that they had lost some time stopping for gas, so Volney proceeded to drive too fast for conditions. Passing through the mountains, Volney couldn't negotiate a curve, and their car went over a 20 foot embankment. Once the car finally stopped bouncing and rolling, they landed at the bottom of the embankment and had to kick the doors open in order to get out. Volney was in a panic, as the lock on the turtleback of their coupe had broken, and everything — including guns and ammunition — was scattered everywhere. Edna recalled thinking that she was all right, but when she bent over to pick up their luggage, she noted blood gushing from her head and into her eyes that temporarily blinded her. Her legs and hands were bleeding, too. Once they located their belongings, they got back into the car, and were trying to get it started, when out of nowhere it seemed, a fellow stopped to ask if they were hurt. They told him that everything was all right, but the fellow insisted on tying his handkerchief around Edna's head, which was bleeding profusely. Their car made it to the next filling station, where they stopped for gas. The attendant asked about the wreck, and expressed concern over Edna's condition. Volney assured him that he was taking her to a doctor. The car wasn't running very well, so by the time they reached the tourist camp in Cheyenne, it was quite late. Meanwhile, the rest of the gang was worried, and feared that something dire had happened to them. Upon their arrival, Freddie wanted to take Edna to a doctor, but she refused to go. The next morning, Freddie went to a drugstore in town and bought bandages and medicine "to fix her up" as best he could. According to Edna's later recollections, Volney — on the other hand — was more worried about the car's health than he was about her health.

Edna was in pretty bad shape and was in a great deal of pain when they reached St. Paul. Once there, she finally saw a doctor, and found out that she had suffered a fractured skull and had two broken ribs. The doctor told her she should have sought medical attention sooner, since, by this time, the swelling to her head prevented the needed stitching required to close the wound. The doctor also let her know that she had run a big risk of getting an infection by letting this condition go unattended for so long.

Volney and Edna rented the first place they could find in St. Paul, but not satisfied with it, they later rented an apartment on Lexington Avenue. It was while living there that Edna first met Bill Weaver and Myrtle Eaton. It wasn't long before Doc Barker arrived in town and paid them a visit. On Christmas day, 1933, Volney and Edna, along with Harry Campbell and Wynona Burdette, had dinner at the exclusive Hollyhocks Club — a Mecca for St. Paul's underworld. And on New Year's Eve, Volney and Edna attended a movie in Minneapolis.

Shortly after the holidays, Doris and Jess returned to Cardin, Oklahoma, for a family visit. Then they moved on to Topeka, Kansas, and rented an apartment at the Senate Apartments under the name of Mr. and Mrs. E. A. Conley. But this would prove to be only a temporary separation before the four of them (Volney & Edna and Doris & Jess) would be reunited again.

Hollyhocks Club – The Hollyhocks Club casino (located at 1590 Mississippi River Boulevard South) was a very popular spot for members of the Dillinger Gang and the Barker-Karpis Gang.

Chapter 22: The Bremer Kidnapping & Its Aftermath

Between the first of the year and January 17, 1934 — the day of the kidnapping of Edward Bremer — Edna saw a lot of Harry Campbell and Wynona Burdette, Bill Weaver and Myrtle Eaton, Arthur "Doc" Barker, Freddie Barker and Paula Harmon, and Harry "Dutch" Sawyer and his wife, Gladys. St. Paul, Minnesota, was Harry's hometown and he pretty much ruled it.

Edward G. Bremer was the target of a Barker-Karpis Gang kidnapping in 1934.

Myrtle Eaton – paramour of Bill Weaver "Courtesy of the Collection of Rick Mattix"

William Weaver "Courtesy of the Collection of Rick Mattix"

On the day of the Bremer kidnapping, Volney Davis was gone for part of the day but was home with Edna that night. Edward G. Bremer was the President of the Commercial State Bank of St. Paul and his father, Adolph Bremer, was a close and personal friend of President Franklin D. Roosevelt. At about 8:20 a.m., Edward Bremer dropped off his 8 year old daughter, Betty, at The Summit School, located at 1150 Goodrich Avenue, where many of St. Paul's wealthiest citizens enrolled their children. A few minutes later, while proceeding on his way downtown to the bank — at the corner of Lexington and Goodrich Avenues — his car was boxed in, as one vehicle cut cross-wise in front of his car while another vehicle came to a stop just behind his car. Several men with guns forced their way into his car, slapped him around and "doubled him up" down on the floorboard, under the dashboard, before driving away. Word spread throughout the day that he hadn't shown up for work at his bank and could not be located anywhere. At approximately noon on January 18th, the broadcast of his disappearance was announced over the radio. It was big news since everyone in St. Paul knew of the prominent Bremer family.

This is the scene where Edward G. Bremer was kidnapped by the Barker-Karpis Gang. The banker had just dropped off his daughter at school and was driving toward downtown, when he was boxed in by two cars, overpowered by the kidnappers, and taken to a hideout in Bensenville, Illinois.

The following afternoon, Volney returned and asked if anyone had been to the apartment while he was gone. When Edna said no, he told her they needed to go to Bill Weaver's place. Freddie Barker, Fred Goetz, Paula Harmon, and Wynona Burdette were all there. Freddie said that the ladies should go home with Edna, as the men had some talking to do. Before sunrise the next morning, Freddie brought Volney home, and then left with Paula and Wynona.

Volney reported to Edna that they had been tipped off by Harry Sawyer that there was going to be a search of some of the apartments, and he further stated that they couldn't risk being arrested. He told Edna to go back to Chicago while he would stay and wipe down the apartment to eliminate fingerprints before leaving. Edna didn't want to drive all the way to Chicago alone since she was sick, and she knew that the roads were going to be very slippery. Volney agreed to get someone to drive her — a man who she later learned was "Shotgun" George Zeigler (the alias for Fred Goetz). Volney then informed Edna that George would drive her to Chicago, and he would also help her locate an apartment.

On their way to Chicago, George gave Edna the phone number of a man named Willie Harris, whom he said would help her out in finding a place to live. He also let her know that Paula and Wynona had already left St. Paul, also driving to Chicago. While traveling through Wisconsin, George spotted a car that was pulled off to the side of the road that he thought might be the car that Paula and Wynona were traveling in. George pulled over and stopped and — sure enough — it was them. Paula was crying about driving on the slippery roads, and was angry with Wynona because Wynona wouldn't let her drive. Wynona said she wished she could travel to Chicago with Edna and George and just let Paula drive by herself.

Once George and Edna finally got the other women settled down, Edna told them she would be getting an apartment in Chicago and they would be welcome to stay with her. She then gave Willie Harris' phone number to Wynona, and told her to call him immediately when they arrived in Chicago because Willie would let them know where she was staying. George and Edna drove on that night until they arrived at a small rooming house in Hammond, Indiana, where her next contact would meet her on the following day. George instructed Edna to register under the name of Mrs. E. J. Snyder, which she did. After telling Edna that Willie would meet her the following morning, George left in Volney's Ford coupe. The next day, shortly before noon, Edna overheard Willie asking for a Mrs. Snyder while he was standing at the front desk. After she introduced herself as Mrs. Snyder, Willie told her that George had sent him for her, and he drove her to Chicago in his Ford coupe. He took her to an apartment at 6212 S. University Avenue on Chicago's South Side, where she again registered under the name of Mrs. E. J. Snyder, and Willie promptly departed. She later learned that Willie's last name was Harrison — not Harris.

A day or so after Edna took up residence in the apartment, Wynona and Paula showed up in the evening. They said they had a difficult time in both finding her and getting in touch with Willie. They had checked into the Fullerton Plaza Hotel, at 1829 W. Fullerton Avenue, on the north side of Chicago. All three of the women drove to the hotel in the Chevrolet sedan that Paula and Wynona had driven in from St. Paul, and moved their baggage back to Edna's apartment.

The next day, January 24th, Volney arrived in the car that he had previously loaned to George. He only stayed a couple of days before departing again. That night, undoubtedly after a few drinks, Paula started antagonizing Edna again regarding Volney "… chasing around with other women." Edna told her that even if that were true, it wasn't any of Paula's business, and she needed to keep her big mouth shut. Then Paula started going on about how much money Volney owed Freddie. Edna finally hauled off and smacked Paula across her face, and yelled at her to "… get your ass out of my apartment. There is no way I'm going to live with you." The next day, Volney was returning just as Paula was moving out (eventually to her own apartment at 6708 S. Constance — about a mile and a half away), and noticing Paula's bruised face, he asked Edna what happened. Edna told him the story, but he didn't have much to say about it. Volney remained there for several days, and during this time he took Edna and Wynona to the Chicago Downtown Loop District to see the sights. This was the first time in her life that Wynona had been to the Downtown area of Chicago.

The next time Volney left, he again did not tell Edna of his destination, but left her by saying that he would see her soon again. She knew that something was going on and the gang had good reason to worry. Volney was wearing a bulletproof vest and was heavily armed. Willie Harrison came by once to check on Edna and Wynona. And Doc Barker also came by the apartment one day for a visit.

Volney continued to come and go for two or three days at a time. Once, when he was at the apartment, Wynona asked him when her "Buff" (her way of referring to Harry Campbell as her boyfriend), was coming back to her. Volney told her he had no idea where her "Buff" was. But, Wynona wouldn't let it go, and kept hounding him about her "Buff's" whereabouts, until Volney finally became so agitated with her, he told her to "… shut the hell up," and not to ask him again.

The next time Volney went out of town, Freddie came by to see how the girls were getting along. He also asked Edna about the argument with Paula. Edna told him to ask Paula about it. A few days later, Volney returned for several days before leaving again.

Volney had been absent once more for a couple of days, when Edna read in the newspaper of Edward Bremer's release, following the payment of the ransom money. Volney returned the following day with Doc Barker, Freddie Barker, Alvin Karpis, and George Zeigler — all acting as nervous as cats. They knew they had "over-played their hand" with regard to the Bremer kidnapping. In the past they had always seemed confident and self-assured about the jobs they pulled, but this time it was different. A day or so later, Harry Campbell finally showed up. This was the first time that Edna or Wynona had seen Harry since the day he left St. Paul. Harry only spent a couple of days in their apartment before taking Wynona with him to Toledo, Ohio.

About 10 days later, around February 20th, Edna and Volney relocated to Aurora, Illinois, renting an apartment at 415 E. Fox Street, under the alias names of Mr. and Mrs. Hanson. They had no specific reason for choosing Aurora as their destination, other than the fact that they wanted to be alone, and in a smaller town. Volney didn't want anyone knowing where they were except for Mother Barker and her son, Freddie. Edna believed that the Barkers had the $200,000 ransom money in their possession.

Soon after moving to Aurora, Edna went to the Riverside Café & Tavern, which was owned by a man named Matt Kirsch. Previously, Edna had known another man, by the name of Corey Bales, also of Aurora, whom she had met in Montgomery, Illinois, back in 1929. She mentioned his name, and Matt said he knew him. He asked Edna if she wanted him to give Corey a call, which of course, she did. After making contact, Corey met with Edna and Volney — whom she introduced as Curly Hanson — at the tavern, later that evening. Afterwards, they all went to Corey's house where they met his girlfriend, Violet Gregg. Corey and Violet were living at 202 High Street, in Aurora, and the two couples soon became very friendly.

When Corey and his friend, Matt Gleason, opened their bookie joint on South Broadway in Aurora, Volney went to work for them running the craps table. This illicit establishment was located upstairs, above a fruit stand on South Broadway, near Main Street. Corey operated the gambling room, and Matt ran the bookmaking end of it. There was also a man named Johnny who operated the blackjack table. Volney was making good money there and was also enjoying his work.

When Bill Weaver and Myrtle Eaton found out that Volney and Edna were in Aurora, they followed them there, and rented an apartment from Volney and Edna's landlord, Frank Burkel, on Claim and High Streets.

Around this same time, Edna and Volney also became good friends with a man named Ted Smith, who owned a tavern near the railroad tracks, lived in their neighborhood, and shared a parking garage with them. Also about this time, Volney sold his Ford coupe, which was registered under his true last name of Davis, and bought a 1930 Buick sedan, registered under the name of G. R. Hanson.

Fred Goetz alias "Shotgun" George Zeigler

Soon after the March 20, 1934, gangland killing of Fred Goetz (alias "Shotgun" George Zeigler) in Cicero, the story hit the newspapers. A couple of evenings later, around 9:00 p.m., Volney and Edna, along with Violet Gregg, were returning home when they noticed two figures on their front porch. Volney told Edna to go to Violet's place until he contacted her. The next morning, he told Edna that the late night visitors had been Kate Barker and Irene Dorsey Goetz, Fred Goetz' moll. Edna could tell that Volney was upset about something. He told her he didn't like the idea of Kate — whom he usually referred to as

156

"Mother" — bringing a strange woman to where he lived. He was so aggravated, in fact, that he talked about relocating to a new apartment the very next day.

Mother Barker had come to seek Volney's help regarding her son, Freddie. She said the heat was on, and her son, Freddie, and Alvin Karpis had recently undergone operations to obliterate their fingerprints. "Freddie's in so much pain he's out of his head," Mother Barker said. She said, "I want you to go back with me, Volney."

Dr. Joseph P. "Doc" Moran – Gangland doctor "Courtesy of the Collection of Rick Mattix"

Dr. Joseph Moran had performed the surgeries in his room at the Irving Hotel in Chicago, with his nephew, James Wilson, assisting. The nephew hoped that the money he made from the gang would pay for his medical school training. It had also been said by some that the two had also performed plastic surgery on the faces of Freddie and Alvin, but Edna didn't think that their faces had changed at all.

By this time, most of the ransom money had been buried in the garage of Irene's uncle, Simon Cinotto, in Wilmington, Illinois. Freddie and Alvin, still recovering from their surgeries, were concerned over the security of the ransom money, so they sent Volney Davis to dig it up for them. Around March 23rd, Volney moved the ransom money to Freddie's apartment in Chicago.

Meanwhile, Edna was also suffering with some health issues. She was not only having female problems, but was also experiencing excruciating pain due to ingrown toenails, so she had no choice but to see a doctor. In April, she saw both Dr. Goodman, and Dr. E. L. Lee, both having practices in Aurora. Dr. Goodman later told FBI agents that he operated on both of Edna's feet, cutting out her ingrown toenails. She was accompanied by Volney Davis, and while the operation was being performed, it was reported that Volney fainted. Dr. Goodman proceeded to revive Davis with water. He readily identified pictures of them both and said he knew them as J. E. Hansen and wife. Dr. Goodman went on to say that he visited the "Hansen" apartment at 415 E. Fox Street on four or five occasions subsequent to April 12th, to change the dressings on Edna's feet. On each of these visits he saw Volney at the apartment, but there was no one else there.

Dr. E. L. Lee, whose office was in the Aurora National Bank Building, also told federal agents that on April 11th, and again on April 12th, a woman, identifying herself as Mrs. J. E. Hansen (Edna), was examined by him. She gave her address as 202 High Street in Aurora. Informing agents of the seriousness of her condition, Dr. Lee said he advised her to return for an operation, and, after the surgery, for her to plan to further remain in the hospital for one to two weeks. According to Dr. Lee, Mrs. Hansen agreed to this plan but did not return after her second visit on April 12, 1934.

Author's note:

Edward Bremer's 8 year old daughter, Betty, (nicknamed "Hertzy"), who was dropped off at The Summit School just minutes before her father was kidnapped, attended the school for 13 years, including kindergarten. After receiving her undergraduate degree from Wellesley College, followed by the completion of her Masters Studies at the University of Minnesota, she returned to The Summit School as the kindergarten teacher. At the time of her death in 2009, she had been married to Robert Johnson for 56 years.

Irene Dorsey Goetz' Downward Psychological Spiral — And Her Amazing Comeback

The gangland slaying of Fred Goetz outside of the Minerva Restaurant in Cicero, Illinois, on Tuesday evening, March 20, 1934, sent his wife, Irene Dorsey Goetz, into a physical and emotional tailspin that continued for over four terrifying months before her psychological condition stabilized, and she started back on a journey to normalcy.

When Fred Goetz, himself a former Capone "Chicago Outfit" gangster and also a member of the infamous Barker-Karpis Gang, was gunned down, he was with Irene. The shotgun blasts to his face made recognition impossible, so the positive identification by the coroner had to be made through his fingerprints.

Over the next few months, Irene's physical, emotional, and psychological condition deteriorated due to the death of her husband, the manner in which he was killed, the fact that she was a witness to the carnage at the time he was killed, and the fact that she still had some unresolved issues with her parents who had strongly advised her not to marry Fred Goetz 10 years earlier, when she was only 18 years old.

Sometime during the first few weeks of June, 1934, Irene, an attractive 28 year old school teacher in Wilmington, Illinois, a far south suburb of Chicago, disappeared seemingly into thin air from her home in Illinois, according to her mother, Mrs. James Dorsey.

During the time of her disappearance, she authored and sent the following rambling, incoherent, letter:

160

"No contacts no signing partner to settle read and think. Use your wits, neither cloud is under control and all need Indian orders wait for them. Answer yes at once."

Irene Dorsey

Larne Hotel

San Francisco, California

Note: There was no hotel in San Francisco named the "Larne Hotel."

Then, in early August, 1934, Irene was found wandering in a dazed condition in the Oakdale District of Stanislaus County, California, and was immediately admitted as a patient to the nearby County Hospital in Modesto, California.

According to Jay A. Rydberg, the Superintendent of the County Hospital at the time Irene was admitted, her mind appeared to be totally blank and she was suffering from a severe case of amnesia.

After a few weeks, while she was under observation, she recalled that her first name was Irene.

With this simple recollection on Irene's part, the first stages of her recovery had begun!

After a few more days of observation, her memory started to return to the state where the doctors were able to contact her mother, Mrs. James Dorsey, also a resident of Wilmington, Illinois. Mrs. Dorsey arrived a few days later and was able to complete her daughter's identification and to arrange for her release from the hospital on August 23, 1934.

According to Mr. Rydberg, the doctors at the County Hospital determined that the most likely immediate cause of Irene's illness was from the nervous shock to her system caused by her husband's recent slaying.

Chapter 23: The Shoot-out At Little Bohemia Lodge

From mid-March through mid-April of 1934, Volney Davis had been making a series of daily trips to Chicago from their apartment at 415 E. Fox Street in Aurora, Illinois, to help Mother Barker take care of Freddie. When he came home on Wednesday, April 25th, he said to Edna, "Rabbit, go to your girlfriend's place for a couple of days. There was a gun battle at Little Bohemia Lodge (in Manitowish Waters, Wisconsin) a few days ago and one of Dillinger's boys was shot. They can't find a place for him, so he's gonna come here."

Little Bohemia Lodge - getting new windows and repairs after the shoot–out.

The newspapers were filled with the amazing story of how the John Dillinger Gang had shot their way out of a trap at Little Bohemia Lodge on Sunday, April 22, 1934 — a lodge in a remote area of northern Wisconsin.

The wife of the owner of the lodge had managed to get word to the authorities that the Dillinger Gang was hiding out there. Federal agents were dispatched to the scene, and they mistakenly believed that their presence had been given away when the owner's dogs began barking. Little did the agents know that the dogs were always barking at something, so the gang inside didn't pay this any undue attention. A few minutes later, some agents, upon seeing a car approaching them as it was leaving the lodge, believed that the gangsters were inside the car. After the agents' alleged unsuccessful attempts to have the occupants stop the car, they proceeded to open fire, hitting all three, and killing one. Unfortunately, these men were just innocent customers who were departing the lodge, and Dillinger and his crew were still inside.

The gang may have ignored the sounds of the dogs, but the machine gun fire got their attention fast. At least one of the gang members fired at the agents from a cabin near the lodge (reputed to be "Baby Face" Nelson), before John Dillinger, Homer Van Meter, and John Hamilton exited out of the rear windows of the lodge, jumped off the rear roof, and ran for the woods in a northerly direction, along the shore of Little Star Lake. "Baby Face" Nelson ran in the opposite direction and wound up at a neighboring resort — holding the owner hostage in his own house. Tommy Carroll, another gang member, managed to elude everyone. When all was said and done, the federal agents were surprised to learn that the gang had escaped out of the unguarded rear of the lodge, and quickly proceeded to steal cars and then move on, while federal agents were shooting hundreds of holes into the unoccupied building — at least, unoccupied by the Dillinger Gang men.

"Baby Face" Nelson was approached by a carload of officials who, after having been delayed, were just arriving to the area. "Baby Face" ordered them out of their car at gunpoint. After following his instructions, he proceeded to fatally shoot Agent W. Carter Baum, and injure Agent J. C. Newman, as well as the local constable, Carl Christensen. "Baby Face" Nelson was the innocent looking kid that Edna had remembered as "Jimmy." In fact, up to this point, he was the only member of the Dillinger Gang that Edna had met.

The following day, Minnesota police spotted the Dillinger Gang's car between the cities of St. Paul Park and Hastings, headed in a southeasterly direction, back towards Wisconsin. At one point in the pursuit, the Minnesota police began firing at the group with their rifles. One bullet pierced the trunk of their car, and struck John Hamilton in the lower back, about an inch or so to the left of his spine, and about an inch or so above his belt line. The Dillinger Gang again managed to escape this encounter, and desperately searched for medical treatment for the injured Hamilton, once they were able to put some distance between themselves and their pursuers.

John "Red" Hamilton

John Dillinger tried to seek medical help for his pal, John "Red" Hamilton, but Doc Moran turned them away because they were "too hot."

John Hamilton's gunshot wound was very serious and he was losing a lot of blood. He later died at the apartment of Volney Davis and Edna Murray in Aurora, Illinois.

Edna went to stay at her girlfriend's place, and Volney went back to Chicago. He later returned home to their Fox Street apartment in Aurora, along with John Dillinger, Homer Van Meter, and the mortally wounded John "Red" Hamilton. Harry Campbell and Doc Barker followed in Doc's car.

The G-men didn't have any idea at the time that Hamilton was wounded. He was at Edna's and Volney's apartment for three nights and two days before he died from his injuries at about 3:00 p.m. on Friday, April 27, 1934. Volney and Doc Barker purchased some entrenching tools and proceeded to start digging a grave for Hamilton near sundown in an isolated spot near Oswego, Illinois, and finished digging the 3½' x 3' x 6' grave at about 6:30 p.m. that same night. On their way back to the apartment, at about 6:45 p.m., they purchased about 10 cans of lye from a grocery store. Then, at about 9:00 p.m. that same night, Volney, John Dillinger, Harry Campbell, Doc Barker, and Homer Van Meter took John Hamilton's body to that isolated gravesite near Oswego and buried him. They poured lye on his face and hands in order to help prevent any possible identification.

Volney brought Edna home as soon as the gang returned to their Aurora apartment. "Rabbit, the guy kicked," Volney announced, meaning that Hamilton had died. That's when Edna found out what had taken place.

When Edna walked into her apartment, she saw that Dillinger, Van Meter, Doc Barker and Harry Campbell were all still there. She never felt as sickened in all her life as she did when she walked through her apartment. Disinfectant powder was everywhere. It was on the bathroom floor, in the bedroom, and even on her bed, but the odor was still overwhelming. Dirty bed linens and pillows were piled all over the floor. The kitchen sink was overflowing with dirty dishes, and Edna's dresser was covered with medicines and bandages. When she opened the closet door, a dirty spade used for digging Hamilton's grave fell out and hit her on the foot. Edna felt it was just another horrible death experience where one of the gang was just buried and forgotten like one might bury an old stray dog. No comfort, no doctor, just dirt in your face. This was the one question that Edna feared the most — what would happen to her if she died while on the lam with the gang? This brought back her dreaded thoughts of ultimately ending up in a grave in "potter's field."

Edna went into the kitchen first and started cleaning up the mess, when Volney and Doc came in to help out. She worked all night trying to get the place clean, and rid the apartment of the foul stench. Volney took the dirty linens and burned them in the furnace in the basement, and purchased new ones the next morning.

The next day, Saturday, John Dillinger and Homer Van Meter stayed close to the radio. They kept it dialed to the "short wave" stations and every so often a broadcast would come through about Dillinger's gang and the shoot-out at Little Bohemia Lodge. It was thought that both "Baby Face" Nelson and Tommy Carroll were still hiding out in the woods near Manitowish Waters, the scene of the shoot-out. The federal agents were in hot pursuit, but still didn't know that law enforcement officers had mortally wounded John Hamilton. The federal agents spent a great deal of time and effort hunting for a man who was already dead.

WANTED   WANTED

South Bend police made this picture of John Hamilton in 1937 when he was arrested there for bank robbery. He made the mistake of trying to hide out in the same block in which the chief of police lived.

John "Red" Hamilton – Wanted

John Dillinger was now the hottest man in the country — with all of Hoover's army after him — and there he was sitting on a sofa in Edna's and Volney's apartment. To Edna, the most nerve-wracking part of it all was the machine guns that Dillinger and Van Meter kept laying across their legs or leaning against their chairs, not to mention the fact that they were continuously wearing bulletproof vests and seemed to be just waiting to respond to the first sign of trouble. Thankfully, they stayed in the living room most of the time, and Edna didn't need to go in there very often. Whenever she was around Dillinger, she said "… he gave her the creeps, with his sneering, snarling, crooked smile and his piercing eyes. He didn't have much to say, and when he did speak; it was usually just cursing and swearing." Edna felt that Dillinger had no respect for women, and just knew that if she crossed him, he wouldn't hesitate to shoot her down and throw her in a grave like he did his pal, John "Red" Hamilton.

Dillinger gave Edna the creeps with his "… sneering, snarling, crooked smile and his piercing eyes."

An announcement came over the radio that "Baby Face" Nelson had kidnapped an old Indian couple by the name of Ollie and Maggie Catfish,

168

and made Ollie drive "Baby Face" out of the wooded section near the shoot-out. Dillinger laughed when he heard that and said to Van Meter, "Well, at least 'Baby Face' ain't hungry. He's got plenty of catfish with him." Edna didn't see the humor in it.

Dillinger and Van Meter had no car, but needed one, and needed one, fast. There was no more time to waste — they had to get a car and get out of that apartment that day, if possible. That afternoon, Edna and Volney drove to Chicago in Doc's car. Volney knew some boys in the car stealing business, and he bought a stolen Ford from them for Dillinger. He drove the Ford back to Aurora, while Edna drove Doc's Buick.

Upon arriving home late that afternoon, there was news on the radio and in the evening paper that worried Edna and Volney even more than the presence of Dillinger and Van Meter in their apartment. John J. "Boss" McLaughlin was arrested that day in Chicago for handling some of the ransom money from the Bremer kidnapping.

It was found out later that leading up to McLaughlin's arrest, he had given William E. Vidler, a Chicago bookie, some small denomination bills from the Bremer kidnapping to be exchanged for larger denomination $100 bills. Vidler exchanged $1,000 at the Uptown State Bank in Chicago on April 23rd and an alert teller matched the serial numbers on the bills and the bank officials notified the FBI.

Again, on April 26th, Vidler exchanged ten $10 bills for a $100 bill at the City National Bank and Trust, in Chicago. The serial numbers on these bills were also matched to the Bremer kidnapping ransom money and the FBI was again alerted. During the transaction, Vidler mentioned that he was a bookie, and this turned out to be a valuable clue for the FBI in locating him.

Vidler was arrested that same afternoon at his Chicago office, located at 226 S. Wells, and indicated that he was exchanging this money for "Boss" McLaughlin. The FBI kept this story quiet until April 28th when they arrested McLaughlin. It should be mentioned that Vidler later was acquitted of having any involvement in the Bremer kidnapping.

Everyone in the Barker-Karpis Gang was very concerned about the arrest of McLaughlin since he knew too much, including the locations where most of the gang lived.

One of the first of the gang to fall into the law, Boss McLaughlin was picked up in Chicago as he attempted to change ransom bills.

One of the first of the gang to fall into the hands of the law, John J. "Boss" McLaughlin was picked up in Chicago as he attempted to launder some of the ransom money from the Edward Bremer kidnapping.

An associate by the name of Russell Gibson was supposed to come to see Volney on the night of the 28th to exchange clean money for the ransom cash, since Gibson and McLaughlin were laundering the hot money for the gang. When Gibson didn't show up at the expected time, everyone assumed that McLaughlin "sang." They all expected the G-men to swoop down on them at any time. The rest of the ransom money was in a suitcase in their clothes closest.

All of the men sat in the living room with the lights turned out. Volney's and Edna's apartment was on the first floor so they could just step out of the window and onto the street if necessary which is the reason that they usually tried to rent apartments on the ground floor. And they always tried to make sure that there were several ways out of the building. This apartment had three large windows in the living room. Doc Barker sat in front of one window and Dillinger and Van Meter had the other two covered. Harry Campbell was keeping watch from a window in the back bedroom. They all held onto machine guns. Volney occasionally took a stroll up and down the street, walking back and forth, and every so often he would sit on the porch. He was the designated outside lookout.

Edna was sitting in their bedroom when Volney suddenly came running in, yelling, "Doc, I think we got it. I believe they are here. A car pulled up on 4th Street, two men got out and walked up the street. There's even another car on Fox street. Three men got out of that car." He then ran to the clothes closet, jerked out the large suitcase, and put it in the middle of the living room floor.

"Rabbit, you get out of here. Go get in my car," he ordered. "Let's all get ready."

Doc Barker could see that Volney was going to pieces. He sharply instructed Edna, "Rabbit, you stay right where you are. Don't leave this apartment. If fireworks start, you get behind me and this 'tommy' and I will take you outta here."

Volney regained control of himself, stating, "Well, maybe you better stay here, Rabbit. If we have to shoot our way out, you grab that bag sitting there and try to get to one of the cars with it."

Edna was in a state of sheer panic. She knew she was trapped in a hornet's nest and all hell was about to break loose any second. When Doc told her to stay put, he meant what he said. One false move and she would be out of the way. He wouldn't put up with someone making any stupid moves that would jeopardize all of them.

Doc cursed as he lifted his tommygun and quickly pointed it towards the window. He saw two of the men cross the street, and one of them then lit a cigarette. He took this as a signal for the G-men to rush the house.

"Don't do that, goddamn it," Dillinger yelled at Doc. "Wait until we're sure we're right. Then we'll give it to them!"

Doc lowered his gun. The room was so quiet that Edna could almost hear herself breathe. Everybody was armed to the teeth with machine guns and .45 caliber pistols. Harry Campbell had a high-powered rifle. Homer Van Meter was the coolest of them all, laughing and making wisecracks in order to ease the tension.

Homer Van Meter – The wisecracker – Edna said he was the coolest of them all

Soon a car pulled up in front of their apartment. Inside was Russell Gibson and Jimmie Wilson, who was another member of the Barker-Karpis gang who had participated in the robbery of the Peoples Bank of Mountain View, Missouri, on October 7, 1931. They knocked on the door and Doc jerked it open. Their faces paled when they saw the room full of men with guns pointed at them.

Russell "Rusty" Gibson "Courtesy of the Collection of Rick Mattix"

Gibson told the boys they were all getting jittery and nervous for nothing. He did, however, say that it would be best for them to get out of town as soon as possible. No one ever did figure out who the mysterious men on the street were. Those men never knew how close they came to getting mowed down by the gang.

Early the next morning, on Sunday, April 29th, John Dillinger and Homer Van Meter walked out of Edna's and Volney's apartment for the last time. They had no luggage, but they carried two machine guns wrapped in a blanket. They left in the stolen Ford automobile that Volney bought for them, and Edna was never so glad to see someone leave. She, thankfully, never saw either of them again.

As for Volney and Edna, it was also time for them to "move on", since they couldn't depend on "Boss" McLaughlin keeping quiet for much longer.

Author's note:

Ellen Poulsen, author of "Don't Call Us Molls — Women of the John Dillinger Gang," once told me:

"Edna wasn't the only woman who felt the way she did about Dillinger. Mrs. Audrey Voss would agree with her. She was the proprietress of Voss' Birchwood Lodge near the Little Bohemia Lodge. Audrey thought Dillinger was a very unpleasant man. She mentioned the bad way he looked at her, just as Edna did. And she was also very happy to see the last of him. It could be that the charisma he had when he was just released from prison and still feeling exhilarated, had quickly disappeared once he became like a hunted animal, leaving with guns in blankets, like the last episode of The Sopranos."

The Reports Of The Sightings And The Whereabouts Of John Hamilton After April 27, 1934, As Reported To The U. S. Bureau Of Investigation

The 101 page internal report issued by the U. S. Bureau of Investigation (later renamed as the "FBI") as described below, lists the alleged sightings and reports of sightings of John Hamilton after the events of the shoot-out in, or near, Hastings, Minnesota, on April 23, 1934, and continues through August 20, 1934, with additional alleged reported sightings.

The summarized FBI report which follows, if accurate, would contradict the statements made by Volney Davis to FBI officials the following year, in August of 1935 — in which Davis stated that John Hamilton died in Aurora, Illinois, within a few days of being shot by Minnesota law enforcement officials near the town of Hastings, Minnesota. Davis also stated that Hamilton was buried within a few hours of his death in a makeshift grave near Oswego, Illinois.

With regard to John Hamilton, the following is a summary of every reported sighting, every reported statement of his whereabouts, and every reported statement of his physical condition, as reported to the U. S. Bureau of Investigation.

Source Document:

U. S. Bureau Of Identification

File Number: 62-29777-3607

For the Period: July 1, 1934, to August 20, 1934

174

Prepared By: Special Agent V. W. Peterson, Chicago, Illinois

Approved By: Special Agent S. P. Cowley, Chicago, Illinois

Some preliminary events leading up to John Hamilton's injuries suffered at Hastings, Minnesota, are as follows:

January 15, 1934. As a member of the Dillinger Gang, during the robbery of the First National Bank & Trust Company, in East Chicago, Indiana, John Hamilton was shot at least twice. It was stated by Jean Burke that once Joseph "Doc" Moran successfully treated Hamilton's wounds, his recuperation was further aided by one of Hamilton's female friends, Pat Cherrington, reportedly at the home of Art Johnson's aunt, at 5740 S. Homan Avenue, in Chicago. Jean Burke also added that Art Johnson was, reportedly, an errand boy for the Dillinger Gang. (page 19).

March 13, 1934. As a member of the Dillinger Gang, during the robbery of the First National Bank, in Mason City, Iowa, Hamilton was once again hit — this time in the shoulder. In this instance, his recuperation time was rather short, since the wound was apparently not as serious as first thought. Within 40 days, he was vacationing with members of the Dillinger Gang in Manitowish Waters, Wisconsin.

April 23, 1934. John Hamilton was shot by Minnesota law enforcement officers near Hastings, Minnesota, on the day after the shoot-out at Little Bohemia Lodge, which was located in the northern Wisconsin town of Manitowish Waters.

And now, the reports of the alleged sightings and/or whereabouts of John Hamilton as reported to the FBI after April 27, 1934, through August 20, 1934, follow:

July 6, 1934. Mr. James Richards, a bartender at the Oasis Dance Hall and Tavern in Michigan City, Indiana, noticed that at about 11:00 p.m., John Dillinger, John Hamilton, and "Baby Face" Nelson were inside the Oasis Dance Hall and Tavern while he was tending bar. He said that he mentioned this to the police on duty that night — although he did not specify the actual time of the night that he talked to the police. The next day, Mr. Richards reported this sighting to the local Chief of Police (COP), Mr. Kibbe, and the sighting was also reported in the Michigan City newspapers on that same day. Mr. Richards was discharged from his position as bartender at the Oasis Dance Hall and Tavern three days later, on July 10, 1934. (page 92).

July 9, 1934. Louis Piquett, who was John Dillinger's lawyer, had his chief investigator, Art O'Leary, direct some unnamed informants to an address at 7923 South Shore Drive on the southeast side of Chicago, where they met John Dillinger. Subsequently, in a taxicab ride from the above address to a location near "North Avenue and Harlem Avenue," John Dillinger reportedly told the unnamed informants that Hamilton had been very seriously wounded (at Hastings, Minnesota), but was receiving excellent care. Dillinger reportedly added that Hamilton was unable to walk. (pages 16-18).

176

July 25, 1934. Special Agent J. S. Johnson telephoned Special Agent V. W. Peterson in Chicago, stating that a Mr. D. E. Wynn, a fingerprint expert for the Indiana State Police, noted that it is claimed that John Hamilton is currently living across the street from 1456 Baldwin Avenue in Chicago (apparently one of Dillinger's reported alleged addresses before he was killed a few days earlier in Chicago).

According to the FBI report, Chicago Police Captain John Stege stated that he still had his men covering this address at the time that this report was completed, even though there was no such address listed in Chicago even remotely close to this stated address. (page 52).

July 25, 1934. In response to a question posed to Louis Piquett by some unnamed informants as to the whereabouts of John Hamilton, Piquett stated positively that Hamilton was already dead. He also allegedly asked the unnamed informants not to say anything about Hamilton's death to Homer Van Meter. (page 21).

July 28, 1934. A letter dated July 26, 1934, from Special Agent in Charge, William Larson, of the U. S. Bureau of Investigation's Detroit Office, arrived at the U. S. Bureau of Investigation Office in Chicago. The contents of the letter were not revealed to the public, but the letter was sent as the result of an interview with Kathryn Kelly, the wife of George "Machine Gun" Kelly. Both were currently serving life sentences for the 1933 Urschel kidnapping in Oklahoma City. The letter alerted the Bureau to investigate an address at 6837 S. Jeffery Street in Chicago. (Author's note: At the time, the proper nomenclature for addresses on Jeffery was "Avenue" — which was later changed to its current designation as a "Boulevard." It was never named "Jeffery Street.")

Since the Bureau agents couldn't locate this specific address, Special Agent R. G. Gillespie of the Chicago Office contacted Mr. N. Drinnan, Superintendent of the South Shore Post Office Substation located at 2207 E. 65th Street, and requested that he ask the appropriate letter carrier if there was such an address on the 6800 block of south Jeffery.

The carrier, John Carlson, stated that no such numbered address existed on Jeffery, and Special Agent Gillespie stated that no further inquiry was deemed advisable at this time, pending additional information (which never arrived). (page 10).

The reason why this event is included in this section regarding the sightings of John Hamilton, is to also show that the Bureau, in their efforts to accumulate as much information as possible, was very sloppy and inefficient in validating the information that they were given.

In this example, not only was the specific address of 6837 S. Jeffery nonexistent, whether one referred to Jeffery as "Street" or "Avenue" or any other designation, as evidenced by both Bureau agents and Post Office officials, but also the address of 2207 E. 65th Street has also never existed!

The area enclosed in the equivalent rectangle of "65th Street to 67th Street" and from about "2000 East to about 2500 East" is occupied by the Jackson Park Golf Course — and this golf course has existed well before the events of 1934, continuing to the present day. Beyond the area of this rectangular area to the north and east is Lake Michigan.

The U. S. Bureau of Investigation would have been better advised to have invested some money in purchasing maps, and perhaps a few additional proof-readers.

August 1, 1934. Special Agent R. D. Brown visited with William Doig, the Chief of Police (COP) of Spring Valley, Illinois, regarding the current location of Joseph "Doc" Moran — since "Doc" Moran's brother lived in that town. One of the underlying reasons for this visit by Special Agent Brown was to gather information on the possibility that "Doc" Moran might have been treating John Hamilton for his injuries.

One interesting sidelight of this visit was that COP William Doig told the FBI agent that it was widely known by local townsfolk that "Doc" Moran had abruptly left Chicago on the day that the Chicago newspapers "headlined" the story of the arrest of John J. "Boss" McLaughlin for laundering money from the Bremer kidnapping, and Moran arrived in Spring Valley a few days later — on, or about, May 1, 1934. (page 99).

This gives added credence to Volney Davis' statement to the FBI regarding the death of John Hamilton and his subsequent burial, the abrupt and documented unplanned departures of both himself and Edna Murray, of John Dillinger and Homer Van Meter, as well as Doc Barker — all of whom abruptly left Volney's and Edna's apartment in Aurora, Illinois, on April 29, 1934.

All of these hurried departures, including "Doc" Moran's quick getaway from Chicago, occurred well within 48 hours of John

Hamilton's actual death and burial **AND WAS VIRTUALLY CONCURRENT** with the day of the arrest of John J. "Boss" McLaughlin, as stated, and later confirmed, by Edna Murray.

August 3, 1934. Some unnamed informants stated that their son saw Homer Van Meter, John Hamilton, and possibly "Baby Face" Nelson in a dark Buick sedan near South Bend, Indiana. (page 24).

August 10, 1934. Nicholas Kominakis (aka Nicholas Cummings) of Cicero, Illinois, called Melvin Purvis, Special Agent in Charge of the Chicago Office, to tell him that Ray Campagna (brother of Lou "Little New York" Campagna) informed him that Hamilton was being taken care of by the "Little New York" mob in Chicago, as requested by Jake Guzik, who, at the time, was currently incarcerated in the federal penitentiary in Leavenworth, Kansas.

The Proof That John Hamilton's Body Was Actually Buried In John Hamilton's Grave

After the embarrassment that the FBI suffered from the shoot-out at Little Bohemia Lodge in Manitowish Waters, Wisconsin, on April 22, 1934, the entire FBI, under the direction of J. Edgar Hoover, was determined to bring the five escaped outlaws to justice as quickly as possible.

Over the next several months, there were thousands of sightings of these outlaws — both real and imagined — but no "sighting" of John Hamilton ever led to his arrest. The other four outlaws were all dead in less than eight months after their escape.

This led to a cottage industry of speculation and intrigue.

Where was John Hamilton — has he robbed any banks lately — have there been any recent sightings of him — what gang is he now affiliated with?

The story of the death of John Hamilton follows, and the interesting ironic twist of the story of his death is that he was not the last of the five to die — but rather, he was the first of this group of five outlaws to die. And his death occurred within a week of the gang's escape from the Little Bohemia Lodge.

As an interesting sidelight, Stephen King, in one of his great and very entertaining books, entitled *"Everything's Eventual: 14 Dark Tales,"* devotes a 42-page chapter on Hamilton's death, entitled, *"The Death of Jack Hamilton."*

In Stephen King's brilliant "True Crime" genre fictionalized version of the escape of John Dillinger, Homer Van Meter, and

Jack (John) Hamilton, the story is written in the first-person, as told by Homer Van Meter as he describes the slow and painful death of Jack (John) Hamilton after being shot by police near St. Paul, Minnesota, the day after their escape from Little Bohemia Lodge in northern Wisconsin. In this fictionalized account, Van Meter includes the refusal of Joseph "Doc" Moran to treat Hamilton upon the group's arrival in Chicago.

This threesome of hunted outlaws is then given refuge by Volney Davis, who offers to let them stay at the apartment that he and Edna Murray rent in Aurora, Illinois.

While at their apartment, Hamilton dies a few days later, in lapses of delirium and dementia.

The Shoot-out in Wisconsin and the Escape

The shoot-out at Little Bohemia Lodge on the evening of April 22, 1934, in the remote northern Wisconsin town of Manitowish Waters, brought even more embarrassment to the FBI. Not only had the five Dillinger Gang members escaped, but the federal agents managed to shoot three innocent civilians — John Hoffman, an oil station attendant from Mercer, Wisconsin; John Morris, a Civilian Conservation Corps Camp Cook; and Eugene Boisoneau, a Civilian Conservation Corps Camp Advisor and Foreman — killing Boisoneau instantly.

Adding to the carnage, during his escape, "Baby Face" Nelson killed a federal agent, W. Carter Baum; he severely injured another federal agent, J. C. Newman; and he also severely injured a local constable, Carl Christensen.

After the FBI agents interrogated the molls of the gang members at the Little Bohemia Lodge the following morning, they

182

then had the names of the five fugitives and quickly proceeded to send out "Wanted Posters" across the country. J. Edgar Hoover, the Director of the FBI, and his agents were determined to bring these criminals to justice.

The initial results in bringing these outlaws to justice were as follows:

On June 7, 1934, Tommy Carroll was killed in Waterloo, Iowa, by local police officers.

On July 22, 1934, John Dillinger, the leader of the Dillinger Gang, was killed in Chicago, Illinois, by FBI agents, with assistance by some East Chicago, Indiana, police officers.

On August 23, 1934, Homer Van Meter was killed in St. Paul, Minnesota, by four police officers, including the local chief of police.

On November 27, 1934, "Baby Face" Nelson was mortally wounded in the "Battle of Barrington" — a suburb northwest of Chicago — and he died later that night. During the gunfight, he managed to kill FBI Special Agents Herman Hollis and Sam Cowley.

With the death of "Baby Face" Nelson, J. Edgar Hoover thought that as of November 27th, they had accounted for 4 of the 5 outlaws being hunted down from the Little Bohemia Lodge fiasco.

J. Edgar Hoover, as well as the entire FBI bureaucracy was wrong — **dead wrong!**

In spite of the fact that the FBI had agents actively trying to find John "Red" Hamilton for well over a year after the Little Bohemia Lodge shoot-out, it never occurred to them that he was already dead — and he was dead well within a week of the shoot-out.

On May 2, 1934, the blood-stained getaway car that Dillinger, Van Meter, and Hamilton had traveled in to Chicago was found abandoned at 3333 N. Leavitt Street — a few miles from "Doc" Moran's residence. It was reported by various gang members that "Doc" Moran had refused to treat Hamilton due to the severity of his injury. The FBI failed to "pick up" on this clue, although some jumped to the erroneous conclusion that perhaps it could have been Dillinger who was injured. This rumor lost traction on July 22, 1934, when Dillinger was gunned down in Chicago.

The Burial and the Exhuming of the Grave

Those Giving Testimony

Frank Burkel

50 S. 4th Street

Aurora, Illinois

The previous Landlord of Volney Davis and Edna Murray

Volney Davis and Edna Murray

415 E. Fox Street

Aurora, Illinois

F. M. Groner

Coroner of Kendall County, Illinois

Submitted the Coroner's Report for the deceased on August 30, 1935

Dr. J. C. Sawyer, DDS

320 Center Street

Michigan City, Indiana

Dentist assigned to Inmates at the Indiana State Penitentiary (from 1925 to 1933)

Maintained and kept Dental Charts on all inmates needing and receiving dental work

Between June 7, 1935 — when Volney Davis was given a life sentence at Leavenworth Penitentiary — and late August, 1935, he volunteered information to the FBI regarding the burial location of the body of John Hamilton.

Volney Davis stated that he helped bury the body of John Hamilton, who had been shot by Minnesota law enforcement personnel in, or near, Hastings, Minnesota, on April 23, 1934, a day after the shoot-out at Little Bohemia Lodge in Manitowish Waters, Wisconsin. He stated further that John Hamilton later died of these injuries a few days after being brought to his (Volney Davis') apartment in Aurora, Illinois.

So this left the FBI with three questions:

A. Can Volney Davis point out the actual location of the grave?

B. Is someone still in this grave?

C. If there is someone in this grave, is it John Hamilton?

185

Answers:

1. Volney Davis showed the FBI where the grave was located, based on aerial photos taken after he described the general vicinity of the location of the grave. The body was recovered on August 28, 1935.

2. The location of the grave was close to where Volney lived at the time. It was just a short drive from his apartment — about six miles south of Aurora, Illinois, and about a mile and a half northeast of Oswego, Illinois.

3. The actual grave was 3 to 4 feet deep. This is exactly what Volney told the FBI agents. Once the body was exhumed, at about 4:00 p.m. on the afternoon of August 28, 1935, it was immediately transported to the Undertaking Parlor of J. B. Thorsen, in Oswego, Illinois. The autopsy commenced that evening.

4. According to the Coroner, F. M. Groner, the decedent's height was 5'8½" and his estimated weight at the time of his death was 160 pounds. This is an exact match with Hamilton's height based on his records from the Indiana State Penitentiary at Michigan City, Indiana, where he had been incarcerated, from March 19, 1927, until his escape, on September 26, 1933. The coroner's estimate of the decedent's weight of 160 pounds was based on the position where his belt was buckled, which indicated 36 inches in girth. While these height and weight measurements, by themselves, cannot prove conclusively that the body in the grave was that of John Hamilton, they do rule out other potential people.

5. The Coroner, F. M. Groner, said that the decedent could not have lived long — a few days perhaps — with the injuries sustained if that person was not treated very quickly by highly trained, and highly competent, medical professionals. There was evidence of gangrene, a ruptured spine, and an infection to the wound which was about an inch above the beltline and just about an inch to the left of the spine. This diagnosis is consistent with the fact that after being injured on the 23rd of April, the decedent expired well within one week.

6. Volney told the FBI that he and Doc Barker picked up 8-10 cans of lye on their way back to the apartment after digging the grave at about sundown on the day that John Hamilton died. When the body was exhumed, the cans which contained the lye were also found in the grave.

7. At the time that the body was exhumed, FBI Agents Earl J. Connelley, R. D. Brown, D. P. Sullivan, J. M. Jones, as well as Dr. F. M. Groner, the Coroner of Kendall County, noted that the body was resting on its left side. Later that evening, during the autopsy, it was noted that both the right index finger and the right middle finger of the deceased were missing.

Last incarcerated in the Indiana State Reformatory at Pendleton, Indiana, Hamilton had escaped on Sept. 26, 1933, from the Indiana State Penitentiary in Michigan City, Indiana.

In the fingerprint records of John Hamilton, taken at the Indiana State Penitentiary, there were no fingerprints of his right index finger or his right middle finger due to the fact that he lost major parts of these fingers as a youth.

There were three possible explanations for the body of the deceased to be missing these two specific fingers and bones on his right hand:

A. The missing two fingers and bones on the right hand of the deceased were missing at the time of death.

B. The missing two fingers and bones on the right hand were removed after the death of the deceased, but before the deceased was buried, or

C. The missing two fingers and bones on the right hand were caused as a result of the lye being poured on the body of the deceased while the deceased was in the grave.

The possibility of item "B" occurring seems to be absurd on its face due to the fact that if someone wanted to eliminate the fingerprints of the deceased by removing the deceased's fingers, then all of the fingers would have been removed — not just the two fingers indicated.

The possibility of item "C" occurring seems to be extremely remote because if the deceased was lying on its left side, it would make it all the more unlikely that the lye would have caused the complete removal of these two fingers, including the bones, on the deceased's right hand. The fact that these two fingers were the only two that were missing **AND** that they

188

were on the deceased's right hand, gives even added credence to the likelihood that the body in the grave was missing those two fingers at the time of death — and that the lye did not cause the disappearance of the bones on the right index finger or the right middle finger, due to the added fact that once the lye initially flowed in a downward direction, it would then be quickly dissipated and diluted once the dirt was shoveled back into the grave.

This evidence of the two specific missing fingers and bones, on the right hand — and only those two fingers and bones, **to the exclusion of the remaining three fingers and bones on the right hand** — while the body was resting on its left side, points very strongly to the conclusion that the body in the grave was missing those fingers at the time of burial.

It follows then, that possibility **"A"** above is the only logical conclusion — namely,

The missing two fingers and bones on the right hand of the deceased were missing at the time of the deceased's death.

8. Volney Davis told the FBI that Hamilton was buried in a blue serge suit and his (felt) hat was also placed in the grave. When the body was exhumed, the deceased was wearing a blue serge suit, and there was also a felt hat lying on top of the deceased.

9. According to Volney Davis' landlord, Frank Burkel, he and Edna Murray moved out of their apartment at 415 E. Fox Street on April 29, 1934. The decedent had to be buried prior to the day that Volney and Edna vacated their apartment.

10. Again, according to Volney's landlord, Frank Burkel, Volney Davis was seen burning sheets and pillow cases in the basement furnace a few days before they vacated their apartment on April 29th.

11. When it's impossible to make a positive visual identification of a deceased person because of the process of decomposition after an extended period of time, it is extremely helpful to compare the deceased's teeth with dental records since *"... teeth are the most durable part of the body and they'll remain after most of the body is destroyed. Teeth are an excellent forensic tool."* (Dr. Joseph R. Cwikla, DDS, DMD — Forensic Odontologist)

Dr. J. C. Sawyer, DDS, was a dentist who had a private practice at the time that John Hamilton's body was exhumed on August 28, 1935. Between the years 1925 to 1933, Dr. Sawyer served as the dentist to the inmates of the Indiana State Penitentiary (ISP). In 1931, he performed some dental work on two of Hamilton's teeth — numbers 20 and 9 under his "mirror image" numbering system, or — numbers 29 and 8 under the later accepted UTNS system. Fortunately, when Dr. Sawyer discontinued his practice at the Indiana State Penitentiary, and went into a private practice, also in Michigan City, Indiana, he kept the dental charts on all of the patients at the ISP. While the autopsy was being performed, Dr. Sawyer initially compared his dental charts with those of the decedent's teeth. It looked like his charts matched John Hamilton's teeth, so Dr. Sawyer had a few specific teeth comparisons he tested.

12. Dr. Sawyer compared the lower right bicuspid tooth (UTNS tooth number 29 — Sawyer's now outdated

"mirror image" numbering system code referred to it as number 20). This tooth that Dr. Sawyer filled in 1931 was the critical and definitive match for him to state conclusively that the body in the grave was the same John Hamilton who was incarcerated at the Indiana State Penitentiary in 1931, when he received the needed dental work described above. The other tooth that Dr. Sawyer treated required a very small filling (UTNS number 8 — referred to as number 9 on Sawyer's "mirror image" numbering system code), and that too was a match.

Based on the thorough review of the dental records compared with the actual teeth of the deceased, the one tooth that left absolutely no doubt that it was John Hamilton who was in the grave, was UTNS tooth number 29!

Digging up the remains of John Hamilton – 8-31-35 "Courtesy of Estella Cox"

After receiving directions from Volney Davis, FBI agents, with the assistance of local law enforcement officials, discovered the body of John Hamilton, covered with a striped canvas cover, in this grave near Oswego, Ill. "Courtesy of Estella Cox"

Chapter 24: Dr. Joseph Moran's Surgical Blunders

The move out day for Volney and Edna from their apartment at 415 E. Fox Street in Aurora, Illinois, was Sunday, April 29, 1934.

Only hours after John Dillinger and Homer Van Meter departed Edna's and Volney's apartment in Aurora, Illinois, Volney told Edna that he needed to take a trip to Toledo, Ohio, and asked her to go home to Oklahoma for a while. He gave Edna the phone number of the Casino Club in Toledo as the number where she could reach him.

At about this same time, Bill Weaver and Myrtle Eaton had also decided to leave Aurora. Myrtle had left for Des Moines, Iowa, even though she told Edna the previous day that she wasn't feeling well and not up to traveling. Bill Weaver also left town, but Edna didn't know his destination.

Edna stayed with Violet Gregg and Corey Bales for a few days before flying to Tulsa. Upon her arrival, she contacted her son, Preston, and shortly afterwards, she located Doris, who was still living with Jess Doyle. After they all visited their families in Oklahoma, all four of them traveled back to Aurora, Illinois, in Jess' Nash automobile. Preston and Edna stayed with Violet and Corey for about ten days, while Doris and Jess rented an apartment — under the name of E. A. Conley — in the same building as Bill Weaver and Myrtle Eaton previously lived.

Matt Kirsch, who owned the Riverside Café & Tavern, and had reunited Edna with her old friend, Corey Bales, opened the Fox Gardens in Aurora. As he had done for Volney at their bookie joint on South Broadway, Corey got Preston the job of operating the craps table. Preston was only 18 years of age at the time, but had no problems in learning the job.

Although Preston resided at the Fox Gardens, he spent a lot of time at the home of Corey Bales and Violet Gregg. Sometimes, when he wasn't working the craps table, he would fill in as a decoy — otherwise known as a shill — at the poker tables.

Around the middle of May, 1934, Volney sent word to Edna to join him in Toledo. She checked into the Algeo Hotel and called the Casino Club, asking for "Curly," the name he went by in Toledo. After having been informed that Curly wasn't there at the time, but was expected shortly, Edna decided to just go there and wait. It was about three hours before he finally arrived. He looked ill and his hands were all bandaged up. Edna's first thought was that he had gotten into a fight. They spent that night at the Algeo Hotel, and Volney told her all about the operations that Dr. Joseph "Doc" Moran had performed on his, and Doc Barker's, fingertips and faces. The next day they rented a place at the Jarvis Apartments, and Doc Barker moved in with them. He and Volney both had little cuts under their ear lobes, but their operations hadn't changed the way they looked at all, at least, in Edna's opinion. They both told Edna how the "heat" was now really on since the Bremer job, and she should have her fingertips operated on too. "That'll be a cold day in Hell," she told them. "Look at your fingers. Doc Moran is no better than a butcher." Curly had to admit that Doc Moran was drunk when he operated on them.

Dr. Joseph P. "Doc" Moran

James Wilson, a medical student and nephew of Doc Moran, was supposed to come to their apartment every day to change the dressings on Volney's and Doc Barker's fingers and faces. However, sometimes he wouldn't show up for days at a time, so Edna had to change the dressings for them. She even had to feed them since they were absolutely helpless and couldn't use their hands at all. Their fingers looked like raw meat, but all their suffering appeared to be for naught. Their faces didn't look any different and their fingerprints returned to look exactly as they had before.

When the bandages were finally removed and the boys could go out again, they headed straight back to the Casino Club where most the gang regularly hung out. Freddie Barker and Alvin Karpis had their surgical operations performed on them a month or more prior to the operations performed on Volney and Doc, so they were now back on the scene, along with Freddie's girl, Paula Harmon (or "Paula the Drunk," as Alvin referred to her); Alvin's girl, Dolores Delaney; Harry Campbell and his girlfriend, Wynona Burdette; Doc Moran's nephew, James Wilson; as well as Willie Harrison — who had gotten Edna her apartment in Chicago the previous January.

Around June 1, 1934, Volney drove Edna back to Aurora, Illinois, so that she could make arrangements to have the operation she still needed. And besides, he was getting awfully nervous about all the "heat" on the gang — and wanted to get out of Toledo. However, Edna didn't have the operation because, as usual, the doctor she went to — Dr. Freeds, of the Christ Hospital — wanted to review all of the records of her previous medical treatment, and, of course, she couldn't provide those records without revealing her true identity.

It was also around this time when Corey Bales informed Volney that he had received two letters from a man named Nichols, who lived in Glasgow, Montana — a town that was booming. Corey said he wanted to go there and start a business, and Volney also expressed an interest in this venture.

Shortly thereafter, Volney and Edna left Aurora, Illinois, and went to Ohio where Volney had rented one of the cottages on Lake Erie, near Sandusky. He told her he had rented this place for her to recuperate, under the assumption that she was going to have the prescribed surgery.

Bill Weaver and Myrtle Eaton were already living there when Edna and Volney arrived. Harry Campbell and Wynona Burdette followed shortly thereafter and they also rented a cottage nearby. Before long, they were visited by other gang members on numerous occasions, including: Doc Barker; Alvin Karpis and Dolores Delaney; Freddie Barker and Paula Harmon; and Jimmie Wilson.

Most of the gang hung out at a club near their cottages on Lake Erie, and they soon made this area their new headquarters. Once when Edna and Volney were there, they were sitting at a table with Freddie Barker, Russell Gibson, and Doc Moran. Moran was angry because he said that they promised him that Bill Weaver would have his fingertips operated on, but Weaver had not yet scheduled an appointment. Doc Moran made it clear that he needed the money. He was very drunk and started yelling. Freddie had enough of Moran's yelling, and told Doc Moran that he had done a lousy surgical job on all of their fingers. He also told Doc Moran that he stayed drunk all the time, and did too damn much talking. At this point, Doc Moran was infuriated, and he told Freddie that he would not be bawling him out like that if he knew what was good for him. "I've got you all in the palm of my hand," Moran boasted.

Russell Gibson spoke up and tried to calm him down by saying, "You're drunk, doctor. Come on let's go for a boat ride. You'll feel a lot better with some fresh air." Gibson then turned and winked at Edna. She knew what that wink meant. The gang had been using a fast motorboat that belonged to an acquaintance of theirs, later acknowledged by several gang members to be that of Ted Angus, of Toledo. Doc Moran was too drunk to even realize what Gibson had said, and he "fell for the bait." He made the fatal mistake of threatening desperate men who didn't think twice about killing anyone. Freddie Barker, Russell Gibson, and Doc Moran all drove off in Gibson's coupe. In a couple of hours, Freddie Barker and Russell Gibson returned to the club, minus Doc Moran.

Author's note:

On September, 26, 1935, a badly decomposed body washed up on the shores of Crystal Beach, Ontario, Canada, absent its hands and feet. The body was later identified by the FBI, through dental records, as that of Dr. Joseph P. Moran.

Late in July, 1934, Volney and Edna returned to Aurora, Illinois, to visit with Corey Bales and Violet Gregg and to find out if Corey was planning on going to Glasgow, Montana. Violet informed them that Corey had been gone for about a week, and she had already received a couple of letters from him. In one of the letters, Corey remarked to Violet that things looked so good in Glasgow that he had decided to start a business there.

Upon hearing this news, Volney also became very enthused about going to Glasgow, Montana. As soon as Volney and Edna returned to Sandusky, Ohio, he started to make preparations for the move. He first went to Cleveland, Ohio, and made a deal to trade in his Buick sedan for a Chevrolet truck.

Around the end of July, while at the lake cottages, Volney and Edna, along with Bill Weaver and Myrtle Eaton, were playing horseshoes in the back yard. Freddie Barker and Alvin Karpis showed up and joined them. Two little girls, named Winnie and Betty, who Edna believed were related to Myrtle, were staying with her and Bill at the time. While Freddie and Alvin were playing horseshoes, Volney went swimming in the lake with the girls. When he returned, Edna saw him walk up to the rear of the house, where he was talking to Freddie. Edna was sitting on the porch and just happened to go into the kitchen to get something, when she overheard them in a heated argument over something that Freddie's mother supposedly said about Volney. She heard Volney say, "I'm a man and I cover all the ground I stand on. I wouldn't bring my mother into an argument. You would be a motherfucker (sic) if you didn't hold up for your own mother, but I still say she is a damn liar."

After Freddie and Alvin left, Volney told Edna that he was getting tired of that "old lady" lying about him, and that she just always seems to cause a lot of friction whenever she's around.

Edna tried to console Volney, telling him to just try to forget about it. He said he was through with the whole damn bunch, and didn't want to have any more to do with them. He decided that he and Edna, together, would go their own way from this point on. Edna assumed that Volney had previously confronted Mother Barker about not yet getting his split of the Bremer ransom money. Volney was tired of waiting, and felt he wasn't getting a square deal. He was absolutely livid when they drove back to their cottage that night. He told Edna, "Rabbit, I'm gonna get my money tomorrow night. I'm gonna meet Freddie and this time I'm gonna get my cut." Edna knew things were headed for a showdown.

Chapter 25: Leaving The Barker-Karpis Gang

Edna and Volney both knew all too well what it meant to have "misunderstandings" with members of the gang. When Volney left the cottage in Sandusky, Ohio, the next evening, it was "even money" if he would even come back home alive. Freddie Barker was a killer and would not hesitate to shoot either, or both, Volney and Edna. It would make no difference whatsoever to Freddie that Volney had assisted in the Bremer kidnapping. There is no such thing as a "pal" when thieves fall out. Volney was ready to kill, too, and Edna knew that Volney was not about to give Freddie the chance to shoot first.

"Don't open the door to anyone, Rabbit, not to anyone," Volney warned Edna before he left for Freddie's cottage. "If I have trouble with Freddie, then I may have trouble with Doc and Karpis too. But if that little redheaded son-of-a-bitch (meaning Freddie) says one word to me, I'll shoot the fucker in the head." Volney then handed Edna a .45 caliber automatic pistol. "If I get shot, they'll come up here and take you for a ride," he warned Edna. "If any of them come up here, use this rod and shoot to kill. That's what they would do to you. Don't ask questions or take any chances — just let 'em have it."

She knew that Volney was telling her the truth. Edna knew how the gang operated. If they killed Volney, they would surely rub her out next. They would know that Volney had told her where he was going, and that she could put the finger on them. She knew too much — just as Doc Moran knew too much.

Edna turned out all the lights in the cottage. She stood there with a drink in one hand, and the .45 caliber automatic in the other. Now she had time to think, and her thoughts were running away with her. She had another drink, but she still couldn't stop shaking. Regardless of the fact that, in the past, she drank and danced and shared good times with the gang, there was no doubt in her mind that "… they would take me out and throw my 'dead ass' in a grave to rot, and they wouldn't lose any sleep over it."

About an hour after Volney left, Edna still remained sitting there, clutching the 45 caliber automatic, and jumping at every little sound. All of a sudden, she heard a car drive up and peeked. She nearly fainted in relief. It was Volney! He had gotten his split of the Bremer ransom money. He was now finished with the gang.

The boys were also upset with Bill Weaver, and were giving him the cold shoulder because he and Myrtle had children visiting with them at the lake, and the gang did not approve of this. Everyone was uneasy and on edge. It was time to split up.

By this time, most of the gang had their pictures in the newspapers as suspects in the Bremer kidnapping. It was bad enough that Hoover's army was after them, but added to that, was the fact that anyone could easily recognize them from newspaper or detective magazine photos, and could turn them in.

Shortly after Volney's confrontation with Freddie, Volney and Edna were packing their things when they were visited by Harry and Gladys Sawyer, accompanied by Willie Harrison. Harry, who ran St. Paul's underworld, had sheltered the gang in St. Paul, and also orchestrated the Bremer kidnapping. He and Gladys had picked up Willie Harrison somewhere along the way. Willie told them he was out on bond on a rape charge in Hammond, Indiana. He had an attitude that Edna never liked — and also, most of the gang didn't trust him. Doc Barker took care of him later on, though, when on January 5, 1935, he murdered Willie and threw his body into a burning barn near Ontarioville, Illinois.

Volney and Edna left Sandusky, Ohio, around August 1, 1934, in their Ford V-8 sedan, en route to Buffalo, New York, just to get away for a while. It was late in the afternoon on the day of their arrival, and Edna's feet were bothering her, so she wanted to lie down and rest as soon as they checked in to the hotel. Volney decided to go for a walk and have a beer or two. He returned to the hotel room a few hours later.

The next morning they drove to Niagara Falls, New York, where Volney sent a postcard to his folks in Neosho, Missouri. After spending a few days there and letting their heads clear up, they decided that Volney should accept the partnership deal that Corey Bales had offered him in Montana.

Their next stop was Cleveland, Ohio, to pick up the panel truck that Volney had previously purchased. From there, Edna drove their Ford sedan back to Aurora, Illinois, where she stayed with Violet Gregg at the Fox Gardens. Meanwhile, Volney drove the Chevrolet truck back to Cardin, Oklahoma, to pick up Edna's son, Preston, after they had decided to take him with them. After spending one night at Violet's, the two women left Aurora in the Ford sedan, on their way to Glasgow, Montana, by way of St. Paul, Minnesota. On their way there, they came upon some slippery pavement near Minot, North Dakota, and the car flipped over. As a result of the accident, Edna and Violet both had to spend a couple of days in the hospital. Edna was far more worried about her identity being discovered than she was concerned about her injuries. She used the name of E. J. Powell because the Ford sedan was registered under that name. Violet telephoned Corey in Montana and informed him of their predicament. Corey came to their rescue the following day, by train, and took them to Glasgow, Montana, where the three of them registered at the Rapp Hotel.

Volney and Preston arrived the following day and the five of them rented a furnished house — nearly 30 miles from Glasgow — in Hinsdale, Montana. Volney, Corey, and Preston immediately went to work at Rennick's Beer Tavern, running a gambling operation. Volney and Corey were also making arrangements to construct their own combination "beer tavern and dance hall" in Glasgow. Volney estimated that by the time the place was completed, it would cost him about $6,000.

After about three weeks in Montana, Edna took Preston and left. She and Volney had another fight due to problems with how the money was being split up in the gambling operation. Edna felt that Preston wasn't getting his fair share for the work he was doing. She and Preston traveled by bus to Kansas City, Missouri, where they stayed with Doris and Jess on 39th Street, near Main Street.

Author's note:

During the month of September, 1934, Paula Harmon, Wynona Burdette, and Gladys Sawyer were all arrested in Cleveland, Ohio. The information obtained from them, according to FBI files, was the first definitive data shown in files that indicated that Edna Murray and Volney Davis were traveling together.

It wasn't long before Edna received a letter from Volney, in which he told her he didn't believe that it was right for her to run off like she did while he was making a sincere effort to stay in a legitimate business. Edna replied by telling him that she didn't like living in Montana, but she was coming back there to get the Ford sedan. It had been repaired by then and Volney had picked it up in Minot, North Dakota, and taken it back to Glasgow, Montana. Edna took a bus to Minot, and from there she took the train to Glasgow, arriving around October 1st. While in Glasgow, she saw that the tavern and dance hall that Volney and Corey were building — called "The Hollywood Inn" — was almost finished.

Edna was in Glasgow for about a week before she and Volney drove back to Aurora, Illinois. While in Aurora, Volney received information that two men had recently been making inquiries concerning him. He knew that these men had to be police officers, since his former gang had no reason to be looking for him in Aurora.

From there, Volney and Edna drove to Kansas City and sold the Ford sedan for $400. The following day, Volney gave Doris some money and told her to go to the Noel V. Wood Motor Car Company on McGee Street and purchase a new Pontiac Sedan under the name of Grace R. Hansen, giving Belton, Missouri, as the address. Volney had previously gone to this same Pontiac Agency and looked over the cars, picked out a particular sedan, and had given Doris the description of it. He also had gone to Belton and rented a post office box on the previous day. Volney couldn't trade the Ford in on the Pontiac because it was registered under the name of E. J. Powell, and he wanted to discontinue that alias name, and to again use the alias of Hansen.

After the purchase of the new Pontiac, Volney and Edna drove back to Montana. Along the way they stopped in Welliston,

205

North Dakota, where they had to have the car serviced. Volney told Edna to wait there while he went to Glasgow alone, to find out if anyone had been inquiring about him there, in his absence. He returned to Welliston the next day and told Edna that Corey had informed him that someone had been asking for him at Rennick's place in Hinsdale, Montana — where he, along with Corey and Preston, had first worked, after arriving in Montana. He then told Corey that he had violated his parole and couldn't stay there for fear of being arrested.

From Welliston, North Dakota, they drove back down to Kansas City, and visited briefly with Jess and Doris for about an hour. They then traveled to Muskogee, Oklahoma, to see Edna's brother, Harry. Volney's purpose for making this visit was because he wanted to persuade Harry and his wife, Sybil, to go up to Glasgow to see how things were being run and to take care of his interest in the business. Harry and Sybil agreed to travel to Glasgow and do what they could to help. Edna and Volney remained in Muskogee for only a few days before they returned to visit with Doris and Jess in Kansas City.

Less than a week later, they rented apartment #12 at the Zelda Apartments, located at 3213 Broadway, in Kansas City, under the name of G. R. Hansen. During this time, Volney associated primarily with Jess and one of his friends, Jack Langan.

Around the first of November, Volney and Edna had yet another argument, and Volney left for a few days. Edna didn't know where he went — or how he got there — but he left the car with her. In any case, he returned before Thanksgiving and they had Thanksgiving dinner with Doris and Jess, and Preston — who had come up from Cardin for the holiday.

In mid-December, Volney told Edna he was going to Chicago and asked her if she wanted to go with him. She didn't know why he was going, but since he didn't offer to tell her, she decided not to ask. Volney had slowed down and paid particular attention to a barbeque stand outside of Bensenville, Illinois. There wasn't anyone around and it appeared to be closed. Volney drove back to Aurora, but went back to the same barbeque stand in Bensenville later that evening. Edna assumed that this was the place Volney meant when he said that he was "… going to Chicago," since Chicago was only about 20 miles away. They had visited this place one time a couple of months earlier when Volney introduced her to a man named Elmer. It was situated on a four lane highway just outside of Bensenville and she thought the owner was a German man.

Edna would later find out that the man she was introduced to, Elmer Farmer, was an associate of the gang, and had helped to locate the house in Bensenville, owned by Harold Alderton, that was used by the gang to hold the kidnap victim, Edward Bremer.

On their way back to Kansas City, near Pontiac, Illinois, Volney and Edna had an accident. This accident was, again, caused by those darn "slippery highways" — probably aided by a good amount of alcohol being consumed by the driver. They contacted a garage, and a wrecker came to the scene and towed their car to the first small town south of Pontiac. There, the minor damage was fixed for about $12. They stayed overnight in the local hotel and drove to Kansas City the next day.

About two days before Christmas, Edna and Volney drove to her brother's house in their Pontiac sedan. Harry and his wife, Sybil, were living at 206 E. Adams Street in Pittsburg, Kansas, at that time. According to Edna, their reason for the trip was to "… learn from Harry how things were going in Glasgow." Sybil's brother, sister, and father were all there visiting for the Christmas holidays. Harry informed Volney that his tavern in Montana wasn't being run very well, and it wasn't making any money. He also told him that a man named "Gip" was working there for Corey. Edna recalled that this same fellow had also worked for Matt Kirsch at the Fox Gardens in Aurora.

Edna and Volney went back to Kansas City for Christmas, spending the day with Doris, Jess, and Preston, who had come in from McPherson, Kansas, where he was working for his uncle, Earl Stuchlik, Doris' ex-husband. A few days after Christmas, Earl drove to Kansas City to pick up Preston, and take him back to McPherson, Kansas.

Years later, Edna distinctly recalled the day the newspapers carried the story of the killing of Russell Gibson, and also the arrest of Byron Bolton on January 8, 1935, in Chicago. Bolton, who was involved as a lookout in the Saint Valentine's Day Massacre in Chicago, Illinois, on February 14, 1929, later teamed with the Barker-Karpis Gang in the Bremer and Hamm kidnappings, and would eventually "sing" on everybody. Volney read the news first, and showed it to Edna, indicating to her that he was acquainted with Byron, whose name was also stated as Monty Carter.

Also in January, Volney personally applied for a new 1935 license plate for the Pontiac, at which time he used the name of G. L. Harper, and gave his address as P. O. Box 12, Raytown, Missouri, after having rented this box just prior to applying for his registration.

208

Around this same time, Jess and Doris moved to 23 Warner Plaza, in Kansas City, Missouri, living under the aliases of Mr. and Mrs. Stacey. Jess sold his Buick coach for about $450 and purchased a 1933 Chevrolet coupe and he registered this car also under the alias of J. C. Stacey.

When the news hit on January 16, 1935, concerning the killing of Freddie and his mother, "Kate" Barker, by FBI agents down in Florida, Volney felt very badly. He didn't want to talk about it. He just told Edna that he guessed Freddie must have acquainted himself with someone who gave him away. A few days later, when the newspapers published the story of Doc Barker being arrested in Chicago, Volney was really upset. Even though Doc and Volney had had their share of arguments and disagreements, they had been real close friends for many years. Volney then told Edna that if he ever got into a similar spot such as the one that Freddie and his mother found themselves in, he would surrender, rather than attempt to shoot his way out. Edna tried not to think about either option.

5-19-35, in a county jail cell in St. Paul, Minn. – after receiving his life sentence for the Bremer Kidnapping – Arthur "Doc" Barker told reporters he would like "one good drunk" before confinement in a federal prison. "Courtesy of the Collection of Rick Mattix"

Chapter 26: Bad Years For Outlaws And Gangsters: 1934 & 1935

The Barker-Karpis Gang had first been linked with the Bremer kidnapping on February 9, 1934, when Arthur "Doc" Barker was identified as one of the kidnappers. His fingerprint was found on a gasoline can, and flashlights used by the kidnappers were traced to a St. Paul, Minnesota, store. Later, one of these store clerks was able to identify Alvin Karpis from one of his mug shots.

Shortly afterwards, Fred Goetz (alias "Shotgun" George Zeigler) was killed outside of the Minerva Restaurant in Cicero, Illinois, on the evening of March 20, 1934. It was general knowledge at the time that he was talking too much about some of the past crimes he was involved in. It remains uncertain whether his killers were members of the Barker-Karpis Gang, friends remaining loyal to George "Bugs" Moran, or on orders from Frank Nitti, who had succeeded Al Capone and was eliminating a number of the "Capone Outfit" loyalists. Police found a $1,000 bill in one of Goetz' pockets which allegedly was compensation from the Reno gamblers — afraid to handle the Bremer kidnapping money.

Then a John Dillinger associate and former member of the Barker-Karpis Gang, by the name of Eddie Green, was ambushed and mortally wounded on April 3, 1934, by federal agents in St. Paul. His wife, Bessie, was arrested at the same time, and after she was sleep-deprived for days, and threatened and tortured, she ultimately told the federal agents everything she knew about the St. Paul underworld. Eddie Green, for his part, managed to hang around for a week or so, basically in a state of near delirium, and shared information freely with agents until he died in a St. Paul hospital on April 11, 1934.

Then, following a gun battle with federal agents at Emil Wanatka's Little Bohemia Lodge on April 22, 1934, in the northern Wisconsin town of Manitowish Waters, John Hamilton, who was mortally wounded in Minnesota the day after the escape, was brought to the apartment of Volney Davis and Edna Murray in Aurora, Illinois, where he finally expired on April 27, 1934. And as previously stated, he was buried in a gravel pit near Oswego, Illinois.

Federal agents in Chicago arrested John J. "Boss" McLaughlin on April 28, 1934, for laundering ransom money collected in the Bremer kidnapping.

Bonnie Parker and Clyde Barrow were ambushed and killed by Texas and Louisiana lawmen just outside of Gibsland, Louisiana, on May 23, 1934. They weren't affiliated with the Barker-Karpis Gang, but the newspaper headlines they made were a constant reminder that the "laws" were getting better at their job by the day.

Tommy Carroll met his "Waterloo" in the city of Waterloo, Iowa, on June 7, 1934. A day after he and his girlfriend, Jean Delaney, checked into a tourist camp in Cedar Rapids, Iowa, an alert gas station attendant notified the local police that Carroll's car contained some suspicious spare license plates. When detectives Emil Steffen and P. E. Walker walked over to question Carroll, he made the mistake of reaching for his gun, and after dropping it, he ran into a nearby alley where he was shot four times, and died a few hours later at a local hospital. Jean

212

Delaney was arrested and convicted of felony parole violation, and was sentenced to a year and a day in prison.

Tommy Carroll "Courtesy of the Collection of Rick Mattix"

John Dillinger, while accompanied by Anna Sage (the "Woman in Red") and Polly Hamilton, was gunned down by federal agents just outside of the Biograph Theatre in Chicago, on July 22, 1934. Anna Sage had previously made a deal with the FBI to set up Dillinger, in exchange for the reward money as well as to keep her from being deported to Romania. She was awarded $5,000 (half of the reward money), but was unable to keep from being deported back to her former country of origin, Romania.

Dr. Joseph Moran, the gangland doctor, was last seen alive in late July, 1934, when he left a nightclub on Lake Erie, in the company of Russell Gibson and Freddie Barker. Freddie Barker later told Edna that Dr. Moran went on a one-way boat ride. As previously noted, his badly decomposed body washed up on the shores of Crystal Beach, Ontario, Canada, on September 26, 1935, absent his hands and feet.

Homer Van Meter was shot and killed in St. Paul, Minnesota, on August 23, 1934, by a group of four assailants — the current St. Paul Chief of Police, Frank Cullen; the former St. Paul Chief of Police, Tom Brown; and two detectives of the St. Paul Police Department. A federal agent later stated that while he was in the morgue, he saw Van Meter's money belt containing several thousand dollars, before it disappeared. It was eventually discovered that Van Meter had been set up for this killing by Tom Brown, who was on Harry Sawyer's payroll, and was upset because he had not received his share of the Bremer kidnapping ransom money. Brown was later fired from his job once his ties to the underworld were exposed.

Gladys Sawyer, Paula Harmon, and Wynona Burdette were all arrested after creating a drunken disturbance in the bar of the Cleveland Hotel, in Cleveland, Ohio, on September 5, 1934. Wynona later rejoined Harry Campbell and they went to Florida. Gladys rejoined her husband, Harry, in Mississippi. Freddie Barker's moll, Paula Harmon, suffered a nervous breakdown after being interrogated by FBI agents daily, for three solid weeks (September 5-25, 1934). After a short stay in a local hospital, she returned to her parent's home in Port Arthur, Texas. Once there, her condition continued to deteriorate to the extent that she was ordered by the court to the State Hospital for the Insane at Rusk, Texas, where she was admitted on January 20, 1935, and remained there for the next 18-20 months. Upon her release, she returned to her parents' home.

Charles "Pretty Boy" Floyd was shot and killed on October 22, 1934, by federal agents, led by Melvin Purvis, on a farm near East Liverpool, Ohio. The federal agents were aided greatly by local law enforcement officers.

Lester Gillis (aka "Baby Face" Nelson), killed federal agents Sam Cowley and Herman Hollis in a gun battle in Barrington, Illinois, on November 27, 1934, and was, himself, mortally wounded in this gun battle. Nelson had been the last major member of the Dillinger Gang who was still at large at the time of his death. Although Nelson escaped from the gun battle scene — still alive after being shot 17 times — he died later that night. His intensely devoted wife, Helen Gillis, who rarely left his side, was with him during the gun battle that ended his life. "Baby Face" Nelson's nude body, wrapped in a blanket, was found late the next morning alongside the St. Paul Cemetery in the town of Niles Center (now Skokie), Illinois. His wife immediately surrendered to the FBI and — after a year in jail — she worked at several jobs, raised her two children, and never remarried.

A wristwatch and a pair of octagon-shaped glasses were all that was identifiable on the charred remains of Willie Harrison, killed on January 5, 1935, and found a few hours later in the ruins of a burned-out barn near Ontarioville, Illinois. Federal agents reported rumors that Harrison talked too much and was killed by "Doc" Barker and Byron Bolton of the Barker-Karpis Gang. "Just like Doc Moran," Edna said, "he didn't know when to keep his mouth closed."

"This is a helluva time to be caught without a gun," Doc Barker told federal agents as he and Mildred Kuhlman were arrested as they were leaving their apartment at 432 W. Surf Street in Chicago, Illinois, on January 8, 1935. Inside their apartment agents found the machine gun that was stolen in August of 1933 during the South St. Paul payroll robbery. Doc Barker's capture was withheld from the press in order to allow authorities to investigate the whereabouts of Volney Davis, Freddie and Kate Barker, Alvin Karpis, and any other members of the gang who were still at large. News of Doc Barker's capture would have alerted all of the gang members to move on, and would have hindered the investigation.

Arthur (Doc) Barker learned about
crime from his mother, Kate Barker.
Her training brought about her own
death at G-men's hands and put Doc
in jail for life as a Bremer kidnaper.

Arthur "Doc" Barker "Courtesy of the Collection of Rick Mattix"

About 4 hours after Doc Barker's arrest, federal agents surrounded an apartment at 3920 N. Pine Grove Avenue in Chicago, and commanded the occupants to surrender. Russell Gibson chose to fight it out and was fatally wounded in the ensuing gun battle.

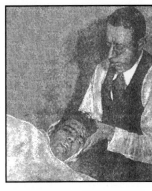

Russell "Rusty" Gibson – in the morgue

Byron Bolton, along with Gibson's wife, Clara Fisher Gibson, as well as Ruth Heidt, the ex-wife of Willie Harrison, all surrendered during the raid. Agents later found an arsenal of weapons in this apartment along with a Florida map with the Ocala region circled.

Eight days later, on January 16, 1935, agents surrounded the house where Freddie and Kate Barker were living on Lake Weir near Ocklawaha, Florida. Defying the federal agents' demands that they surrender, Freddie fired on the agents with a machine gun. When tear gas was lobbed into their house, the Barkers were forced to vacate the first floor and to move to an upstairs bedroom. Thousands of bullets were fired into the house for 4 hours. Then, after a lull of about 45 minutes, the federal agents sent the Barkers' handyman, Willie Woodberry, inside the house to see if anyone there remained alive. Willie found Freddie and his mother lying dead on the bedroom floor. Newspaper accounts erroneously reported that Kate Barker was found dead, gripping a "smoking machine gun." Thus, the legend of "Ma" Barker began.

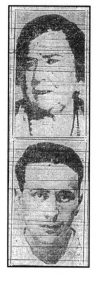

Kate & Freddie Barker "Courtesy of the Collection of Rick Mattix"

Kate and Freddie Barker were laid out in a mummified condition in the Ocala morgue for months. When George Barker, Kate's husband, was finally able to recover his wife's and son's money from the government, he transported their bodies home for burial in the Williams Timberhill Cemetery in Welch, Oklahoma.

Elmer Farmer, who arranged for the use of the kidnap hideouts in Bensenville, Illinois, in both the William Hamm and Edward Bremer abductions, was also arrested on January 16, 1935. The following day, January 17th, ex-bootlegger Harold Alderton, in whose Bensenville, Illinois, home Edward Bremer was held, was arrested in Marion, Indiana. Both men confessed to their involvement in the Bremer kidnapping.

After a gun battle with police officers on January 20, 1935, Alvin Karpis and Harry Campbell escaped from the Dan-Mor Hotel in Atlantic City, New Jersey. Girlfriends Dolores Delaney and Wynona Burdette weren't so lucky though, as both were captured.

Volney Davis, Alvin Karpis, Arthur "Doc" Barker, Harry Campbell, Elmer Farmer, Harold Alderton, Willie Harrison, Harry Sawyer, Phoenix Donald (aka William Weaver), and Byron Bolton were all indicted on January 22, 1935, for the kidnapping of Edward G. Bremer and transporting him across state lines.

Edna Murray, Dr. Joseph P. Moran, Oliver A. Berg, John J. McLaughlin, Myrtle Eaton, James J. Wilson, Jess Doyle, William E. Vidler, Philip J. Delaney, and an individual identified as "Whitey" (later determined to be Bruno Austin), were also indicted on January 22, 1935, for conspiring with one another and with deceased conspirators Fred Goetz, Fred Barker, Russell Gibson and Kate Barker in the planning and execution of the kidnapping of Edward Bremer.

The future did not look promising for the remaining outlaws and gangsters who were still at large.

Wanted – With a price on their head, the heat is on. "Courtesy of the Collection of Rick Mattix"

Chapter 27: The Shot That Brought Them Down

Since leaving the Barker-Karpis Gang, Jess Doyle had joined forces with John Langan, Jack Rich, and Clarence Sparger — all criminals in the Kansas City, Missouri, area. Among other crimes, they had robbed a U. S. Mail truck in Coffeyville, Kansas, on September 22, 1934. It was shortly after this mail truck robbery, when Edna and Volney returned to Kansas City, that Jess introduced Volney to John Langan and Jack Rich. After recently having had a "falling out" with Freddie Barker, which led to his leaving the Barker-Karpis Gang, and later finding out that his venture in Montana was no longer a viable option, Volney Davis decided his last remaining hope at this time was to join up with Jess Doyle and his friends.

On January 30, 1935, Volney Davis, John Langan, and Jack Rich robbed the Montgomery County Treasurer's Office in Independence, Kansas, of $1,938.

The boys didn't know that this would be the last job they would ever pull together.

Outlaws don't stay in one place for very long, and, add to that, the fact of Volney's evolving state of increasing episodes of paranoia, the result was that he and Edna had the job of "moving quickly from one place to another" down to a science. They didn't possess many personal belongings; they lived primarily out of their suitcases; and they traveled from one furnished apartment, hotel, or tourist camp, to another.

On Saturday, February 2, 1935, Volney and Edna moved into apartment #209 at the Beaumont Apartments, which was in the 3000 block of Baltimore Street, in Kansas City. Before they left their previous apartment at 3213 Broadway, in Kansas City, Edna and Volney read in the newspapers that Volney had been indicted in St. Paul, Minnesota, in connection with the Bremer kidnapping case. "That's a tough break for us, Rabbit," Volney told Edna. He believed that the government had no case on him, although his association with members of the Barker-Karpis Gang reflected badly on him.

The following Tuesday morning, February 5th, Volney made an appointment for 1:30 p.m. that day for Edna at the beauty parlor located on the corner of 31st and Main Street. Volney had taken their Pontiac in to the United Motors Service garage, located at 27th & McGee, the day before, for servicing. He was told it would be ready by noon, on Wednesday. Edna returned from the beauty parlor at about 3:00 p.m. and found Volney already at home. He told her he was going to walk over to Jess and Doris' apartment at Warner Plaza, and ask Jess to take him to Raytown, Missouri, to see if he had any mail, since he was expecting his registration card for the Pontiac. Jess drove Volney back home at about 4:30 p.m. in his Chevrolet coupe.

After Volney and Edna had dinner that night, they walked to the Crown Drug Store at 31st & Main to purchase a few articles, and then they walked home and went to bed.

The next morning, Wednesday, Jess awakened them around 7:00 a.m., with the news that Doris was in jail for shooting a woman. He brought a newspaper with him, and all three of them read the story in disbelief. Then at around 11:20 a.m., Volney left the apartment to pick up his Pontiac from the garage. He and Edna had intended to pick up her laundry that afternoon, and then to drive over to his post office box in Raytown, Missouri, to find out if the Pontiac registration had arrived from the state capital in Jefferson City, Missouri.

Doris Stanley (aka Vinita Stacey) after her arrest in Kansas City – Tight lipped, both women added few clues as to the motive of the shooting. "Let Mrs. Taylor tell about it," suggested Mrs. Stacey (Doris Stanley). "I do not know Vinita Stacey," Mrs. Taylor said from her hospital bed. "Courtesy of the Collection of Rick Mattix"

Later that day, around 6:00 p.m., Edna was starting to become very anxious and concerned because, not only was Doris in jail, but also Volney had yet to return home. After taking a cab to a location near the United Motors Service garage, Edna then walked to the garage and peered inside a window to see if she could see their car, but was not successful in being able to spot it. By this time, her worst fears seemed to have come true — she now was convinced that Volney, too, had been arrested. She then rushed home to pack all she could into just a few bags. Jess, likewise, returned to his and Doris' apartment to quickly pack his bags.

Jess picked Edna up from her apartment and they left in his car. They drove around Kansas City for several hours, going by Edna's and Volney's apartment to see if there were any lights on, in hopes that Volney might have returned in the meantime. Not knowing what else to do, they finally decided to drive to Edna's Brother's (Harry) house in Pittsburg, Kansas.

They arrived at Harry's around 1:00 a.m. on the morning of February 7th, and informed the Stanleys of all the events that had just happened — Doris being in jail and Volney most likely having been arrested. Of course, Harry and Sybil were also deeply concerned with regard to this unfortunate turn of events. All four of them sat up half the night, discussing why Doris shot this woman; where Volney could be; what the future held for them; and what they should do next.

At 8:00 a.m. that morning, Jess returned with a newspaper and read that he was now being sought as a fugitive. This worried him a great deal, and he quickly made up his mind to leave. He asked Edna if she wanted to go with him, but she refused, as she was becoming physically ill because of this turn of events. She said Jess didn't say where he was going — or if, or when, he might return.

At this point, Harry decided to go out to purchase a bottle of liquor. He returned about ten minutes later, saying someone was chasing Jess and shooting at his car. Several minutes later, Edna saw three men drive up to the front of the Stanley home. Shortly thereafter, two men entered the house and promptly arrested all of them, but not before Edna threw her .32 caliber automatic pistol on the sofa. It turned out that these two men were Special Agents from the Federal Bureau of Investigation.

Edna gave the agents a statement after her arrest but, otherwise, she remained as tight-lipped as possible. The agent typing her statement then added the following to his report:

"In connection with the above, it should also be noted that in several places it is quite probable that Edna Murray is not

telling the truth or at least is concealing certain facts known to her, especially concerning her contacts and those of Volney Davis during the past three or four months."

HELD IN THE BREMER KIDNAPING. 2-15-35

Edna Murray, the "kissing bandit," and Jess Doyle, who are held in the Wyandotte County jail in connection with the Edward G. Bremer kidnapping at St. Paul. Doyle, an acquaintance of Alvin Karpis, surrendered following a battle with federal and Crawford County officers at Pittsburg, Kas, a week ago. Edna Murray, who escaped from the Missouri penitentiary while serving a 25-year term, is the sweetheart of Purdney Davis, who escaped from federal officers at Yorkville, Ill, while being taken to Chicago. She is a sister of Viruta Stacey, being held in the Jackson County jail for the shooting of Helen Rush.

Jess Doyle and Edna Murray in the Crawford County Jail at Girard, Kansas, on February 15, 1935, before being transferred to the Wyandotte County Jail in Kansas City, Kansas.

Chapter 28: Volney Davis Escapes While In Custody

In the days following Volney Davis' arrest, which was, at first, mistakenly believed to be Jess Doyle's arrest, the country's newspapers were rampant with stories.

After the arrest of Doris (whose name was believed to be Vinita Stacey) for the shooting of Frances Taylor (whose name was believed to be Helen Rush), the confusion later cleared up and the names were correctly sorted out so that the "Vinita" in question was, in reality, Doris, the sister of Edna Murray. This led the G-men to conclude that the chances were good that the rest of the gang was close by; which, consequently, led to Volney Davis' arrest. At first, the authorities thought they had Doris' boyfriend, Jess Doyle. Not only was the FBI confused, but they also had the newspaper reporters confused, as well as some of the gang and their associates.

Preston, who was recovering Volney's car from Corey Bales in Montana, first read the wrong story — that Jess Doyle had been arrested. The next day he read the correct version of the story — that Volney and his (Preston's) Aunt Doris had been arrested. Next he read that his mother, Edna, as well as Uncle Harry Stanley, Aunt Sybil (Mary) Stanley, and Jess Doyle were all in jail. He had a long drive home, and a lot of time to think about this new development. Would his mom go back to prison to finish her 25 year prison sentence? Would Volney ever get out of prison? Why have they charged Jess with the Bremer kidnapping? What will happen to Aunt Sybil, who doesn't even belong in jail? Aunt Doris must have had a real good reason to shoot Frances Taylor, but what could that reason have been?

Earl Stuchlik, Aunt Doris' ex-husband, had gone up to Montana to accompany Preston, and also to drive Volney's car back. Neither Preston nor Earl wanted to be in too close a proximity of the police. At this point, it appeared that most of Preston's family, as well as their "significant others," were behind bars. Preston and Earl then decided to travel to the home of the Stanley family's attorney.

The newspapers were loving this story and had a difficult time keeping up with the readership demand in the immediate Pittsburg, Kansas, area. This was the most excitement enjoyed in this part of the country in quite a long time.

The following are excerpts that were found to be quite entertaining and informative from various "period" newspapers:

Pittsburg, Kansas
Pittsburg Headlight Newspaper
February 7, 1935
<u>"JESS DOYLE IS IN GIRARD JAIL"</u>

"Bremer Kidnap Suspect in Voluntary Surrender This Morning"

"PREVIOUSLY EVADED G-MEN IN CHASE AND GUN PLAY HERE — Three Other alleged associates, Held in Pittsburg Lockup — Man Said to Be H. C. Stanley, One Woman His Wife: Other Gives Name as Edna Murray; Sought In Kansas City."

"Jess Doyle, wanted by the Department of Justice in connection with the Bremer kidnapping case at St. Paul, Minn., was lodged today in the Crawford County jail at Girard and three of

the desperado's associates, a man and two women, were held in the Pittsburg jail as the culmination of swift developments here this morning.

"Capture of the three in Pittsburg, and the subsequent voluntary surrender of Doyle, climaxed a swift motor car chase and gun battle on residential streets in the south part of the city in which Doyle, two federal operatives, and Ross Armstrong, Chief of Police, figured.

"Kansas City police yesterday broadcast an order for the arrest of Doyle, after his trail was picked up there in connection with the shooting of Mrs. Helen Rush there Tuesday night. Mrs. Vinita Stacey was arrested by Kansas City police in connection with the shooting."

GET NAMES OF TWO

"Pittsburg police reported that the man arrested in Pittsburg this morning is H. C. Stanley, and one of the women, his wife, Mrs. Sybil Stanley. The second woman, an attractive blond, who smoked cigarettes almost constantly after her arrest, gave her name as Edna Murray, (of) Kansas City.

"Doyle, 34, successfully evaded officers here shortly after 8 o'clock this morning when he succeeded in escaping in his car, a Chevrolet coach, after the officers attempted to arrest him and gave chase when he fled. During Doyle's successful break for freedom, several rounds of ammunition were fired by federal agents and Police Chief Armstrong in an ineffectual effort to halt him.

"Then, later, Doyle voluntarily surrendered by telephoning the sheriff's office at Girard, according to the Pittsburg police *version of the case. His car became stuck in the mud on a dirt road near Cherokee, (Kansas), it was reported, and the officers hurried to Cherokee to take him into custody and escort him to jail at Girard.*

"Federal agents, it was said, had been watching activities of the Stanleys for some time, believing they had some connection with the bandit gang of which Doyle is charged with being a member.

"However, the Department of Justice men kept their plans to themselves, and even after the four were behind bars this afternoon, the federal agents declined to discuss the case. It was understood they decided to close in on their quarry this morning, but Doyle was just in the act of leaving in his car, and the officers followed close behind."

Through Gunfire

"The desperado made his escape through a barrage of withering gunfire from a machine gun manned by one of the Department of Justice men and rifle shots from a weapon wielded by Chief Armstrong. Residents of the neighborhood, attracted to their front porches by the round of firing, quickly ducked for shelter when the actual battle was noticed.

"After reaching the intersection of Quincy and Walnut, the desperado turned into Quincy Court, according to a version of the chase given by officers. Department of Justice men swung their big car across the intersection, believing they had their prey trapped.

"The suspect reached for two guns in the seat beside him. Officers at this point opened fire. A charge from the rifle held by Chief Armstrong shattered the windshield of the car as the

228

desperado backed the machine away, then swung around the larger federal car and sped north on Walnut."

A Stream of Lead

"Federal men poured a stream of lead into the rear of the speeding car. Bullet holes were noticeable as the slugs found their mark in the rear of the coupe — just above the "turtle," according to reports.

"As the suspect continued to dash away at a high rate of speed, the bullets from the officers' guns apparently falling short of their intended mark, the officers then jumped into their own car and started in pursuit. Trace of the fugitive's machine was lost at Walnut and Kansas, where the desperado headed west.

"The chase was witnessed by a large number of persons, including passengers in taxis. The shooting was heard over a wide area and the police telephone was kept hot with inquiries as to the nature of the disturbance."

House Was Watched

"The East Adams address has been under watch for the past two months. Stanley has been under suspicion for the past year for alleged harboring of criminals, including Raymond Hamilton, Texas killer under sentence of death, and Alvin Karpis, Public Enemy No. 1, and wanted in the Bremer kidnapping case.

"Federal agents were reported to have suspected Stanley of harboring a number of criminals who allegedly paused here in their flight from officers elsewhere.

"Officers today expressed the belief that Stanley was attempting to aid Doyle in getting away from Pittsburg this morning when the desperado was encountered by the officers.

229

"It was reported that a sister of Stanley was an associate of several of the "big time" criminals, including Doyle.

"The "G" men refused to let any information out regarding the case. No one was permitted to talk with the prisoners.

"A steady line of persons came to the police station to learn first hand just what had transpired. The stream of visitors held up all morning, but federal men were tight lipped."

Crawled Under Bed

"Reuel Griffin, employee of the Midland Theatre and student at the college, doesn't care for machine gun fire for an alarm clock.

"Griffin, who rooms at 122 West Quincy, was awakened shortly after 8 o'clock this morning. When the first round of firing awakened him, Griffin said he could not imagine what was taking place. A second impulse was that one of the "horse operas" had come to life. But the third suggestion to come to his mind was the best, Griffin said. It was the idea to crawl under the bed.

"The shooting originated almost in front of that address. Several other persons in the house ran outside at the initial firing, but quickly retreated to cover.

"A woman living on East Adams stated today that the Stanleys moved into the house at 206 East Adams a little before Christmas. She added that she had not paid much attention to her neighbors since they had not offered to mix with other people."

Booked As Doyle

"Federal agents at Girard this afternoon declined to make any official announcement about the case, referring inquirers to the

Department of Justice offices in Kansas City. They said details would have to come from there.

"On the jail blotter at Girard, the arrested man was listed as "Jess Doyle, Kansas City." The time of the booking was 11:15 a.m.

"From other sources here, it was learned the federal men have been on the trail of Doyle for a month, and have known that he was coming and going from the Stanley home.

"At Girard, Doyle was held incommunicado on the third floor of the jail. Inquirers were not permitted to go beyond the second floor.

"Among Doyle's effects, which were in possession of officers, were two rifles, one an automatic, a sawed-off shotgun, and three suitcases. On one of the rifles there was a bullet mark which officers said apparently was made during Doyle's flight from officers in Pittsburg this morning."

Surrender Details Vague

"Details of Doyle's surrender still were somewhat vague late this afternoon. The only information elicited from official sources was that his car mired in the mud near Cherokee, (Kansas), and that he telephoned Girard to surrender.

"Eight federal agents were in Girard this afternoon. It was said only five of them had been working on the Doyle case. The man in charge was Agent (Delf A. "Jelly") Bryce.

"Late this afternoon it was reported that the car Doyle abandoned in the mud was being brought to Girard and would be placed under lock and key in a garage there. A wrecker was sent out to bring the car to Girard from near Cherokee, (Kansas)."

Kansas City
Feb 7, 1935
PART OF THE GANG ACTIVITY

"A theory, that the shooting of Mrs. Helen Rush, 27, in critical condition in a hospital here, was the outgrowth of gang activities, was advanced today by T. J. Higgins, Chief of Detectives.

"Higgins said Mrs. Helen Rush and Mrs. Vinita Stacey, 32, who was charged with assault with intent to kill today in the shooting of Mrs. Rush, were believed to have been the companions of members of a recently-organized criminal gang.

"As charges were being filed against Mrs. Stacey, a report was received from Yorkville, Ill., that her sweetheart, Jess Doyle, sought in the Bremer kidnapping, has escaped from federal agents there."

Author's Note:

This story was printed when the police "thought" they had Jess Doyle, but actually had arrested Volney Davis. After being arrested in Kansas City, Volney escaped in Yorkville, Illinois. Also — at that time, few persons knew that Vinita Stacey was an alias for Edna's sister, Doris, — who was actually 34 at the time, not 32.

Companion of Langdon

"Mrs. Rush was known as the companion of John Langdon, (should be Langan) who is being sought with (Russell) "Spike" Lane as suspects in the robbery of an Osawatomie, Kansas bank, Higgins said. Still another member of the group, he said, is Jack Rich, also being sought in bank robbery charges.

232

"Mrs. Stacey remained silent on the cause of the shooting. 'Let Mrs. Rush (alias for Frances Taylor, the girlfriend of John Langan) tell about it,' she said.

"Police abandoned an earlier theory that jealousy was the motive for the shooting, pointing out that the two women and their companions had lived in apparent accord in the same apartment building here.

"Earl Stuchlik, recently released from the Kansas prison, also was being sought in connection with the case. Higgins said he was believed to have been connected with Langdon (should be Langan) in a liquor running enterprise, and said police were investigating the possibility the shooting followed a dispute over division of the proceeds."

Confirmation Lacking

"R. B. Nathan, head of the department's office here, also refused to say whether the man who escaped at Yorkville was Doyle. It was learned at the airport here, however, that a pilot had been engaged yesterday to fly two federal agents and a prisoner to Chicago, and (the) belief (that) the prisoner was Doyle was generally expressed.

"Mrs. Rush is also known as Frances Taylor. Prosecutor W. W. Graves, Jr., said murder charges would be filed against Mrs. Stacey if the victim did not recover. A hold order for Mrs. Rush, who was arrested in October, 1933, on a charge of attempting extortion, has been filed, police said. Mrs. Rush jumped bond in that case and was a fugitive at the time she was shot.

"Mrs. Stacey, arraigned today, was returned to jail when she was unable to furnish $15,000 bond set on the assault charge, and $1,500 on a charge of carrying concealed weapons. Her preliminary hearing was set for February 19th."

Aurora, Ill.
Feb. 7, 1934
Slugs Way to Freedom

"*A federal prisoner who last night escaped from his guard in Yorkville, Ill., near here, was the object of an intensive search through Northern Illinois counties today.*

"*A mix-up of police messages had authorities hunting the wrong man for four hours. Federal agents refused to identify the escapist, and Chicago police set out to hunt Jess Doyle, wanted in the Edward G. Bremer kidnapping at St. Paul.*

"*A report of Doyle's capture at Pittsburg, Kansas, came later in the day, but the agents would give no hint as to the identity of the prisoner who fled.*"

Arrested In Kansas City

"*Doyle, believed arrested in Kansas City, was being brought to Chicago by airplane. Unable to locate the municipal airport at Chicago, the pilot, Joseph Jacobson, made a forced landing on the farm of E. L. Matlock, near Yorkville, 50 miles southwest of Chicago.*

"*With their prisoner handcuffed, the agents drove to Yorkville in the motorcar of William Ford, a farmer, and entered the hotel where one of the agents placed a call for the Department of Justice Office at Chicago.*

"*While his companion was phoning, the second agent led Doyle to the hotel bar and removed the handcuffs.*"

Seizes Opportunity

"*'The officer ordered two beers,' Grace Larrison, a waitress who witnessed the escape, said. 'The prisoner sipped his beer slowly and seemed to be watching his guard's movements. Suddenly, just as the federal officer raised his glass, the prisoner struck him on the chin and the officer fell to the floor.'*

"'Like a flash the prisoner turned around and leaped through the closed window into a side yard. I saw him race out the gate and across the street where he jumped into a motorcar and drove away while the agent kept firing at him through the window.'

"Witnesses said he performed a half-flip, landing on his feet. Outside, Bretthauer, a grocer, had left his new sedan parked with the motor running. Doyle raced to it and drove away.

"Later the sedan was found abandoned ten miles East of Wheaton, 25 miles to the West of Chicago.

"D. M. Ladd, agent in charge of the Chicago federal men, declined to identify the escaped man.

"R. B. Nathan, Chief of the Division of Investigation's Kansas City offices, maintained the same silence, not even admitting that his men had captured Doyle."

Tulsa, Oklahoma
Pittsburg Headlight
February 7, 1935
"Pickup" Order

"A general "pickup" order was issued here today by Tulsa police for two unidentified men, bandaged, apparently wounded and armed with two machine guns, who were seen driving a 1934 green sedan, bearing a New York license.

"A police broadcast advised "caution" in approaching the car.

235

"Tulsa officers declined to say whether they believed the men might be Raymond Hamilton, Texas desperado reported wounded in an encounter with Dallas officers Monday night, with a companion, or Alvin Karpis and Harry Campbell, Tulsa, who recently made a spectacular escape from an Atlantic City police trap.

"Word of their presence was received from a sandwich shop operator who reported the men insisted on being served in their car. He saw bandages about their heads and the guns in back of the machine

"After being served, he said, the men headed north out of town.

"A general warning and description of the men and their car was sent to Southern Kansas, Kansas City, and Southwestern Missouri, and Oklahoma."

It seemed as though the police were not sure who they had captured and who they had not yet captured.

Chapter 29: Edna Starts To Feel The Repercussions

After Edna Murray's arrival in the Crawford County Jail in Girard, Kansas, she was feeling even more emotionally spent and physically sick. When the Federal Agents arrived at the jail, things were about to get a lot worse for her. The agents had enacted a standard procedure that had to be carried out for new inmates. Edna was taken into a room with a matron who gave the order for her to undress. Edna had no option other than to oblige this request. It didn't matter that her nerves were so shot or that she was shaking like a leaf — not to mention that her abdomen was cramping and aching — and she felt as though her insides were going to fall out. Edna had no choice — she had to follow the rules of the procedure.

She began taking her clothing off, one article at a time, and handing each item to the matron. The matron, in turn, handed the items around the corner to the young male federal agent in the adjacent room. He was inspecting the garments for possible hidden items, but Edna thought that he was stretching his neck a little further around the door than necessary, each time he received another piece of clothing.

"Being in the prime years of my life," as Edna later told the story, she was at this time wearing a sanitary napkin and belt. She had removed everything else, except this last necessary item. When ordered by the matron to remove that item too, Edna just wasn't in the mood for this undue harassment, and was becoming more irate with each passing second, in part, because of the agent in the adjacent room. He kept peeping around the corner at her, and was not shy about his curiosity. Edna carried out the matron's order. "If you need this so goddamn bad, here it is," she told the matron, as she plastered the extremely blood-soaked sanitary napkin right in the middle of the matron's chest. At that point, the matron screamed, "Look what you did to me!" Agent "Peeping Tom," from the next room, then appeared in full view and hit Edna with a blow that sent her sliding — nakedly — across the cold tile floor.

This wasn't the first, or the last, time that Edna would receive "brutality" from a federal agent. "But," she boasted years later, "by God, it was the most fun I'd had earning it," as she threw her head back, laughing loudly, before taking another drag off her cigarette.

Although her criminal career ended after her apprehension in Pittsburg, Kansas, on February 7, 1935, Edna never quit feeling the repercussions from her crimes and her underworld associations. For the remainder of her life, she was watched and followed, constantly kept under surveillance, suspected and questioned concerning various crimes, and often, subpoenaed to court. Once the Federal Bureau of Investigation (FBI) has a file on you, you will never be free of their watchful eye.

Special Agent in Charge, D.M. Ladd, wrote a letter regarding Edna to J. Edgar Hoover which in part, stated:

"While awaiting her appearance as a witness on behalf of the Government in the recent trial of Harry Sawyer, William Weaver and Cassius McDonald at St. Paul, Minnesota, Edna Murray appeared to be in poor physical condition. She is reported to have a cancer of the breast which has become aggravated in the past year. She has lost approximately twenty-seven pounds in

the past six months and it is doubtful whether she will continue to live for any considerable period of time.

"The attention of the Bureau is directed to the weakened physical condition of Edna Murray in view of her value to the Government in any future prosecutive (sic) action to be had either in the Bremer case or in the Hamm case."

Very truly yours,

D.M. Ladd,

Special Agent in Charge

February 24, 1936

In Response to Special Agent Ladd's letter, Mr. J. Edgar Hoover wrote:

Re: Alvin Karpis with aliases,

Fugitive, I.O. #1218, et al;

Edward George Bremer-Victim

Kidnapping

Dear Sirs:

Reference is made to the personal and confidential letter of February 24, 1936, from the Chicago Bureau Office in the above entitled case, advising of the recent interview with Byron Bolton at St. Paul, Minnesota, and the concern pertaining to the poor physical condition of Edna Murray as observed during her appearance as a witness on behalf of the Government in the recent trial of Harry Sawyer, William Weaver and Cassius McDonald at St. Paul, Minnesota.

The Bureau, of course, is in accord with your suggestion to the effect that these two individuals will undoubtedly be of invaluable assistance to the Government should prosecutive (sic) action be inaugurated against any of the persons responsible for the kidnapping of William A. Hamm, Jr. However, no affirmative action can be entertained by the Bureau suggesting a more suitable place of incarceration for these persons. Of course, every possible courtesy should be shown both these persons by Agents of the Bureau, but nothing should be done which will border upon the infringement of the duties of another Governmental agency.

Very truly yours,

John Edgar Hoover,
Director

Author's note:

If Grandma Edna actually did have breast cancer, then I, as her granddaughter, would have heard of, or seen, the telltale signs. She wasn't a bit modest or bashful around me, and when watching her dress and undress, I never saw anything to indicate that she ever had breast surgery. She may have had a hysterectomy, and it's possible that she may have had uterine cancer. She often complained of having had a lot of female

240

problems which possibly could have been confused with breast cancer. Her problems could have been the result of the sexually transmitted disease that she cursed Volney for giving her!

Edna was promised good health care, under the condition that she would testify on the government's behalf. But, even as ill as she was, she agreed to their terms only after Volney confessed.

In his statement, Jess Doyle, would "give up" much more information than could ever be squeezed out of Edna.

KISSING BANDIT WON TITLE WITH OFFERS—NOT KISSES

EDNA MURRAY

In this article written by a St. Paul, Minn., reporter, Edna was quoted as saying, "All my life I've been a good girl. All my life I've been a victim of circumstances." Edna admitted her love for Volney Davis dating back some 14 years. She said that in the most recent years they had lived in many parts of the country. Edna said she kept house for Volney while he worked at odd jobs and "made an honest living in gambling games."

Chapter 30: Jess Doyle Tells His Story

After being transferred from the Crawford County Jail in Girard, Kansas, to the Wyandotte County Jail in Kansas City, Kansas, Jess Doyle gave the following information to the FBI on February 15, 1935:

Stating his name as Jess Doyle, alias E. A. Connley, alias E. V. Connley, alias J. C. Stacey, he told federal agents that he was born in Elberton, Georgia, in 1900, and had never been married. He stated that he had not seen his parents since 1926, and he didn't know if they were still living at that time.

Jess informed agents he had met Doc Barker and Freddie Barker in 1915 or 1916 in Tulsa, Oklahoma, when they were teenagers. He was later arrested in Tulsa in 1920 for car theft, and was sentenced to the Oklahoma State Penitentiary at McAlester for 13 years and 4 months.

After receiving an early release from the Oklahoma State Penitentiary on July 28, 1926, he later met up with Freddie Barker and his older brother, Herman, in South Coffeyville, Oklahoma. They went into the business of operating a bathhouse resort called Radium Springs, east of Claremore, Oklahoma, in the northeastern part of the state. It was a large hotel with numerous small cabins, in addition to the bathhouse.

Jess was arrested again in January, 1927, in Parsons, Kansas, for burglary, and received a 5 to 10 year prison sentence.

Author's note:

This particular robbery was of the Pfeiffer Jewelry Store in Parsons, Kansas, and occurred in October, 1926. When Jess and Edna were both arrested on February 7, 1935, The Parsons Sun Newspaper ran the following articles:

Parsons, Kansas
The Parsons Sun
February 7, 1935
"Believed to Be Pfeiffer Burglar"

"Although Frank Pfeiffer and Parsons police are not positive that they are correct, they are convinced in their own minds that the Jess Doyle who is in jail at Girard is the same Jess Doyle who was convicted in district court here in March, 1927, and sentenced to the Kansas penitentiary from which he later was paroled. The Pfeiffer Jewelry Store was robbed one night in October, 1926, safecrackers entering through the ceiling and robbing the safe. A short while later Jess Doyle was arrested and brought to Parsons where he was convicted of participation in the robbery. He had one of the Pfeiffer watches in his pocket and burglary tools identified as those used on the Pfeiffer safe."

Parsons, Kansas
The Parsons Sun
February 7, 1935
"Knew Barkers in 1926"

"Then in September, 1927, the Pfeiffer Store was held up by Ray Terrill, Danny Daniels and Ralph Scott. Terrill held up the store principally for 'revenge,' it is believed, because Mr. Pfeiffer was largely instrumental in getting Doyle "sent up" for the previous job. Later Terrill was captured and is (currently) in the Oklahoma penitentiary. A. A. (Danny) Daniels was captured in Colorado and led the sensational prison break there a few years ago when he shot himself after killing several guards. Scott was caught and convicted in district court here and is believed to be in the Kansas prison now. (One fact that helps convince Mr. Pfeiffer and local police that the Jess Doyle who escaped last night is the same man who was in the robbery here, is that when he was tried, his alibi was that he was at a health resort in Northern Oklahoma at the time of the robbery. That "health resort" really was a hangout at that time for the famous Barker gang, and thus it is evident that the Doyle in the local robbery was a companion of the Barkers who participated in the Bremer kidnapping.)"

Jess went on to tell the agents that while he was in the Kansas State Penitentiary, he became acquainted with Alvin Karpis and another convict by the name of Lawrence DeVol. When Jess arrived, Freddie Barker was already in prison, convicted of burglary. Jess did Freddie several favors, and before he was released, Freddie told Jess that he would watch the newspapers to see when he got out, and would meet him in Kansas City, Missouri, in front of the Majestic Hotel, on the day he was released.

Upon his release from prison on June 17, 1932, Jess then proceeded directly on to Kansas City, Missouri, by streetcar. He waited for Freddie Barker all that day at the Majestic Hotel, until Freddie finally showed up at 8:00 p.m. that evening. Freddie took Jess with him to the Country Club Plaza Apartments, where he, his mother, and Alvin Karpis were all sharing an apartment. Freddie then gave Jess $500 for clothes and living expenses.

During this period of time, the Citizens National Bank in Ft. Scott, Kansas, was robbed of $47,000, and, according to Jess, this was how he remembered the event:

The robbery occurred on June 17, 1932, the same day he was released from the Kansas State Penitentiary. He stated that, to his knowledge, the following men participated in the robbery: Thomas Holden, Francis Keating, Harvey Bailey, Larry DeVol, Alvin Karpis, Freddie Barker, and Bernard "Big Phil" Phillips. On the night that Freddie took Jess to his swanky apartment, he saw all of these men there. At one point, Freddie went outside by himself and returned with a large laundry bag. Mother Barker and Jess were sitting on the porch when the loot was divided, and Jess later saw all the men with large quantities of money. Freddie told Jess later that evening that the money he had brought into the apartment was from the Ft. Scott Bank robbery.

Mother Barker and Alvin Karpis left that night for St. Paul, Minnesota. Francis Keating, Thomas Holden, and Harvey Bailey were later arrested in Kansas City on July 7, 1932. Freddie Barker, Larry DeVol and Jess Doyle went to a tourist camp on the main highway on the northern outskirts of Kansas City.

Later, upon arriving in St. Paul, the guys met Alvin Karpis and Kate Barker in a car on a street near Harry Sawyer's Green Lantern Saloon, located at 545½ Wabasha Street. Freddie and his mother rented an apartment on Grand Avenue in St. Paul, and Alvin Karpis and Jess stayed with them. Larry DeVol rented his own apartment nearby. According to Jess, a few weeks later, he, along with Freddie and his mother, and Alvin Karpis moved to the Twin Oaks Apartments in St. Paul.

According to Jess, around this same time, Freddie Barker was successful in getting his brother, Doc, a conditional pardon from the Oklahoma State Penitentiary through an attorney by the name of Lester, from McAlester, Oklahoma. Freddie and Doc were subsequently instrumental in procuring a Leave of Absence for Volney Davis, also from the Oklahoma State Penitentiary, and Jess believed that the negotiations were likewise made through the same attorney, Lester.

Jess went on to say that after Doc Barker was released from prison, he first went to visit his father in Neosho, Missouri, then went to St. Paul to live with them, Jess and Freddie. Shortly after Volney's release, he also went to St. Paul, and soon thereafter accompanied Mother Barker on a visit to her sister's home in California.

Around this same time, the Third Northwestern Bank of Minneapolis was robbed by the gang, and according to the information Jess Doyle gave to the federal agents, this is what happened:

This robbery occurred on December 16, 1932, and Freddie and Doc Barker, Larry DeVol, Bill Weaver, Alvin Karpis, Verne Miller, and Jess Doyle all participated. Freddie, Doc, Alvin, and Jess were all living in St. Paul at this time. They held a meeting in a garage in Minneapolis shortly before the robbery, and Jess — wearing a chauffeur's cap — drove the other men to the bank in a Lincoln Sedan. He drove the car a short distance down the street while the others entered the bank. Shortly thereafter, he saw Larry DeVol come out of the bank to act as a lookout. A few minutes later, the others emerged from the bank and, simultaneously, a squad car pulled up in front of Larry. He fired at the officers with a machine gun, killing two of them. When Jess saw the others coming out of the bank, he drove to where they were, and they all got in. Verne Miller took the driver's seat, — replacing Jess' position — and drove away.

As they were making their getaway, the police fired at their car and punctured two tires. Verne drove at a rapid rate of speed to a park in St. Paul, where they abandoned the Lincoln. Freddie instructed Alvin and Jess to take off on foot, telling them he would meet them at the apartment, later on. They took a cab, and as they were leaving, Jess heard several shots fired a short distance away. Alvin and Jess proceeded on to their apartment, and sometime later, Freddie and Doc arrived. At this time, Freddie gave them their split. Jess was under the impression that the money was previously divided in Larry's apartment.

Jess heard, through conversations with Freddie and Doc, that when they were changing cars in St. Paul, someone in an automobile tried to get their license tag number and one of the gang members shot him in the head. Jess claimed he didn't know who "cased" this job, nor did he recall the amount of his split. None of their boys were wounded.

Jess told the officers that on the following night, Larry DeVol was arrested while drunk in his apartment, and was charged with participation in this robbery. Jess believed he pled guilty and received a life sentence.

Larry DeVol "Courtesy of the Collection of Rick Mattix"

Harry Hull, who was living with DeVol at that time, notified the boys of Larry's arrest the following morning. At Freddie's suggestion, all of them — with the exception of Verne Miller — left St. Paul and drove to Reno, Nevada.

Upon their arrival in Reno, Freddie connected with Earl Christman who, in turn, had a contact who could help launder their hot money. Volney Davis and Mother Barker were in Reno when they all arrived.

While in Reno, Harry Hull, who was now living with Jess, stole about $250, plus some of his clothing and then just disappeared. Jess anticipated that Hull would be going to Kansas City, so Jess and Doc — with revenge on their minds — hopped on a plane for Kansas City to recover the stolen money.

When they left Reno, Volney Davis gave Doc Barker a message for him to give to Volney's girlfriend, Edna Murray, who he heard had recently escaped from prison in Jefferson City, Missouri. Volney thought she would go to Kansas City, and he wanted to reconnect with her.

While making inquiries at various places in Kansas City in an effort to find Harry Hull, they met Earl Doyle (no relation to Jess), who operated a business in Kansas City. Jess had previously met him in South Coffeyville, Oklahoma, when Earl was operating a nightclub there with Tom Hill. Jess believed that Doc Barker had known Earl in Tulsa, Oklahoma, many years before. Earl Doyle took them to Edna Murray's apartment in Kansas City, and that was when Jess Doyle first met Doris, Edna's sister, who he believed was using the last name of O'Connor at the time. Jess stated that he and Doris started keeping company, and when he left Kansas City, he told her he would be back soon.

According to Jess, he and Doc Barker returned to Reno, Nevada, by train and shortly thereafter Volney, Mother Barker, and Doc took a trip to California. Freddie Barker and Alvin Karpis followed in another car, but all of them returned to Reno about a week later.

Jess and Doc left Reno in early January, 1933, and went to St. Paul, Minnesota, where they rented an apartment with Freddie on Grand Avenue, as Jess recalled. Earl Christman and his girlfriend, Helen Ferguson, also came to St. Paul at this time and had an automobile accident on the way. They rented an apartment on Marshall Avenue, near Cleveland Street. About his third day in St. Paul, Jess came home from the movie theater one evening and found Gladys Sawyer, the wife of Harry Sawyer, sitting in her car in front of the building. She stopped him and asked where Freddie Barker and Alvin Karpis were. When he responded that he didn't know, she stated that Jess better look them up because the police were planning a raid on their apartment the following morning.

Knowing that Harry Sawyer was well-connected politically in St. Paul, and Gladys would have access to such inside information, Jess went downtown immediately to look for Freddie and Alvin, but could not find them. When he returned, Gladys was still there and she told him that Freddie and Alvin had been there, but had already left, and they would meet him at the "joint" — meaning Harry Sawyer's place — the Green Lantern Saloon.

When Jess arrived at the Green Lantern, Freddie and Alvin told him they had seen Volney, Doc and Mother Barker, and that they were already on their way to Chicago. The three men then left immediately for Chicago in Freddie's Chrysler Sedan. On the way, they met Earl Christman and Helen Ferguson. Freddie got out of his car and talked with them for a few minutes, but Jess mentioned to the authorities that he didn't know what the conversation was about. They then drove straight to Louis Cernocky's roadhouse at Fox River Grove, Illinois, some 40 miles or so northwest of Chicago, Illinois. (Louie's place later became a popular gathering spot for the Dillinger and Barker-Karpis Gangs, and it was Cernocky who reportedly sent Dillinger and Nelson to Emil Wanatka's Little Bohemia Lodge, in northern Wisconsin, with a letter of introduction, in April of 1934.)

When they arrived at Fox River Grove, Volney, Doc, and Mother Barker were already there. Jess then met Frank Nash and his girlfriend, Frances Luce, both of whom were living at Louie's place. Shortly thereafter, Earl and Helen arrived. All of them stayed at Louie's that night, and on the following day, Freddie, Doc, Alvin, and the women went to look for apartments.

A few days later, Eddie and Bessie Green appeared at Louie's, and Jess met them for the first time. Jess stayed at Louie's place

251

for about a week and then went to look for an apartment in Maywood, Illinois, since he was planning on bringing Doris up from Kansas City, Missouri, to live with him. He found a furnished apartment on 5th Avenue about two blocks south of the Edward Hines Hospital on Roosevelt Road.

On or about March 30, 1933, Jess and Freddie drove to Kansas City, Missouri, to meet up with the rest of the gang, who had left for that city several days previously. They robbed the Fairbury, Nebraska Bank on April 3, 1933, and Freddie and Doc Barker, Volney Davis, Alvin Karpis, Eddie Green, Earl Christman, Frank Nash, and Jess Doyle all participated.

At this time, Freddie, Doc, Earl Christman, and Alvin Karpis were all living at the Home Apartments in Oak Park, Illinois, with Mother Barker and Earl's girlfriend, Helen Ferguson. Volney Davis and Jess were living with Edna and Doris at Jess' apartment in Maywood, Illinois. Frank Nash was living at Louie's place in Fox River Grove, Illinois, with his soon-to-be wife, Frances.

The boys had gone to Kansas City two or three days before the robbery took place and rented a furnished apartment near 45th and Main Street in Kansas City. Jess believed that it was Doc Barker and Volney Davis who made the arrangements for this apartment. Once Freddie and Jess arrived in town, they lived in this apartment until the day of the robbery. The eight men drove to the bank in two cars, with Freddie driving a Chevrolet Sedan and Jess driving a Buick. Doc, Volney, Alvin, Eddie, Earl, and Frank entered the bank, while Jess parked his Buick on the street nearby. Freddie was parked in back of Jess' car.

Shortly after the gang entered the bank, Earl Christman came outside to act as a lookout. A few minutes later the rest of the gang emerged from the bank, and as they were getting into their waiting cars, Earl was shot and wounded.

Jess drove his car to a point 15 miles away, where they switched cars with one they had previously parked there. Alvin then joined the group in the other car, and Doc and Volney returned to Kansas City with Jess. They went straight to their apartment, abandoning their car a couple blocks from the building.

That night, Freddie came to Doc's apartment and told Doc and Jess to return to Chicago, stating he would take care of the car they had abandoned.

Doc and Jess immediately took a train to St. Paul, Minnesota, since Doc wanted to see Harry Sawyer. They remained in Harry's place only a few hours, after which a fellow named Tom, who worked for Harry Sawyer, drove them to Louie's place in Fox River Grove, Illinois. Freddie Barker, Alvin Karpis, and Frank Nash were already there when the group arrived. It was at this time that Freddie told Jess that Earl had been shot. Freddie also gave Jess his split of the loot at that time.

The next afternoon, Freddie and Doc left Oak Park, Illinois, and went to Kansas City. Two or three days later, Volney Davis returned alone and told Jess that he had been in Kansas City on business. A few days later Freddie and Doc returned, and at that time Freddie informed Jess that Earl Christman had died.

When Freddie and Jess arrived in Kansas City two or three days prior to the Fairbury, Nebraska, bank robbery, Jess immediately went to see Doris and found Volney there visiting Edna.

Jess gave Doris the keys to his automobile and told her and Edna to drive to the apartment he had rented in Maywood, Illinois.

When Doc and Jess returned from St. Paul the day after the Fairbury bank robbery, they went directly to Louie's place and found Doris and Edna there. That night, Freddie and Jess got into an argument because Jess wouldn't get drunk with Freddie. Freddie believed that Doris was keeping Jess from drinking and that Jess was preferring Doris over him. Jess said he drove home in Freddie's car that night, and on the following day, Freddie came to his apartment for his car and the keys. Other than that, Freddie didn't have much to say to Jess.

The next day when Volney returned from Kansas City, he told Jess that Freddie wanted to speak to him. For the next few days, Jess said he went to Freddie's apartment in Oak Park, but each time, Mother Barker said he was out of town. After about four days, Jess said that Freddie must have returned, since he saw him with Eddie Green leaving the Home Apartments.

Jess then confronted Freddie and told him that Volney had said that Freddie wanted to talk to him. Freddie appeared to be very angry and said, "Never mind, you and I are through." That's all that Freddie said.

A couple of days later, while they were at Louie's place, Freddie danced with Doris and told her what a "sap" Jess was for falling for a girl. Doris became very angry and swore at him.

The following day, Alvin and Freddie came to Jess' apartment and Freddie accused Jess of bad-mouthing him to Doris. Jess denied it, and Freddie called him a liar, then abruptly left. That was the last time Jess saw Freddie until he came to his apartment in Minneapolis, Minnesota, about seven months later.

Jess said that prior to Freddie becoming angry with him, Freddie had given him money, off and on, totaling about $5,000.

Jess said that he and Doris, and Volney and Edna, were together most of the time in Maywood until the latter part of June, 1933. Around the end of May, Jess and Doris went to Cardin, Oklahoma, and picked up the boys, Preston and "Little" Mott, and brought them back to Maywood with them. They took the boys with them to the World's Fair in Chicago, before moving back to Kansas City at the end of June.

Jess and Doris went to say good-bye to Volney and Edna, and while at their apartment, they met Verne Miller and his girl-friend, Vivian Mathis, and her daughter, Betty. Jess said he had actually seen Verne and Vivian once or twice at Louie's place a few weeks earlier.

Jess said when they left Maywood, Illinois, they spent a few days with Doris' family in both Cardin and Commerce, Oklahoma, before continuing on to Kansas City, Missouri.

Upon their arrival in Kansas City, they rented an apartment at the Tattershall Apartment Hotel.

Late that summer, they left Kansas City and went back to St. Paul and they checked into the St. Paul Hotel under the name of K. A. Connley.

Shortly thereafter, Jess met Eddie Green in a gambling joint near the St. Paul Hotel. Eddie suggested that Jess and Doris go fishing with him at a place called Three Lakes, which was close to Crosby, Minnesota. The four of them — Eddie, Bessie, Doris and Jess — later stayed at this lake for about 35 days in virtual seclusion. They liked the lake so much that when they left, all four of them — at Eddie's suggestion — moved to a cottage they rented on a lake about 25 miles South of Minneapolis, where Eddie and Bessie had previously stayed. This was around September 1, 1933. Jess recalled that on the day they left Three Lakes, they stopped at a filling station and read about the payroll robbery in St. Paul. Eddie and Jess talked about it and Eddie remarked, "I wonder who in the hell pulled that (job)?"

About a week after they moved, Doris received word from her brother that their father had died. She flew back to Cardin, Oklahoma, for his funeral.

Doris was receiving her mail in care of General Delivery, St. Paul, and Jess and Eddie were making frequent trips to St. Paul to pick up her mail for her. On one occasion, Eddie got drunk in Harry Sawyer's Green Lantern Saloon and told Harry where they all were living. This made Jess pretty nervous.

After the cold weather set in they gave up their fishing lake and Jess and Doris rented an apartment in Minneapolis, at the Whiteside Apartments, on Girard Street. Eddie and Bessie rented their own apartment, nearby, on Freemont Street. Jess thought it was around October 1, 1933, when they began frequenting Harry Sawyer's Green Lantern Saloon. He recalled seeing Tommy Carroll and "Baby Face" Nelson there. Jess and Doris continued to spend a lot of time with Eddie and Bessie during this period, and Jess remembered that on a couple of occasions when they visited Eddie Green's apartment, Tommy Carroll and Homer Van Meter were there.

Shortly after Thanksgiving, in 1933, Volney and Edna paid Jess and Doris a visit in Minneapolis. They had a car accident on their way and, as a result, Edna suffered two fractured ribs. Jess took Edna to a doctor in Minneapolis, and she stayed with Doris and Jess for a couple of days.

During Edna's visit, Freddie Barker showed up at Jess' and Doris' apartment. Jess assumed he had gotten their address from Volney. Freddie wanted to know what Jess was doing palling around with Eddie Green. Freddie then informed him that he had heard that Eddie had beaten up his own mother. Jess responded by telling Freddie that he knew this wasn't so, because he had just seen her, and she was doing fine. Freddie then became enraged and said that Jess was siding with Eddie and making a fool out of him. Later, Volney told Jess that Freddie was "cussing him out" and also saying that Jess preferred Eddie Green over him. Jess guessed that Freddie must still be upset over Jess preferring to be with Doris than getting drunk with him back in Fox River Grove, Illinois, at Louis Cernocky's roadhouse.

Bill Weaver and his girlfriend, Myrtle Eaton, also visited Jess and Doris on several occasions throughout this period, but the only people Doris and Jess visited were Eddie and Bessie Green, and on a couple of occasions they all went to Eddie's mother's house for dinner.

One evening on January 15, 1934 — two days before the Bremer kidnapping — Freddie Barker returned to Jess and Doris' apartment, warning them that they had better move if they knew what was good for them. Freddie didn't explain why, and he left before giving Jess a chance to ask him any questions.

Jess immediately went over to Eddie Green's place and told him what happened. He told Eddie he didn't know what was going on, but he was leaving town. Jess planned on taking Doris back to Oklahoma for a visit, and Eddie and Bessie offered to accompany them. Eddie had previously expressed an interest in seeing the zinc mines in Oklahoma that Jess had told him about.

All four left the following morning in Jess' car. They drove straight through to Commerce, Oklahoma, arriving late that night. Bessie and Eddie stayed at Doris' and Edna's brother's (Mott) house, while Doris and Jess went to Cardin to stay with her mother, Louie Nettie Stanley.

They spent about a week in Oklahoma, and while they were there, they read about the Bremer kidnapping in the newspapers, which had occurred on January 17, 1934. Jess and Eddie discussed the kidnapping and Eddie was convinced that the Barker Gang pulled that job, since he knew they were in St. Paul at the time — and furthermore, he didn't believe that anyone else in St. Paul would have been capable of pulling a kidnapping on such a grand scale as this was. Jess also believed that the Barker Gang was responsible for the kidnapping of Bremer, and that Freddie told Jess to leave St. Paul so that he would not be in town when the kidnapping occurred. It may have been an act of kindness on Freddie's part, Jess later told the authorities.

Moving on, Jess and Doris — still in the company of Eddie and Bessie Green — relocated to Topeka, Kansas, where they rented apartments at the Senate Apartment Hotel. Eddie and Bessie left Topeka about three weeks later and returned to St. Paul.

The day after Eddie and Bessie left, Doris and Jess went back to Commerce, Oklahoma, where they lived with Mott for a few months, lying low.

Around the end of May, 1934, Doris received a call from Edna, who was then living in Aurora, Illinois. According to Jess, Edna told Doris she was going to have an operation and she wanted Doris to come and be with her.

After driving to Aurora in Jess' Buick Victoria Coupe, the couple registered at the Riverside Hotel under the alias name of E. V. Connley. They stayed at this hotel for about a week, before moving into an apartment that they rented from a man by the name of Burkel. Jess saw Volney a few times during this period, but he wasn't living in Aurora. On one of these occasions, Volney gave Doris $250 to give to Jess. Volney had borrowed money from Jess from time to time while they were in St. Paul and Reno — in late 1932 and in early 1933 — totaling about $800.

Jess also recalled that while they were in Aurora, he and Doris went to visit Corey Bales. Edna had introduced Corey, along with Matt Kirsch, to Jess, as some friends from her past. Freddie Barker and his mother, accompanied by a heavyset guy named Willie, also came to Corey's house while they were there. Mother Barker said that they just stopped by to see how they were getting along, but Freddie didn't have much to say. They all spent a considerable amount of time drinking at the Fox Gardens, along with Volney and someone named Jimmy that he had brought to Aurora with him.

After about a month, Doris and Jess returned to Commerce, Oklahoma. Shortly thereafter, Mott Stanley received a letter from Volney in which there were enclosed two money orders for $100 each. Though issued in Mott's name, the money orders were actually intended for Jess, as part of the money that Volney still owed him.

Jess and Doris left Commerce, en route to Salina, Kansas. From there they drove to Wichita, Kansas, before going back to Cardin, Oklahoma.

Jess said he did a little gambling around this time and won about $200. They moved to Kansas City in August, 1934, first living in an apartment on Campbell Street. Later they moved to an apartment at 4112 Locust Street, under the name of E. A. Connley. They lived there for several months.

After living on Locust Street, Jess and Doris then moved to an apartment located at 23 Warner Plaza, apartment #7. There, they went by the names of Mr. and Mrs. J. C. Stacey, living there until February 5, 1935, when Doris was arrested following the shooting of a woman claiming to be Mrs. Helen Rush.

Author's note:

Special Agent John L. Madala commented in his FBI report that, "... relative to possible contacts and associates of Volney Davis in this vicinity, Jess Doyle apparently was more willing to offer assistance, in his respect, than Edna Murray."

Chapter 31: Doris Ends Her
Silence — Becomes An Informant

Around February 1, 1935, Volney Davis sent Edna's son, Preston (Paden), to Glasgow, Montana. He was accompanied by his uncle, Earl Stuchlik (Doris' ex-husband), to see what Corey Bales was doing with their club, the Hollywood Inn. Edna's brother, Harry, who had been there previously, had reported back to them that things weren't being run very well, and the place was losing money. But that wasn't the half of it! Once Preston and Earl arrived there, they quickly found out that Corey was nowhere to be found, since he had sold the place and returned to Aurora, Illinois.

Then on February 6, 1935, while Preston and Earl were in Montana, they read in a newspaper that Jess Doyle had been arrested — but then escaped — from two federal agents. At this point, they had yet to learn that it was Volney Davis — and not Jess — who the agents had actually captured, before he escaped.

On their way back to Kansas City, Preston was driving his own 1933 Chevrolet coupe, while Earl was returning Volney's 1934 Chevrolet panel truck that he had left in Montana. They picked up another newspaper en route and learned that Doris, Jess, Volney, and Edna had all been arrested and that it was Volney — and not Jess — who had escaped.

Preston and Earl then decided to head for Topeka, Kansas, to confer with Hugh Larimer, an attorney who Preston had known for most of his life. Larimer had done legal work for various members of the Stanley family since 1925, when Preston was still a young lad.

Before going to see Larimer, Earl stored Volney's panel truck in a private garage.

Preston and Earl then met Hugh Larimer at his office in the First National Bank Building in Topeka. They told Larimer that they had Volney Davis' truck that they brought back from Montana, and that they wanted to leave the registration papers with him for safekeeping. They also told him that they wanted him to represent Edna, Doris and Jess. He was also asked to defend Preston's Uncle Harry and Aunt Sybil, and, as it turned out, the latter two people mentioned were the only ones Larimer did end up representing.

At the time Preston left the title papers for Volney's truck with Larimer, he explained that he didn't want them on him in the event that he should be arrested. Preston, Earl, and Larimer traveled to Kansas City to see Preston's relatives who were behind bars. Larimer was unable to see Edna or Jess, but he did get a chance to see Doris. She had somehow managed to smuggle some money and jewelry into the jail, and gave Larimer $450 and a diamond ring to give to Preston.

After visiting with Doris in jail, all three — Preston, Earl and Hugh Larimer — then continued on to Ft. Scott, Kansas, where Harry and Sybil Stanley were being held. Larimer wouldn't ride with them because he felt it was too risky because they were "hot." Larimer decided to take the train instead, and to later meet them at the hotel.

Larimer was representing Harry and Sybil, so Preston and Earl, feeling that they had done all they could do for them, decided to leave Ft. Scott and return to Kansas City.

On February 27, 1935, shortly after Preston and Earl had returned to Kansas City, Earl was arrested while driving Preston's 1933 Chevrolet coupe near Twelfth and Broadway. He had entered the car at 4915 Troost Avenue, the residence of Russell "Spike" Lane, a former nightclub operator. Upon noticing that he was being followed, he drove around the streets of Kansas City in an attempt to elude his pursuers. Failing to escape from his pursuers, he was stopped by special agents R. P. Shanahan and M. Kremer, and subsequently taken in for questioning.

Earl Stuchlik was then booked into the South Kansas City Police Department on charges of investigation for the government. He was transported the following day to Topeka, Kansas, where he was charged with a parole violation and held until March 2, 1935, when he was turned over to Federal Probation Officers in Kansas City, Kansas. On May 27th, Earl was received at the U. S. Federal Penitentiary in Leavenworth, Kansas, to finish out his sentence for counterfeiting.

William H. Davenport, Operative in Charge of the Division of Secret Service of the Treasury Department, in a letter to the Record Clerk at Leavenworth Penitentiary, stated in part that *"... Earl Stuchlik was arrested by agents of the Bureau of Investigation on February 27, 1935, for suspicion of being implicated in car thefts and the shooting of a woman companion in Kansas City, the woman being implicated in kidnapping and bank robbery. And it was because of this arrest that he was sentenced on May 22nd under the probation granted him on the counterfeiting indictment."*

Earl spent another 18 months in prison but was probably only guilty of being with the wrong people, in the wrong place, at the wrong time.

A couple of items found under the seat of Preston's car also didn't help matters at all where Earl was concerned. There was a flashlight taped up so that only a small beam of light could be seen, similar to one that would be used in burglary jobs. And then there was the other issue of a beer bottle found, containing nitroglycerin.

Upon entering the residence of Russell "Spike" Lane, officials found several pints of nitroglycerin concealed under the kitchen sink. At that time, Lane was arraigned on a federal charge of harboring and concealing Volney Davis, who was a suspect in the Bremer kidnapping case, and who had also escaped from federal custody in Yorkville, Illinois, while being transported from Kansas City to Chicago. Investigators had refused to reveal what part the nitroglycerin was to play in the activities of the gang.

Once they had properly disposed of the nitroglycerin, the agents returned to the apartment occupied by Spike Lane, and conducted a more thorough search. There, they found a safety deposit box rental receipt for box #130, at the Parsons Safety Deposit Company, 1804 Broadway, Parsons, Kansas, that had been tucked under one of the bottles of nitroglycerin. The receipt, dated January 8, 1935, and signed by F. W. Wilson, was for a period of one year.

Immediate inquiries were made at Parsons, Kansas, by Special Agent L. S. Vandover, where it was found that this Safety Deposit Company was operated by an elderly woman in the rear of a mercantile establishment. She informed the agents that on February 17, 1935, a burglary had occurred in her establishment, during which time approximately 40 safety deposit boxes, including box #130, had been entered by boring out the lock, and consequently, all of the contents were removed. This woman had no information or description of the person renting the box, and indicated that her ledger, which contained all the information, had also been stolen during the burglary. The Parsons Police Department believed this to have been a local burglary job.

Following Earl Stuchlik's arrest in Kansas City, Preston's car was confiscated by the County Sheriff, Thomas B. Bash. With no hope of getting Earl out of jail, Preston went back to the home of his Grandmother, Louie Nettie Stanley, in Cardin, Oklahoma.

From her jail cell in Kansas City, Missouri, Doris wrote the following letter to Jess Doyle, who was incarcerated in St. Paul:

Dearest Jess,

Please Dear don't give up. Your note made me feel badly. Perhaps I don't understand the procedure there. But I know we can prove we had no part in that kidnapping.

Do you have a lawyer? If so, have him write particulars to address on enclosed card. Yes Jess, you are quite right. We should be happy tonight instead of miserable. But I feel I did my bit as oft times my suggestions were never considered, and silence is what I got in return. And I often wondered why. But since this miserable catastrophe I can only think of your condition. If you have enough to eat, if you are warm, your kindness and the love I hold for you. Why should you write you have lost me? When you wrote me not to implicate you in anything, I could not understand your meaning. For if you ever did anything, it was before I met you. I know you could not have while we were together.

265

I plan to make a bond here next week. If the government takes charge of me no doubt I'll be up. I don't know why they should, but they were quite angry at me when they left, so I expect most anything. Said you had told them we knew you had been indicted. But I know I didn't know and don't believe you said as much.

I got my rings back, and saved the money by an unexplainable miracle. I can arrange to send any part or all of it to you.

I want a lawyer to see H. C. and Sybil. They are quite sick. Where is your car? Why don't you try and have this lawyer get it?

Were the papers correct on your capture? I have my doubts. You looked so tired in your pictures. Made my heart ache.

I haven't heard from home only indirect. Every thing is okay. One of the Gov agents said he was going down to take your ring and pin and question them. Did you give them your ring? Write me something about yourself. I am fine only lonesome for you.

Love Ever   Doris

11-P.M. Just brought Earl in, arrested him this A-M in Preston's car. Put him in the death cell which joins the girls. I have been talking with him. He said it is awful the things they can imagine. Put investigation as the charge. I'll let you know what they do.

He said they told him Preston had been stealing. Earl did not know that Edna bought the car for him. One of the colored girls is singing, (for all we know we may never meet again) and how it hurts.

D.

Author's note:

The card referred to in the second paragraph had Doris' attorney's name and address on it.

It read:

Ralph S. Latshaw, Lawyer

416 Scarritt Building

9th and Grand Ave.

Kansas City, Mo.

Phone: Victor 7644

Residence phone, Valentine 8100

After a couple of weeks, and some time to think over the situation, Preston decided to visit Hugh Larimer in Topeka, again in an effort to try to get his car back from Sheriff Bash in Kansas City. He told Larimer that he wanted him to sell his car as well as the panel truck that belonged to Volney Davis. Larimer advised Preston that in order to protect himself, it would be necessary for him (Preston) to sign the car over to Larimer, and for Preston to write him a letter, acting as though he was not in Topeka when he wrote this letter. Larimer dictated the letter as he wanted Preston to write it. Then Larimer had him sign the name of J. E. Hanson on the papers for Volney Davis' truck, as this was the name in which it was titled. Larimer then agreed to sell both vehicles, charging Preston $25 for each.

Preston put his trust in Hugh Larimer because of the past assistance he afforded his family, mainly in helping them get out of bootlegging charges. But, unbeknownst to Preston, Larimer

267

was as crooked as they come, and was a man without any moral code or concern for anyone other than himself. With most of the elder Stanley family members in their own "hot water" situations, Larimer took advantage of their plight, knowing that no one else was going to come to Preston's rescue, and consequently, Larimer could profit at his expense.

Upon being interviewed by federal agents in April of 1935, Larimer stated that he had been the Stanley family attorney, representing Mott Stanley, Harry Stanley, Edna Murray, Doris O'Conner (her current alias name) and another sister whose name he couldn't recall. Because there was no other sister, perhaps Larimer was referring to Mott Stanley's wife, Helen Stanley, or possibly, he was referring to Harry's wife, Sybil. He also said he was acquainted with Preston Paden and his uncle, Mott Stanley, and had recently spoken with him, and he had him bring Preston to Topeka, where he had Preston sign over ownership of his Chevrolet in exchange for legal services which had been rendered. This latter statement was a lie. Larimer told the FBI that Volney Davis would most likely be contacting Preston, and he went on to say that he didn't know Jess Doyle and had not seen Doris O'Conner for some time until the fall of 1934, when she came to his home in Topeka. She was with Volney Davis at the time, who he only knew as "Curly." He had only seen Davis on two occasions and had been advised by Earl Stuchlik and Doris O'Connor, since their apprehension, that Volney Davis, Edna Murray, Jess Doyle, Doris O'Conner, John Langan and Frances Taylor were closely associated. Frances had told Doris that she had been talking too much, according to Larimer.

Being the crooked attorney that he was, he must have had some ulterior motives for making these statements.

Larimer also informed the FBI that should Preston Paden be taken into custody by the bureau, Volney Davis would endeavor to assist him in escaping.

Less than four months after Doris was arrested for the shooting of Frances Taylor (who went by the alias of Helen Rush) she was released from jail, and even talked authorities into letting her pick up Jess Doyle's belongings. She had actually been in federal custody on two separate charges. One, of course, was for the shooting of Frances Taylor, and the other charge was for harboring a fugitive, namely Jess Doyle. In total, she was held in the Jackson County Jail, in Kansas City, Missouri, from February 5, 1935 until June 1, 1935.

While incarcerated, Doris was interviewed by Federal Agent W. F. Trainor on several occasions. She had furnished no information upon her arrest, and had maintained her demeanor of absolute silence. Agent Trainor indicated, though, that Doris might possibly be used as an informant. He further noted that even though it was evident that she had complete information and knowledge regarding the workings of the Barker-Karpis Gang, and the probable whereabouts of those who were now being sought, she stated that there was only one thing she could be relied upon to do, and that was to give information as to where they could find Volney Davis. She appeared to be upset with Davis, because she believed that he had her nephew, Preston Paden, with him, and would most likely drag him into a major crime in the future. Agent Trainor had his own theory that Doris was angry with Volney because she suspected him of having furnished information as to the identity of Jess Doyle, "… which, as a matter of fact, is true," stated Trainor.

Walter Holland (aka "Irish" O'Malley)

On April 2, 1935, in an interview with Doris, she informed Agent Trainor that a friend of Volney Davis, Edna Murray, and Jess Doyle — and who was residing at 4915 Troost, Kansas City, Missouri, as of February 5, 1935 — was Walter Holland, alias "Irish" O'Malley, Identification Order number 1200. She further stated that Lloyd Doyle (no relation to Jess Doyle) and Vivian Chase had been residing with O'Malley and another woman. She also stated that Volney Davis and Jess Doyle secured the stolen traveler's checks that came from the Okemah, Oklahoma bank robbery from this group of individuals. Doris expressed doubt that Volney Davis was in on the Okemah bank robbery, and said she knew positively that Jess Doyle was not in on the job. She felt quite sure that O'Malley, Lloyd Doyle, and Vivian Chase were then in Kansas City and that Volney Davis was, in her opinion, with them. She stated that upon her release from jail, she intended to immediately make personal contact with all four of them, and once she did, she would notify Agent Trainor of their location.

Doris also agreed to supply the desired information, but only on the condition that it be treated as absolutely confidential at all times, and also that she would not have to deal with more than one agent. Agent Trainor then proceeded to give Doris his telephone number, and also the telephone numbers of two other agents in the event that she could not reach him. This was all agreed upon, only with the understanding that her assistance would never become known.

When she was taken to the U. S. Marshal's office in Topeka, Kansas, to pick up Jess Doyle's money, Doris saw Hugh Larimer, and he gave her $100 to give to Preston for the sale of his car. Larimer told her that he hadn't sold Volney's truck yet, but when he did, he would send the money to Preston.

Following Doris' release, she and her nephew, Preston, traveled to McPherson, Kansas, where they took up residency. Preston called Larimer several times asking him whether or not he had sold the truck. Larimer's response was always **"No"** to this question. Finally, Preston went to Topeka to get the truck. He met Larimer at his office and Larimer told Preston that he could not get the truck because the man who owned the garage was at the show. But, then, the next morning, Larimer changed his story, and told Preston that he had, in fact, sold the truck, but was keeping the money because he thought Earl Stuchlik owed it to him. Preston then told Larimer that the truck belonged to Volney Davis — not Stuchlik — and that Volney Davis and Alvin Karpis had driven him to Topeka, and if he didn't give him the money, they would kill him (meaning Larimer).

Preston, of course, had made this story up to scare Larimer. Larimer responded by telling him that if he didn't get out of his office immediately, he was going to call the police. Preston reacted, by saying, **"No, I'm the one who's calling the cops!"** Instead, he then called his aunt Doris, who was "madder than a hornet," and she told Preston that she was leaving McPherson, Kansas, immediately, and coming to Topeka.

Once Doris arrived in Topeka, and after talking to Hugh Larimer, she was really fired up. She threatened Larimer by saying she was calling Special Agent A. E. Farland of the Department of Justice, to inform him of what was happening. In an effort to calm Doris down, Larimer suggested that they all go to Leavenworth and speak with Earl Stuchlik, and see if Earl didn't agree that he owed Larimer the money. Preston and Doris did go to Leavenworth, but Hugh Larimer never showed up. Doris then called the Department of Justice, but was unable to get in touch with Special Agent Farland. After repeated unsuccessful attempts to make contact with him, Preston and Doris returned to McPherson, Kansas, the next day.

Chapter 32: Preston Paden Joins In With Volney Davis And Jess Doyle

Born during World War I, raised during the "Roaring Twenties," suffering through the "Dust Bowl" in Oklahoma, and now entering the "Great Depression," Preston had seen a lot, but nothing like what was yet to come.

Preston was 16 years old when his mother, Edna "The Kissing Bandit" Murray, escaped from prison for the third, and final, time. Once she was able to contact him, it was decided that he would join her and her "Barker Gang" of outlaws. He was misled by his mother and other relatives at his very young age, to believe that a life of crime was an exciting and profitable venture. All of the male role models in his life, except for his ill grandfather, were outlaws and gangsters.

Just because he dropped out of high school didn't mean he wasn't smart. In fact, Preston had an unusual knack for numbers. He could make calculations in his head with amazing accuracy without any assistance from adding machines or calculating devises. His Aunt Doris was always fascinated by his mathematical ability and knew that some day they would be able to use this ability for profit in the gambling trade.

Preston was actually much closer to his Aunt Doris than he was to his mother, Edna, so he usually stayed with Doris and Jess Doyle. Doris had a good mind for business and liked to be in charge — which didn't set very well with most of the men. It was Doris who actually figured out where Preston's talents could be most useful, and encouraged him into working in the bookie operations at the youthful age of 16 years old.

Edna was jealous of all women, but she was especially jealous of the relationship that her son had with his Aunt Doris. She had been jealous of Doris' good looks and intelligence since they were growing up as kids, but her son's great fondness of her sister made her furious. It was pretty easy to see why Preston would choose his aunt over his mother. Doris was charming and funny, having a great wit about her, and just enjoyable to be around. Edna, on the other hand, seemed to be intoxicated most of the time and/or high on something — or suffering from withdrawal because she wasn't high on something. She could be laughing hysterically one minute and crying in the next minute. According to Edna, life was implicitly unfair for her because she had been dealt a bad hand from the start. She felt that she should never be held responsible for anything that happened to her, and it was always somebody else's fault when something went wrong. In Edna's mind, anything bad that happened to her had always been the result of either a misunderstanding, or someone unfairly accusing her of a misdeed. She was apt to change her mood at the drop of a hat, and she was rather depressing to be around at times.

When Edna would start crying the blues about Preston spending more time with Doris than he did with her, he would give it his best shot at being with her for as long as he could bear it, before finally making some excuse to leave. It was after one of these times when he returned to Cardin, Oklahoma, to visit his grandparents who had raised him. His Grandpa Stanley was ill, but he was not expected to die anytime soon. Preston had gotten into a scrap with another kid in Picher, Oklahoma, which landed Preston in jail. It was on September 5, 1933, when the unexpected happened — Grandpa "Charles" Stanley, at the age of 75, died from a heart attack. Preston was devastated over losing the only father figure he had ever known. As an act of compassion, he was let out of jail on a "Leave of Absence" for his grandfather's funeral.

Doris had received word of her father's death and had traveled from their fishing lake cabin at Three Lakes, Minnesota — where she and Jess Doyle were staying with Eddie and Bessie Green — to attend her father's funeral with her grieving family in Cardin. The entire Stanley family was on edge, however — fearing that the G-men would track them down, possibly forcing a big shoot-out.

Edna, on the other hand, hadn't been notified of her father's death, which was something that she never forgave Doris for. Whether or not Doris knew how and where to contact Edna is debatable, but it also could be possible that she didn't want to deal with Edna's outbursts, along with the grief that everyone was already suffering. Doris was like her father in so many ways. Everyone in the family knew she would take his death very hard.

The G-men didn't make an appearance, Edna missed her father's funeral, and Nicholas Drew "Charles" Stanley was peacefully laid to rest.

Even though Preston returned to jail after the funeral, he escaped from the jail on the very first night. The event of his grandfather's death seemed to be the beginning of Preston's new nihilistic attitude. After his escape from jail, Preston left Cardin, Oklahoma, for quite some time.

Preston was still a young lad when he first heard stories about Dillinger, "Pretty Boy" Floyd, and the Barker Gang. The gangster stories were told as if these men were some kind of heroes, robbing and stealing, and engaging in gunfights with the law. Then, all of a sudden, one day, here he was, right in the midst of some of the most talked about outlaws in the whole country. But even though he knew there were guys who would love to be in his place, he always had a "gut feeling" that this lifestyle just wasn't right. He never felt good about mistreating or hurting anyone unless he needed to for his own self-defense or self-preservation. Yet, when one of the Barker Gang said, "Come on kid, we can use your help," he didn't feel like he had any other options.

In September of 1934, about a year after his grandfather's death, Preston was visiting with his Grandma Louie, in Cardin. Jess Doyle, Volney Davis, and John Langan were living in Kansas City, Missouri. They had asked Preston what he knew about the money transfer from the Miami, Oklahoma, bank, to the Picher, Oklahoma, bank, on Saturday mornings. Preston told them he would run over to Picher — only about two miles away — and find out as much as he could.

Preston said, *"On this particular morning during September, 1934, Jess, Volney, and John drove down in a Dodge, and parked about a half mile down a dirt road from my Uncle Mott's house. That was the day before the robbery — and we drove to Afton, Oklahoma, where we got a tourist cabin for all of us for the night. Early the next morning we had breakfast in Afton, and then we drove to a cemetery between Miami and Commerce, Oklahoma. We had the tag number of the Chevrolet used to carry the money and we waited until we saw it go by, on its way to Miami. We stalled along, out on the highway, until it passed us, then we took out after it. A woman was driving, and a man was in the front passenger seat. They 'ranked' to us (meaning looked us over or checked us out) just before we got into Commerce, and they started driving fast — but we stayed close to them as we went through Commerce. Jess was driving, John was in the front seat, and Volney and I were in the back — with Volney on the right side. When we hit on the curve between Commerce and Cardin, she opened the Chevrolet up and we took out — trying to catch her. Volney and I were masked with black silk stockings. Volney had on brown union-alls over his suit, and I had overalls over my suit. We stayed crouched down, coming through Commerce, and when we hit the second curve between Commerce and Cardin, Jess said to 'raise up' and we would take them. He caught the Chevrolet on the curve, and just as we got up to them, John stuck a shotgun out the window. When he did that, the young woman pulled the emergency brake and stopped the car. Volney and John got out — John had a shotgun and Volney was carrying a pistol. Volney 'poked them up' and got them out of the car, and they turned their backs to us. John searched the car, pulled the silver out and set it down. There were a bunch of windshield stickers in the car, which he mistook for money, so he put them with the silver in our car. When Volney said 'put up your hands,' and asked the boy where his pistol was, the young man said it was behind his ear, and the woman said, 'He said pistol, silly, not your pencil.' Then he told them where it was, and John got it out of the dash pocket of the Chevrolet. We took the keys of the car, and the woman's purse, then went to the north, up a dirt road. John threw the keys and purse out along the road somewhere. We drove straight to Kansas City, where we cut (split up) the money* at the Blackstone Apartments. There was $1,165, all in silver, and we cut it even four ways."

In another story Preston told, he said, "*Volney Davis had a 'square' Pontiac. He wanted another car, so one night shortly before Christmas, 1934, Volney and I were riding around in the Pontiac, looking for a car to steal. At the Safeway Market, near 40th and Main, Volney saw a man get out of an Oldsmobile. We could see that the motor was running and Volney said, 'There, it's just the kind of a car that we want.' He got out (of the Pontiac), got in the Oldsmobile, and drove it off. I followed him in his Pontiac. Volney took the Oldsmobile to his garage, and then went to get Jess Doyle and John Langan. Jess and John had kept a hot Dodge in their garage, which they stole in Osawatomie. When Volney showed them the Oldsmobile, they decided to dump the Dodge in Kansas City, Kansas, and put the Oldsmobile in its place.*"

Preston then continued, "*A few days later, Volney, John, Jess, and I started to Oklahoma. Volney, knowing where some machine guns were kept in a fire station, said we were gonna get the town afire, and then get the machine guns. We had 20 gallons of gasoline with us. A short distance out of Kansas City, we had a wreck. We flagged down a 1934 tan Ford Coach, and took it away from a young fellow who was driving, and the elderly couple he had with him. They had a quart of homemade wine in their car. We left the Oldsmobile there with the 20 gallons of gasoline in it. We drank the wine, and we kept the Ford Coach for quite some time. It had a mailman's sticker in the dash box, and it was the car we used in the Blankenship robbery. Volney told me that he eventually left this Ford in Ft. Scott, Kansas — and I think he said that he burned it — but I am not certain.*"

Preston hung out with Volney "Curly" Davis, Jess Doyle, and John Langan — accompanying them on several of the jobs that they pulled — including the robbery of the Drexel State Bank, in Drexel, Missouri, on December 13, 1934, and the robbery of O. K. Blankenship and his brother, E. K. Blankenship, in North Kansas City, Missouri, on January 13, 1935.

One of their car theft jobs went something like this, according to Preston. *"Volney Davis had a hot Ford that he and John Langan and I had been using. Volney and I spotted an Oldsmobile Sedan, black with a built-in trunk and six wheels, while we were driving around in Independence, Missouri, one day. This was the kind of car that we wanted, and we were in Volney's Pontiac at the time. Volney sent me over to see if the car was locked. It was, so we stayed there for what seemed like forever before a man came and got in it. We followed him until he drove up to a school house that was under construction, where he got out and went into the school. I went to check the car and found that it was locked again. Volney said that he didn't want to take the car then, because we were in his Pontiac, which was a 'square' car, and he didn't want any heat on it. We figured we would have time to get back to Kansas City and trade cars before the guy left the school. When we got into Kansas City, Volney decided he wanted to go get Jess to drive the Oldsmobile for us. Jess wanted to take John along, so the four of us headed back to the school house at Independence, in the Ford. The man was still in the school when we got there, so we parked near a vacant house that was close by, went in the house, and waited. When we saw him coming out, we jumped in our car and drove up to him, while he was still about 10 feet from his car. Volney jumped out, showed him his pistol, but didn't put it on him, and told him to get in our car.*

Jess and John took the man's keys to his car, got in it, and drove off. I sat in the back seat, put the man in the floor of the back seat, and put my feet on him. Volney drove the car and I told the man, 'Don't look at me or I'll shoot your head off.' I blindfolded him with Volney's handkerchief after I tore the laundry marks off. The man said, 'Boys, you can have my car and money and everything, but please don't take me out in the country and leave me.' Volney was joking around and said he believed he wouldn't bother to tie him up — he would just shoot him. We drove him out in the country, took him up into some timber, and tied him to a tree with clothesline rope. While Volney was tying him up, I went through his pockets and found $15. Volney said don't leave him anything to call or get a taxicab with. I started to take his watch, but Volney said not to because it would only get me in trouble. We went back to Kansas City and met Jess and John at Jess' apartment. They said they had put the car in the garage behind the Plamor Hotel."

Preston said that sometime later he and John were together in Joplin, Missouri, and he asked John whatever happened to that Oldsmobile. John said, *"They wrecked it. They had used it to rob the Montgomery County Treasurer's Office at Independence, Kansas, on January 30, 1935, when they got $1,938. Jess had driven them down to Independence and Volney was driving on the way back. It was sleeting and Volney ran into a car that some "niggers" (sic) were pushing up a hill."* John said that *"... one of these "nigger (sic) girls" said 'Officers nothin, look at them gettin' those license tags.' Volney had previously told them that they were officers chasing bank robbers. They got out on the road and heisted a 1934 Chevrolet Coach, set the Oldsmobile on fire, and drove back to Kansas City in the Chevrolet. Then they* *put the Chevrolet in a garage near the Blackstone Apartments in Kansas City."* He also said that later, *"... the keys to it were found in his apartment and he knew they would trace those keys to the Chevrolet, then to the burned Oldsmobile, and he would get a rap on the Independence, Kansas, job."*

John also told Preston that Al Sherwood had selected the "mark" (target) at Independence, Kansas.

Several months before the Independence job, Volney, Jess, and Preston drove to Parsons, Kansas, to look over a mail robbery. They didn't see the money come in, so Volney said, "Let's drive to Coffeyville and ask Al Sherwood about it." Al was an "old hand" at robbery. He had been a member of the Terrill-Barker-Inman Gang back in the early 1920s. Their favorite scheme was backing a stolen truck up to a bank and winching the entire safe out — taking it away to crack open at their leisure. Al had been in and out of prison — once escaping from a train that was en route to the Oklahoma State Penitentiary in McAlester, on St. Patrick's Day, March 17, 1927.

At South Coffeyville, Oklahoma, they talked to Tommy Hill at his saloon. He said that Al Sherwood wasn't there. He was living at a tourist camp in Coffeyville, Kansas, where they found him at home. After talking to Sherwood, Volney and Jess told Preston that he (Sherwood) was going on the "mark" at Parsons.

In the early spring in 1934, when Preston was living in Wichita, Kansas, with his Aunt Doris and Jess Doyle, Jess was telling him about an attempted bank robbery in Topeka a few months earlier, in January, 1934. The way Jess told it, Eddie Green was given the "mark" from Attorney Hugh Larimer, in

Topeka. At that time, Eddie and Jess were friends, but later fell out, and Jess was not in on the attempt.

Preston said that at one time, Jess and his Aunt Doris, as well as Eddie and Bess Green, all lived at the Senate Apartments in Topeka. He remembered that Doris and Jess were in Commerce, Oklahoma, visiting with his Uncle Mott and Aunt Helen Stanley. Someone came over from Pearl's Barbecue, which was next door to Mott's house, and said that someone was calling for Jess. Jess came back and said it was Eddie Green, "wanting to see him." Jess later read about a bank robbery where they got the banker at his house and made him open up the bank — Jess said that was the job Eddie was "wanting to see him" about.

Later, in the fall of 1934, when Preston was living with Doris and Jess at the Blackstone Apartments in Kansas City, they were going under the aliases of Mr. and Mrs. Conley. John Langan had an apartment on the floor above them. Preston heard Jess and John talk several times about a mail robbery that had taken place a short time before, in Coffeyville, Kansas. From the conversations, Preston learned that Jess Doyle, John Langan, Jack Rich, and Clarence Sparger took part in this robbery that occurred on September 22, 1934. This was a "stickup" of a mail truck just as the truck was leaving the depot. There was supposed to have been $49,000 in this mail, but they said they only got $4.00 out of it. Just as they were about to make the "heist," they discovered that they had a flat tire, and Sparger and Rich did not want to go through with the robbery, but Doyle and Langan did, so they went ahead with the robbery. Jess was doing the driving and Langan, Sparger, and Rich made the "heist." They were using a 1934 Ford V-8 Sedan, which Preston thought they had stolen in Kansas City, Kansas, shortly before the robbery.

Jess and John were so angry with Sparger and Rich because they wanted to back out of the job, that they planned to kill them if they would have gotten the expected $49,000 haul. They burned the mail sacks somewhere along their way back to Kansas City. Preston thought the $4.00 was in a registered letter.

When Preston told this particular story in the fall of 1936, he said that he believed Jess Doyle was currently serving a 10 year sentence in the Nebraska State Penitentiary at Lincoln, Nebraska; that John Langan was serving a 10 year sentence at the Missouri State Penitentiary at Jefferson City, Missouri; and that Clarence Sparger was serving a 25 year sentence, he thought, at Leavenworth, Kansas, since he was wanted on the Neosho Bank robbery when arrested. He also thought that Jack Rich was serving time at Leavenworth for the Neosho Bank robbery.

Preston L. Paden – Young Gangster

Chapter 33: Life In Sapulpa, Oklahoma

Sapulpa, Oklahoma, looking down Dewey Avenue - "Route 66"

Edna's youngest brother, Gloyd Augusta "Ginney" Stanley, married a fine young lady by the name of Jewel Sullivan, and they settled in Sapulpa, Oklahoma, where they raised their family, with their first born arriving in 1923.

Gloyd Augusta "Ginney" Stanley – Uncle Ginney always had a smile! "Courtesy of Bill Stanley"

Sapulpa was the county seat of Creek County, and it was named in honor of "Chief" James Sapulpa, a full-blooded Lower Creek Indian from Alabama, who came to Indian Territory around the year of 1850, and established a trading post about one mile southeast of the present community. In 1886 the Atlantic and Pacific Railroad — later named the St. Louis and San Francisco Railway — extended its line from Red Fork, Oklahoma, to this area. The place became known as Sapulpa Station, in honor of "Chief" James Sapulpa, who had befriended the railway workers. A post office was later established here on July 1, 1889, and the town was incorporated on March 31, 1898. The Euchee Mission Boarding School was built about a mile east of Sapulpa, in 1894, with its purpose being to educate American Indian children. Due to the benefit of these railroad activities, as well as the local natural resources such as walnut trees, clay, petroleum, natural gas, and sand used for glass manufacturing, Sapulpa experienced a rapid growth during its first three decades — 1890 to 1920.

Chief James Sapulpa

In 1926, plans were made for the creation of a road stretching from Chicago to Los Angeles — a 1,500 mile "ribbon of concrete," now referred to as "The Mother Road" — and for many years this two-lane stretch of highway was the main thoroughfare that carried travelers across our nation. Sapulpa was privileged that "Route 66" ran through its heart, and tourists would often stop by and visit its restaurants and shops. Back then, people learned their U. S. Geography by driving their cars from city to city while on vacation, and mingling with the local town folks. They were intrigued by this particular town's name and wanted to know how to pronounce "Sapulpa."

Ginney's house always seemed to be full of guests. Whether it was the neighborhood kids mooching cookies from Jewel, or family and friends popping in, guests were always welcome. Jewel could stretch a pot of stew farther than anybody, and wouldn't let a guest leave her house hungry.

After the death of Preston Paden's dear Grandpa Stanley and Preston's subsequent escape from jail in Picher, Oklahoma, he was constantly hanging out with Edna and Volney, and/or Doris and Jess, and also worked for his uncle, Earl Stuchlik, in McPherson, Kansas. Preston also liked spending time with his

Aunt Jewel and Uncle Ginney whenever he could. He was fond of his cousins and enjoyed doing special things for them.

One time, he heard of a new ice cream shop on the corner of Maple and Dewey Streets so he gathered up all his little cousins and took them there to get some ice cream cones. Preston knew this was a treat that they rarely experienced. One of the kids spotted a "double-headed" cone, and asked, "What's that, Preston?" Preston answered, "That's what y'all are going to get your ice-cream in," and then he proceeded to order a big double-dip cone for each of them. The Stanley kids never forgot that act of kindness.

One hot summer day in the year of 1934, a panel truck — with about eight fishing rods tied to the top of it — came rolling in the driveway of the Stanley house on South Birch Street in Sapulpa. Out stepped Preston Paden and Volney Davis. They said that they had come by to visit for a few days, and do some fishing. Volney would get up every morning, get dressed, and take the Stanley's dog for a walk, even though he always wore a vest to cover up his gun and shoulder holster. After breakfast, on the day they were leaving, after Preston and Volney had loaded up the panel truck, Aunt Jewel and the kids walked with them out to the car. Volney turned to Jewel and said, "Miss Jewel, you treated us so fine, and I never enjoyed anything as much as your biscuits, and I been keepin' track — I think I had about ten of them, and they oughta be worth at least $10 apiece." Then Volney proceeded to hand her a $100 bill. She almost fainted. That was the most money there was in the whole world as far as she was concerned. She, at first, refused to take it, but Volney insisted. Preston and Volney then left for Montana, and Jewel fed her family for a long while on that unexpected gift.

The Stanley kids never forgot the visits from their Aunt Doris or Aunt Edna while they were growing up. One time in particular, Edna and Volney came through the door all excited about something. At least Edna was excited, because she never stopped talking the whole time while she sat her little Pomeranian dog down, took her fur coat off, and she and Volney both threw their guns on the couch. Volney told Jewel he sure could use some eggs and biscuits, and Edna was busy pouring herself a drink.

It wasn't as if everything was "prim and proper" around their house all the time. Uncle Ginney was a "Stanley" too, and when times were tough, he would do whatever it took to feed his family. Aunt Jewel was raised in a good home and she was a good and loving wife who put her children first. Ginney drove a taxicab during Prohibition, and it was said that he delivered a lot more bottles of whiskey than he did passengers. And looking back on their childhood memories, most of Ginney's children remember riding with him when he would drive to pick up his cases of whiskey in Joplin, Missouri, or Fort Smith, Arkansas.

Grandma Louie Nettie Stanley and Grandson Preston L. Paden

Sometimes Preston, or Edna, or someone else in the family, would pick up Grandma Louie in Cardin and bring her to visit at the Ginney Stanley residence. Her grandkids all loved their Grandma Lou. She would keep them entertained with something all the time, even if it was just her routine way of doing things. She was also a creature of habit, and you didn't mess with her habits. Ginney was in big trouble with his Mother Lou if he forgot to bring her "Creomulsion" or "Black Draught" when he came home from work.

And you best keep quiet on Sunday mornings while "Brother Oral" was on the radio. Grandma Lou never missed sending Brother Oral (Evangelist Oral Roberts) his $2.00 donation after his weekly Sunday morning radio program.

Grandma Lou and her baby, G. A. "Ginney" Stanley

Grandma Louie Nettie – Such a sweetheart – She always kept us in stitches.

Chapter 34: The Drexel, Missouri, Bank Robbery In 1934

Preston recalled robbing the Drexel, Missouri Bank and related his story to officials as follows:

"The car we used in the Drexel, Missouri, bank robbery was a 1934 Oldsmobile 8 Sedan," according to Preston Paden. *"We stole this car at 40th and Main, in Kansas City, Missouri. This car was a big black sedan with six wheels, a trunk rack, and it had a heater in it. Jess Doyle and Volney Davis had a trunk put on the rear. We kept this car in a private garage at 39th and Broadway, in an alley across from the Blackstone Apartments."*

Preston continued, *"Volney got the car and brought it to Locust Street (on the evening of December 12th). Jess, John Langan, and I got in the car with two sawed-off shotguns, a high powered rifle — and we all carried pistols. We also had a crowbar, a chisel, and a hammer, if needed, to get through brick walls. John Langan was wearing a dark blue suit and a tan hat. Volney Davis had on a gray suit, grayish-blue topcoat, gray hat, and was wearing a pair of galoshes or overshoes. Jess Doyle wore a heavy blue double-breasted overcoat and a gray hat. I was wearing a grayish-blue suit and a tan topcoat. About 10:30 p.m. we started our trip from Kansas City to Drexel, Missouri, intending to get there about midnight. We had trouble with the fuel pump so it was about 3:00 a.m. (on December 13th) when we finally arrived. We drove up behind the bank, and John and Volney got out. Jess and I drove to the local high school and turned right for three blocks, then left for two miles. Volney and John walked down the railroad tracks to where we were, carrying all their tools and guns. It was almost daylight when they got there, and they said they couldn't get in the bank because they didn't have time. They had broken into a store next door to the bank, and tried to get through the wall into the bank."*

Preston said that they decided that since the bank would open soon, they would just hold-up the damn place. As they drove to town, Preston and Jess let the other two boys out at a café and went to fill the car up with gas. They then drove up a side street, close to the bank, where they waited for it to open.

According to Preston, *"Volney and John Langan walked to the back of the bank and ran a crowbar through the door. Then they ran around to the front to see if an alarm went off. Since it didn't go off, they went back to the back door, broke in it, and just waited for the employees to come to work. When the employees came in, Volney and John put them "to work," just as if nothing was wrong. I was across the street in front of the post office. A postal employee of small stature was loading sacks of mail into a postal truck. He had a pistol, and I noticed that he kept watching me. Jess was down the street with the high powered rifle, and it would have been bad if the postal employee had 'shook' me.*

"I waited across the street where I was in a position to see into the bank window and see the vault. The time lock had gone off when the man who opened the vault came in to work. John put a gun on him and told him it was a robbery and to open up. The man got excited and started to grab at John's gun. Volney said he was fixing to shoot the bastard, but John got him settled down. When I saw the man open the vault, I started for the car. Jess was right with me, and he jumped under the wheel. We pulled up behind the bank in the alley. Volney was coming out

292

first, with John right behind him. John had a big pasteboard box in his arms that he had filled with bills, money trays, and silver coins. Just as they were coming out of the bank door, a big fellow was coming down an outside staircase from the building next door. When he saw what was going on, he turned and started to go back up the stairs. Volney hollered at him, putting his gun on him, and told him since he was bothered with "nose trouble," he wanted him to go along and ride on the side of the car. But on the way to the car, the fellow got a building between him and Volney and was running down the alley. Jess told me to bring him back, so I jumped out with a sawed-off shotgun and chased him down. We put him on Volney's side of the car, where Volney could watch him. Volney told him if he jumped off he would shoot him through both kidneys. However, after we went about two blocks, Volney just pushed him off."

Preston went on to say that they then went back to Kansas City, and just as they were near the Missouri-Kansas state line, down close to the old police station, Volney and Preston took the paper money, while Jess and John took all the silver — and they put it in their coat pockets and went to a saloon. Jess and John put the car in a garage. After Volney and Preston had a drink, they took a cab to Volney's and Edna's apartment, got Volney's car, and went to Jess' apartment to split the money. Preston concluded with the statement that *"... the take from the Drexel Bank job was around $2,500, and we split it four ways."*

Chapter 35: The Blankenship Brothers Robbery

Preston said, *"In January of 1935, I was living in Kansas City, Missouri, staying with Jess Doyle and Doris Stanley. We were living in an apartment that I believe was at 4012 Locust Street. In the same building, in another apartment, John Langan and Frances Taylor were living — using some Irish name. Jess Doyle and Doris Stanley were known as Mr. and Mrs. Conley. My mother, Edna Murray, and Volney Davis were living on Broadway, south of 32nd Street. They had a ground floor apartment, in the second apartment building from the north, in the row of apartments on the east side of Broadway. They were known as Mr. and Mrs. Hansen."*

Preston went on to say, *"While living there, Volney Davis got the 'mark' on two old men by the name of Blankenship ('O. K.' and 'E. K.'), who lived at Winnwood Beach, (Missouri), and who were supposed to carry $30,000 around with them. Volney and I drove over there one night in his Pontiac, and he sent me to the house to knock on the door, just to see if they would answer at night. I got the name of a neighbor, off a mailbox, and when they answered the door, I asked them about these people. They told me where they lived, and I thanked them and went back to the car. Volney and I then drove back to Kansas City.*

"About a week later, Jess Doyle, John Langan, and I were at Jess Doyle's apartment, when Volney came over in his Pontiac. We all got our guns and left with Volney. John had a .38 revolver, Jess, Volney, and I each had a .45 Colt automatic. Also in the car, was a 303 automatic rifle and a sawed-off Remington automatic shotgun. We went to Volney's apartment on Broadway, and left the Pontiac parked out front.

"Volney had a 'hot' Ford Coach which he had stolen in Kansas City, and kept in a garage in back of the Plamor Hotel. We walked from the apartment to this garage and got the Ford. We had the rifle and shotgun in cases that we carried with us.

"When we left the garage in the Ford, it was about 6:00 or 7:00 o'clock in the evening. Volney drove the car, Jess was in the front seat with him, and John and I were in the back seat. We drove to North Kansas City, using the bridge near the airport, and on to Winnwood Beach. We drove to the Blankenship's house and Jess and John went up to their door. Volney and I could hear what was said. John knocked on the door and someone said, 'What do you want?' Langan said he wanted to talk to Baker, or some 'off the wall' name, and they said he had the wrong house and wouldn't let them in.

"John and Jess came back to the car, and we started back to Kansas City. Volney asked John why he didn't go in, and what the hell did he say 'Baker' for, instead of Blankenship. I don't remember just what John's answer was. Volney also asked Jess why he didn't go in the house, and Jess said, 'That old man had a pistol.' And Volney said, 'You've got one too, haven't you?' Then Volney said if it would have been him, he would have kicked the door in and gone on in. 'What the hell do you think we went out there for? We went out to rob those people, didn't we?' Volney drove back to the Plamor, and we put the car in the garage and walked back to Volney's apartment, then he took us home in his Pontiac.

"At about 6:00 o'clock the next morning, (January 13ᵗʰ), Volney came to our apartment and asked Jess and me if we wanted to go on over there and get that money. He said that he

hadn't slept all night thinking about it. He said for me to go over to John's apartment and get him up — which I did. Volney was already in the Ford when he came over. I got John up, and we hurried and dressed and went out and got in the car. We had our same guns that we had the previous night, but I don't think we had the shotgun and the rifle.

"We drove to North Kansas City, to Winnwood Beach, and right up in front of Blankenship's house. Volney had a brass colored badge, and he, John, and Jess went up to the front door. They sent me around to the back door. Volney knocked on the door. I don't know who answered. Volney had gotten the tag number on the Blankenship car and when the door opened, Volney gave them the rush act; said 'I'm an officer,' showed them his badge, and said, 'Who has been driving that maroon colored Ford?,' and told them the tag number. The three of them crowded into the house, and I went around to the front and followed them in.

"Inside, we found two old men, a girl (later determined to be Mrs. Orville, a niece of the Blankenship brothers) who looked to be about 20 to 22 years of age, but was probably (much) older, as she had (about) an 8 year old boy (later determined to be 10 years old), and a husband, who looked to be in his late 20s or early 30s. He had a dark complexion, was taller than I, heavy set — and looked husky enough to be a wrestler. The girl, I believe, was the niece of the Blankenship brothers.

"The kitchen and dining room were together, straight back from the living room. They had been eating breakfast, and Volney had them all on their feet when I got inside. He called the big guy from the kitchen, saying, 'You've been driving that car, too, haven't you?'

"All of them had come into the living room, with the four of us, when Volney, Jess and John 'drug' their pistols — and told them to 'lay down on the floor.' One of the old men put up a 'scream' about it — said he had never been arrested in his life, and he didn't think officers were supposed to treat people like this. They all got down on the floor, however, and John went into the bedroom — which was off to the right of the living room — tore up some sheets, and started tying these people up.

"Both of the Blankenship men looked to be past 70. One of them said he could not lay down because of his rheumatism — but he finally got down after Volney convinced him he didn't have it so bad. I also remember one of these old men told the other, 'Eddie, you've got your feet in my face.' We tied them all up and the mother of the little boy kept screaming that she wanted the little boy near her. When Volney finally 'boxed' her, and then laid the little boy by her, her husband started to get up. Volney asked him if he wanted to be 'boxed' too, so he laid back down. I helped tie the big guy up with some baling wire that I found. He reached in his overalls pocket for something, and I told him to jerk that hand back out. Volney jumped over there and put his pistol right in his ear. He didn't make a move after that.

"Jess and I stayed in the living room with these people, while Volney went out in the kitchen and poured out the flour, sugar, etc., thinking he might find some money in there. John went in the bedroom and found their money, in a striped canvas sack, pinned with a safety pin, under the mattress. The sack was made out of mattress cover, and contained $2,500 — a $100 dollar bill on the outside, and $2,400 in tens and twenties, mostly tens — ten in a bundle, each bundle tied with a rubber band — and the

twenties were in bundles of five. The rubber bands were so old they had stuck to the money. John searched the old men and took their purses, where he found several $5 pieces, and some $5 gold pieces that had been used for watch charms. He also got an old $50 bill and an old $20 bill out of their pockets. These were the old type bills — larger than the new bills. One old man had several things wrapped up with names of them — one an old silver dollar. We also got a Spanish type .38 pistol and a .410 shotgun pistol. Volney and I later threw these in the river. John put their purses back in their pockets, keeping the money, of course.

"As we left, Volney told them we would look at their car, and if it hadn't been wrecked, we would come back in and untie them. The young man knew we were robbing them, but the two old men seemed to think all the time that we were officers.

"We were back to Kansas City at Volney's apartment, by about 9:00 o'clock that morning. Jess and John went inside, while Volney and I put the Ford in the garage. After we walked to the apartment, we 'cut' the money. The guy that gave Volney the 'mark' got the gold and the 'old time' money, probably $150. I don't know who this was — Volney took care of that part. The rest was split even, and I got $500 and something for my share."

Chapter 36: The Bremer Kidnapping Trial

Edna Murray & John J. "Boss" McLaughlin being escorted by a federal agent from a "Paddy Wagon" to the courtroom of Bremer Kidnapping Trial. "Courtesy of the Collection of Rick Mattix"

Edward G. Bremer, President of the Commercial State Bank of St. Paul - in his office.

The Bremer Kidnapping Trial was held across the street from the kidnap victim's office.

St. Paul, Minnesota
Local St. Paul, Minnesota, Newspaper
May 6, 1935

"From April 15, until May 6, 1935, those indicted in the Bremer kidnapping were on trial in St. Paul, Minnesota. 'Doc' Barker and Oliver Berg were sentenced to life. Elmer Farmer and Harold Alderton got 20 years. John J. "Boss" McLaughlin, Sr., was sentenced to 5 years for money changing, but charges were dropped against his son, John Jr. James Wilson, Sr., (Dr. Joseph Moran's nephew), also got 5 years. William Edward Vidler and Philip J. Delaney were acquitted. Charges were dropped against Jesse Doyle and Edna "The Kissing Bandit" Murray, but Edna was returned to the Women's State Prison at Jefferson City, Missouri, to complete her 25 year sentence for highway robbery — with two additional years (added on) for escape. And Doyle was turned over to Nebraska where he will be tried of the Fairbury Bank robbery. Byron Bolton pleaded guilty to the kidnapping and testified against the other (Barker-Karpis) gang members. His sentence was deferred until later. Bruno "Whitey" Austin, another of the alleged money changers, was discharged by court order."

Author's note:

Jess Doyle was turned over to the State of Nebraska, where he was tried and sentenced, for the Fairbury Bank robbery. Also, Bruno "Whitey" Austin would later be convicted of murder in Illinois and sentenced to life.

"A blonde in a gingham dress described Byron Bolton, the Barker-Karpis Gang gunner, as '... a sneak who redeemed his ticket for the hot seat with lies.'

302

"The blonde was Edna (Rabbit) Murray, who, with Jess Doyle, was freed of complicity in the kidnapping of Edward G. Bremer, St. Paul banker.

"Lounging in the matron's reception room in Ramsey County Jail (in St. Paul), both Mrs. Murray and Doyle spoke freely about the Bremer kidnapping trial in which they sat as defendants for fifteen days.

"They shook hands, chatted and joked with each other, and posed for pictures.

"'How would you feel if you were freed in a case like this?' asked Edna, when she was queried about the dismissal of charges.

"'Well, I feel swell, of course,' she added, exhaling cigarette smoke. 'I expected to be exonerated, although I didn't expect the charges to be dismissed.'

"Doyle touched off a cigarette and grinned when asked how he felt about it.

"'Boy, it's a relief,' he said.

"Both were in court Monday when Bolton took the stand as a government witness and named Harry Sawyer, one-time St. Paul underworld kingpin as the "finger" man in the Bremer abduction. Bolton also identified Volney Davis as one of those who "stood by" as three members of the Barker-Karpis gang kidnapped the banker in January, 1934.

"'Bolton's testimony,' said Edna Murray 'was the only damaging stuff I heard at the trial. He is a sneak,

who traded with the government. He is trying to escape the hot seat (electric chair) down in Chicago for the St. Valentine's Day massacre. He traded lies for his ticket to the hot seat.'

"*The jet-eyed Bolton's identification of Davis angered the blonde.*

"*'He named Volney and he knows that Volney wasn't mixed up in the actual kidnapping,' snapped Edna. 'So far as Volney's being mixed up in the money changing, I don't know.'*

"*Edna asserted that she and Davis were occupants of a St. Paul apartment on the day Bremer was kidnapped. Davis, she said, first heard about the abduction at a drug store where he had gone for some whiskey to treat her cold.*

"*'Volney couldn't have been in on the kidnapping because he didn't get up early enough,' she added frankly. 'I heard it on the radio and when Volney came back I told him. He said that I had better get out of town because I couldn't stand an arrest, but he could.' Being wanted in Missouri for her escape from prison, Edna decided to leave for Chicago that day, she said.*

"*Edna was apparently a little perturbed about being removed to Missouri. She said, 'I'm not guilty. I was framed and I'm going to reopen the case when I go back. I am perfectly innocent of the charge.'*

"Just before she changed clothes for the picture, Edna disclosed that her 18 year old son was at the trial last week and left St. Paul on Saturday night. Her husband, Jack Murray, was still in the Missouri prison serving a 25 year sentence for the same charge on which she was convicted.

"Doyle said the appearance of his name on the Bremer kidnap indictment '... always will be a mystery to me. I can't figure out why it was there,' he said. 'My name wasn't mentioned once during the trial.'

"The slender, nervous Doyle, (who was) captured by federal agents (in Cherokee, Kansas) near Girard, Kansas, a few weeks before the trial began, is anxious to 'get going' on the two robbery charges confronting him.

"'I wish that (the) county attorney over in Minneapolis would bring his witnesses here and have 'em look me over,' he said, discussing his alleged connection with the robbery, December 16, 1932, of the Third Northwestern National Bank (of Minneapolis). 'There isn't a witness who can truthfully say I had anything to do with that robbery.'

"Doyle also could be tried on charges of participating in the holdup of a bank in Okemah, Oklahoma. 'I was on an operating table in Kansas City the day that robbery took place,' he said.

"Doyle said he once lived in Minneapolis and that he was deer hunting in Minnesota in December, 1934.

He said he 'was on the way to the coast' when Bremer was kidnapped.

" 'What did you think of Bolton's testimony?,' Doyle was asked.

" 'I think he's a government agent,' he replied, laughing."

Edna Murray Injured on Her Return to Missouri

Jefferson City, Missouri
Local Jefferson City, Missouri, Newspaper
May 13, 1935

"Mrs. Edna 'The Kissing Bandit' Murray, the triple escape queen of the Missouri State Penitentiary, was returned here today after narrowly escaping serious injury while being brought back from St. Paul, Minnesota.

"Mrs. Murray, whose 'in again, out again' career began here in 1925 when she began a 25 year sentence for first degree robbery in Kansas City, and Deputy Sheriff Robert Scholten, who was returning her, suffered bruises Sunday when their automobile collided with another car near Toledo, Iowa.

"She was turned over to Missouri authorities Saturday, after having been questioned in connection with the Bremer kidnapping case.

"The widow of 'Diamond Joe' Sullivan, who was electrocuted in the Arkansas penitentiary, she first escaped in May, 1927, and was gone for four years. Later, she got away again, but was captured here the next day.

"She escaped December 13, 1932, with Irene McCann, slayer of a Carthage jailer, and (she) was captured in Pittsburg, Kansas, last February.

"Mrs. McCann voluntarily surrendered about a year ago."

Edna Murray-- smiling for photographers in St. Paul after testifying against the Barker-Karpis Gang. "Courtesy of the Collection of Rick Mattix"

Chapter 37: Bootlegging In Kansas, Circa 1935

While living with his Aunt Doris in McPherson, Kansas, during the summer of 1935, Preston Paden helped her run her tavern, which was located just outside of town. Most of the time, he kept busy running "hooch" (bootleg alcohol) to keep her business supplied.

Sheriff Ralph McPhail had been contacted by federal agents concerning Doris Stanley's activities regarding the operation of her tavern in his county. He was asked to keep in touch with her regularly, relative to obtaining information about fugitives that the feds were seeking. It was of his belief that the G-men were trying to trade Jess Doyle for Alvin Karpis and Harry Campbell, and that apparently they had told Jess Doyle and Doris Stanley that they could get a parole for Jess if either of them could furnish information leading to the apprehension of the remaining fugitives in their case load.

Sheriff McPhail stated that he allowed Doris to run her tavern in the county until September, 1935, when he began to realize that she was merely "leading him on" so she could continue to remain in business. Consequently he ordered her out of the county in late September of 1935, at which time she relocated to Lyons, Kansas.

Sheriff McPhail was further advised that Helen Stanley, sister-in-law of Doris Stanley, was currently serving an indeterminate sentence at the Kansas State Penitentiary in Lansing, Kansas, on a liquor violation. He stated that he did not know the present whereabouts of her husband, Mott Stanley.

Author's note:

Uncle Mott Stanley and Aunt Doris Stanley were partners in a restaurant & tavern operation in, or near, McPherson, Kansas. "Little" Mott, Doris' son, told me of that venture and said that they had gotten into some trouble over the selling of liquor. That would explain why Aunt Helen, Mott's wife, was sent to the penitentiary in Lansing, Kansas. Helen may have taken the fall for all of them because neither Mott nor Doris could have afforded another conviction.

Aunt Doris Stanley & her son "Little" Mott Farrell

J. Edgar Hoover's boys never gave up on trying to learn something from Doris' activities. They spent a lot of time and money believing that they could get her to tell them where to find the rest of the Barker-Karpis Gang. From the time she was released in Kansas City, on June 1, 1935, they would pick her up for questioning at every possible opportunity.

Any informant or agent could come up with a story and the government boys would be on top of it in a heartbeat. A hog thief named Earl Feneman, who had done some time in prison with Jess Doyle, concocted a story about Jess telling him that Alvin Karpis and a friend named Harry "Buddy" Campbell would stop by Doris' place in McPherson every once in a while. Not only did federal officials pull Jess out of the penitentiary in Nebraska and take him to the Jefferson County Jail in Fairbury, Nebraska, for questioning, but they also sent their men to McPherson, Kansas, to spy on Doris. They secured a room in a hotel in McPherson and, through some means or other, got Doris to go to that hotel room and talk to them because the sheriff thought she might be able to assist them. But the only information they obtained from Doris was that she was "on the outs" with the McPherson County Sheriff, Ralph McPhail, since he had picked her up on a previous minor charge.

Jess said that he only vaguely remembered who Earl Feneman was. Jess went on to say that he hadn't talked to Feneman about any of Doris Stanley's activities. He said that he had been playing the role of "the lone wolf" since being incarcerated, and he anticipated that he would keep on playing that role until the day that he is released. He said he doesn't talk to the other convicts any more than absolutely necessary, but just enough to get along with them. He added that he never talks to them about Doris Stanley.

For months, government agents plagued Doris' place of business. They questioned her, they questioned her patrons, and they even showed them pictures of John Langan, Russell Lane, Clarence Sparger, and Jess Doyle. They returned with pictures of Alvin Karpis and Harry Campbell. They found every reason imaginable to interview and question Doris and her employees.

By keeping Doris under constant surveillance, the feds knew her every move. Mr. Hoover was advised that during February, 1936, Doris Stanley, using her correct name, purchased a 1935 Plymouth Coach from Stoss & Evans, a Plymouth Agency in Great Bend, Kansas. Also that Ermin "Curly" Griffin and Preston

Paden have been seen driving the car in Great Bend, Kansas, on several occasions, and that Griffin and Paden were very unreliable individuals and that they couldn't be trusted.

Any person that made the mistake of even so much as speaking to Doris or Preston was put under the watchful eye of Hoover's G-men.

Chapter 38: Preston Paden's "Hit-And-Run" Accident

The evening of January 11, 1936, wasn't much different than any other Saturday night except that Preston Paden was running a little late with his delivery of bootleg whiskey for his Aunt Doris' tavern just outside of Lyons, Kansas.

He was headed east, approaching the northwest corner of the square in Lyons just before 9:00 p.m. Maybe he was driving a little too fast or maybe he just wasn't paying enough attention to the road. Then, all of a sudden, seemingly out of nowhere, his car struck three girls while they were crossing the street. A bit uncertain as to what had just taken place, he looked back to see the three girls getting up from the street. The only thing he could think of at that moment was to get the whiskey out of the car. Aunt Doris had always said, "Whatever you do, ditch the whiskey before the 'laws' catch up with you." He made a bee-line for the house, unloaded the whiskey, and was trying to decide what he should do next. He knew he had to turn himself in, and he was afraid that one of the girls might be badly hurt, but he wasn't sure how to explain his "leaving the scene" in the first place. He wanted to talk to his Aunt Doris before he made any decision.

As Preston's vehicle had continued on after striking the girls, several witnesses wrote down the license number. This led to Preston's arrest shortly after the accident, at a house 5 miles north of Lyons. Alberta Smyers of Little River, as well as Betty Jo McCabe and Ruth Blakey, both of Lyons, were all struck by the car. All three girls suffered numerous scratches and bruises, but none of the girls had any broken bones or serious injuries.

Preston L. Paden

Upon Peston's arrest, no liquor was found in his car, but a quantity of liquor was confiscated by officers at the house. Action on that charge would come later, according to the officers.

On the same evening, at about the same time, another hit-and-run accident occurred between Chase, Kansas, and Ellinwood, Kansas. George Sedore suffered broken bones in his left ankle and left leg when he was struck while changing a tire on his truck on the open road. After the car that hit him continued on without stopping, Sedore still managed to get back into his truck and drive to the nearest hospital in Lyons.

All of this uncivilized behavior in one evening, including the acts of drivers leaving the scenes of accidents, had riled up the citizens of Lyons.

The next day the Lyons Daily News read, in part:

"Citizens of Lyons were startled out of their lethargy upon hearing of two accidents Saturday night caused by members of a contemptible class of motorists, hit-and-run drivers. The fact that apparently no one was critically injured makes the offense(s) no less serious, and it does not lessen the need for some sort of adequate traffic regulation here. Parking in the centers of the streets, inadequate speed regulations, and inadequate stop signs coming onto the highway constitute acute hazards. These things,

314

together with the fact that an extremely large number of people haven't the mental equipment ever to be anything but a menace to public safety on the road, make it dangerous for everybody, including pedestrians and careful motorists. And careful motorists apparently haven't any better chance of steering clear of accidents than the careless driver(s), as the morons who are behind the wheels of cars are no respecters of persons."

Preston was thrown in jail again and this wasn't good. He and his Aunt Doris Stanley had just been in court the previous month for the possession of, and the selling of, intoxicating liquors. Her tavern had been raided on October 18, 1935, and they were both out on bond after having appeared in court on December 2, 1935. They were scheduled to go to court on these charges in just a few days — on January 17, 1936.

Even before making his previous scheduled court date, Preston was brought before Justice of the Peace, L. H. Lanham (who was also the Sheriff) on January 14, 1936. His bail was set at $1,000 and he was thrown into the Rice County Jail, in Lyons, Kansas. This case was continued until January 24th; then until February 13th; and again, until April 7, 1936.

Preston was in the newspapers again on January 16, 1936, when he was admitted to the Lyons hospital by ambulance early that morning for medical treatment.

The following day, January 17th, looking a bit roughed-up, Preston was brought into the courtroom so that he and Doris could face their "Unlawful Possession of Liquor" charges. The County Attorney entered a "dismissal without prejudice" motion with regard to the case against Doris Stanley. The remaining defendant, Preston LeRoy Paden, thereupon "took the fall" and voluntarily entered a plea of guilty of unlawful possession of intoxicating liquors. Preston was fined $100 plus court costs, and sentenced to serve 30 days in jail.

Aunt Doris had persuaded Preston that it would be best for them if he pled guilty because the judge would go easier on him than her since he was only 19 years of age.

Once again, Doris walked.

Chapter 39: The Killing Of Night Marshal Ben Wiggins

Kansas Newspaper Headlines
March 30, 1936
"NIGHT MARSHAL KILLED ON DUTY"
"Body of Ben Wiggins is found in an alley this morning"

"He had come upon robbers about to rifle safe of a business house"

"Ben Wiggins, 45, Lyons, (Kansas), Night Marshal, was shot and killed sometime early this morning apparently by burglars whom he surprised while they were in the act of burglarizing the Williamson-Booker Furniture Store on the west side of the Square.

"Wiggins' body was found by a dishwasher, on his way to work at the Blue Front Café, nearby, a few minutes before 6 a.m. Evidently the shooting had occurred several hours before. Wiggins' body was in a pool of drying blood, about six feet outside the back door of the furniture store, on the wooden loading platform.

"Detectives and Special Investigators were in route to Lyons from all parts of the State. Word was received that Special Officers Ben Jones, Argubright and Grant of the Santa Fe Railroad were on the way to assist. The State Police Patrol was sending its fingerprint expert and a detective. Others were expected to come, and nothing was being left undone in an effort to track down and bring the criminals to justice.

"At the Coroner's Office, the bullet that had gone through Wiggins' body was found between his back and the shirt that he was wearing. There was a gash and bruise above the right

317

temple, on his forehead. The single bullet wound was in his chest just below the hollow of his neck and bore evidence of having been fired at close range, as though the weapon had been placed directly against the officer.

"As to what had transpired, the scene inside the building gave mute but concise evidence. From the double rear doors where the officer fell mortally wounded, it was forty feet to an inside partition that separates the warehouse room from the store proper. In the store, just inside this partition, is a safe of medium size. The combination was knocked from this safe and a steel pinch bar and a heavy all-steel screwdriver were lying on the floor. The rear doors that had been barred from the inside were standing open.

"Wiggins' hat was lying on the very threshold of the doorway, six feet away from where his body had been. Six feet inside the doors, a single, what was originally thought to be a .32 caliber, empty cartridge was lying. It was believed that the shot was fired from an automatic pistol, in which event the automatic ejection of the shell would have tossed it about the distance between the doorway and the point at which it was picked up.

"Whether the wound on his forehead was inflicted before or after the shooting was a matter of conjecture with investigating officers. It was apparently done with a piece of iron or some other heavy, rather blunt instrument.

"Examination of the officer's hat showed that the felt had been cut entirely through at a point corresponding to the position of the wound on the forehead. That injury was found, in the autopsy, to have been merely a scalp laceration and not a skull fracture. Just below the main wound on the head was a bruise

at the eyebrow line, which Coroner Louis Booker, and the two physicians assisting, said could have been caused by the same instrument and the same blow as it followed downward.

"The autopsy disclosed the exact course of the bullet. It had entered near the center of the chest just below the neck and had ranged diagonally down the body, coming out to the left of the center of the back. It had barely pierced the flesh where it emerged, and was found inside the officer's shirt, having failed to pass through his clothing. In coursing through the body, the bullet severed the upper aorta, (the) main artery leading from the heart. No other vital organs were pierced. There were distinct powder marks on the flesh around the bullet wound, proving that the shot was fired at extremely close range. The bullet corresponded with the empty cartridge found at the rear of the store.

"If Wiggins was first slugged as he stepped through the door, reeled back and fell to the loading platform, and while lying there outside the door was shot, then the empty cartridge was flipped at least 15 feet and through the open doorway by the ejector. Those experienced with automatic pistols of that kind say that such was highly possible. If he was shot after being first struck over the head, then it would appear likely that the burglars may have been someone known to the officer and that they shot him to prevent being identified later.

"(The) source of the tools left behind by the murderers was a matter upon which the authorities spent considerable time. It was first reported that a local garage had been burglarized, but a check there and an examination of the tools by the management, brought out that they had not come from that place. No one else had reported

the loss of such tools. The pinch bar was old but bright from constant use and the steel screwdriver appeared to be new.

"Nelie Corland, the dishwasher who found the body, said at the time that he came to work it was just getting daylight and that the body was in plain sight, almost at the edge of the alley. He didn't know at that moment that it was Wiggins, although he said he had seen the officer several times and noticed a resemblance. He also didn't know he was dead. He hurried to the café to tell other employees what he had seen and the Sheriff's Office was notified at once.

"It was believed that City Councilman, Robert Hall, had been the last person to see Wiggins (alive). He had talked to him for a few minutes at about midnight, before Hall went home to bed.

"Officers were having trouble figuring out how the burglars had gained entrance to the furniture store. None of the rear windows had been broken out and the rear doors apparently had not been forced, but had been unlocked from the inside after the burglars had gotten in.

"Further strengthening the supposition that Wiggins was attacked by a lookout in the burglary was the fact that just inside the rear doors were several cigarette stubs, lying close together on the floor as though someone had been standing there, smoking one cigarette after another in nervous fashion.

"All clues in the case were being gathered carefully by City Marshal George Fox, the slain officer's immediate superior, Sheriff Art Estabrook and Under Sheriff Ray Nodurft, and by Superintendent N. S. Wiggins, and E. S. Ford of the State Reformatory at Hutchinson, Kansas. Mr. Ford, the photographer and fingerprint expert at the reformatory, was endeavoring to obtain prints from the safe and tools left behind by the murderers.

"Ben Wiggins had been the Night Marshal in Lyons for only 15 months, but he had a reputation for being vigilant at his job. This was his first experience at being a peace officer, and he made it a careful practice to examine the front and rear doors of all businesses at frequent intervals during the night. Although often finding doors left unlocked by careless business owners, there had been no robberies in the business district during the time he was in office.

"Officer Wiggins' gun, a .38 caliber Colt revolver, was in its holster when his body was found. He was accustomed to wearing it under his leather jacket, and there was no indication that he had attempted to draw it. It was fully loaded."

"Wiggins was survived by four sisters; Mrs. Calvin Cook, Mrs. Arch Morris and Mrs. John Lantow of Lyons, Kansas, and Mrs. Roy Doran of Covina, California. Another sister, Mrs. Fred Wohlford, passed away only two weeks before her brother's death, and Mrs. Doran had just returned to California. Ben Wiggins was a brother of Seth Wiggins, who died several years before him. He had been reared on a farm a few miles northeast of Lyons where he was born (on) May 4, 1891. He had never married."

Kansas Newspaper Headlines
March 31, 1936
"SEARCH FOR CLUES"
"Many Officers From Over the State Aiding In Wiggins Slaying Case"

"Kansas had sent some of its best talent to Lyons to aid local authorities in their efforts to track down the murderers of Night Marshal Ben Wiggins. Included in the group who came to Lyons

to assist were, A. P. Keeling of the State Police Force, finger-
print expert for that organization; Special Officers Grant and
Argubright of the Santa Fe Railroad; Parole Officer Docking
and Bertillon System expert, Ford, of the State Reformatory;
N. S. Wiggins, Reformatory Superintendent; Vance Houdyshell,
Chief of Police at Great Bend, and M. W. Murdy, Barton County
Sheriff.

"In the meantime only a few clues of substantial nature were
in the hands of the officers. One of the more interesting developments was the finding of the slain officer's flashlight. Carl
Aldridge, a 13 year-old Lyon's boy, had picked up the flashlight
and brought it to the sheriff's office. He had found it on a pile
of tin cans and other bits of junk just across the alley from the
spot where the body was found. He said he had found it about
3 o'clock in the afternoon, just before he turned it in. Indications
were that the (flash)light had been thrown and the lens and rim
holding it had been broken.

"Strangely, the Aldridge boy was the lad who only a few days
before had turned in to the Sheriff, the two medical bags that had
been stolen from Dr. L. J. Beyer's car the night before. He had
found them in a ravine in back of the White Swan Laundry.

"Several of those working on the Wiggins case, earlier in the
day, had searched the same ground where the boy said the flashlight was found in plain sight. Whether the light had been there
all the time but simply had not been noticed, or whether it had
been tossed there later in the day was an interesting and baffling
angle to the case.

"Robert Hall, Councilman, who was thought to have been
the last person to see the night marshal alive, said he had been

in the habit of "making the alleys" with Wiggins on one of his trips each night, and that Sunday night was the first time he had failed to accompany him in several months.

"It had been the officer's habit to make a tour of the front doors in the business district about 10 to 11 o'clock and try all of them to determine whether any had been left open by accident. Then sometime between midnight and 1 o'clock he usually made a trip through the alleys, examining back doors. Again, before daylight, he would make at least one more regular tour of the alleys. It was the early trip during which Hall accompanied him, he said.

"Speculating upon what happened on the fatal night, Mr. Hall said that Wiggins usually was cautious, and that he had been advised always to carry his weapon in his hand when making the rounds through the alleys. On one of his most recent trips, Mr. Hall recalled, Wiggins had found the rear door of the Williamson-Booker Store open. Upon closer investigation, he learned that there had been an ambulance call and the doors had not been barred after the ambulance had been run out, due to the need for hurrying. Mr. Hall believed that (incident) was in his mind when Wiggins investigated the unlocked door at the furniture store. He thinks that Wiggins merely went into the room far enough to see if the ambulance was there and that he was slugged as he started in.

"Louis Booker, of the Williamson-Booker (Furniture) Store, advised officials that the murder of Night Marshal Wiggins was committed during a burglary that could have netted the robber-murderers comparatively little. There was only about $80 in the safe, he said."

Author's note:

On the same night as the Wiggins murder in Lyons, Kansas, a key Barker-Karpis Gang member, namely Alvin Karpis, — currently "Public Enemy No. 1" — made news headlines from Hot Springs, Arkansas, as shown below.

Topeka, Kansas Newspaper
March 31, 1936
"STATE PATROL IS PURSUING KARPIS"
"Public Enemy No. 1 Is Believed To Be In Arkansas Now"
"Director of The Kansas Highway Patrol There When The Fox Escaped"

"Announcement that a raid of officers in an attempt to capture Alvin Karpis, Public Enemy No. 1, at Hot Springs, Ark., had failed to apprehend the accused Bremer Kidnapper was made last night to the office of the Kansas Highway Patrol. Wint Smith, director of the Kansas Highway Patrol, telephoned the information to his assistant, Frank Stone. 'Smith said he believed Karpis had been there but had left,' Stone announced. The raid was made early March 30. Smith arrived at the scene after it was made."

Chapter 40: Paden And Mallory Arrested For Burglary

April 4, 1936
"ARREST TWO ON BURGLARY COUNT"
"PRESTON PADEN AND HENRY MALLORY HELD IN COUNTY JAIL"
"Accused of Burglarizing Store Where Officer Wiggins Was Found Dead"

"Two men were being held in the Rice County Jail in default of bond, charged with burglary of the Williamson-Booker Furniture Store, behind which the lifeless body of Night Marshal Ben Wiggins, was found, slugged and shot.

Henry Mallory

"The two men were Preston LeRoy Paden, 20, and Henry Mallory, 36, both of whom gave their address as Lyons, Kansas.

"Following five days of feverish activity on the part of city, county and state officials and a number of special officers who were endeavoring to run down any and all information leading to a solution of the case, the arrests were announced by Sheriff Art Estabrook and Officer A. P. Keeling of the State Highway Patrol.

"Commenting on the arrests, Officer Keeling said the burglary charge was for the purpose of holding the men, pending more complete investigation into the case.

"Paden was out on bond awaiting sentence from district court after pleading guilty on February 24, 1936, to a charge of leaving the scene of an accident. At the time of his plea in district court, Judge Ray Beals deferred sentence until April 7th. In the meantime, Paden had been at liberty on a $1,000 bond.

"Mallory, who had been in Lyons for only a few months, had no criminal record except for a few minor run-ins with the Wichita police, so far as could be determined. According to Officer Keeling, he was known to have paid three stiff fines in Wichita, at least one, for drunken driving.

"Investigation into Paden's record disclosed nothing previous to the charge mentioned. Both men had come to Lyons from Oklahoma and both had been identified with a "Drink Stand" just west of the city on U.S. Hwy 50 North. Information had also been released that both, Paden and Mallory, had been confined for two days at the Barton County Jail in Great Bend, Kansas, where they had been questioned before being transferred to Rice County."

April 7, 1936

"Preston Paden was sentenced to the State Reformatory for leaving the scene of an accident, when a car he was driving struck and injured three girls at the northwest corner of the public square on January 11th."

Preston L. Paden

326

Chapter 41: The Details Of The Killing Of Ben Wiggins

It takes only one second — **one foolish and thoughtless second** — to damage the lives of so many people. And such was the case on the night of March 29, 1936.

Having just served his 30 day sentence for taking the fall for both his and Doris' liquor violations, Preston Paden, who was then out on bond, still had another court appearance to make. He had yet to face the charges for leaving the scene of an automobile accident with the three girls just outside of Lyons, Kansas. That incident, too, was directly related to his employment with his Aunt Doris. Had he not been transporting illegal liquor for her, he would not have left the scene of the accident without, at first, stopping to find out if the girls were hurt. Upon reflection, he felt that he had only himself to blame, and he was just grateful that Doris had been able to bail him out. Attorney's fees, bail bonds, and court costs were starting to mount up though, as were Preston's concerns about his future.

On the evening of March 29, 1936, Preston Paden, Henry Mallory, and Ermin "Curly" Griffin rolled into Lyons, Kansas, from Joplin, Missouri. Mallory got off at the Snider Cabin Camp at the west edge of Lyons, and Paden and Griffin continued on to Great Bend, Kansas, where Griffin lived. Paden and Griffin then met Dee Herbold, also from Great Bend, at a beer parlor. Paden and Griffin, after having traveled all day, were already weary when they started drinking. According to Herbold, they started talking about making some easy money. As more beer was consumed and the conversation continued, the idea of cracking the safe at the Williamson-Booker Furniture Store was starting to seem to be a lot more attractive. The three returned to Lyons, picked up Mallory, and they planned their burglary while at Doris Stanley's place, where Paden and Mallory were employed. Griffin wanted to check the furniture store out so he went there first. He came back and said that he got into the store without a problem, but he would need some help in cracking that safe.

All four of the men got into Doris Stanley's car because it was bigger than their coupe. They left it parked a half a block west of the rear entrance to the store. Herbold was positioned as the lookout at the rear door, holding a .380 caliber pistol that belonged to Mallory. Paden, Mallory, and Griffin then went into the front room where the safe was situated.

In a blundering attempt to open the safe, Griffin was attacking it with a hatchet, as Paden and Mallory stood by. They heard a shot followed by a warning to "… get the hell out of there." Herbold and Griffin proceeded to run across the lot to where Doris' car was parked. Paden and Mallory fled to the south and down the alley to Commercial Street and continued on foot to Doris Stanley's place at the west edge of town. Shortly after they arrived there, Herbold and Griffin showed up on foot due to the fact that they weren't able to get into the car because Paden had the only set of car keys. Griffin then took Paden back uptown and let him out close to Doris' car so that he could drive it home. It wasn't until later that the other three men got the story from Herbold as to what actually had happened.

According to Herbold, an officer had stuck his head in the rear door, throwing his flashlight beam onto Herbold. Herbold then struck him on the head with the point of his gun. Herbold said he must have jarred the safety off when he struck the officer's head, and, as the officer was staggering and going down, the gun fired, hitting the officer. As the gang was leaving, one of the men picked up the officer's still lit flashlight, turned it off, and threw it across the alley.

Needless to say, this wasn't the way this burglary was supposed to go down. Griffin and Herbold later returned to Great Bend in their coupe. Paden and Mallory, although they had a room rented at the Snider Camp, followed them to Great Bend before going on to Larned, Kansas, to spend the night.

Preston was the youngest of the four burglars, and he thought that he was not naïve in any way, but up to this point, he had never been sentenced for a felony. Ermin "Curly" Griffin, an oil worker from Great Bend, known as a bootlegger, had previously served a 17 month sentence in the Missouri State Penitentiary in Jefferson City, Missouri, on a grand larceny charge. Henry Mallory, age 36, had been arrested a time or two in Wichita, Kansas, for drunkenness. Dee Herbold, 33, a stonemason from Great Bend, had been arrested twice in his lifetime, once for fighting and once for buying liquor. None of the men had bargained for the events that would unfold from that night in Lyons, Kansas.

Unable to take back their foolish and thoughtless behavior, unable to bring life back into the body of the man they left lying dead, and unable to find forgiveness even from themselves, they all had fled the scene of the crime.

Chapter 42: Paden And Mallory Bound Over For Trial

Night Marshal Ben Wiggins

On April 28, 1936, in a preliminary hearing before Justice Harvey Rimmer, Preston Paden and Henry Mallory, charged with the murder of Night Marshal Ben Wiggins on the morning of March 30, 1936, were bound over to the District Court for trial.

Up until this time, investigators had been closely guarding any information they had obtained concerning this case.

It seems ironic that Louis Booker was both the Coroner as well as the victim of the attempted furniture store robbery. He testified briefly as to the burglary and the finding of the body of Night Marshal Wiggins. He was followed by Dr. R. Leonard, who described the slain officer's wounds, as they were determined by an autopsy.

There was testimony designed to show that a car that Paden had been driving had been parked on South Pioneer Street, just south of the Conoco Filling Station and a half a block to the rear of the furniture store, at about 10:00 p.m. on the night of the burglary, and again, at about 1:00 a.m. the following morning.

Sheriff Art Estabrook testified that he had traced fresh footprints from the rear of the furniture store across the vacant lot leading to the place where the car had been parked.

A. P. Keeling of the State Police, who had been heading the investigation, testified that the bullet from Officer Wiggins' body had been of the same caliber as an empty shell found at the murder scene. He said that the gun was a .380 caliber — a somewhat unusual caliber — and it had been previously thought to be a .32 caliber. This evidence was the first indication the public had that the slaying was not committed with a common .32 caliber pistol.

Roy Lee, a former Lyons hardware merchant, identified Mallory as the man who had purchased a clip for a .380 pistol from him about two weeks prior to the murder. He said he first ordered, and later called for the pistol when it arrived by mail at the hardware store.

Lloyd Benefiel, a clerk at the Benefiel Hardware store, identified Mallory as having purchased .380 caliber shells from him on two occasions shortly before the murder.

Connecting the activities of Mallory and Paden on the night of the crime, Officer Keeling stated that both had acknowledged to him, when questioned, that they had made a trip to Joplin, Missouri, together on the few days preceding the murder, and that they had spent the evening and night of March 29th and 30th together. He testified that they had answered his question as to their hour of retiring that night, and that his investigation had determined that they had retired at a much different hour.

Mallory and Paden would be coming up for trial in the September term of the District Court.

Chapter 43: The Paden-Mallory Trial — Days 1 & 2

Preston LeRoy Paden and Henry Mallory went on trial in District Court in Lyons, Kansas, on Wednesday, September 9, 1936, charged with the murder of Lyons Night Marshal Ben Wiggins early on the morning of March 30, 1936. Selection of a jury turned out to be a long and tedious affair just as had been expected. In preparation for such a circumstance, a venire of 76 people had been called for duty, and only 13 of those were selected, of which 12 would ultimately deliberate. Many of the jurors had disqualified themselves by declaring that they had reservations against capital punishment. Since Kansas had enacted a new law providing that a jury may recommend death for a convicted murderer, selection of a jury in such trials was made all the more complicated. No one radically opposed to the death sentence could qualify to be a member of the jury.

District Judge Ray H. Beals was appointed as the Presiding Judge, and Howard Fleeson was appointed as the Lead Prosecutor in this case.

L. E. Quinlan, an attorney for the defense, announced on the first day of the trial that his co-council would be Cliff Holland of Russell, Kansas. This was the first time Mr. Quinlan had disclosed the name of his assistant.

The Paden-Mallory Trial was regarded as the most fascinating murder case in Rice County, Kansas, in more than 20 years. And added to that, the public knew very little about either defendant, except from hearsay.

Preston Paden, only 20 years old, had no previous criminal record of a serious nature except a conviction for leaving the scene of an automobile accident — an incident that occurred in Lyons, Kansas, shortly before his arrest on the current murder charge.

Following his arrest on the murder charge, he was taken before the District Court and sentenced to the Kansas State Industrial Reformatory (KSIR) in Hutchinson, Kansas, on the auto accident count, and had remained there since, while awaiting trial on the current murder charge.

It quickly became known that he was the son of Edna Murray, known in Missouri as **"THE KISSING BANDIT,"** who was currently confined to the Missouri State Penitentiary in Jefferson City. But so far as known, Paden had no criminal record prior to the case for which he was sentenced to the reformatory. He had been employed at the lunch and drink stand of his aunt, Doris Stanley (sister of Edna Murray), at the west edge of Lyons for several months, and officers further stated that he was also under suspicion as a bootlegger.

As for Henry Mallory, except for two or three arrests in Wichita, Kansas, for drunkenness, he seemed to have no prior criminal history. He was said to have been employed as a field foreman for an oil company in McPherson County just before coming to Lyons, Kansas, last winter for employment at the Stanley establishment.

Just why Paden and Mallory were so quickly placed under arrest was never fully disclosed by the authorities. Their arrests followed soon after the arrival of A. P. Keeling, the fingerprint expert of the State Highway Patrol, who had been assigned to the case as a special investigator. Mr. Keeling, as well as dozens of other officers from all parts of the state who went to work on the case, would not disclose to the press why Paden and Mallory had initially been suspected. This situation, likewise, added to the heightened public interest in the trial.

Merle Gill of Kansas City was introduced as an expert witness by stating that he had been a professional firearms expert since 1927, and had maintained a laboratory for that work since 1923. As a ballistics expert residing in Kansas City, he had previously examined more than 1,500 exhibits for the Kansas City Police Department and for the U. S. Department of Justice. He told the court of having examined guns belonging to many notorious criminals — among them being Harvey Bailey, George "Machine Gun" Kelly, Albert Bates, Charles A. "Pretty Boy" Floyd, Alvin Karpis, and many others. He said that he had worked on over 150 cases just in the state of Kansas.

Mr. Gill's testimony was of a highly technical nature — about the first of that kind that had ever been offered in a local courtroom.

Upon questioning by the prosecution, Mr. Gill explained exactly how he identified the murder weapon as being a Colt .380 caliber pistol by the rifling marks on the bullet, which he said could have been made by no other gun. He stated that he had examined the empty cartridge found at the scene, as well as a shell from the box in question, in order to see if the knurling around the cartridges was the same.

At the suggestion of Prosecutor Howard Fleeson, Mr. Gill described the appearance and purpose of the knurling around cartridges, which he said was put there with a special tool for the purpose of creasing the shell in such a way that would prevent the bullet from sliding down too far into the case, thus causing

335

it to fire improperly. Mr. Gill further stated that the knurling is done with a machine that employs a small tool that is made by hand. It must be of soft metal, he said, in order not to damage the shell metal, and therefore each knurling tool can be used on only about 200 shells before it is removed from the machine and discarded. He further stated that each tool leaves a mark that will have its own unique properties under microscopic examination, and that these characteristics change gradually from the first of the 200 shells to the last, so that by microscopic examination, their order of being knurled might be re-established, if all the shells were on hand for comparison.

Continuing with his expert testimony, Merle Gill offered two greatly enlarged photographs, which were shown to the jury at close range. Each of the photos, he said, was of two shells — on one picture the knurling of the murder cartridge appeared in the top half of the photo, with a shell from the box of cartridges matched against it in such a way as to definitively establish that they were made by the same knurling tool, and therefore belonged to a group of 200 shells (or four boxes of 50 shells each).

The other enlargement was of the same type — one half of the picture showed what he said was the cartridge found at the scene, and against it, the knurling marks of a shell of the same kind, picked at random from a supply in his own laboratory, which he said showed that the two knurlings did not match in any way.

When Mr. Gill was asked by the prosecutors what conclusion he was able to draw from his findings, he replied "... that they (the empty cartridge and shell represented as being from the box) were made by the same knurling tool."

In reply to a question from Defense Attorney Quinlan, Mr. Gill said that he had "… no idea where the other 150 shells might be." **Then, Mr. Gill was asked if he could tell any two cartridges apart.**

Merle Gill emphatically answered, "Yes."

Before being dismissed, Mr. Gill was questioned as to what his fee was for testifying in this case. "My charge," he said, "is $100 per day — and if I have to stay over (until) tomorrow it will cost another $100." Attorney Quinlan then remarked: "We'd better let him go."

A moment later Prosecutor Fleeson addressed the court: "May we dismiss this $100 per day witness?"

Judge Ray Beals adjourned court for the day at 5:20 p.m.

The case re-opened shortly after 9:00 a.m. on the following morning, Thursday, September 10th, with the state calling more of its witnesses. Roy Lee, a former Lyons hardware dealer, identified the defendant, Henry Mallory, as the man who had come into his store on, or about, March 10, 1936, and asked for a cartridge clip for a .380 caliber gun. Mr. Lee testified that he didn't carry shells or clips for .380 guns in stock because this was "… an unusual gun in this part of the country" He said that he was obliged to order the clip since he had none in stock, and that about three days later the purchaser called for it.

Ray "Red" Nodurft, acting Sheriff of the County at the time of the crime, took the stand and remained there for most of the morning session. He testified in detail to observing the body of the slain Night Marshal, Ben Wiggins, after being summoned to the scene of the crime by telephone. With the assistance of blueprint maps presented in evidence by the State, Sheriff Nodurft described the scene at, and near, the rear of the Williamson-Booker Furniture Store on the west side of the Square, where Mr. Wiggins' body was found.

An objection by the defense that "... Sheriff Nodurft's description of the appearance of the body was gruesome ..." was overruled by the court, and Sheriff Nodurft continued by saying that Mr. Wiggins was lying on his back, with his head facing north, and with his body parallel to, and close to the edge of the alley, nearest the store doors. He said that Mr. Wiggins was lying "face up," with his eyes partially open, and arms extended along the sides of his body, with palms upward. He described the officer's clothing, stating that he was wearing a leather jacket, and that his gun was still in its holster.

Sheriff Nordurft said that he then examined the body, and found two wounds on the right side of the forehead, and that he could detect no life in Mr. Wiggins' body.

Sheriff Nordurft followed with an identification of a number of objects as being those observed at, or near, the store's safe when he went there to telephone the other authorities. Among these articles, all of which were introduced as exhibits, was a metal screwdriver, a wooden-handled screwdriver, the combination dial of the safe, two tops of the safe's hinges, and a steel wrecking bar.

Sheriff Nordurft also testified of finding footprints of two men, starting at the alley and leading in a general northwesterly direction through the half block of open ground to Pioneer Street, directly to the back of the store. He said the tracks were 45 to 48 inches apart.

Asked whether he formed an opinion concerning them, Sheriff Nordurft replied, "Yes, the two birds that killed Ben Wiggins were running from the scene of the crime."

Testifying as to his presence when the defendants were arrested, Sheriff Nordurft said that they were placed under arrest at the cabin of Doris Stanley at the Snider Cabin Camp at the west edge of the city on the night following the crime. He testified that a gun had been found there in a dresser drawer and that Preston Paden had claimed ownership of the gun. Sheriff Nordurft further stated that the cabin bore the appearance of being the abode of the defendants.

As something of a surprise to the courtroom, came Sheriff Nordurft's description of a meeting and conversation between the defendant, Preston Paden, and Night Marshal Wiggins, which he stated took place about January 11th or 12th, 1936.

Defense attorneys entered strenuous objections to admission of a statement of an alleged conversation between them, but their objections were overruled by the court, and Sheriff Nordurft continued on with his testimony.

Sheriff Nordurft said that Ben Wiggins and Preston Paden had met in the office of the county jail, and that Wiggins had said to Paden, "If I had been there I would have shot you out from under that wheel." Sheriff Nordurft then quoted Paden as having replied, "Perhaps you will have that chance, Mr. Wiggins."

Author's note:

Although this incident was not further related in court, the particular conversation that was referred to, took place at the time of Preston's arrest for his "hit-and-run" accident in Lyons, Kansas.

Chapter 44: The Paden-Mallory Trial — Day 3

Interest in the Wiggins Murder Trial intensified after the testimony given on the first two days of the trial. On Friday, September 11, 1936, the courtroom was filled by 8:15 a.m. as interest in this case was starting to skyrocket, and people wanted to arrive early in order to be certain of getting seats. Scores of people, unable to get into the courtroom, stood outside in the hallway — many of whom peered through the courtroom doors.

Since the defense attorneys protested that the jurors were allowed to go to their respective homes on the night of September 9th, the jurors were kept together on the night of September 10th, in the custody of Bailiff Charles Ward. They were taken to a hotel in Little River, Kansas, because lodging could not be found for them in Lyons, Kansas.

Witnesses for the State were expected to consume most, if not all, of the time this day. The greatest interest of the attending public was fast becoming the answer to the question, "What will the defense present?"

Dr. L. J. Beyer had testified the previous day in describing the condition of Ben Wiggins' body before and during his autopsy. After relating that he, along with Dr. R. Leonard and Coroner Louis Booker, conducted the autopsy, he concluded that in his professional opinion, Night Marshal Ben Wiggins had been dead for at least 6 or 7 hours prior to the start of the autopsy which was initiated at about 9:00 a.m. on the morning of March 30th. He also stated that, in his opinion, the gunshot wound had been the actual cause of death and that the wound on the forehead would not have, in itself, been fatal.

Prosecutor Howard Fleeson handed Dr. Beyer the .45 caliber gun that allegedly had been the property of Preston Paden, and asked the physician whether the butt of the gun might have caused such a wound, had the weapon been used as a club. The defense objected to this question, and the objection was sustained by the court.

Rice County Attorney for the Prosecution, Ed Wahl, asked the witness if, in his professional opinion, he had any idea what sort of a weapon might have caused the head wound, and Dr. Beyer replied, "I think it was caused by a gun."

The Coroner, Louis Booker, was then summoned to the stand. He described his first view of the deceased body after having been called to the scene a few minutes after it had been found by Nelie Corland, a dishwasher at the nearby Blue Front Café. Mr. Booker also expressed that, in his opinion, the bullet had been the actual cause of Night Marshal Wiggins' death.

At this juncture, several articles of clothing worn by the slain officer on the night of the murder were placed into evidence. They included the officer's leather jacket, which showed no bullet holes, his bloodstained shirt with a bullet hole at the neck, and the bloodstained underwear with a bullet hole at the back where the bullet came out through the undergarment but failed to break through the back of the shirt next to it. These bullet holes were all pointed out by Mr. Booker to the jury.

Mr. Booker then described the conditions around the Williamson-Booker Furniture Store safe which, he said, gave evidence of an attempted burglary, and related the manner of closing and fastening the rear doors of his establishment. He said that the doors had been barred from the inside but that the fastening was so loose that the doors might have been opened by slipping the bars, by reaching through with some object from the outside.

Mr. Booker continued by stating that he had known both of the defendants for several months prior to the murder, and that they had both been in his store several times for various purchases.

Next on the stand was A. P. Keeling, a Kansas State Highway Patrolman, who was shown the .45 caliber revolver. Replying to questions put by the prosecution, he said that he had obtained the revolver at the cabin of Doris Stanley, the location where, and the time when, he had arrested Paden and Mallory. He added that Paden had claimed ownership of the gun at that time. Patrolman Keeling was then asked if he could ascertain as to where the gun came from, and he replied that he had found it in a dresser drawer at the Stanley cabin.

Officer Keeling was then dismissed and M. L. Woolsey of Picher, Oklahoma, was summoned as the next witness. He identified the gun as one that he had formerly owned, and said he had sold it to a Mr. Tobe Renick, also of Picher.

Tobe Renick was called to the stand as the next witness. He, too, identified the weapon, and the defense started a series of objections to every part of his testimony, with the judge replying he would hear what the witness had to say and then rule as to whether the testimony would be stricken. The protested testimony was that Renick had loaned the gun to Paden between December, 1935, and January, 1936. Mr. Renick stated that Paden had remarked that it "… looks like a punch board gun …" and that he had replied that it was all he had and that he was welcome to borrow it if he liked. Mr. Renick said that he handed Paden the gun and he (Paden) took it out to his car to show another person in the car. He related the ensuing conversation between Paden and the other man, saying Paden had asked, "Which one do you want?" And the other man replied, "I'll take the big one."

Defense Attorney Quinlan moved that all of the testimony of the two Oklahoma men be stricken from the record, and the court sustained him in part, but allowed the portion containing the conversation between Paden and the other man (in the car) to stand.

Mrs. Minnie Patterson, who said she lived a half a block north of the murder scene, testified that she was unable to sleep on the night of the murder and heard a gunshot from the direction of the murder scene at approximately 1:20 a.m. She said the shot rang out clearly and she was sure that it was not from the backfiring of a car.

Lucille Scotton was the State's next witness. She testified that she was employed by Doris Stanley at the time of the crime, and was well acquainted with the two defendants. She said that she also could describe Doris Stanley's car, a black Plymouth Coach, and had seen Paden drive it many times. Replying to questions by the prosecution, Miss Scotton related that on the night of the murder she had been riding around town in the company of her sister, Mary Scotton, and Mary's friend, a man named J. R. Castetter. She also stated that she had seen Doris Stanley's car twice during the evening, the first time at about 10:00 p.m., parked just south of the Conoco filling station on Pioneer Street, half a block west of the scene of the murder. She said she next saw it at the cabin of Doris Stanley, about 11:30 p.m. on that same evening. She further testified that she had again seen the car about an hour later, still at the Stanley cabin, after she had been taken to her own cabin in the same camp. She said that she saw the car at the time when she started to walk over to the Stanley cabin, then changed her mind when she observed that there was no light on in the cabin.

An effort by the State to wring from Lucille Scotton the statement that Paden resided at the Stanley cabin did not succeed. She replied she did not know in which cabin Paden was living.

Mary Scotton, sister of Lucille, was then put on the witness stand. She stated that she was living in Lyons, Kansas, but working in Chase, Kansas, at the time of the murder, and that she knew both defendants. She further testified that J. R. Castetter called for her where she roomed, at 122 North Pioneer Street in Lyons, Kansas, about 9:00 p.m. on the night of the murder. She said they went to the Snider Cabin Camp to pick up Lucille, and then the three of them went for a ride. She told the court of seeing the Stanley car parked just south of the Conoco Station, after which, she said, they went to a show, and afterward saw the same car at the Conoco Station again at about 10:45 p.m. She said that there was a comment among them about the car at that time — just a passing comment. She identified the car by its license number, and quoted this number as being "48-343."

Mary Scotton then said she saw the car a third time that night — a little after 11:00 p.m. — when they took Lucille home, at which time she said it was parked at the Doris Stanley cabin. She testified that she and Mr. Castetter remained at the cabin camp only an additional 15 or 20 minutes, prior to driving out. She said neither she nor Mr. Castetter entered Lucille's cabin.

On cross examination, Mary Scotton testified that they had arrived at the camp about 11:15 p.m., and that she reached her home at about 11:45 p.m.

The next witness, J. R. Castetter, a friend of Mary Scotton, told a similar story to that related by the girls about riding around that night and seeing the Stanley car parked near the Conoco Filling Station.

Mr. Castetter added that, after he took Mary home — which time he estimated to be about 1:00 a.m. — he then drove around the block enroute to his home, and again saw what he believed to be the same car in question, parked at about the same place as he had seen it before. He declined to say positively that it was the same car but said that he believed it was.

Homer Sharpe, the County Treasurer, was summoned with auto license records to show that the tag number of the Doris Stanley car was, indeed, "48-343." He was not cross-examined.

Mrs. J. R. Scott of Oil Hill, Kansas, testified that on the night in question she occupied a cabin immediately south to that of Doris Stanley. Mrs. Scott testified that she had some teeth pulled that day and consequently was unable to sleep well that night. She added that she heard a car, or cars, come and go from between the cabins several times during the night. She was not cross-examined.

Mrs. Claude McCoy of McPherson, Kansas, testified that prior to her marriage she had several dates with Preston Paden in McPherson in July of 1935. She was allowed to testify, over

346

objections of the defense, that Paden had been in the habit of carrying a gun at that time. She was shown two pistols, a large one and a small one, and asked to say which gun most resembled Paden's gun. She indicated that Paden's was the smaller weapon of the two. She said that she saw the gun only twice, once when they were out riding, and another time at a "Chicken Inn" when Paden "pulled it."

Earl Phillips, Manager of the Champlin Filling Station at Great Bend, Kansas, was put on the stand and identified two screwdrivers — allegedly found at the scene of the crime — as having been his property by showing, as evidence, the monograms he had etched on them with an electric needle as a means of identification. He said that he had put these markings on the tools about three months prior to the time of the crime. He added that he was acquainted with both Mallory and Paden and that the two defendants had been in the station at various times.

He said that one of their visits was between March 7 and March 10, 1936. He further stated that he first became aware that one of his tools was missing about a week later, on March 18th, but he had no recollection as to when the other tool disappeared from his station.

Phillips said he saw Paden at his station about three times, once accompanied by Mallory, at which time "Curly" Griffin of Great Bend was also with them.

On cross examination by Defense Attorney Holland, Mr. Phillips testified that the station was at a busy corner and that many motorists stopped by there.

Victor Horning, also an employee of the Champlin Filling Station, next took the stand and positively identified the burglary tools. He also identified Mallory as having been in the station in March of 1936, and said that during one particular week, Mallory was there about four or five times. He further stated that Mallory once was in the company of "Curly" Griffin and another man who he could not identify.

Horning testified that on one occasion Mallory brought a car to the Champlin Filling Station for service because something was "loose" on the car. The car was then taken into the grease room where it was jacked up. This was the room that contained the station's rack of tools. Horning said that he didn't remain in the room all of the time that the car's owner was looking at the car. On cross examination, he, too, admitted that there were many persons who "came and went" at the station.

T. E. Roberts of Newton, Kansas, an employee with the Sharpe Motor Company, testified to having telephone conversations with Mallory several times prior to March 31st, with reference to the purchase of a new car, and said that Mallory had been told very clearly that he must have the down payment on the car when he called for the car. He stated that the estimated down payment was 33% of the selling price of $700. He said Mallory came there on March 31st, which was the first time he had met him in person, and that he took Mallory to a local finance company, but Mallory didn't get the car. Mr. Roberts was not allowed to answer this question as to why Mallory didn't get the car because of objections by the defense which were sustained by the court.

J. C. Suderman, of the Newton Finance Company, told of talking to Mallory about the car at his office on March 31st. He quoted Mallory as saying he couldn't make the down payment at that time but would be back on the next pay day, which Mallory said would be April 18th. Suderman further stated that Mallory told him he was employed by the Tri-State Drilling Company.

The most sensational incident of the trial thus far came when Leonard Booker, an inmate of the Kansas State Industrial Reformatory (KSIR) at Hutchinson, Kansas, was brought into court and asked to take the oath. He held up his right hand, but after the oath was read, he said, "I will not swear to tell the truth." Turning to Judge Beals, he said, "I refuse to testify in this case."

Disregarding Leonard Booker's comment, Judge Beals ordered him to the stand to be questioned. Booker was asked by the prosecution if he was working in his father's store, the Williamson-Booker Furniture Store, in February, and the first part of March, 1936. Booker stated that he was working there at the time, and that he knew both defendants. When he was asked if he carried a key to the store, he again answered in the affirmative.

Attorneys for the two sides were at loggerheads at this juncture over the State's efforts to draw a statement from Leonard Booker. Prosecutor Howard Fleeson asked him point blank whether he ever had a conversation with Paden in which Paden had propositioned him with regard to his father's store. On that point, Booker said, "I refuse to answer."

The court ruled that there was no way of compelling him to answer, and he was finally dismissed from the stand.

Chapter 45: The Paden-Mallory Trial — Days 4 & 5

At the opening of the Saturday afternoon session of District Court, in which Preston LeRoy Paden and Henry Mallory were being tried for the murder of Night Marshal Ben Wiggins, the courtroom was again packed with both the interested and the curious. The overflow crowd, standing in the lobby, was the largest to show up to date.

Sheriff Art Estabrook, who had been on the witness stand when court recessed for the dinner hour on Friday night, resumed his testimony as court convened.

The officer's testimony was largely based on the results of his investigation of the footprints found leading westward, across the vacant lot, from the scene of the crime. He said that there were two sets of tracks a few feet apart and that the individual steps were over 40 inches apart. Sheriff Estabrook also testified that the slain officer's gun was in its holster when he first examined the body, and that his "sap" was still in a pocket. He then explained that a sap is the same as a "blackjack," a weapon of heavy weight padded with leather, used in trying to knock people senseless.

On cross-examination, Sheriff Estabrook told of observing a third set of tracks, closer to the Scheib residence just south of the vacant lot. He said this set of tracks was not very plain. He was questioned at length about the different footprints by Defense Attorney Clifford Holland.

J. A. Applegate of Oklahoma City, a drug sundry salesman, took the stand for a minute, testifying to having seen Mallory at the Champlin Filling Station in Great Bend, Kansas, on

March 12, 1936. He said that he had been acquainted with Mallory for some time, having known him previously in Blackwell, Oklahoma.

N. S. Wiggins, Superintendent of the Kansas State Industrial Reformatory (KSIR), was next placed on the stand, and testified regarding his viewing of the footprints in the vacant lot, and of the position of the empty cartridge found on the floor of the rear room of the furniture store. At the suggestion of Prosecutor Fleeson, Mr. Wiggins also testified as to the circumstances surrounding Roy Lee's identification of Mallory at the county jail as the man to whom he had sold an ammunition clip for a .380 caliber gun. He said that Mr. Roy Lee was taken upstairs at the jail to where the prisoners were kept, and he viewed all of the 8 to 10 prisoners there.

L. A. Holloway, the Clerk of the District Court, then took the stand. He said that he had been present at the time that Paden and Mallory were arrested, and testified that he had heard a conversation between Paden and Patrolman A. P. Keeling in regard to the keys to Doris Stanley's car. Mr. Holloway quoted Officer Keeling as asking Paden whether there were two sets of keys to the car, and he said that Paden replied in the negative, stating that there was only one set of keys and that he had them in his possession.

The cross-examination of this witness was confined by the court to the one point in question — the conversation about the keys. Defense Attorney Quinlan asked him whether Paden had told Patrolman Keeling where he stayed on the night of March 29th. The State objected and the objection was sustained by the court.

Officer Keeling was then recalled to the witness stand. Questions were put to him by the prosecution relative to his knowledge of firearms. He testified that the .380 or .38 caliber gun has more "knockdown" power and less penetration than the smaller .32 caliber gun. When Officer Keeling was asked for his professional opinion regarding the distance from the gun to Officer Wiggins' body when the shot was fired, he stated that he thought it was about 6 inches or less.

Officer Keeling told of several conversations he had with Mallory, and quoted Mallory as telling him that he had never bought any .380 shells in one conversation, and in another conversation he said that he had bought such shells. He also quoted Mallory as saying he had not purchased an ammunition clip for a .380 gun.

Concerning the questioning of the defendants at Great Bend, Kansas, shortly after their arrest, Officer Keeling stated that Mallory told him that on the night of the murder, March 29th, he had arrived in Lyons, Kansas, between 5:00 p.m. and 6:00 p.m. that evening; he had gone to the Snider Cabin Camp where he took a bath; then placed a call to Newton, Kansas; and then had gone uptown for supper. Upon his return to the cabin camp, he went to bed in his cabin between 8:00 p.m. and 9:00 p.m. At least, that was the story that Officer Keeling said that Mallory told him.

Then the officer related that Mallory told him that Preston Paden had come in between 11:00 p.m. and 11:30 p.m. on that same night, and had gone to bed in the same cabin as Mallory, and remained there for the rest of the night.

Officer Keeling then told of questioning Paden along similar lines. He said that Paden reported that he was in Cabin No. 9

on the morning of March 30th. He also quoted Paden as saying that he had talked to George Snider that night, had found Doris Stanley's cabin locked, and had then gone to Cabin No. 9 and had gone to bed, and that no one else had seen him during the night.

In the cross-examination of Officer Keeling by Attorney Quinlan, there followed several minutes of repartee and verbal conflict between the two that had the courtroom crowd breathless when it was not otherwise chuckling. Attorney Quinlan launched an attack against the patrolman, which was clearly intended to show Officer Keeling had arrested Paden and Mallory without following proper procedure as to warrants, and had held both suspects for too long a time without the benefit of legal counsel.

Officer Keeling, in his response, contended that he did not know that he was obliged to tell them they were entitled to counsel, and repeated the contention several times while the attorney attempted to elicit a confession from him that he knew he had acted improperly.

Asked directly if he had a warrant when he arrested the two, Officer Keeling replied, "Only a search warrant."

A moment later, while being questioned along related lines, Officer Keeling volunteered: "It might help you if I said these men were arrested for investigation."

"You can help me by just answering my questions," Attorney Quinlan retorted.

There was laughter in the courtroom and Judge Beals instructed the Bailiff to keep order, even if obliged to remove those who made undue commotion.

Again there was a clash between the witness and the attorney when Officer Keeling was asked to supply a date, and he replied that the attorney could "… get it off the warrant."

"You can get it off the warrant," Quinlan snapped.

Officer Keeling said he did not have the warrant with him.

Judge Beals ended the argument by reaching for the files in that case, and looked up the point in question by himself.

The heated questions and answers continued to fly as the defense attorney questioned the officer on one occasion about taking Mallory to the Kansas State Industrial Reformatory at Hutchinson, Kansas, for a prolonged period of questioning.

Officer Keeling admitted that Mallory had been questioned at intervals over a period of about 48 hours. When asked whether Mallory had had any sleep during that time, Officer Keeling replied: "I don't know. I wasn't there all the time."

Officer Keeling acknowledged that Mallory had been in a room, being questioned when he — Officer Keeling — had gone to bed late one night, and that Mallory was in the same room as before when Officer Keeling awoke the next morning, with Mallory still in the presence of officers. But Officer Keeling said that the defendant appeared to be in good condition, both physically and mentally.

The defense attorney ended his cross-examination with the question: "Have you ever been arrested?"

"No Sir," Officer Keeling replied.

"Never in your life?" Attorney Quinlan repeated.

"No Sir!" was the emphatic answer.

Lead Prosecutor Fleeson took over and asked Officer Keeling whether the defendant, Mallory, had always maintained that he stayed in Cabin No. 9 on the night of the crime. The patrolman said he had.

"Was he given food and water during the questioning?" the witness was asked, and the reply was in the affirmative.

Officer Keeling also testified that Mallory had told him that he had been employed tending bar for Doris Stanley during the preceding six months.

Attorney Quinlan questioned him further, asking whether Mallory had also told him that during the year prior to that he had worked as a pumper and earned $1,700.

Officer Keeling said he could recall no such statement, but could not say definitely without looking at his notes on the case. He was allowed to obtain his notes from the prosecutor's table, and after looking them over said he could find no notation of a statement about the amount of money Mallory said he had earned the previous year.

Attorney Quinlan then addressed the court, asking that a copy of Mallory's statement, as taken while he was being held at Great Bend, Kansas, be given to the defendant by the State.

Judge Beals appealed to the State to give him a copy through courtesy, but said he would not order that such be done.

George Snider was the next, and last, witness on the stand during the afternoon.

Snider testified that on the night of March 29th, he had first talked to Mallory about 9:30 p.m., when Mallory called to him asking him if he would open up the office so that he might place a telephone call. He said he remained at the office with Mallory for about 10 or 15 minutes, and that after the telephone call, Mallory walked south into the camp and Snider returned to his basement living quarters.

Snider further testified that he saw Mallory later that night about 11:00 p.m. when Mallory asked Snider if he had any cabins available. Snider said that he told Mallory, "No. 9 is open," and that Mallory paid him $1.00 for it and asked him whether he should sign for it.

Snider said he told Mallory that the record book was in the basement and that if it was satisfactory he, Snider, would sign for him, and that Mallory had agreed.

Snider said he returned to the book and, being unable to spell "Mallory," wrote "Preston Ray" in the book since Mallory had said Preston was to spend the night there also. He said he had written it "Preston Ray" because he did not know Preston's last name.

Asked whether he had seen Preston that night, Snider replied that he had heard his voice, about 9:00 p.m., when Preston called to him asking whether there was hot water.

Snider then replied to questions put by the State as to his conversations the next morning. He said his wife was washing and asked him to go to Cabin No. 9 and get the sheets. He said that when he went in to the cabin at about 8:00 a.m., he saw that the bed was in good order and thought it was just like his wife had made it the day before. So he returned and told her she wouldn't have to wash those sheets.

Upon cross-examination, Snider was asked by Attorney Quinlan what he had written opposite Preston's name in the register, and was told it was "Ellinwood, Kansas," and "2 p.m."

Attorney Quinlan then demanded, "Did they (meaning the authorities) ask you to say it was 2 p.m.?"

Snider replied, "They asked me if I was sure that I hadn't made a mistake. That it wasn't 2 a.m. (I had meant), and I said it wasn't. And that if I made a mistake, and had to pay a penalty, I would."

Snider further testified that he did not know whether Doris Stanley's car was there that night. Neither did he know whether the defendants were in the cabin they rented from him, and if so, at what time they left it.

Attorney Fleeson questioned Snider again. "Has your wife a particular way of making up the beds?"

"Yes," Snider answered. Then he related how she folded down the top sheet, and how she placed the pillows.

"Were there any wrinkles in the sheets when you looked at them the next morning," he was asked.

"I didn't get down and examine them with a magnifying glass," he said. "But I didn't see any."

Lead Prosecutor Fleeson asked the witness to relate just what it was that the authorities had said to him in regard to the time that he wrote in the record book.

George Snider answered by stating, "They wanted me to be positive (as to) what time it was (when) they came in."

Shortly after the end of Mr. Snider's testimony, the court adjourned for the day.

The murder trial of Preston LeRoy Paden and Henry Mallory, which had occupied half of the previous week in District Court, convened again on Monday, September 14, 1936.

A.P. Keeling, the Kansas State Highway Patrolman, was again placed on the stand by the State as the morning session opened. Mr. Keeling had testified several times before and was called back only to say that Mallory, when being questioned over a long period of time at the Kansas State Industrial Reformatory, was kept in the residence quarters of the Reformatory Superintendent, and was further questioned as to what would happen to a .380 caliber shell when a gun of that size is fired. Patrolman Keeling answered that the shell would automatically be ejected by the gun.

On cross-examination, Patrolman Keeling was asked whether there were one or two rooms in the Doris Stanley cabin where the defendants were arrested, and he replied that there were two. Asked whether there was a bed in each room, Keeling responded by saying that there was a large bed in one room and a small bed in the other room.

The State announced that it rested its case at 9:30 a.m.

Ivan L. Stone was the first witness called by the defense. He qualified as an expert in safe repairing, and said he had been called to the Williamson-Booker Furniture Store the morning following the crime, and described what he had found regarding the condition of the safe. He testified that the manner of the attempt at opening the safe was similar to the manner in which attempts had been made on several other safes in that vicinity subsequent to the arrest of the defendants.

In his cross-examination of Mr. Stone, the Prosecutor, Howard Fleeson asked if the manner that was used in opening the safe was that of a novice. Mr. Stone replied in the affirmative. Mr. Fleeson then asked the witness whether a man who had once tried it that way and failed, might attempt the same method again, but the question was objected to by the defense and the objection was sustained by the court.

The second and last witness for the defense was A. B. Martin of the George Lantz Clothing Store. Mr. Martin brought with him a device for measuring feet to determine shoe sizes. In open court, both defendants were brought forward and had their right shoes removed. The witness measured their feet and announced their shoe sizes as 8-A for Mallory and 5-A for Paden. There was no cross-examination and it was evident that the intention of the defense attorneys was to show that the shoe sizes, as determined in court, were not in agreement with the shoe sizes of the footprints found leading away from the scene of the crime, as described by witnesses for the State.

Then the defense announced that it rested its case at 10:10 a.m.

Judge Ray Beals then read the court's instructions in the case to the jury.

Before the attorneys began their final arguments, the court ruled that each side may not exceed a 3 hour time limit for this purpose. If the entire time was used by both sides, that might prevent the case going to the jury before late afternoon.

County Attorney for the Prosecution, Ed Wahl, used only about 30 minutes of his time before noon, with court recessing at 11:50 a.m., and set to resume at 1:00 p.m.

In his opening remarks, Prosecutor Wahl outlined the state's testimony in a more related and coordinated fashion than it had been given by the witnesses, because of the necessity of using the witnesses in a somewhat haphazard order and unconnected manner.

Up to the time of the noon recess, Prosecutor Wahl had only emphasized one point of the testimony, namely, a contention that the renting of Cabin No. 9 was for the sole purpose of the defendants attempting to create an alibi in advance.

Continuing his argument after court reconvened after the lunch hour, Prosecutor Wahl gave a further reminder of certain points in the evidence in a quiet and dignified tone and stated the following before turning his remaining time over to the Lead Prosecutor, Howard Fleeson: *"My years of experience do not compare with those of the other attorneys in this case, and consequently you have heard no oratory in my remarks."*

In opening his argument, Lead Prosecutor Fleeson thanked the jury for the close attention it had given to the testimony; he thanked the court for its expected impartiality; and he thanked the defense for its fairness during the trial.

Prosecutor Fleeson then pointed to the testimony of witnesses for the State who had told of overhearing a conversation of the defendants relative to a "big and a little gun," went into the matter of the shoe measurements to say that witnesses for the State had, in effect, described the sizes, and discussed the statement of a defense witness regarding the manner in which amateurs are apt to try to enter safes.

"There is only one issue in this case," Prosecutor Fleeson **stated emphatically, "and that is whether the defendants are guilty (of first-degree murder). There is no halfway point such as a second-degree murder conviction would indicate. They are either guilty of first-degree murder or not guilty at all."**

Acknowledging that the case was made up largely of circumstantial evidence, Prosecutor Fleeson added: *"Circumstantial evidence is often the most valuable kind. A criminal does not summon witnesses, ordinarily, when he's about to commit a crime."*

Prosecutor Fleeson then presented to the jury his interpretation of a number of portions of the testimony. He called attention to the parked car, the ammunition purchase and testimony of the ballistics expert, the identification of the stolen tools and their unique monogram, and the failure of Mallory to make the initial payment on a new car the day after the crime, as he had been quoted as saying he would be able to do.

Prosecutor Fleeson attributed the failure of the State to offer definitive fingerprint evidence to the fact that the defendants were "smart enough to wear gloves." And the reason for the unoccupied Cabin No. 9, he reasoned, was due to the fact the defendants spent the rest of the night outside somewhere looking for a good hiding place for the murder weapon — a weapon which was never found.

He called attention to the testimony of Patrolman A. P. Keeling, saying that the officer had been most fair, even to the point of quoting the defendants in their own behalf and reporting the confession of only one incriminating admission by them — the acknowledgment of Mallory that he had purchased some .380 caliber shells.

During a ten minute recess for the jury, Defense Attorney Quinlan entered objections to several points in the Prosecutor's (Howard Fleeson) remarks, namely: **Prosecutor Fleeson's statement that Doris Stanley did not dare take the stand to**

**testify regarding possession of the keys to her car; a state-
ment that he would be interested to learn (from the defense)
where the defendants spent the night, following the crime;
a statement that no person appeared to contradict the fact
that they were not in Cabin No. 9; that Patrolman Keeling
"knew" the defendants were guilty when he arrested them;
and that it was up to the defendants to tell the police where
the gun was hidden.**

The court sustained the objection as to Doris Stanley's failure
to testify and that Keeling **"knew"** of their guilt, but promptly
overruled a motion by Attorney Quinlan that a mistrial be
declared because of the statements. Upon their return, the jury
was instructed by the court to disregard the points on which the
defense had been sustained.

Attorney Cliff Holland commanded the floor to sound the
opening volley for the defense. He charged that both he and the
jury were confronted by a "fearful responsibility" and reminded
the jurors of their oath to try the case from the evidence presented only. Attorney Holland then said, *"The future lives of this
19 year old boy and this other young man are in your hands. The
attorneys have done their best by them and by you and to be fair
with the State of Kansas. We know innocent men have been hung
or put in prison. We are not asking for your sympathy, but if they
have not been proven guilty they should walk free."*

Attorney Holland characterized the incident of the identification of a "small gun" by Mrs. Claude McCoy, a former girlfriend
of Paden, as an attempt to prejudice the jury. He added that,
by law, the defendants are not bound or required to prove their
innocence.

363

"You don't want to send men to the scaffold on doubtful evidence," Attorney Holland pleaded. *"Ben Wiggins, himself, would not want it that way. He would not ask that such small, unrelated circumstances be used to send men to their death."*

"Every circumstance in this testimony," Attorney Holland contended, *"could be proven against at least two or three other people."*

Referring to the testimony that the two sets of footprints were of uniform stride, Attorney Holland reasoned: *"Would a tall and a short man (such as the two defendants) take such a uniform stride in their flight?"*

Then Attorney Holland pointed to a number of alleged weaknesses and inconsistencies in the State's testimony. He charged a lack of merit to a number of statements, such as J. R. Castetter's lack of being positive in identifying the car he saw parked near the murder scene; discrepancies in the time set by Mr. Castetter and Mary Scotten and her sister, Lucille Scotten; an alleged admission of "The Third Degree" (48-hour questioning period) given to Mallory; differences in testimony regarding the dates of sale of shells given by witness Lloyd Benefiel at the preliminary hearing and again at this trial; as well as the testimony of Mrs. Patterson that she heard the shot but saw no one near where the sound originated. In addition, Attorney Holland listed a few other minor points of his stated perceived inconsistencies in testimony.

Attorney Holland declared that, *"The State has been proving our case by acknowledging that the defendants told questioning officers where they had spent that night, and had stuck to that story even in the face of long (hours of) questioning."*

Attorney Holland used his closing argument as an opportunity to present a contention upon which he had been laboring throughout the trial in the cross-examination phase of witnesses. Each witness testifying as to the footprints was questioned regarding one specific print that stepped into some hedge brush or a hedge limb lying on the ground. In his argument, Attorney Holland argued that the officers should have made a minute inspection of this brush which, he said, must have caught at least a microscopic bit of clothing on its thorns that should have been subjected to the same meticulous examination to which the empty cartridge was put.

Attorney Holland characterized it as something very peculiar that one of the two screwdrivers found at the burglary scene had not even been noticed — let alone picked up — until several days later. He was implying that police may have planted evidence.

"This is a peculiar case," Attorney Holland remarked. *"The State would have you believe their witnesses on some points, but not on others. The State violated the rights of Defendant Mallory by taking him to the Kansas State Industrial Reformatory at Hutchinson, Kansas, for questioning without allowing him counsel or having a commitment for him to the reformatory."*

In an objection by the State to a remark by Attorney Holland, *"... the defendant's bond had been set at only $10,000 by the Justice of the Peace ... "* was sustained by the court as not having been introduced in the trial.

Defense Attorney Holland was then followed by the Lead Defense Attorney in the trial, Attorney L. E. Quinlan.

"I am sorry to say," Mr. Quinlan began, *"that I am going to have to make some remarks about some folks connected with this case."*

Then Attorney Quinlan launched into a severe criticism of the prosecution and a number of its witnesses. *"There has been a deliberate attempt to introduce improper material — the worst such example I have ever heard in 20 years of practicing law,"* he declared. *"It is an insult to the intelligence of you jurors to ask you to convict upon the evidence that has been offered."*

"The prosecution says they have been fair," he said. *"The best way to show a man you are being fair with him, is to act that way."*

He remarked about the question of reasonable doubt on the matter of the burglary tools, and deplored the sort of testimony given by the witnesses from Oklahoma brought here *"... with your money and mine."*

After flaying Patrolman Keeling for alleged unfair tactics in the case, Attorney Quinlan charged the State with being lax in not making plaster impressions of the footprints found at the scene, or at least the State should have made an attempt to match the tracks made on the ground with the feet of the defendants after they had been arrested.

Some of the same points criticized by Defense Attorney Holland were reaffirmed and pointed out by Lead Defense Attorney Quinlan, particularly the gun identification by Mrs. Claude McCoy, Mr. Castetter's apparent contradictions, and Mrs. Patterson's testimony that she saw nothing unusual in the direction of the shot.

Defense Attorney Quinlan said that the cost of prosecuting a case on such evidence was a shame. He said that comparisons offered by Ballistics Expert, Merle Gill, presented a type of evidence upon which juries do not convict. Furthermore, he declared that it was not logical to think that if the defendants had carried two guns to the crime scene, that they would have thrown away the smaller gun and kept the larger gun, especially where it could be easily located.

Defense Attorney Quinlan insisted that *"This case is built on suspicion alone. Where were you, or you, or you, on the night of March 29th?,"* he asked. *"Probably not one of you could tell us. There has not been one positive statement made by the prosecution in this case. You can't conscientiously say the State has proved beyond a reasonable doubt that these men are guilty."*

In rebuttal, Lead Prosecutor Howard Fleeson said: *"I have practiced law only about 15 years, but in that time I have observed that when an attorney has a losing case, he tries the attorney on the other side, for he has nothing else to talk about."*

"The question in this case," Prosecutor Fleeson continued, *"is not that of my fairness, but the guilt of these defendants. I warn you that if they are acquitted, it may mean that they will go out in life to do the same thing again."*

He then opened a discourse in which he presented an explanation for the discrepancy in the time element of seeing the defendants' car, as testified to by three witnesses, by saying that in two instances the Scotten sisters were simply mistaken as to the correct time. Defense Attorney Quinlan then scoffed at Mary Scotten's statement that Mr. Castetter had taken her, his date, directly home after delivering Lucille to her abode, as being unnatural. *"Of course,"* Prosecutor Fleeson said, *"Mary was his date, and not until Lucille had been left at home, did they have any time alone together that evening. Naturally they went for a ride first."*

As to Mr. Castetter's identification of the car he had seen around 1:00 a.m., Prosecutor Fleeson called attention to the fact that all three had seen it and remarked about it earlier in the evening as being sufficient proof that he would be able to properly identify it a short time later.

Prosecutor Fleeson continued, *"Attorney Holland advises you that Defendant Paden is only 19 years old. What difference does that make? You know by reading the papers that many of our outlaws today are young men. Does that count in their defense?"*

Prosecutor Fleeson met a defense challenge on the length of the strides in the two sets of footprints being of the same measurement, by insisting that, of course, they were substantially the same length because the two men were running together. He said that the footprints had not been preserved because they were too soft for plaster impressions, as stated in the testimony.

Regarding the matter of Mallory's *"50-hour questioning,"* Prosecutor Fleeson termed this merely a *"smoke screen by the defense to cloud the issue."*

Mrs. Patterson's failure to observe anything other than the shot she heard was attributed by Prosecutor Fleeson to her own testimony that *"she was not looking for anyone, nor was she thinking there was murder in the area, but in fact was just gazing more down the highway and into the alley."*

As to the defense plea that the jurors themselves might not be able to say where they were on the night of March 29, Prosecutor Fleeson reasoned: *"If you had been asked on April 1st or 2nd, where you were on that night, you could have known. You might not have known exactly what hour you retired, but you certainly would have remembered where you spent the night, and you would have told the truth about it, especially if faced with the gravity of a serious charge."*

"The defense has said," Prosecutor Fleeson continued, *"that no State witness has been positive. What about the statement of George Snider that the bed in Cabin No. 9 had not been slept in? What about the identification of the filling station's tools? What about the positiveness of the falsehood about when the defendants went to bed, the positiveness in the identification of the car, the tracks leading to the car and away from the crime, the bullet and the cartridge, the knurling on the murder shell? Mallory's ordering a new car and not being able to pay for it when the time came, and his falsehood in saying he worked for the Tri-State Drilling Company?"*

"We have clinched the fact," Prosecutor Fleeson said, *"that there was only one set of keys to the car, that the tracks ran toward that car, that the burglar tools came from a place frequented by the defendants, that they had plenty of opportunity to steal these tools, and that the .45 caliber gun did not come from a punch board, as Paden said."*

Prosecutor Fleeson then dramatically enacted his personal interpretation as to what had happened as Ben Wiggins was slain on the night of March 29th, or early on the morning of March 30th. In this scene, he contended that Paden had been standing guard at the door, in possession of the .380 gun, and that Night Marshal Ben Wiggins, while walking through the alley, observed that the door was ajar. *"As he started to look in,"* Prosecutor Fleeson related, *"Paden struck him on the head with his gun, intending (only) to knock him out until he and Mallory, who was inside working on the safe, might be able to get away. But Officer Wiggins, not badly injured, started to get to his feet, and it was then that Paden put the gun against the officer's body and fired the fatal shot. Calling to Mallory, they fled the scene."*

Prosecutor Fleeson concluded by stating, *"These who killed must stand before the bar of justice. We have proven by circumstantial evidence, beyond all reasonable doubt, that these men are guilty. Not one bit of this evidence is sufficient proof, but taken all together they are. The State has made its case. It is now up to you citizens, with a duty to perform."*

Chapter 46: The Paden-Mallory Trial Verdict

In a swift and decisive manner, the murder of Ben Wiggins, a popular Lyons, Kansas, Night Marshal, was avenged on Monday night, September 14, 1936.

All twelve male jurors in the case filed out of their room at 10:30 p.m. to announce their verdict — guilty of first-degree murder against each of the defendants, Preston LeRoy Paden and Henry Mallory, and further, their recommendation that both be incarcerated for the remainder of their lives.

It was a hard-won victory for the police officers and the State's Attorneys. Days, weeks, and months of tedious effort had marked their determined efforts to bring the murderers of the beloved peace officer to justice.

A. P. Keeling of the Kansas State Highway Patrol; Sheriff Art Estabrook of Rice County, a special investigator on the case; other members of the Kansas State Highway Patrol, as well as other county officers and other authorities in many Kansas localities, all had worked painstakingly long and hard hours to accomplish the end result in the interests of justice and on behalf of civilized society everywhere.

Lead Prosecutor Howard Fleeson, County Attorney Ed Wahl, and Assistant Prosecutor, Carl Tebbe, had delivered this vast array of evidence — circumstantial though most of it was — to the court and jury in a most powerful way. The jury's speedy agreement was their assurance that the effort of these three men had been successful.

There was another side to this story — that of the Defense Attorneys in this case.

No less energetic was the work of the counsel for the defendants — Attorney L. E. Quinlan of Lyons, Kansas, and Attorney Cliff Holland of Russell, Kansas. They labored earnestly and, no doubt, sincerely. Their alertness during the trial and their forceful pleadings to the jury were a match for the dynamic energies of their opponents, but their abilities were, in the end, no match for the mountain of evidence with which their defendants were confronted.

Upon receiving the case at 5:20 p.m. on Monday, September 14th, the jury began its deliberations immediately. A few ballots were taken, followed by an hour's recess for supper. Returning to their task of responsibilities at hand, they balloted again and again, each vote drawing them nearer to the final result. Then at 10:15 p.m., they signaled to the Bailiff, Charles Ward, that they were ready to report their verdict to the court.

After the defendants and court attachés had been called in, the jury was summoned from their room. There was a complete stillness about the courtroom that "spoke volumes" regarding the tenseness of the situation.

Glenn Lackey, the foreman of the jury, stepped forward at the command of Judge Ray H. Beals and handed him a sheaf of papers containing the jury's findings.

The court read aloud: "We the jury find the Defendant, Preston LeRoy Paden, guilty of murder in the first degree and recommend that he be sentenced to the (Kansas) State Penitentiary for life."

The defendant, Preston Paden, gave no outward sign of emotion. He sat half slumped in his chair idly twirling the laces of one shoe, a pose and a habit he had assumed throughout much of the trial. His face was somewhat whitened and the corners of his mouth drooped perceptibly. That was the composite of his reaction to the verdict.

The court read again a verdict of identical nature against the other defendant, Henry Mallory. And again there was no reaction from the defendant to indicate that he was greatly moved — nothing more than a slightly pained expression on his face which had been in evidence since the court had announced its finding against Preston Paden.

Henry Mallory's gray-haired mother, who had arrived for the first time the previous day, Sunday, from her home in Blackwell, Oklahoma, sat beside him as the verdict was announced.

The jury had deliberated altogether for less than 4 hours, not including the hour in which they were eating supper.

On the day following the verdict, it was reported in and around the court house, that on its first ballot, the jury had stood at "4 for conviction with the death penalty" to "8 for conviction, but with opposition to the death penalty."

On the second ballot, only one juror remained who voted to assess the death penalty.

On the third ballot, not a single juror voted to access the death penalty.

The seven ballots that followed were all on the question of "conviction with a recommendation of life imprisonment."

It was related that there was never even one ballot cast for anything less than first-degree murder for either of the defendants.

It was the second time in the September Term of the Rice County District Court that a jury had declined to assess the death penalty — the other instance being that of William Davis, who was sentenced to life imprisonment for the murder of his brother-in-law, Frank Rains.

The sentence was not immediately announced, and it was presumed that Paden and Mallory, as well as Davis, would hear their sentences from the court the following Monday when the September Term was reconvened.

Chapter 47: Herbold & Griffin Also Given Life Sentences

A swift final solution of the Ben Wiggins murder case came at Great Bend, Kansas, on the night of Friday, September 18, 1936, when Dee Herbold, a 33 year old brick mason, confessed to the actual killing, and a short time later at Lyons, Kansas, when Ermin "Curly" Griffin, also of Great Bend, Kansas, gave officers a statement acknowledging that he took part in the crime.

Herbold and Griffin ultimately followed the precedent set by Preston Paden and Henry Mallory, who had earlier in the week been found guilty of first-degree murder by the District Court jury trying their case. Paden was the first to give the full and correct version. Henry Mallory, after hearing Paden's statement read to him, admitted its truth.

Dee Herbold

At the Rice County Jail, where Paden was taken from the Kansas State Industrial Reformatory (KSIR) in Hutchinson, Kansas, Mallory and Paden sat down before a stenographer and out-lined the entire case. Paden told the story almost exactly as he had given it at Hutchinson the day before, and Mallory nodded assent, or occasionally corrected him on a minor detail. When finished, both Paden and Mallory affixed their names to the document.

A few minutes later, Griffin was brought in from his cell and was confronted by the two convicted men and their confession. Griffin sat quietly as the paper was read to him. He was then asked by Patrolman A. P. Keeling whether he had anything to say, and Griffin answered, *"No, I guess not."*

No further effort was made at that time to get Griffin to talk. Instead, Officer Keeling, Sheriff Art Estabrook, and several others, including a reporter for the News, went to Great Bend, Kansas, where Herbold was being held in the custody of Police Chief Vance Houdyshell.

As Herbold was brought from his cell into an office, Patrolman Keeling said to him, *"Herbold, we have a story here which I think you might want to hear. I'll have the girl read it to you."*

As the reading of the Paden-Mallory statement began, Herbold took a seat and gave the narrative close attention. He sat almost motionless, except for a frequent blinking of his eyes, and heavy breathing.

At the conclusion of the narrative, Patrolman Keeling addressed the Great Bend officers, and asked them to remove Herbold to Chief Houdyshell's private office. This was accomplished by two policemen, and before Keeling could gather up his records and follow them, they had returned to say that Herbold had *"... come clean, admitting he was the slayer."*

Patrolman Keeling and the stenographer joined Herbold in the small office and the questioning began.

Herbold was allowed to tell his story in his own way. He began at the point where the burglary of the Williamson-Booker Furniture Store had been discussed at Great Bend earlier on the night of the crime. He said that Griffin and Paden had asked him whether he would like to make some easy money. He said he asked them what kind of money and they replied, *"A little job over at Lyons. It doesn't amount to much."*

Herbold said he had been drinking; otherwise he would not have gone. He said that he did not know what sort of a job it was to be until he arrived at the store, and then did not even know the name of, or the nature of, the store's business.

He related that upon their arrival in Lyons, Mallory appeared not to be intending to go along with them, and loaned them his gun, but later Mallory changed his mind, and decided to join the group. Herbold said that after they all had gained entry into the store — the rear door of which was already open by the time Herbold arrived — they discussed which one would guard the back door, and finally decided that Herbold should take Mallory's gun and stand guard.

Herbold said in his statement that the time of their arrival was around 11:00 p.m., which, although an earlier time than the prosecution's contention of 1:20 a.m., coincided with the statements of other witnesses involved, that the group entered the store on, or before, midnight.

Standing at the rear doors while the others went far inside the building to the safe, Herbold said that he recalled several times wondering to himself, *"What the Devil am I doing here?"* He said he thought seriously of walking away, but concluded that since he had started something, he should go through with it.

He said that he believed that the other three had been inside the store for only about half an hour when he heard footsteps coming down the alley — which turned out to be those of

Night Marshal Ben Wiggins. As Officer Wiggins tried the door, Herbold said he thought of holding it shut, but somehow became confused and didn't do it. When the officer pushed open the door, Herbold said that Wiggins threw his flashlight beam inside and to the south, fully upon him.

"As he did that," Herbold continued, *"I struck him with the end of the gun, which I was holding by the grip. I had the gun on safety and I think as I hit him it must have been jarred off that position, and I believe I must have pulled the trigger accidentally just as he fell back. I had no thought of killing him. Honestly, I would rather it had been me than that officer."*

Herbold then related how he and Griffin ran across the vacant lot located behind the rear of the store to where the four had parked Doris Stanley's car in which they had previously driven downtown from the Snider Cabin Camp. They found it locked and the keys gone, so they continued on foot to the Snider Cabin Camp to meet Paden and Mallory who *"... must have run down the alley."*

Upon their return to Great Bend, Herbold said that he and Griffin first buried the gun a short distance northeast of that city. A day or two later they went back and dug it up, and as Griffin drove away, Herbold took the gun apart in as many pieces as possible. Then, he said, they continued to drive along the road. Every so often, Griffin would stop the car and Herbold would get out and proceed to bury a piece of the weapon. *"I buried the pieces as deep (into the ground) as I could dig with my hands,"* he said. *"There were so many stops of this kind that I honestly doubt whether I could take you to any one of the (buried gun) parts."*

Concluding the narrative, Herbold told Officer Keeling, *"You may not believe me (to be) sincere, but I want to tell you I would have given myself up for this "long ago" if it had not been for my wife and two children. I have the finest wife in the world. She has known from my actions that something was wrong, and I hate it for her sake."*

"You have no idea," Herbold continued, *"how it is to have something like this on your mind. It would be with me every minute of the day while I was working. Then when I would come home at night I would try to sleep. Counting sheep or nothing else helped very much. I couldn't sleep. I don't know what this is going to mean. If it means the rope, that's all there is to it. It will just have to be."*

After Herbold finished his statement, Officer Keeling said, *"Herbold, I want to congratulate you on coming clean on this matter. You have eased your conscience, I know, by telling the full truth. I am sorry for you because you are sorry for what you have done. I have seen many murderers in my time, and I think I can tell when one is really penitent."*

In the questioning, Herbold, who grew up in Great Bend, was asked whether he had ever been mixed up in any other crimes. He replied, *"I have been arrested only twice before in my life — once for fighting and once when I had just bought a bottle of liquor."*

Mrs. Dee Herbold was sent for, at the prisoner's request. Out of common decency, most of those who had been in the room listening to his confession, stepped out as she came in to the room. Those who were obliged to remain on guard, later said that although she was plainly crushed, Mrs. Herbold bore the news of the confession with admirable bravery.

One point that investigators had never quite understood was quickly cleared up by Herbold, who, by the way, was the only man in a position to correctly answer this question. It was how Officer Wiggins' body happened to be lying several feet outside the rear door of the building, when the position of the ejected shell, being inside the room, showed the shot had been fired from inside the building, or at least in the doorway.

Herbold answered the question by saying that after the shot was fired, Wiggins staggered and reeled backward, finally sprawling upon the rear porch in the position in which his body was found the next morning.

He also verified the statement of Paden and Mallory that the officer's flashlight, still in his hand and burning, was snatched up and thrown out into the vacant lot by Griffin.

Herbold also said that Officer Wiggins groaned only once after the fatal shot was fired.

After returning to Lyons, Kansas, the officers brought Griffin into the sheriff's office to be confronted by Herbold. As they met and exchanged greetings, Herbold said, *"Curly, I have told them exactly how it happened."* Then Herbold related an outline of the confession at the request of Officer Keeling.

When he had finished, Officer Keeling turned to Griffin and asked, *"Is this right Curly?"*

Griffin replied, *"I don't care to make a statement until I have talked to a lawyer in the morning."*

Herbold looked at Griffin for a moment and said, *"Curly, I first thought of fighting this thing, myself. I even had a lawyer*

*coming up from Wichita to see me tomorrow. I had an alibi
arranged in my mind. But then I got to thinking that I would
have to ask my wife and others of my family to perjure themselves to help me, and that might mean they would be sentenced
to several years in prison."*

Griffin still declined to talk.

A little later, however, Griffin said he would like to speak to
Officer Keeling privately.

When they returned, Griffin answered in the affirmative to a
number of questions based on the truth of Herbold's statement.
But when it came time to signing a statement, he again demurred,
saying he still preferred to wait until he had talked to an attorney
the following morning.

Shortly after noon on Saturday, September 19, 1936, Curly
Griffin signed the statement of his involvement in the Ben
Wiggins murder and was immediately sentenced to life in prison
along with his other three co-conspirators.

Had Curly Griffin not signed the statement of guilt on
September 19th, he ran the risk of being charged with the
crime — that very day — then having a jury trial and, finally,
under the recently enacted Kansas State Law on Capital
Punishment, he could have been given the death penalty by
the jury. And it would be very likely that a "Curly Griffin"
jury would have little or no leniency for him, due to the fact
that there was no doubt about his guilt in the Ben Wiggins
murder case.

Curly Griffin finally correctly reasoned that he had two
options, both of which were bad. He could request a jury trial

and risk being given the death penalty or he could sign the statement of guilt and be given a life sentence.

Curly Griffin wisely chose the latter option — that of a life sentence.

Ermin "Curly" Griffin

Chapter 48: Prisoners Transferred To
Kansas Penal Institutions

Early on Sunday morning, September 20, 1936, the largest group transfer of first-degree murderers from Rice County, Kansas, to penal institutions within the state, occurred when five first-degree murderers, all sentenced to life imprisonment, left the county in the custody of police officers.

The five convicts were William Davis, found guilty and sentenced for the murder of his brother-in-law, Frank Rains; Preston Paden and Henry Mallory, found guilty and later confessed in connection with the burglary-murder of Night Marshal Ben Wiggins of Lyons; and Dee Herbold and Ermin "Curly" Griffin, who also pleaded guilty to the Wiggins murder.

Of the five, only Paden did not go directly to the state penitentiary. At the time of his conviction, he was serving a term in the Kansas State Industrial Reformatory (KSIR) in Hutchinson, Kansas, for leaving the scene of an accident. The reformatory, therefore, had first rights to him and could hold him there until the completion of his term before releasing him to the Kansas State Penitentiary.

Only one of the five men, Ermin "Curly" Griffin, was found to have a previous criminal record of any consequence. He told the court that he had previously served 17 months in the Missouri State Penitentiary at Jefferson City, Missouri, on a grand larceny charge.

Paden had never been sentenced for any offense other than the one for which he was serving time in the reformatory. Mallory was found to have been arrested in Wichita, Kansas, a few times for minor offenses. Herbold, who formerly lived in the Raymond Community of Rice County, and had grown up in the Great Bend area, had previously been arrested only twice, and both times for minor counts. William Davis had no previous criminal record.

It is interesting to note that of the five men convicted of murder, only two were actual murderers. Dee Herbold confessed to the Wiggins slaying, and William Davis killed his brother-in-law, Frank Rains.

The other three men being incarcerated on September 20th, and being given life sentences, were murderers only in the broader technical and legal interpretations of the law.

Kansas laws specified that in the event of a murder committed by one of a group of people engaged in the commission of another crime, all members of the group were to be deemed equally guilty of first-degree murder.

Chapter 49: Conditions At The KSIR In Hutchinson, Kansas

 **"Hutch" - The Kansas State Industrial Reformatory**

After being convicted of leaving the scene of an accident, Preston Paden, who had only been behind bars for a mere few nights in city or county jails in his whole life, found himself in a completely new and different world upon entering the Kansas State Industrial Reformatory (KSIR) in Hutchinson, Kansas.

Even though his attorneys had always stressed that it was important that he pretend to be a bit younger than his actual age, and the newspapers had said that he was only 19, Preston was, in fact, 20 years old when he first passed through the gates of the reformatory. One might believe that it was easier doing time in the reformatory at Hutchinson than it would be in one of the federal prisons, but that wasn't the case. The federal prisons followed the rules. The state wasn't under federal regulations and their employees had to meet few, if any requirements. On top of that, state prison employees weren't paid very well, and, as a result, many state reformatory guards treated the prisoners as they pleased.

The first order issued to Preston, as told to him by an old battle-axe that seemed to find a sadistic measure of enjoyment in her job, was, "Drop your britches, boy." And things only went further downhill from there.

At the next station, Preston received a big gunnysack filled with straw that was tied with a piece of string around the top. After being led to the cell house, and being assigned his cell, Preston was informed that the wooden bench in his cell was his bed, and the gunnysack of straw was his mattress. Funny looking mattress, he thought. But after jumping on it, stomping on it, rolling on it, and kicking it, it finally resembled the beginnings of a mattress. The discomfort of the feel of it was the good news. It was nothing compared to the bugs and fleas that came out and bit him after he attempted to sleep on it. Every once in a while, the prisoners were given some sort of ointment to rub on their bites, and possibly kill the bugs that were crawling all over them. This may have helped for a short time, but it certainly wasn't the long-term cure that the inmates were praying for.

The dining hall operated under the "code of silence." Once everyone sat down to eat, a bell would ring which meant that complete silence was to be maintained during the meal period. Preston missed the first meal he was to have in the dining room. It seemed as though a big colored fellow working the chow line was under the impression that Preston was a candidate to perform some sort of sexual favors for him. After hearing "You gonna be my Bitch," Preston knew that he needed to handle this situation without delay or Grandpa Stanley would undoubtedly turn over in his grave. A fist to the face, a rearranged nose, and blood splattered all over the food was the perfect prescription for sending Preston to spend time in solitary confinement. He was satisfied that he had done the right thing, though, in maintaining his self-respect and self-esteem.

Preston had heard Volney Davis, and some of the other boys in the gang, talk about "Hutch," and how Alvin Karpis had done time there a few years back. He knew it wasn't the kind of place where you could let your guard down. The worst thing was that the place was full of "snitches," and the convicts there were the worst snitches of all.

Unless you have spent time in prison, you have no idea what it is like. It is the epitome of "Hell on Earth." Right off the bat, you are going to get your ass kicked like it has never been kicked before. It is inevitable. It is part of your sentence. It goes without saying that you will fight until you are unconscious and maybe, just maybe, you will wake up. Some of the old timers call it "showing heart," but whatever you want to call it, either you will do it, or you will die, or you will wish you were dead.

Not unlike animals, men are born with testosterone. They will find relief for their urges in one form or another. The weak will suffer unless they are of the few that like to be the "Bitches." When that is the case, those will be the ones to satisfy the men, to do their laundry, to cater to them, and, of course, to please them sexually.

Even if they've found their place, and have their "Bitch," or are comfortable with being someone else's "Bitch," there is always the dreaded cage that they live in, day after day. It isn't called the "Pen" by accident. Living in a pen like a caged animal for months, and then years, has a powerful effect on a man like nothing else that could be done to him. A few have the stamina to carry on and wait for the day that they are released. Many go stark-raving mad and kill themselves or kill someone else, or cause someone else to kill them. A huge percentage of prison inmates are like "ticking time bombs," wired and ready, waiting for the smallest thing to set them off. If they weren't crazy when they were initially incarcerated, they most likely will be if they stay there long enough.

The prison system in our country is, and always has been, a pitiful excuse for reform. If a kid going into the penal system isn't yet an expert at committing crime, he will be when he gets out. If, upon entering, he wasn't physically strong enough to fight off the misfits, then he will become mentally warped for life by their abuse. If he innocently fell for the gang protection system, then he will be owned by the gang for the rest of his life. He will always be indebted to the gang and liable to carry out their orders to "kill or be killed."

The only people who are released from prison with any of their sanity intact are those who fought for their life, retained their self-respect, and vowed to never put themselves into a position that would return them to this "Hell on Earth."

Chapter 50: Preston Paden Tells The Whole Truth

It didn't take Preston Paden (register number 12184) very long to figure out the system and determine that if he kept his nose clean and minded his own business, he might have a chance of someday being on the other side of the prison walls before becoming an old man.

One of his first jobs at the Kansas State Industrial Reformatory — also known as "Hutch" — was general cleaning duties in the kitchen. As he worked himself up in the ranks, he eventually became one of the cooks. Then after learning the basics of cooking, he discovered that he seemed to have a natural knack for, and a general liking of, cooking activities. He started adding his own touches to some of the plain and bland institution foods, which soon increased his popularity with the inmates. Preston was turning the former old, boring, dreaded, meals into healthier and more palatable meals than the inmates had previously been accustomed to. He also started feeling a little bit better about himself, but even though he would forever criticize himself on the mess he had made of his life, he was now more determined than ever to turn his life around and be a productive member of society.

After several months of incarceration, Preston was still boiling mad over being ripped off by Attorney Hugh Larimer. Larimer had cut the lock off of the door to the garage that stored a vehicle belonging to Volney Davis; then he proceeded to sell the vehicle; and he then kept all of the proceeds of the sale for himself. In addition to that, Larimer recovered Preston's car from Sheriff Tom Bash and sold it for considerably more than the $100 that he returned to Preston.

When Preston first requested to speak to someone about the illegal activities of Larimer, it caused quite a stir at the Bureau of Investigation. Even J. Edgar Hoover was alarmed and requested an investigation into the matter. The excitement concerned some confusion of the coincidence that the FBI had an agent with the same name as Attorney Hugh Larimer. This was eventually straightened out and it was confirmed that the former Bureau agent, Hugh Larimer, and the Attorney, Hugh Clifford Larimer, were, in fact, two different and unrelated people. And, there was even one more Hugh Larimer in Topeka — Hugh Dillon Larimer — who was the father of Attorney Hugh Clifford Larimer.

Preston was told that the FBI would investigate Attorney Hugh Larimer if Preston would answer some questions for them. Since his mother, Edna Murray, had been returned to prison to finish her 25+ year sentence, and just about all of the gang had been incarcerated by now, Preston thought that he couldn't hurt anybody by simply trying to help himself out, and also to clear his conscience. Even Jess Doyle had told his story, and Volney Davis had "caved in" and spilled his guts.

Preston told the authorities what he knew of Attorney Larimer being in cahoots with the outlaws, stating that Larimer not only represented outlaws when they needed an attorney, but was also involved in — and sometimes the actual instigator of — their crimes. One example given was that Larimer, and a Kansas City attorney by the name of Buddy Middleton, were behind an alleged extortion plot for which Frances Taylor (aka Helen Rush), was convicted in Topeka, Kansas. Frances Taylor had attempted to extort money from a prominent Topeka lumber businessman through photographs of her and the businessman in acts of sexual perversion. Preston remembered hearing from John Langan and Earl Stuchlik that Frances Taylor and her co-conspirators tried to extort $10,000 from one man and probably hefty sums from a few other unsuspecting men as well. The plot had been engineered by Hugh Larimer, and Preston had heard Larimer and Earl Stuchlik discuss the plan in the Missouri Hotel in Kansas City. At that time, Larimer said that the reason they were unable to get the money from the "old men" was because it was becoming known on the streets that Frances Taylor was "hot" and she could not afford to take the chance of being recognized by appearing in court.

In order to clear his conscience, Preston proceeded to tell the FBI all he knew of his gang's former activities, and also what his involvement had been in each specific activity. By doing so, he made some fellows who had previously been wrongly convicted of crimes, very happy.

The stigma of arrest and felony charges against four men for a crime in Clay County, Missouri, nearly two years earlier, was removed when Preston told the correct story of the Blankenship Brothers robbery in Winnwood Beach, Missouri, on January 13, 1935. Preston gave his statement to Wint Smith, Attorney for the Kansas State Highway Commission and also Director of Motor Vehicle Inspectors, and to Joseph Anderson, one of Mr. Smith's officers. The robbery of O. K. Blankenship and E. K. Blankenship had resulted in convictions for Art Corey, of Kansas City, Missouri; James Wilson of Winnwood Beach, Missouri; and Dode Reffert and Roy Richardson, both of Birmingham, Missouri. Preston's confession named John Langan, who was currently confined in the Missouri State

Penitentiary at Jefferson City, Missouri — and also was wanted in Wyandotte County, Kansas, for shooting a deputy sheriff; Jess Doyle, who was in the Nebraska State Penitentiary; and their leader, Volney Davis — one of the members of the Barker-Karpis Gang involved in the Bremer kidnapping; and Preston also named himself as one of the robbers.

Again, Preston, in wishing to wipe his slate clean, reached far back into his childhood memories in order to understand why it was absolutely necessary for him to confess to all the crimes that he was aware of.

He recalled that although "Grandpa Stanley" was a very educated and smart businessman, and "Grandma Stanley" was a very sweet and loving lady — for whatever reason — most of their children turned out to be non-law abiding citizens. Most of the adult Stanley children enjoyed partaking of alcoholic beverages, even to the point of forming an addiction to alcohol. The passing of the Volstead Act, and the beginning of Prohibition most certainly influenced their decisions to break the law. Preston grew up among a family of bootleggers, rumrunners, lawbreakers, and drunks. He knew what was safe to talk about and when to keep his mouth shut. He knew that the "laws" meant trouble and you don't give "coppers" any information. From his skewed perspective, his mama was always in jail because of the "laws," or she was on the lam and running from the "laws."

As a result, Preston grew up to have no respect for the "laws."

When he was about 8 or 9 years old, Preston and his cousin, "Little" Mott, were staying on Old St. Joe Road, about five miles north of North Kansas City, with "Little" Mott's mother, Doris, and her husband Earl Stuchlik. Preston recalled that the

392

Stucklik's operated a thriving bootlegging operation from this location. Fisher Paris, formerly of Abilene, Kansas, owned the place, and his wife's father lived on the next farm to the north.

George Chase, Gus Nichols, Sammy Hoyt, and Tom Underwood would frequently visit Doris' and Earl's place. One day, George and Gus were bragging about how the four of them had robbed the Kaw Valley State Bank in Topeka, Kansas, and their car had broken down on the road during their escape, forcing them to kidnap a truck driver and making him drive them to Kansas City.

Later on, when Doris and Earl moved from the Kansas City area to St. Paul, Minnesota, they were accompanied by George Chase and Gus Nichols. Preston had fond memories of that time because it was on the 4th of July that George Chase gave him a $20 bill and Preston said that was the most money he ever had in his life.

When Preston was telling this story in 1936, he said that at the time, to his knowledge, Gus Nichols was currently serving time at the Stillwater State Prison in Stillwater, Minnesota; Tom Underwood was serving his sentence at Alcatraz Penitentiary; Sammy Hoyt was doing time at Jefferson City, Missouri; and George Chase was dead.

Another story that Preston recalled hearing about was the July 26, 1932, Concordia Bank Robbery — actually, the Cloud County Bank in Concordia, Kansas — that was reportedly robbed of $250,000 in cash and bonds. Jess Doyle had told him that he, along with Freddie Barker, Alvin Karpis, Larry DeVol and Earl Christman robbed the bank of some $22,000 in cash. However, this robbery didn't go off without a hitch — since they had some unexpected trouble with the Vice President of the bank. He was reluctant to open the vault, so the gang proceeded to beat him with their .45 caliber pistols. This beating had gone on for several minutes or so, and was not very productive, when Freddie Barker had an idea! He grabbed a female stenographer and threw her down on the floor at the VP's feet. He then told the VP that he was going to shoot her head off if the VP didn't open the vault at once. At this point the VP said he would gladly open the vault but he wasn't physically able to, due to the violent beating he had just received. He then told the gang the combination, and the gang opened the vault themselves. Once they retrieved the money, the gang immediately left and drove directly to Harry Sawyer's place in St. Paul, Minnesota. This was the way that Preston remembered hearing the story when he was 16 years old.

A more detailed version might have included that the Vice President of the bank — Josiah C. Peck — was pistol whipped on the face and head so severely that the blood ran into his eyes and impaired his vision so badly that he was unable to see well enough through the blood to read the combination lock's dial. Therefore, an employee of the bank, Ida Cook, opened the vault as Peck recited the combination numbers to her.

After filling their bags with the cash and securities, the gang grabbed three female employees of the bank, namely Ida Cook, Marie Frederickson, and Nelda Appleby. The three women were ordered to ride on the running boards of the car as the gang wound their way through town and out to the highway. Throwing roofing nails out on the roads behind them, the gang hoped to flatten the tires of any police vehicles that might be in pursuit. Once on the highway, the female hostages were released and received an apology from the bandits for using improper language and treating them so disrespectfully.

Preston and his mother, Edna Murray, were both witnesses and gave testimony at Coffeyville, Kansas, in connection with the mail robbery case there. Edna later pitched a fit, wanting to be paid for those services. Dwight Brantley, Special Agent in Charge, advised Mr. Hoover that enough money had already been spent for transportation and guards for her on that case. Edna never did receive any remuneration in exchange for her testimony as a witness acting on behalf of the prosecution.

In another aspect of Preston's life where he wanted to become a productive member of society, he decided to turn much of his attention to educating himself.

One thing that the inmates were allowed to do after they had completed their workday duties, was to read. Since Preston had always enjoyed this activity, and decided that he could also further his education in this manner, he read more books while he was incarcerated than he had in the previous 20 years.

Preston read just about any book that he could get his hands on. Since he was the cook, he read many books about foods and famous restaurants. He could tell you that the "Waldorf Salad" originated at the Waldorf-Astoria Hotel in New York City and consisted of equal parts — diced apples, halved and seeded red grapes, diced celery, halved English walnuts and mayonnaise. And he could also tell the listener that "no substitutions were allowed."

The original creator of the "Waldorf Salad" — Oscar Tschirky — was not a chef at the Waldorf-Astoria Hotel, although many people assume he was; but rather, he was the maître d'hôtel at the Waldorf-Astoria Hotel at the time.

Because of the medical books he read — originally trying to diagnose his own lung condition — Preston became quite knowledgeable in the field of medicine. Later in life, he was known to assist both family and friends with his medical knowledge, particularly those who couldn't otherwise afford a doctor's care. He didn't try to prescribe medications, but had an excellent concept of "what to do" and "what not to do" as far as home care was concerned. He also could tell his neighbors when it was time for them to stop trying to treat themselves, and to seek professional medical attention — short of depending on the hospital emergency room to tend to their needs. But if the hospital was their only option, Preston would tell them that they should go to the hospital before the condition worsened or became grave.

In addition, Preston probably could have passed an accountant's exam after reading all the books he read in prison about accounting.

That too, was an area of his expertise — **NUMBERS!**

Preston was really good with numbers and he would continue to use that ability later in his life.

Chapter 51: World War II —
And The Merchant Marine

The Merchant Marine is collectively comprised of those non-naval ships that carry cargo or passengers or provide maritime services as well as the civilian crewmen and officers who sail those ships. During World War II, the ships and men of the United States Merchant Marine transported vast quantities of war material, including the supplies, equipment, and troops needed to fight and win that war across the oceans of the world. The men of the U. S. Merchant Marine were civilian volunteers who nonetheless died in equal or higher proportions as compared to the rates of any branch of our uniformed military services. As the Armed Guard with whom they sailed, the men of the Merchant Marine helped make the Allied victory in World War II possible.

In 1940, the Merchant Marine numbered about 55,000 people — all volunteers. A massive recruiting effort brought in retired seafarers who were able to ship out immediately on the newly launched Liberty Ships. The U. S. Maritime Service officially took youngsters who were as young as 16 years old — and they took some with one eye, one leg, or even those who had heart problems. Many men who were too young or too old for the other services, or who were physically unfit for the other services, applied for, and were accepted into, the Merchant Marine.

The Merchant Marine mariners signed on for each voyage, which lasted until they returned to a U. S. port, which was usually one year or more in length. They had no paid leave, no vacation time, and no pension benefits. In comparison, the Navy personnel had equivalent or higher salaries, paid leave, disability and death benefits, free medical care for personnel — as well as dependents, free uniforms, and a generous retirement pension.

Merchant Marine mariners were on the front lines from the moment that their ships left U. S. ports and were subject to attack by enemy bombers, kamikaze suicide missions, battleships, submarines, mines, and land-based artillery. Countless mariners performed acts of bravery and heroism far beyond the normal call of duty.

It was often said that the crewmembers of the Merchant Marine ships were the toughest and most courageous bunch of misfits that the seas had ever seen.

Preston L. Paden - Certificate of Service issued on 3 NOV 44.

Preston Paden, upon receiving his parole from his incarceration in the State Industrial Reformatory in Hutchinson, Kansas, signed up with the U. S. Merchant Marine in Port Arthur, Texas, on November 3, 1944, knowing full well that he should have checked into a hospital first. His lung condition had severely worsened since he first began having breathing difficulties, about six years earlier.

His official occupational specialty was that of "Mess Man" — that position as being the performance of kitchen-related duties. That was fine with Preston since he was so proud that he would be serving his country in time of war, and he certainly knew his way around any kitchen very well. Three months later, on February 2, 1945, he was promoted to "Second

Cook and Baker." He was very good at his job, and his crewmen admired his efforts and enjoyed the food he prepared for them. Two months later, on April 2, 1945, Preston was promoted once again, this time to "Chief Cook." It is probable that he was serving aboard a tanker hauling fuel for the Texaco Oil Company about this time. That company, shipping mostly out of Port Arthur, Texas, lost a total of 9 vessels under their flag during World War II.

On June 26, 1945, Preston boarded the S. S. Winfield S. Stratton at the Port of San Francisco, California, and departed four days later, on June 30th, heading for the Philippine Islands.

Uncle Ginney & Cousin Bill Stanley (home on leave) "Courtesy of Bill Stanley"

Just prior to Preston's release from "Hutch," his cousin, Bill Stanley, who served on the submarine, "Bluefish," from 1942 until 1945, was visiting with his Aunt Edna. Bill's father was Edna's younger brother, Gloyd Augusta Stanley, better known as "Ginney" to most of the Stanleys. Ginney had told his son, Bill, that if he was ever in port in San Francisco, he could find his Aunt Edna living there. Sure enough, not only did he find Edna, but also her husband at that time, Carl Memmott, who coincidentally, was one of the welders working on his ship, the "Bluefish."

Carl Memmott, Edna Memmott, shipmate (name unknown), Bill Stanley (Edna's nephew) at a dance hall in San Francisco, Calif. – 1944. "Courtesy of Bill Stanley"

Bill recalled that Edna and Carl lived on Figaro Street, and he remembered that Carl's employer was a big steel company on 3rd Street. Bill's crew was in port in San Francisco for a few days, having required maintenance work performed on the "Bluefish." Edna loved to party, and she had a reason to celebrate every night that Bill was there. He said she would dance all over the floor and would wear him out.

Once, when Bill was taking a little break from Edna's dancing him around the floor, he was leaning on a stack of beer bottle cases that had empty bottles in them. Somebody bumped into him and he accidentally knocked some of the bottles out. One of the bottles still had some beer in it that splashed on a drunken sailor's girlfriend. The drunken sailor started swearing at Bill, and before Bill could even say anything, Edna came over — all 5'1½" of her — swinging the biggest pocketbook Bill had ever remembered seeing. She smacked that sailor upside his head, told him a thing or two, and by the time she was finished — she had her nephew, Bill, winning the war all by himself. The sailor decided he wasn't any match for Edna, and tucked in his tail and left. When Edna's poor little hubby,

Carl, said something about how Edna probably shouldn't have reacted the way she did, she told him, "Shut your mouth, or I'll whip your ass, too."

Bill recalled that one night they went to a dance where all the hillbillies, who worked at the shipyards, congregated. It was called "Dude Martin's Barn Dance," and everybody there was having a good time.

Edna had been dancing Bill all over the dance floor for quite some time, when Carl, who had to be at work early the next morning, told Edna that they needed to go home. Edna let Carl know right away that if he wanted to leave he could "… get his ass out of here, but he would be leaving the keys to the car with her." Bill said poor little Carl just sat there quietly until Edna was good and ready to leave.

Mr. and Mrs. Carl Memmott – Carl was Edna's fifth husband

Bill said Edna was quite a gal, and there was never a dull moment when she was around.

Ruth Evelyn & Mott Clinton Farrell "Courtesy of Bill Stanley"

Edna's nephew, Mott Clinton Farrell ("Little" Mott), who had grown up with Preston, was performing his patriotic duty by enlisting in the Air Force. By making the highest scores on the entrance exams, he was sent straight into flight training. Although he excelled in the training program while in the classroom, he just could never quite cut it while he was actually in the air. It seemed that as soon as his feet left the ground, he was throwing up so violently that he couldn't even take care of himself, let alone pilot a bomber aircraft. He found this to be very embarrassing but could do nothing about it. "Little" Mott was grounded and destined to serve his time in the Air Force sitting at a desk.

Author's Note:

General Douglas MacArthur paid this tribute to Merchant Marine Seamen in the Pacific Theatre of the War with the following tribute:

"They have brought us our lifeblood and they have paid for it with some of their own. I saw them bombed off the Philippines and in New Guinea Ports. When

it was humanly possible, when their ships were not blown out from under them by bombs or torpedoes, they delivered their cargoes to us who needed them so badly. In war, it is performance that counts."

Preston Paden's Merchant Seaman Certificate of Identification – 26 JUN 45

Chapter 52: The Kansas State Tuberculosis Sanatorium

Not far from Preston's hometown of Cardin, Oklahoma, in a small farm and mining community in the southeastern corner of Kansas known as Stippville, the residents were finding themselves in the midst of the Great Depression by the early 1930s. Watching her poverty-stricken family merely exist on a steady daily diet of potatoes and a little milk, the bright and pretty, little Naomi Keith was forced to end her education after the 8th grade. She had graduated as a straight "A" student and wished so very much to go on to high school, but it was not to be. Having four older brothers and four younger sisters, Naomi knew the financing would be impossible. Naomi's father, Jeff Keith, a man in his mid-thirties with his wife, Ethel, and nine children to support, and possessing only the skills of an ordinary dirt farmer, was caught up in this terrible Depression that seemed to engulf the whole world around him. He felt that, at this stage in his family's life, his main purpose was for no more than to protect his family from starvation.

The older boys were doing their share of helping around the farm and sometimes were lucky enough to find small jobs in town that would add a few cents to the family cookie jar. Naomi did all she could to help with the smaller children — heating water for their baths, washing clothes on the scrub board, and helping to keep coal in the potbelly stove in the central part of the house that was their only source of heat in the cold and drafty little farm house. Having four older brothers and being the eldest of the girls, Naomi always seemed to be the one that the brothers picked on. Being high strung herself, and somewhat of a tomboy, Naomi would always try her luck at fighting back, which seemed to encourage the boys' pranks even more. One cold Kansas winter morning, after treading through the snow out to the old outdoor toilet, Naomi discovered after sitting on the cold toilet seat that it suddenly became not quite so cold, and the electric jolt that was next to come, nearly flung her through the door. A tremendous roar of laugher came from behind the toilet where her brothers had heard her screams. They had been up since daybreak, carefully lacing the cracks in the toilet seat with fine copper wire that they had ingeniously attached to an old car battery. Naomi was sure that this was the worst trick they had pulled on her since she was much younger, when they had talked her into sticking her tongue onto a doorknob of their poorly heated house in freezing weather. When Naomi touched her tongue to the doorknob, it stuck fast, and she was sure that half of her tongue stayed on the doorknob when she pulled it away.

Naomi's brothers were an ornery lot, for sure, but Naomi was terribly saddened when her oldest brother died of pneumonia during that long winter in Kansas during the Great Depression. They couldn't do anything for Rolland except to try and keep him warm while watching him die. It was then that Naomi felt she just had to get off that farm or she would just waste away, herself, before long. She longed so much just to have one dress that wasn't threadbare, and, oh, what she would give for a new pair of shoes! She had often carefully cut pieces of coffee tins to the size and shape of her shoe soles, and carefully put them inside her shoes and topped them off with pieces of cardboard to keep from feeling the cold through the holes in her shoes.

Coffee tins came in handy for a lot of things. When cut in tiny strips and wrapped in pieces of brown paper sacks, they were excellent for rolling her hair around, and the ends of the strips would fold over the roll of hair, holding her make-shift curlers nicely in place. Naomi was always very particular about her appearance and could mend or fix anything and make things out of virtually anything.

Upon hearing of a job in town that a girl of her age could fill, one day Naomi decided to walk 12 miles into the little town of Columbus, Kansas. An elderly couple's failing health required the need of someone to cook and care for them. Since Naomi had ample experience of those duties by virtue of being the eldest girl in her family, she seemed to fit the bill and was promptly hired for $2.00 per week, plus room and board.

The days that followed were not always the most pleasant, but Naomi had a knack for making the best of any situation, and she always kept a smile on her pretty face as she toiled through the days. She was up early in the mornings, starting the fires and firing up the old wooden cook stove in the kitchen, preparing the meals, doing the wash, and keeping the house always neat and tidy. The elderly man's health was failing even more quickly than that of his wife, and he coughed a lot and had spells of sweating during the night that soaked his bedding. He kept a pan of water under his bed that was supposed to ward off the night sweats. Naomi had her doubts that the pan of water afforded any cure to the problem at hand, but she kept the pan full of fresh water and changed the wet bedding daily — keeping him as comfortable as possible. One night during the mid-spring season, Naomi, although not feeling so well, herself, as of late, heard the lady of the house calling out for her. The gentleman of the house had passed away in his sleep during the night.

The lady of the house, shortly thereafter — not wanting to stay in the same home after her husband's death — decided to move in with a relative. Naomi returned home to her parent's farm in Stippville, Kansas.

In the fall of 1938, Naomi, suffering from what her mother had been calling a summer cold, began looking very frail and was coughing almost at every breath. But it was only after she began coughing up blood that her father, Jeff Keith, hitched one of his plow horses up to the wagon and took Naomi to the doctor in town. Old Doc Fuller told Jeff that he had seen these symptoms many times as of late. Doc Fuller was certain that Naomi was in the advanced stages of tuberculosis, and both of her lungs were affected. He told Jeff of a tuberculosis sanatorium in Norton, Kansas. He said it had a long waiting list, but he would put Naomi's name on it. He said it would surely be weeks, and probably months, before the sanatorium would have room for her. Naomi was very worried, since she had seen the gentleman that she cared for in town suffer with the same symptoms, and she remembered, all too well, what his fate had been.

It was well into winter before the letter from the Kansas State Tuberculosis Sanatorium (KSTS) arrived. Little Naomi — now, not much more than a skeleton — was put on a train to make the long journey alone. The Keith family had to scrape to come up with enough money just for Naomi's train fare, and there was no money left to allow for anyone to accompany her on the trip. Naomi, who had never been very far away from her family, was frightened as the train pulled away from the station, and she wondered if she would ever see any of her family again. She tried to muffle her cough in order to not attract attention, and pulled the blanket — that the kindly porter had given her — snuggly around her frail weak little body. Naomi's Guardian Angel (the porter) checked on her several times during the night, his white shining teeth being the only part of his friendly black face that Naomi could distinguish in the dark. She had never before been close enough to a colored person to talk to them. He had a funny sort of way of slurring his words as he spoke, but he was very kind and made her feel as though at least one person was looking out

The Norton, Kansas, Tuberculosis Sanatorium

for her on that very long, and otherwise, lonely trip.

The train pulled into the station at Norton, Kansas, just before daybreak. "Dis where you gettin' off, little girl?" the porter asked through those shining white teeth. Seeing that Naomi's knees were so weak that she was shaking as she struggled to stand on her feet, the kind porter scooped her up in his arms as if she was a feather, and carried her — along with her little knapsack — to the taxi waiting to take her to the sanatorium.

Naomi's first diagnosis at the sanatorium was not good. The doctors doubted if she would still be alive at week's end. A female doctor approached her with the possibility of trying an experimental drug. They called it "gold shots" and the doctor continued with the comforting words that, "… it would either help her or do her in." Naomi always had a lot of fight in her, and she wanted to give herself at least a chance.

A young man that she had met at the sanatorium, also in very poor condition from tuberculosis, started the "gold shots" at the same time that Naomi did. He was in a room on the men's floor, directly under her room. They had a string with a clothespin on the end of it that they used to send notes up and down to each other. They would compare notes every day as to how they were feeling. Naomi seemed to be doing much better than her friend on the floor below her. One day when she sent him down a note on the string at the usual time, he didn't respond. She stomped her little foot on the floor, and still received no response. She then inquired through the nurses, and later found out that her friend had passed away in his sleep. She suffered deeply for her friend, and this sad event was something she never ever forgot for the rest of her life.

It was several months before Naomi's strength was built up enough to tolerate the painful "pneumo" treatments. In actuality, the patients receiving these treatments lived "in spite of these treatments," rather than because of them — but this was the recommended treatment of the day. The worse afflicted lung was the first to be deflated, thus letting it rest so it could heal. Each day, for months, Naomi went in the treatment room to have the big needle carefully placed between the wall of her chest and her lung, forcing an ever so tiny amount of air against her lung. Once the lung was sufficiently deflated, the treatment would be only once a month or so, in order to compensate for air leakage and to keep the lung deflated. About 18 months of healing time was allowed for each lung, plus a few more months was required for the deflated lung to return to normal after the treatments were discontinued. Altogether, Naomi would ultimately spend about five years of her life in this sanatorium fighting her own personal war in order to save her own life.

The Kansas State Tuberculosis Sanatorium was built in an ideal location for an institution of its purpose. It was situated about 4 miles East of Norton, Kansas, on a beautiful spot on the Prairie Dog Creek. The altitude was 2,260 feet above sea level and the sun shined an average of 300 days a year. The air was invigorating, and the sanatorium's buildings had an abundance of pure water and a near perfect drainage system. The buildings were situated on 240 acres and arranged around the Administration Building that stood near the center of the campus. Drives and walkways leading to the different parts of the grounds had evergreens and flowers at intervals that created a beautiful and picturesque atmosphere. The sanatorium's buildings and grounds were adorned by lighting that was visible for miles. The cornerstone for the sanatorium was laid on June 14, 1914, and bears the inscription:

"In the health of the people lies the strength of the nation."

If only there could have been room for the 82% of the people that had tuberculosis, and were left to fight it out alone, thereby, infecting others!

Shortly before Naomi was to be released from the KSTS, having received a clean bill of health and just waiting for the total healing and usage of her left lung, she was walking in the gardens adjoining the huge hospital facilities. She spotted a fair-haired young man of slender build who she hadn't seen on the premises before. He appeared to be watching her as she walked, and he had a broad and, sort of a, crooked smile. "Hello there, Red," he said to her. Naomi had dark auburn hair, and when it caught the light of the sun, it did sometimes look as if there was a red glow to it. But in all these years, this was the first time she had ever been called "Red."

Preston's breathing condition did not improve while he was at sea and had caused him to be sent back home for medical attention. The KSTS at Norton, Kansas, was the hospital

The Norton, Kansas, State Tuberculosis Sanatorium Grounds

closest to his home that had the necessary facilities, equipment, and specialists to treat various lung disorders, particularly, tuberculosis.

During his stay at the KSTS, Preston and Naomi spent their free time walking in the gardens and sometimes sneaked into town on some evenings to catch a movie. They soon discovered that their hometowns had merely more than the state borderline between them. Naomi was now 23 years old, and this truly was her very first romance. Unlike any of the guys she knew from home, or had met while at the sanatorium, Preston had an unusual wit about him, and rarely could she hit upon a subject that he wasn't knowledgeable about. She was used to being "the brain," and most men seemed dumb and uninteresting to her. Preston always had something witty to say — a joke for every occasion — and made her laugh more than she had in her whole life. He was six years older than her, had been "around the block" a few times, and appeared to be very confident, and he had never met a girl so fond of life as Naomi appeared to be. He wondered how, after she spent almost 5 years in the hospital, that she could seemingly be so filled with such joy and happiness. Compared to Preston, she had led a sheltered life, but she was so open and natural and genuinely pure. Unlike so many people Preston had been exposed to in his lifetime, Naomi seemed incapable of ever doing anything wrong, or bringing harm to any living soul. He chuckled under his breath when he thought of how she was so unlike his mother, Edna.

After having just about every kind of test the doctors at the sanatorium could come up with, Preston was diagnosed with asthma and bronchitis, but was found to be free of tuberculosis. There wasn't much they could do to treat these conditions, and since his prognosis didn't deem him to be contagious, he was released to go back to his port in San Francisco. Preston and Naomi said their good-byes, and he promised her he would write to her as often as he could.

Once in San Francisco, Preston had a few days with his mother, Edna, before shipping out to the Philippines. He was full of excitement in telling her about his new sweetheart, Naomi. Edna, on the other hand, didn't share his excitement about his new-found love. Even though he explained to Edna that Naomi was cured of tuberculosis and would be going home soon, Edna said, "… he had best stay away from that 'Tuber.'" Preston wasn't really surprised at Edna's behavior. He should have known that she wouldn't want to hear about anyone that he might show more attention to, than her.

On June 30, 1945, Preston shipped out of the Port of San Francisco on the S. S. Winfield Stratton, a freight steamer headed for the Philippines. He kept his promise to Naomi, and not only did he write to her, but he often sent her pretty gifts. Sometimes she would receive soft, hand-embroidered handkerchiefs, or silk scarves made in the Philippines. Once, she received a beautiful handmade silver bracelet with a 1921 silver dollar set in it representing the year of her birth. She had never received such lovely gifts before in all of her life.

On September 2, 1945, Naomi's birthday, General Douglas MacArthur accepted Japan's surrender.

The war was over. Preston would soon be coming home.

Everyone was celebrating the end of World War II and ships were arriving in the ports almost daily. The S. S. Winfield Stratton arrived in Seattle, Washington, and Preston was discharged from his Merchant Marine duties on November 14, 1945.

A few days later, Naomi was collecting the mail from the family mailbox that sat atop the pole standing on the edge of Highway 7 that her father, Jeff, had painted red every spring since she was a little girl. Along with the usual mail and the winter issue of the Sears Roebuck & Company Catalog, Naomi saw a small package addressed to Miss Naomi Bell Keith. She raced to the house, threw the mail on the kitchen table and proceeded to tear open the little package. Wrapped around a tiny blue velvet box was a note that read, *"So that you can't say you didn't have the time, meet me at the Post Office at 5:00 p.m. on Saturday*

414

the 24th. All my love, Preston." Naomi opened the velvet box to reveal the most beautiful tiny gold "Bulova" wristwatch she had ever seen. It was yellow gold with diamond cut white gold trim around it, giving the appearance that it was studded with diamonds. Naomi's mother, Ethel, couldn't believe her eyes when

My Daddy, Preston L. Paden, after WWII – Mama said he had a toothache in this picture.

she saw it. She was sure the watch was all diamonds and gold. She went running to everyone she saw for days, telling them about Naomi's watch, and she idolized Preston before she had ever even met him.

Chapter 53: Preston, Naomi, And Me

Preston LeRoy Paden and Naomi Bell Keith were married in Columbus, Kansas, by Judge David C. Graves on December 12, 1945. Naomi's sister, Mrs. W. D. Dungan (Zelma), was Matron of Honor, and a close friend, C. W. Rogers, was the Best Man.

Naomi & Preston Paden – It's "Mr. & Mrs." Now

Preston and Naomi were ecstatic about having discovered each other; happy that the war was over; and they were looking forward to a long and happy life together. They also knew that Naomi's health was not good enough for her to have children until she had plenty of time to fully recuperate from her long bout with tuberculosis — and then, and only then, to first ask for the medical okay from her doctor.

In short, they knew that they had to be extremely careful, knowing that Naomi should avoid becoming pregnant for the time being.

Uncle Ginney's house in Sapulpa, Oklahoma, had always been a second home to Preston, and he was also very fond of Uncle Ginney's family. Sapulpa, he thought, would be a good place to start his new life with his bride. However, with the war just ending, and the soldiers now returning home, jobs were hard to find and housing was expensive, especially for a couple just getting started. The newlyweds rented an upstairs furnished apartment in the Bell Hotel, located at 17½ East Dewey Avenue, in downtown Sapulpa. The first job that Preston could find was that of a cook at a restaurant within walking distance from their apartment. This was their plan until they could afford to buy a car, after which, Preston could then look for a better paying job.

Naomi was delighted with her new life and her loving husband and their very own little apartment. She enjoyed the city life that she had never been previously exposed to, and marveled at the sights in the nearby city of Tulsa, where they would occasionally visit for an evening out on the town or, at times, just for just shopping. It was the kind of carefree newlywed situation that most young couples could only hope for at that time.

Early into 1946, Naomi was a bit worried when she realized that she was late having her menstrual period. Preston was as concerned and felt extremely guilty, knowing that her doctor had warned them not to let Naomi become pregnant. A visit to the doctor confirmed her pregnancy and she was advised that she should absolutely not give birth to a child, in her condition, at this time. Naomi didn't want to have this abortion so she and Preston talked it over and decided that she had overcome so many obstacles over the years to keep living, that taking this chance now would not be the wise thing to do.

Naomi was admitted to the hospital for the abortion procedure which consisted of performing a spinal block, dilating her cervix, and packing her uterus with gauze soaked in iodine. This packing was left in place for the allotted 24 hours and then removed. As soon as she had regained the feeling in the lower portion of her body, she was released to go home. She wasn't feeling well though, and had a horrendous headache for several days. Her doctor said she would be fine and her body would be back to normal soon.

A few months passed by when Naomi, still not having resumed her monthly periods, began feeling slightly nauseated in the mornings. On a return trip to her doctor, much to his amazement, it was discovered that the previous abortion procedure had failed. The pregnancy was, by now, much too far along to attempt that procedure again. The only other option available was surgery. Naomi was secretly happy that the abortion attempt had failed and she said that if there was surgery to be performed, she would just wait until it was time for delivery and have a caesarian section at that time.

Preston was worried sick about his little wife and their baby. Naomi was confident that all would go well and she was delighted that she was going to get to have her baby after all. The expected date of birth was about September 22nd, so the date of the caesarian section was set for September 2, 1946 — Naomi's upcoming 25th birthday —which allowed plenty of time before she would go into labor in the normal, natural manner.

Then, on a very warm August morning — **August 22, 1946, to be exact** — Naomi awoke feeling full of energy and ready to face a new day. She pulled on her blue jeans that wouldn't quite zip all the way to the top by now, and rolled the legs of her jeans up in "pedal pusher" style. She put on one of Preston's long tail shirts that worked beautifully as a maternity top, stepped into her shoes and headed out to do her grocery shopping.

Feeling relieved that she had gotten her shopping done before the heat of the day had arrived, she climbed the stairs to their apartment with the paper bag containing her groceries. She suddenly experienced an unusual sensation and felt a gush of warm liquid run down her legs. This frightened her, and she then became light-headed and fell into Mrs. Mac's apartment door, after sliding down to the hallway floor. A spry little elderly lady of Scottish descent, with a bit of a Scottish brogue, Mrs. Mac had become one of Naomi's favorite neighbors. Mrs. Mac came to investigate the thud she had heard just outside her apartment door. "Oh my, oh my, what's happened to *me* " Naomi? God bless you child, let's get you inside." It was only minutes before Mrs. Mac — having served as a midwife in her younger years — diagnosed Naomi's condition as being in labor, since her water had already broken. Naomi was afraid that something was wrong because her baby wasn't actually due for another whole month. She imagined all sorts of dire consequences on the taxi ride to the hospital.

Mrs. Mac rode in the taxicab with Naomi, and wisely didn't phone Preston at the restaurant until they had reached the hospital, since that would have meant the loss of valuable time in the process. Naomi, determined as always, made it through the delivery of her baby without experiencing any of the predicted bad side effects of a normal childbirth. Immediately upon his arrival at the hospital, Preston welcomed the announcement that mother and daughter were both doing fine. Naomi and Preston each shed a few happy tears, and couldn't believe that their baby daughter had not only fought the odds of living through an attempted abortion, but also chose her own time to enter this world.

My mother, Naomi, admired the actress Pamela Drake, and therefore chose the first name of Pamela for me. My daddy worshipped his grandmother, Louie Nettie Stanley, who had raised him and his cousin, "Little" Mott, which accounted for my middle name of "Lou." My Cherokee Indian grandfather, George Taylor Paden, who fathered my Grandma Edna's only child, had the honor of giving me my last name.

So in Sapulpa, Oklahoma, on Thursday, the 22nd day of August, in the year of 1946, weighing in at 6 pounds and 12 ounces, with brown eyes and no hair, Pamela Lou Paden entered into this world.

Grandma Edna was pissed, to say the least, when she heard that I was born earlier than expected. It messed up her plans and inconvenienced her considerably, but nevertheless, she boarded a plane to Tulsa as soon as possible. There was no way that she was going to miss out on the limelight of being a new grandmother. Uncle Ginney picked up Edna at the Tulsa Airport upon her arrival and she was firmly planted on the sofa — waiting for us — when we came home. It was a Monday, August 26th, when Preston proudly sat beside his wife and baby in the Buffington Ambulance on their way back to their little apartment.

Among the many visitors to see me were Grandma Edna Memmott (Carl Memmott was Edna's 5th husband); Ruth McEwen (Edna's long time friend); G. A. Stanley (Uncle Ginney); Kenneth Stanley and Norma Jean Stanley (Daddy's cousins); Grandma Ethel Keith (Naomi's mother from Stippville, Kansas); Aunt Wanda Keith (Naomi's sister from Columbus, Kansas); Uncle Dale and Aunt Zelma Dungan (Naomi's sister), and their daughter, Dixie, also from Columbus, Kansas; and Great Grandmother, Louie Nettie Stanley, from Cardin, Oklahoma.

After I was born, and before we headed out west to California, Daddy had to show me off to his Grandma Louie – my namesake.

My Baby Book lists the family and friends that came to visit me. It also includes comments from my parents. Written in his own handwriting, my daddy wrote the following in my baby book:

"This wee Miss has wrapped her tiny arms right around her Daddy's heart."

Awww – I used to carry this in a locket around my neck.

Preston Naomi and me

Chapter 54: California Bound

Sunday, April 14, 1935, started out as a normal, clear day in Guymon, Oklahoma. The temperature was in the upper 80s and the citizens, in their fourth year of drought, went to the Methodist Church for a "rain service." By late afternoon the skies were darkened, but not by rain clouds. Instead, the worst of the black blizzards was about to engulf this town.

At this same time, the Associated Press staff writer, Robert Geiger, was in Guymon, writing a series of articles. In his April 15th release for the Washington, D. C., Evening Star, he wrote, "Three little words achingly familiar on a Western farmer's tongue rule life today in the dust bowl of the continent. **If it rains ..."**

Robert Geiger had just used the term **"dust bowl"** in print for the first time.

Within three months, the term "dust bowl" was being used throughout the nation. For various reasons, the word "Oklahoma" quickly became synonymous with this term.

John Steinbeck's novel, *"The Grapes of Wrath,"* as well as stories and lore about Oklahoma's weather, helped perpetuate Oklahoma's dust bowl image — **"The wind blew the farms away, but we didn't lose everything — we still had the mortgage."**

The word that became synonymous with the migrants, who traveled west from Oklahoma for work, was **"Okie."** Reportedly, Ben Reddick, a journalist with the Paso Robles Press in California, saw numerous "old cars with Oklahoma license plates in migrant camps, reading 'OK.'" On the back of a photo depicting the camps and the autos he wrote the word "Okies," which was published in the caption. With their land barren and their homes foreclosed for unpaid debts, many farm families just gave up and left. The migration was drastic and 15% of the state of Oklahoma moved west. The migrants were generally referred to as Okies, whether or not they were from Oklahoma.

During the late 1930s and into the 1940s, some members of the extended Stanley family and their spouses relocated to various parts of California. Earl Stuchlik's brother, Vernon, was already living in Los Angeles by 1935 at 4273 S. Vermont Street. He and Doris had remained close friends.

About this time, Aunt Doris finally found a fellow who was right for her, and who wasn't into any illegal activities that she was aware of. Uncle James Benjamin "Jay" McCormick was just about as nice a guy as you could ever ask for. Starting out from the bottom as a "rough-neck" on an oil rig, he worked his way up the ladder in the oil field business.

Doris and J. B. McCormick – circa 1940 "Courtesy of Bill Stanley"

Aunt Doris and Jay operated a bar in Torrance, California, at the time.

Uncle Mott and Aunt Helen had also relocated to Los Angeles, California, about this same time.

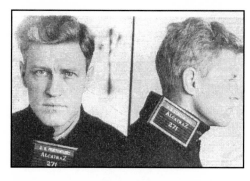

Volney Davis "Courtesy of the Collection of Rick Mattix"

Sometime shortly after being paroled on December 20, 1940, Edna settled farther up north, in San Francisco, California, not far from Volney's residence "On the Rock" in Alcatraz Federal Penitentiary, on Alcatraz Island, just off the coast, near San Francisco.

In late October of 1946, Preston, Naomi and their two month old daughter — me, Pamela Lou — left Sapulpa, Oklahoma, and also headed out west to San Francisco, California, where we lived for nearly two years. Preston worked there in a prestigious chef's position at a very prominent restaurant. It was an enjoyable place to live, and my parents took me for rides on the streetcars and we often visited Fisherman's Wharf where we purchased delicious fresh lobster and shrimp the size of "coffee saucers," as mama would describe them.

Pammy & Preston – Daddy bought me a little lollipop.

Me & Daddy by the Ocean.

Pammy & Naomi – San Francisco Beach

Got my knee up just like my Daddy.

Me & Mama in the Pacific breeze.

Pammy Lou and Grandma Edna – 1947

Grandma Edna giving Pammy Lou a "squeeze" – 1947

Edna had a jealous nature and was even jealous of her own daughter-in-law. She often tried to come between Preston and Naomi, even going so far as to try to interest Preston in other women. When Naomi got word of her mother-in-law's conniving behavior, it was "… the last straw." Out of respect for her husband, Naomi had gone out of her way to tolerate Edna's behavior, and had done everything she could do to befriend her. She had always thought that Edna was probably the worst mother she had ever known — and now this same woman was trying to break up her own son's marriage. Naomi strongly suggested to Preston that it might be better if they didn't live in such close proximity to Edna, and, in fact, another town might even be appropriate. Also, Preston's lung condition wasn't getting any better while living in the damp and rainy weather that was typical of San Francisco.

After discussing his situation with his Aunt Doris, Preston decided that, with some assistance from Uncle Jay, he would give the oil fields in the Los Angeles area a try. Uncle Jay was happy to assist. He liked Preston a lot and always kidded him about his Cherokee Indian heritage by calling him "Quapaw."

Among my first recollections as a child are those of the day in 1949 that we moved into our little duplex house in Long Beach, California. I was almost 3 years old at the time, and I can remember the way the little duplex was laid out, even the way that the new furniture that mama and daddy had bought for it was arranged. The front of the house faced the airport where the planes would fly over our house after taking off. We had a beautiful green lawn that I loved to play on, and we had really nice neighbors next door who had a little boy my age, named

Ramey. We lived on Cherry Avenue, and we weren't very far from "The Pike" that was just the greatest place for kids to go play on the beach.

Aunt Doris, (we called her Aunt "Dode"), and Uncle Jay would visit us often and I just loved these visits. They thought I was pretty special because I was the only little kid they had to spoil. I could do just about anything and Aunt Dode thought it was cute and funny — so I "hammed it up" a lot. Mama and daddy would always give Aunt Dode a report on what I had been doing lately.

One day, my little friend, Ramey, tried to teach me how to go to the bathroom standing up. When mama scolded me for making a mess on the floor, I told her, "… but Ramey does it that way." Ramey also showed me how he could stand on the arm of the couch, unscrew the light bulb in the floor lamp, turn it on and stick his finger in the socket. Mama walked in the room just as the bolt of electricity threw him off the couch, crashing onto the floor. Mama almost had a heart attack and I was pretty scared myself until he got up laughing. I remember hearing mama telling this story to Aunt Doris, and she said that when she told Ramey's dad about it – Ramey's dad was an electrician – he just laughed and said it wouldn't hurt him. Mama said that it might not hurt him at **his** house but it wasn't going to happen anymore at **ours.**

And then there was the day that I found a piece of lead out of an indelible pencil and drew a masterpiece on the living room wall. Mama paddled my behind until it stung for quite a while. When Aunt Dode asked me what happened when I drew on the wall, I told her, "My mama spanked me 'til the "bleed" ran down my leg." Aunt Dode was fighting mad about that until my mama convinced her that was just a terminology I had heard somewhere, and was not what had actually happened.

Preston's health just wasn't good enough for him to be working the oil fields. He tried with all his might, but he just wasn't able to do it. He was very disappointed in himself, but he always had faith in his Aunt Dode.

Doris never lost her love for gambling, and since moving to California, her love of horseracing had become her favorite pastime. She knew all the bookies in the area and had no problem finding someone who needed somebody with a good head for figures. Preston started working as a bookie — and did a mighty fine job of it. He was making around $1,000 a month back in 1949 — which was extremely good money in those days. My mama was a little bit concerned that this activity was illegal, but Aunt Dode said that gambling didn't hurt anybody — and besides, "… it wasn't anybody's business if someone wanted to gamble."

The racetrack at the Alameda County Fairgrounds is the oldest horseracing track in America, dating back to 1858. It is, in fact, older than New York's famous Saratoga Racetrack.

In 1912, the first modern Alameda County Fair was held in Pleasanton, California, when the racetrack owner, Rodney G. MacKenzie, lobbied the California State Legislature to have the racetrack on his property.

Then in 1933, California legalized pari-mutuel betting, and by 1939 pari-mutuel wagering started in Pleasanton, California.

In 1941, the Alameda County Fair ran from July 3rd through July 12th, with 9 of the 10 days scheduled for races, for a total "handle" (money wagered) of $432,644, which, at the time, was a national record. This Fair and Racetrack have continued to set records for money wagered ever since.

In 1949, just before my third birthday, daddy wanted mama and me to see this famous and beautiful racetrack, which was approximately 40 miles from Grandma Edna's apartment on Market Street, in San Francisco. After visiting with Grandma Edna, we then proceeded to the Alameda Racetrack.

I can still remember the racetrack, sitting in the grandstands, looking out in the middle of the track to see a pretty body of water and these magnificent, long-legged pink birds, called pink flamingos. Daddy came to where we were sitting, and brought us something to drink and handed me a candy bar. He stayed in the grandstands with us for a while and told us that he had to go back to work. I'm not sure just what his work there was, but I know it had something to do with betting on the horses.

The very first television set I ever saw was in Aunt Dode's and Uncle Jay's house. I still remember sitting on the floor right in front of it and I was so amazed by the picture on this little round screen. I don't even remember what show we were watching, but I remember being absolutely fascinated by this new technology they called "television."

"Little" Mott Farrell and his wife Ruth Farrell – Doris McCormick and Mott Stanley

"Little" Mott — I called him "Uncle" Mott — and his wife Ruth Evelyn, were also there.

Ruth Evelyn was very sweet and she had the tiniest little feet I had ever seen on a grown person.

That night I decided that I wanted to stay overnight with Aunt Dode and Uncle Jay. That decision lasted until bedtime. It would have been the first time that I had not gone to bed in my own house with my mama and daddy.

So I concocted a plan. I told my Aunt Dode that I didn't feel well. She did everything she could think of to console me, but I just couldn't settle in for the night. Finally, Aunt Dode had to call my daddy to come and get me to take me home.

But, later, as time went by, I did get over being a "scaredy-cat."

Chapter 55: Returning To Kansas —
Then To Oklahoma

"Come on, Pammy," somebody said to me, during what seemed to be the middle of the night. "Come on, baby," daddy said, as he picked me up out of my little youth bed, wrapped my cover around me, and started for the door. Something was said about us going for a visit, and I was soon back asleep in our car.

When I woke up the next morning, our little green Chevy sedan was loaded with what looked like everything that had been in our house, except for the furniture. "Where we goin', daddy?" I asked. "We're going to see a lot of your relatives that haven't seen you for a long, long time," my daddy told me. And then he and mama reeled off a bunch of names of people that I never heard of.

Whatever "Kansas" was, it sure took a long time to get there. Daddy said something about our car tags, and that he didn't want anyone to see them. He would park our car where the tags wouldn't be easy to see when we would stop to eat or spend the night at a motel. I think we were in Colorado when I saw snow for the first time, and daddy pulled off to the side of the road so I could touch it. Then I was taught how to make a snowball — and that led to a little snowball fight, of course. Finally, I tasted some snow and decided that I had done about everything I needed to do with snow. We got back into our car and mama warmed my cold hands and told me stories about all the ways they played with snow in Kansas when she was a little girl. We stayed in a motel in Colorado that first night on the road.

I woke up in the middle of the night in that motel, feeling very thirsty, and walked to the bathroom to gulp down a glass of water. That water tasted awful, and I threw up. The next morning we went into the little café next to the motel and as soon as the waitress brought glasses of water to us, I immediately gulped some of mine down. I had the same reaction as before, only this time I threw up all over the floor in the café. Daddy said that I should not drink any more water, and he ordered some orange juice for me. For years to come, I truly believed that Colorado's water was actually poison.

Mama didn't drive, so daddy did all the driving from the west coast of California to the southeastern corner of Kansas. Sometimes I sat on daddy's lap and helped him drive. He said I was a pretty good driver by the time we reached Kansas. The tops of daddy's fingers were sunburned by then from being on the steering wheel for so long.

Grandma Ethel Keith was tickled to see us when we reached her house on Highway 7 in the little mining community of Stippville, Kansas. I didn't remember her coming to see me when I was born, but she seemed to remember the visit very well. She always seemed happy and spent most of her time in the kitchen, cooking up things to eat. Right after we arrived there, I had to inspect the place, and unknowingly embarrassed my mama to no end when I spotted an old weather stained window in one of the bedrooms and announced to Grandma Keith, "This window is so dirty it's going to get 'fection,' (meaning infection)," which I didn't say correctly.

Grandpa Jeff Keith was sort of a quiet fellow, and spent most of his time plowing or working outside. Grandma Keith acquainted me with country life right away. I thought "… diggin' up sweet taters" was real fun — and so was loading them up with brown sugar, cinnamon and butter — but the very best part was eating them after we took them out of the old cook stove.

I wasn't real sure about getting the chickens ready to cook though. Grandma Keith cornered one of those "young roosters" in the chicken pen and reached down and grabbed him by his head. Before I even knew what had happened, grandma had twisted that young rooster's head off, thrown it over to the pigs, and that rooster was running around squawking and flapping its wings even without its head on! Then she gave the headless rooster a bath in a bucket of boiling water and pulled out all his feathers. After Grandma Keith cooked the rooster, it tasted just like the ones that mama bought in the stores, brought home, and fried.

It seemed like we stayed with Grandma and Grandpa Keith for quite some time. One of my mama's brothers, Raymond, who we called Uncle "Rabb," also lived there. I thought he was very funny. He liked to drink a lot and always seemed to be in a good mood. I can still hear him singing the tune, *"When I lost my baby, I almost lost my mind."* He was a pretty good singer and could really bellow out those old bar tunes.

One night when we were staying at Grandma and Grandpa Keith's house, all of the adults, except for Grandma Keith — so she could babysit for me — went up highway 7 to a big "Dago" party in "Little Italy." That is the only time I ever saw my daddy or my mama intoxicated. My mama spent hours throwing up in grandma's "shit pot" (sic) as they called it, and daddy was doing more crawling than walking — and he and mama were both "cussing" somebody out they called "Gin." Uncle Rabb, who had come home with them, evidently wasn't ready to quit partying yet and then "all hell broke loose" when daddy heard him take off from grandma's house in our green Chevy sedan. Daddy was very upset about that. He just knew that Uncle Rabb would wreck the Chevy, the law would then come into the picture, and daddy would end up in jail. I tried to figure out for many years why daddy was so worried — but I'm sure there was a good reason why we left California in the middle of the night.

One day, we put all of our belongings back into the green Chevy sedan and told everybody goodbye. The whole Keith family was there on the day we left to see us off. I had grown very fond of my Aunt Zelma and Uncle Dale Dungan, and especially of my cousin, Dixie Dungan, who was just one year older than I was. Also, there was Aunt Bonnie and Uncle Chester Keith, and their son, Donnie, who was about two years older than I was; and Aunt Wanda and Uncle Louie Schreiner, who didn't have any children yet. I just loved Aunt Wanda. She made me laugh when she said that Uncle Louie was a fireman and he just peed on the fires to put them out. All the Keith family had a funny sense of humor and they were a lot of fun to be around and were a very loving family.

The stay at Grandma and Grandpa Keith's house had just been a temporary visit and we were headed back to Sapulpa, Oklahoma, where I was born. Uncle Ginney, his wife Jewel, and their family were there to greet us when we arrived. They were to become a big and important part of our lives for several years to come.

I could never forget moving into our apartment in Sapulpa. There were some really wild kids running all over the place. Daddy said they were "wild Indians." I was told that I was a good deal of Cherokee Indian myself, but I thought I would never act like those kids did. Well, I probably did, and I learned to love the Indians and was told by the Indians to dislike the "Niggers" (sic), as they were called back in those days. I didn't know why I wasn't supposed to like the "Niggers" (sic), that's just what the Indian kids told me to do. And the Indian kids said that the Indians really owned Oklahoma, and they were just being nice in letting everybody else live there. But they said that the "Niggers" (sic) had to live on the other side of the tracks and live on "Nigger Hill" (sic). All I knew was that the "Niggers" (sic), if they came into town, went to their own school, sat in the back seats on the buses, used the restrooms that said "Colored," all the while that I was to use the ones that said "White," and the same rule was in effect for drinking fountains. And they always walked half on the sidewalk and half in the street. For a while I thought they did that so they wouldn't rub any black off on the white people.

Our apartment was at 313½ E. Hobson in Sapulpa, and it wasn't that far from the railroad tracks. During the summer, I would walk down the alley and snoop around under the big stacks of railroad ties. One day I met some of the "Nigger" (sic) kids that lived up on "Nigger Hill" (sic). We played together just like any kids would, and I went home and asked my mama why I wasn't supposed to like them. Mama didn't have any reason why I shouldn't like them, and she said that I didn't have to "not like them," but she thought it would be safer for me if I didn't go there and play with them.

My mama and daddy never mistreated anybody because of the color of their skin. In fact, I remember a colored lady that we called Aggie, who swept the apartment building halls. It would be so very hot in the summer, and poor Aggie would be dripping with sweat by the time she got to our end of the hall. My mama would always offer her a glass of ice water, and Aggie would thank her again and again for it. I liked Aggie because she was pleasant, and she was always very nice to me.

Our next door neighbors in the apartment house connected to ours were the Adkins family. They were a real hoot. I thought they were funny from the very first day I met them. We actually became real good friends with them, but they never ceased to amaze me. I can't remember Mrs. Adkins' first name — we just called her Mrs. Adkins. The father of the family was Nat Adkins. The oldest boys were twins, Lee and Lump Adkins. Next was the oldest girl, Natalee Adkins, and her son's name was Jodylee Adkins. Then there was Brookalee Adkins, and her son, Orbylee, and daughter Judy Lee. The youngest of the Adkins kids was Leegus. I don't ever remember meeting any spouses of the Adkins kids, and they all lived at their parent's apartment with their children.

They were a wild bunch for sure. They were Creek Indians, and they drank a lot. The boys were always getting into fights and the girls weren't afraid of much of anything. The only time we ever had any differences with them was one time shortly after I had been given a baby duck for Easter. I named the duck "Little Bit" because not only was he little, but everywhere he went, he left a "little bit." One day I had Little Bit out on the old wooden balcony in a washtub, letting him swim. When he was finished, I dumped the water out and it ran down stairs on the ground below. Natalee must have been having a bad day, or had too

438

much to drink or something, because she came running up the stairs to our balcony screaming about me dumping "duck shit" in their yard. Mama came out and tried to explain to her that it was just clean water that the little duck had been swimming in, and it wasn't going to hurt anything. Nothing was going to settle down Natalee with the mood she was in. I remember being really scared when she started threatening to hurt my mama, and the next thing I knew, mama had a butcher's knife in her hand. Finally, Natalee decided to go home, and I'm not sure but I think I peed in my pants before the whole ordeal was over.

Natalee was a hard person to reason with after she had too much to drink.

Chapter 56: Getting To Know Grandma Edna

My early memories of Grandma Edna are somewhat vague, but I can remember how she looked, how she acted, and things that we did together when she came to visit us in Sapulpa, Oklahoma, particularly in the summer of 1952. We did a lot of visiting with her friends, Ruth McEwen and Clarence — but I don't recall ever hearing of Clarence's last name. Grandma Edna once told me that Ruth and Clarence weren't married to each other — only that Clarence was her boyfriend.

Ruth owned, or managed, an older second story hotel that was more like a rooming house than a hotel. She lived in two of the units on the backside that were across the hall from each other. One unit was composed of one big room that had a living area at one end, and a bedroom at the other. I thought this was where Ruth slept since it was quite nice and fancy — as a lady would fix it. In this unit, she had a big wardrobe with mirrors on the doors, and a pretty vanity dresser with a big mirror in the center and smaller mirrors, on hinges, on each side. I liked to sit in front of this dresser and move the mirrors so I could see all sides of myself. Ruth was nice and gave me combs and bar-rettes and bobby pins, and all sorts of nice things to help me fix my hair.

Ruth's apartment across the hall consisted of a kitchen in one half of the unit, and a small bedroom and sitting area in the other half. This unit looked more like a man's room, and it smelled like cigars, so I thought that maybe Clarence slept in there. We only went across the hall to this unit when Ruth was cooking. Clarence either owned or managed the cigar store and beer parlor that was on the lower level of the hotel. The name of this business was the Lawrence Cigar Store and, along with the hotel, was located in the Dewey Unit Block on the corner of Dewey Avenue and Main Street in Sapulpa.

Once, when Ruth took Grandma Edna and me up to the front of the hotel, I sat on a windowsill and looked down at the parade on Dewey Avenue, which was part of Old Route 66. Both Grandma Edna and Ruth had a "death grip" on me to keep me from falling and I thought the parade below was really neat. We were in a room that some man rented, but Ruth said that he wouldn't mind if we watched the parade from his room.

When Grandma Edna came for visits, she and Ruth would mostly just sit around and talk. I'm not sure if they were long-time friends, but they sure had many things in common dating from years ago, and they talked about people they both remembered. Every now and then, one of them, usually Ruth, would declare that "... Pammy probably needs a soda," and we would go downstairs and get something from Clarence to drink. As we would turn the corner to go into the Lawrence Cigar Store, there would always be a distinct aroma of tobacco smoke coming from the door. One day as we started to go into Clarence's store, there was a big commotion going on out in front, and several men picked up another man — who had apparently suffered a heat stroke — and placed him inside the store on the water cooler. I just sat there on my stool, drinking my root beer, until it was decided that he was going to be all right. This incident was "the talk of the town" for quite some time to come.

One unusual thing that I remember quite clearly when visiting at Ruth's apartment is that sometimes when we were in her kitchen, she would put honey in Grandma Edna's eyes. And after a while, Edna would say, "Yeah, that's better, I can see better now." At the time, I didn't have any idea why Ruth was doing that for Grandma Edna.

Well, about 35 years later, I was diagnosed with a hereditary eye disease called Fuchs' Corneal Dystrophy. About 1% of the nation is afflicted with this condition in which the bottom layer of the cornea does not have a sufficient number of cells to keep the edema pumped out of the cornea. Once the excess fluids are accumulated in the cornea, it is similar to trying to look through a fogged-up lens in your eyeglasses. I was asked by my ophthalmologist if anyone in my family had experienced this condition. It was then that I recalled the "honey" treatment, as described above. My ophthalmologist laughed and said that the honey would have helped to draw out the excess fluid in Grandma Edna's corneas. He said that he would make a note of that to pass on in his documentations.

I am uncertain as to Grandma Edna's marital status at the time of this particular visit in 1952. I think she was married, but she had a boyfriend not long after she arrived in town. I remember him well, and I swear his name was "Hank." That's funny, because her sixth, and last, husband also went by the name of Hank. But this Hank — "Sapulpa" Hank — was in the picture just while Grandma Edna was in Sapulpa. He had a Nash Rambler that was just the cutest car that I had ever seen.

One evening, Grandma Edna and "Sapulpa" Hank took me out to eat. We went in the little Nash Rambler, of course, and after dinner I had ice cream. I was busy enjoying every little lick off each spoonful of ice cream, since this was a luxury my parents couldn't easily afford. Once in a while I would glance up at Grandma Edna, who was playing "kissy-face" with "Sapulpa" Hank in between taking puffs off her cigarette. I was a little bit embarrassed by this "kissy-face" stuff, so I tried to keep my eyes focused only on my ice cream. All of a sudden I found something hard and sharply pointed inside my mouth. I took it out as fast as I could, and while holding it between my fingers, I exclaimed "Grandma, Look!" She said, "Yeah, Honey, it's a piece of ice." "Uh uh, Grandma," I said, "It's a piece of glass!" I had no idea what level of drama I had started by saying that. Grandma Edna, in getting out of the booth, almost knocked "Sapulpa" Hank right off his seat and onto the floor. He was stumbling to catch his balance, and was wearing somewhat of a dumbfounded look on his face. I was probably looking dumbfounded myself, because I didn't know what was coming next, either. Well, Grandma Edna then stuck about 6 of her fingers in my mouth, prying it open to check inside. She asked me, "Are you hurt?! Are you cut?! Are you bleeding?! We'll sue these bastards if you're hurt!" I was trying to say **"No"** but I was having a hard time being understood with so many of Grandma Edna's fingers fishing around inside my mouth.

By this time, everybody in the restaurant was gathering around us, or at least staring at us from where they were sitting. And while I had previously thought that Grandma Edna's "kissy-face" stuff with "Sapulpa" Hank was embarrassing — this new scene, consisting of her sticking both of her hands into my mouth — almost breaking my jaw at the same time — was totally humiliating for me! I had suddenly lost my appetite for any more ice cream — especially since my grandma had washed the nicotine from her fingers into my mouth — and I just wanted to get out of there fast. I finally got the chance to say, "Grandma, I'm Okay! Can we go?" She then asked, "Are you sure you aren't cut?" Then she turned towards the person who was manning the cash register and demanded, "Where's the manager of this establishment?" as she had a hold of my arm, dragging me up to the cash register. In retrospect, it seems like we got our meal for free — but I know I never ever went into that restaurant again — and that was one bowl of ice cream that I will never ever forget eating!

Grandma Edna was always very expressive when she talked and told stories. If she found something to be funny, she would throw her head back and let out a big hearty laugh. She had gold around some of her teeth that was quite visible and shiny when she laughed. On the other hand, if something had upset her or made her angry, she wasn't bashful about spilling out some cuss words, either. Ruth didn't seem to mind though, and she always enjoyed Edna's company when she was in town. When I was listening, Grandma Edna would often say, "Now, Pammy Lou, don't you be telling your mama I told you that!" I would answer by saying, "I won't, Grandma." Usually I kept my word, but sometimes I would ask mama what something meant — and when she'd ask where I heard that from — well, that meant that I had unintentionally "let the cat out of the bag."

Grandma Edna was also a "quick change" artist when it came to changing the subject. She would be talking about "Curly" or "Blackie" or "Gold Tooth Harry," or somebody getting shot, or somebody getting caught — and I would be sitting on the floor, right in front of her, mesmerized by her story, and then she would often say something like, "… and it was the cutest little dress I had ever seen." I thought that maybe Grandma Edna was a little bit goofy the first time that happened. But it didn't take me long to figure out that the "quick change" occurred when my mama was walking into the room.

Grandma Edna also had some bad habits that got on my mama's nerves. One thing in particular is that Edna would walk around barefoot in the apartment most of the time. And then when she was ready to go to bed, she would get a nice clean washcloth out of our cabinet in the bathroom, wet it under the faucet, sit on the edge of the bed, and proceed to wipe her feet off with the washcloth, and then just toss it down on the wood floor.

It wasn't as if we had a full-time maid that came in and picked up the laundry and washed it every day. My poor mama did her best to keep our apartment nice and clean at the least possible cost. We didn't have a washing machine, and we didn't have any transportation. Mama and I would put the dirty laundry in my *"Radio Flyer"* wagon and we would pull it down to the wash house — a few blocks away. We always hung our clothes out to dry on the balcony — or even in the house, if the weather was bad. But when daddy got really ill and mama wouldn't leave him, she washed everything by hand in the kitchen sink, even scrubbing the dirty spots with her bare knuckles. I know that my mama did not enjoy washing the dirty washcloths that Grandma Edna had used to clean her feet.

Grandma Edna also had an irritating habit of cleaning off her makeup on a clean washcloth and leaving it in some haphazard spot — but the foot-washing regimen "took the cake" and was the one my mama hated the most.

446

Chapter 57: Wallace The Cat, And MacTavish The Dog

One summer when daddy was still getting around pretty well, some of the family from California came to Oklahoma for a visit. Some of their time was spent visiting in Sapulpa, where we all congregated at Uncle Ginney's house for picnics and festivities. Grandma Edna wasn't there during that visit. By this time, she and her sister, Aunt Doris, scarcely talked to each other. They had always argued and fought, and the older they got, the more they got on each other's nerves. I would assume that the reason Edna didn't show up for this visit was probably because Doris made sure that she wasn't invited.

Aunt Doris and Uncle Jay McCormick had the most amazing cat that I, or almost anybody, had ever seen. Wallace wasn't just a big cat — he was huge. He was almost as big as most of the neighborhood dogs, and all of the dogs were afraid of him, mainly because Wallace wasn't intimidated by them, and he didn't back off, either. He was Aunt Doris' baby and he was spoiled rotten. He actually thought that he was a person, and not only that — he used the bathroom just like a normal person. I had already heard about his many talents and had seen many pictures that Aunt Doris had sent of Wallace using the "stool" — but I thought the funniest thing I ever saw was when Aunt Doris showed me Wallace's potty chair that they brought with them in the car from California.

After vacationing in Sapulpa for a while, just about everybody went to Cardin, Oklahoma, to visit Grandma Louie Nettie Stanley. Grandma Lou was just a little bit of a thing, but she was pretty feisty. And she wasn't used to, or happy to have, animals in her house -- and especially ones that thought they were people and could use her potty. And even though Grandma Lou did tolerate Wallace in her house — along with his special talents — he eventually did cross the line.

If there is one thing I will never forget, it is the time that Wallace danced his little butt around on Grandma Lou's kitchen table. Lou was fixing a spread of her favorite dishes for her kids, grandkids, and great grandkids that had come to Cardin to visit. She had the table all set, with a few relishes on it, when she glanced towards the table and saw Wallace prancing around and sniffing everything. Talk about quick! Grandma Lou flew across the kitchen and slapped the daylights "… outta that damn cat." But instead of jumping down off the table like an ordinary cat, Wallace slapped at little Lou's arm with extended claws and ripped her fragile aging skin open with razor-like cuts. Lou cried out in pain, and one of the boys came running into the kitchen. That is the last thing — Grandma Lou crying out in pain — that I clearly remember happening from that event. After that, everything became somewhat of a blur. Someone started yelling — and then I heard that one of the boys "… was going to kill that goddamned cat." Aunt Doris responded that it would only happen "… over her dead body." Everybody was screaming and yelling and cussing like I had never before heard in my life. I was petrified. I got as far back in the corner of the kitchen as I could get and I even covered my eyes. There was no doubt in my mind that somebody was going to die because everybody was threatening to kill someone.

Somehow, everybody lived through the "Wallace Incident" unscathed, which was somewhat of a miracle, considering that

Pammy Lou visiting Grandma Lou in Cardin, Oklahoma

half of the Stanley family was drunk — not to mention that they were the craziest family I had ever seen in my life.

That was actually the last time that I ever saw Aunt Doris and Uncle Jay. But, Aunt Doris wrote to us frequently, and she never ever forgot my birthday or missed sending me a Christmas present. She didn't have any grandchildren of her own, and since she treated my daddy as if he were her kid, she also always did special things for me. I was her proxy grandchild.

One thing that always stuck in my mind was the time Aunt Doris shared her winnings from the racetrack with me. Aunt Dode (daddy's name for her) loved to gamble, and always did. Well, I had written to her about a "Win the Puppy Contest" that I won when I was about nine years old. They had a really cute little Welsh Terrier on the Uncle Zeb Show (a kid's show that came on after school on weekdays from the Muskogee, Oklahoma, television station). I wanted to enter the contest, and my mama agreed to it. Well, I wrote a little letter and explained that since the puppy was Welsh, I thought the name "MacTavish" would be just perfect for him. Much to my surprise, and especially to my mama's surprise, I won "MacTavish" as well as 24 cases of Kennel Ration dog food. Since daddy was confined to our apartment and mama never drove or left daddy alone, the minister and his wife, from the church where I went to Sunday school, took me to the television station. I got to be on the Uncle Zeb Show and received my prize of a 6 week old puppy and all that dog food. We had cases of Kennel Ration stashed under our beds for months.

Shortly after I won MacTavish, Aunt Dode went to the race-track and, there on the list of horses for one of the races, was a horse named, of all things, MacTavish. Aunt Doris, being the superstitious gambler that she was, bet on the long shot — on the horse named MacTavish. Her horse came in, in second place and Aunt Dode won a lot of money that day.

Since I was the one that had selected the lucky name, Aunt Dode determined that I was entitled to a share of her winnings. She sent me two very crisp, brand new $20 bills. When I received the money I yelled out, "Holy-Cow! That's the most money I have ever owned in my life." I had the best time ever, shop-ping for new school clothes that year. And, as always, my daddy thought his Aunt Dode was just the greatest.

Doris Stanley – 1940 – 40 yrs. Old

450

Chapter 58: School Days In Sapulpa, Oklahoma

The first day at Washington Elementary School in Sapulpa, during the fall of 1952, was a little bit frightening for me. As best as I could recall, up until that point in my life, I had spent every day with my mama and daddy. But it wasn't long before I was no longer afraid because I quickly made a lot of new friends and I decided that school was fun, after all.

Our first grade teacher, Mrs. Sprague, was short and round and had a jolly personality. Her big crusade, right off the bat, was to have the girls signed up for the "Brownies." I ran home all excited about joining the Brownies — and my mama chose some tactful words for telling me that we couldn't afford the uniforms and the costs of joining. I don't recall that the words she said came as crushing news, but, all these many decades later, I still haven't forgotten the day, the excitement, and later, the disappointment I felt.

Norma Jean Stanley (Ginney's oldest daughter), Louie Nettie Stanley, Pamela Lou Paden, G. A. "Ginney" Stanley, Vicki Lynn Stanley (Ginney's youngest child) – circa 1952

The next year at school, my most vivid memory of second grade was the day my teacher, Miss Young, stormed into the girl's washroom and yanked me off the toilet stool, not even allowing me to wipe myself, and ordered me to pull up my pants and get back in to my classroom. My "hiney" itched all day and I felt from that day forward that she didn't believe a word that I told her. I really wasn't trying to get out of doing my class work, but rather, I was suffering from a severe bout of constipation.

Front row- cousins Karen, Vicki Lynn, and Mike Stanley; Back row- Preston Paden, Ruth Evelyn Farrell, Kenneth Stanley, "Little" Mott Farrell, "Ginney" Stanley, Naomi Paden, and Grandma Louie Nettie Stanley. I was in school and missed being in the picture.

Mama would always shop at "Naifeh Brothers Foods" to buy our groceries. It was one block from our apartment house — straight down the alley. It seemed like The Naifeh Brothers owned about half of the city of Sapulpa. Anyway, in addition to the grocery store, they also owned the apartment building that we lived in, as well as a tobacco company and other businesses. Daddy would take us to Naifeh Brothers in our Chevy coupe, and then he and I would go next door to "Flo's Bar." Flo was a blonde-headed lady that had an all-around good disposition. Daddy wasn't much of a drinker that I ever saw, but he would order a mug of beer to drink while mama was shopping. He would sprinkle salt on the top of his beer and some "big ole" suds would foam up on top. That was when he would let me slurp the salty suds off, before he drank his beer. I thought that was the best thing ever. Flo would always give me a little bag of salted peanuts which made me feel as if I was one of "the gang" at Flo's. There was a nice gentleman that always sat on the first bar stool as you came in the door. His name was Mel Robertson, and I liked him because he always talked to me and told me that I had big brown, and pretty eyes, and I would probably be a movie star some day. I thought that was funny, and I would laugh with him. He had an envelope that he always carried in his pocket that had pictures of his son, Dale Robertson, and Mel said that his son was a movie star. I didn't know much about movies or movie stars, but I liked Mel. I remember one time Mel had just come home from visiting his son in Hollywood and his hair was a lot darker than it usually was. Daddy said not to say anything about his hair. He said Mel wanted to look nice for his son when he went to see him, so he decided to dye his hair.

Sure enough, when I checked on Mel's son, Dayle Lymoine Robertson, I discovered that he was born on July 14, 1923, in Harrah, Oklahoma, to Melvin and Vervel Robertson. He was best known for his role as Jim Hardie in the television series, *"Tales of Wells Fargo,"* as well as his role as Ben Calhoun in the television series, *"Iron Horse."* He starred in 63 films before he retired in Yukon, Oklahoma.

It was around my seventh birthday when I noticed my daddy didn't always feel well, and he seemed to cough a lot more than usual and he used his nebulizer a lot. He didn't laugh and play with me as much as he used to, but he still called me his little "Sweet Petunia." I had no idea what a sweet petunia was, but I knew it had to be good because it started with the word "sweet."

Daddy had a knack for working with numbers and was somewhat of a human calculator. He did all the neighbors' income tax returns for them in the evenings after he came home from work, and sometimes on the weekends, too. Of course he charged them much less than what they would have paid to an accountant.

If daddy wasn't working on something, he was reading since he always loved to read and learn. He was especially interested in books on medicine and general medical knowledge. He usually had a pretty good idea what to do for common ailments, and knew if an illness was severe enough to require a physician's treatment. One time there was a Creek Indian girl in our building who was very ill. Since everyone in our building knew that daddy was very knowledgeable about diagnosing illnesses and recommending the right treatments, the girl's husband came to our apartment to seek my daddy's advice. The couple was very young, and already had one child. The young girl, after believing that she was with child again, had taken some kind of a "medicine-man concoction" that was supposed to abort the fetus. I remember my daddy telling my mama the girl needed to be hospitalized immediately. He said that she probably had set herself up for gangrene, and what she had taken could have killed her. In the end, she survived the ordeal, and all the Indian occupants of our building were very thankful that my daddy had insisted that she see a medical doctor.

Another time that I remember daddy coming to the rescue was one night when I woke up with a nasty case of croup and was very frightened. I would cough and cough and I sounded like a goose. Daddy and mama didn't drink, but most all of our Creek Indian neighbors did drink whiskey. Daddy asked mama to ask one of our Indian lady friends if she might happen to have some whiskey in their house. The lady gave mama a little shot glass full of whiskey. Daddy proceeded to mix up a tiny jigger of sugar, and then he dampened it with whiskey, for me to suck on. That croup was gone in no time.

The next morning, one of the neighbor ladies came over and wanted to know how my croup was progressing. I told her, "Oh, I'm over my croup, but I sure have a nasty hangover." Everyone laughed about that for the longest time.

Mama and daddy seemed to worry about money a lot, especially when daddy had been too sick to go to work. Finally, one day, he was unable to ever go to work anymore.

Mama cried sometimes and always seemed worried. I once heard the doctor say that he would have an oxygen bottle sent to the apartment and he was sorry that he couldn't do more. Mama was beginning to have a lot of chest pains at that time, and that, too, frightened me.

It was a spring day in 1954, when Sapulpa was hit by a tornado. The wind was breaking out our windows, blowing the door off its hinges, and daddy, of course, due to anxiety, on top of his lung condition — and feeling so helpless — was sent into an asthma attack. Mama hooked him up with his oxygen mask, and she and I were doing our best to nail blankets over the windows to keep out the flying debris. We repositioned the door to where it had been before it blew into the kitchen, and secured it by driving case knives into its frame. Mama was having chest pains and sat down on the couch to try to catch her breath. It was then that another window blew out, and a huge "dagger shaped" piece of glass was driven into the wall just above her head. That was the last straw — my courage was totally shattered — and I began screaming. That was the most horrifying storm I ever lived through. Once the bricks quit falling from above the windows and the winds died down, I just held my breath, fearing that this nightmare of a storm would start all over again. The electricity was off, and it was as dark outside as if it were midnight. Mama and I lit some candles and started soaking up the water off the floors with our towels, and then wringing them out by hand into the kitchen sink. When it finally became almost daylight again, we looked outside to see what appeared to be a war zone. The thing that still sticks in my mind to this day is the motorcycle that was parked in front of our apartment house. An electric high line wire had fallen on the motorcycle and literally melted it into the pavement. Trees were everywhere, water was everywhere, and people were crying and bleeding and running around like they were crazy. For years to come, when the skies even hinted of stormy weather, I would start closing the blinds, shutting the drapes, and beginning to look for places to hunker down.

In third or fourth grade, I had a teacher named Mr. Greenfeather. He was one of my favorite teachers because he would tell us about himself living on an Indian Reservation as a child, and how tough it was for him growing up. I felt like I could identify with him somewhat, because my world was taking a turn for the worse, and I was sometimes very afraid of what the future held for me.

I didn't realize it at the time, but I was about to grow up fast. My daddy was likely to have an attack at any time because of his diseased lungs, and my mama would rarely leave his side while he was confined to our home. I acquired the duties of grocery shopping, paying the utility bills, and standing in the commodity line each month to collect our allotted share of "basic foods" that

456

the state afforded us. I will never, ever, forget some of the people that stood in that commodity line and it frightened me just to look at some of them. I feel a lot of shame now for feeling that way, but I was only 8 years old then and I had led a rather sheltered life by the time I first experienced this humiliation. Most everyone in line seemed to have a mean look on their face, and many of them smelled like they never bathed. The mothers with children by their sides always seemed so unhappy with the children and would often yell at them and slap their little faces. And, standing in line, there was always this one particular colored man who was the biggest person that I had ever seen. He was a huge man and towered over everyone else. But it wasn't his size that unnerved me, but rather his left eyeball. It was at least three times larger than the average person's eyeball and it sat in a huge eye socket half way down on his left cheek — and this left eye always looked at me, no matter which way his head was turned, or where I was standing. I felt so sorry for him because of his appearance — but at the same time — I was afraid of him. Standing in that line was the most humiliating thing that I ever had to do, but I never let my mother or daddy know this — and I would fight back tears all the way to the "commodity line." I don't know why I dreaded it so — I should have been grateful, but I was so uncomfortable at just being there. And, to this day, I still don't like white rice, and I don't care if I ever see another box of processed cheese.

There is nothing worse than not being able to get your breath — nothing! Lung disease, especially in a middle-aged person, can almost always guarantee a horrible death. Knowing that he would someday suffocate, surely added to the anxiety that led my daddy into those terrible episodes of turning blue — meaning that he was not being able get enough oxygen into his lungs. I'm not sure what they did that helped him, but the firemen from the fire station, several blocks down the street from us, would come to assist us when daddy was having difficulty breathing. We didn't have a telephone and none of our close neighbors did either. When daddy would have an attack, I would always be the one to run to the fire station as fast as I could possibly run. I would be so afraid that my daddy was going to die that I would run so hard that my heart would pound like it was coming through my chest. The firemen would give me a ride back home with them in the fire truck and we would all run up the stairs and down the hall to the very back apartment where my mama would be comforting my daddy. Maybe it was just the feeling of knowing that someone was trying to do something for him, but the firemen always helped to stabilize him and made him feel better.

I hated the fifth grade, as well as my teacher, Mrs. Hewitt. Not only was I regularly standing in the commodity line by now, but this was also the year that I was put on the "free lunch program." Every day, Mrs. Hewitt would take the lunch count, and then say aloud, **"... and the four, of course."** She was referring to me, and three little smelly, dirty, Creek Indian kids, who were also getting free lunches from the state. For whatever reason, every kid in the class would look at each and every one of the four of us — every time she said those 5 words. Somehow, I just didn't classify myself with the caliber of the three other kids on the free lunch program, since I did not, and would not ever, come to school dirty and smelly. But I had no choice in the matter. I was 9 years old and my parents had suddenly become very poor, and my daddy was very sick. I would never forget Mrs. Hewitt saying **"... and the four, of course,"** and making my heart sink every day that I sat in her classroom.

One area that Mrs. Hewitt could never belittle in me was my mind. I excelled in her class and I placed in the spelling contest for our district. My theme paper won second place in the whole county — and when I stood in front of my class, I could tell funnier stories than anyone else. My literary compositions were my favorite part of class and I would spend hours getting each word to represent the exact thought I wanted to get across. My daddy was my very own living, breathing, talking, and personal library. He could quote facts to backup anything I wanted to prove. He could spell even the most difficult of words, and I can't remember ever having a question that he didn't have the answer for. Realizing that most kids feel the same way about their dad as I did, I do believe that my daddy was exceptionally intelligent. But he sure went through some tough times to get that smart!

Chapter 59: The FBI Comes To Our House

After hearing of how the FBI agents had unfairly and rudely treated my Grandma Edna, along with some other ugly descriptions she had made of the agency, the mere mention of the three letters — **F - B - I** — sent a shiver up my spine. I was mortified the day that three men, dressed in suits, knocked on the door of our little apartment at 313½ East Hobson, in Sapulpa, Oklahoma, and shouted, "FBI — OPEN UP!" Then, when I saw my daddy's frail little body, dressed only in pajamas, walking to the door with his hands held over his head, I was horrified, humiliated, and angry. Daddy, sensing my fear, said, "It's all right, Pammy Lou. You go out and play." I went out on the old wooden balcony just outside our little kitchen window while I felt my heart pounding in my chest, and waited until the three men in suits had left. I don't know what I thought might happen, but Grandma Edna had instilled a fear of the FBI in me, and I just knew something bad was going to happen to my daddy. The FBI men spoke loudly and sounded mean. After they left, daddy told me that they wanted to locate Grandma Edna because of a trial that they needed her to attend. My daddy assured me that everything was going to be okay.

Edna & Henry "Hank" Potter – Edna's 6th husband "Courtesy of Bill Stanley"

According to FBI Files:

"Edna Murray (Martha Edna Potter) was served with a subpoena on July 8, 1954, at her apartment in San Francisco, California."

Joplin News Herald

St. Paul, Minnesota

Thursday, July 8, 1954

"Barker-Karpis Gang's Lurid Career Has Echo"

"Echoes of the notorious Barker-Karpis gang are resounding in a federal courtroom here today as Volney Davis seeks freedom from a life sentence for his part in the kidnapping of Edward G. Bremer, a St. Paul brewer.

"Davis, now a slim and white haired 52 (year old man), was brought here from Leavenworth Penitentiary to present his case before Judge Gunnar H. Nordbye. He has been in prison, first at Alcatraz and then at the Kansas institution, ever since he was sentenced after pleading guilty June 3, 1935. He charges he was denied the services of an attorney.

"On the law enforcement side, another famous name ... Melvin Purvis ... is listed among the government's 30 witnesses. Purvis, then FBI agent in charge of the Chicago office, said his men captured Davis (on) June 1, 1935.

GAINED MORE FAME

"Purvis gained earlier, and more lasting, fame when he and his agents shot down John Dillinger, another headliner of the gangster era, outside a Chicago theatre, (in 1934).

462

"On the stand all day yesterday, Davis told how he grew up in his native Oklahoma with Fred and Doc Barker. Later, when the Barkers joined Alvin Karpis in a wave of crime that claimed headlines throughout the 1920s and early 1930s, Davis said he went along.

"'The Barkers spent thousands of dollars in 1932 to get me out of a life term for murder in Oklahoma,' the witness said. 'After that, I traveled with them and they supplied me with money. But I didn't know their business.'

"Records disclose the Barker-Karpis boys were responsible for slayings, bank robberies, holdups and other crimes in a dozen states. The spree ended when Bremer was snatched from a St. Paul street, with a $200,000.00 ransom paid for his release."

This visit from Grandma Edna was the one when she had just come from testifying in St. Paul, Minnesota, when she complied with her subpoena to testify on July 12, 1954. She was wound up, like a "nine-day clock," according to my mama. Grandma Edna was rattling on and on about the "… good ol' days," telling story after story. Mama, who apparently was wishing Edna would just shut up, kept finding things to occupy my time so I wouldn't be listening so closely. It seems as if Grandma Edna stayed quite a while on that visit. She was more talkative than she had ever been, and told how "Curly" (Volney Davis) now had "white" curls. She spoke of "Blackie" Doyle, Harry Sawyer, and several other people and events at the trial that helped refresh her memory. Somewhere into her conversation, she got off on a rant against Paula "fat witted"

463

Harmon again — or as Alvin Karpis referred to her — "Paula the Drunk." Now if Paula was always drunk, and Edna was never sober — that seems like a good reason why they were fighting all the time.

Edna also seemed to want to blame Aunt Doris for everything that had gone wrong — especially when Doris' shooting of the woman (Frances Taylor) in Kansas City brought the heat down on all of them. Daddy was sticking up for his Aunt Dode to some degree, which only wound up Grandma Edna even more and she then really "hit the roof" and cussed up a storm!

Grandma Edna visited with her friend, Ruth McEwen, at the hotel, just like old times, and I went with her most times because school was out and I always wanted to tag along in order not to miss out on anything.

It was also on this trip when Grandma Edna brought a copy of a gangster comic that she seemed quite proud of. I remember it well — it was the "August, 1954, Issue" of *True Detective (Avon Books) Issue #4.* It had an 8 page story of my Grandma, Edna Murray, with art by Sid Check, and she was featured as "The Kissing Bandit." She had copies of this issue for everyone. Uncle Ginney and his family had one. Of course, Ruth McEwen — grandma's best friend in Sapulpa — had one, and I know we had one. I was totally fascinated with it since no one else in our family had a story about themselves in a detective magazine. I just couldn't believe that this was my grandma they were writing about. Daddy didn't seem to think it was that much of a big deal. My mama wasn't as enthusiastic about this featured article about Grandma Edna as I was — in fact, the last time I remember seeing the magazine was when she caught me reading it for the umpteenth time and said, "Give me that damn thing!" Yes, that was the last time I saw that magazine in our house!

There was an incident that happened during my grandma's visit that I just never understood. Daddy hated taking any kind of medication that might become habit forming, but finally, when his breathing became so labored that it was causing fear and anxiety for him, his doctor convinced him to take a barbiturate that calmed him down a bit. He was also having some difficulty swallowing during these episodes, and I would put one of the "red gelatin" capsules in a little tiny shot glass with some warm water so that it would dissolve. This made it much easier for daddy to swallow. I remember this well, because I had done it so many times for him. Also, we had several of these little shot glasses that were made where daddy used to work in Sapulpa, at the Bartlett Collins Glass Factory, where he was the timekeeper until April of 1954. All of these glasses had funny little sayings on them that represented different terminologies for a shot of whiskey, such as "bottoms up" (with a monkey hanging upside down on it); "a night cap" (with a guy in his nightcap); as well as "just a swallow" (with a swallow bird); and so on. I would read the saying out loud as I would hand daddy his "shot" of medicine. Well, on this particular night, mama was getting daddy's capsule out of his bottle, which was kept in the refrigerator, and she noticed that there weren't very many left in the bottle. This didn't seem right since I had just walked to the drugstore a few days before, for his refill. Mama mentioned this to daddy, and he became very upset. Mama had to crank the oxygen way up for him because he was "cussing out" Grandma Edna — saying he had heard her opening the refrigerator just before she left that evening. She had a date with her latest boyfriend that night and I believe she stayed over at Ruth's place for the rest of her visit. It was about this time that my daddy gave me a dissertation about the evils of drugs — and he told me to never let anybody give me anything, or take anything, unless it's from my own doctor!

I've thought back on that incident many times, and each time I wonder how a mother could steal her dying son's medications, especially when it was so difficult for him to afford the cost for this in the first place. Grandma Edna knew that we did without so many things just so that daddy could have the medications that helped him to be more comfortable — and yet, she stole them anyway.

She must have had one powerful drug addiction!

Chapter 60: Grandma Lou Stanley Passes Away — 1955

I think it was Uncle Ginney that delivered the news to us when Grandma Lou Stanley passed away. It had happened quite suddenly and she had only spent one day at the Miami Baptist Hospital in Miami, Oklahoma, before she died. Her death was attributed to arteriosclerosis, and heart failure.

Grandma Lou – everybody loved her

Louie Nettie Rosadell Waddell Stanley was born in Liberty, Indiana, on September 5, 1867, and died on May 30, 1955, at the age of 87. Grandma Lou was laid to rest in the Baxter Springs Cemetery, in Baxter Springs, Kansas, where her husband, Nicholas Drew "Charles" Stanley, was also buried.

No one ever had a bad word to say about Louie Nettie — although they wondered how such a sweet lady could have had such a pack of ornery kids.

Preston was devastated at the death of his Grandmother Lou. She had been the only real mother that he had ever known. And the worst part for Preston was, with his current medical condition, being tied to his bed by an oxygen bottle was worse than wearing a ball and chain. He was not even able to attend his own sweet grandmother's funeral.

After the funeral for Grandma Lou, several of the Stanley family members came through Sapulpa, Oklahoma, and visited us. Most vividly of all, I remember Uncle Mott ("Little" Mott), daddy's cousin, who was raised with him by their Grandma Lou. Uncle Mott was also very saddened at the loss of his grandmother. And seeing his beloved cousin, Preston, who he had grown up with as if they were brothers, and now currently living like a prisoner — confined to his bed and tethered to an oxygen tank that was, indeed, his lifeline — was absolutely heart breaking.

I remember seeing tears run down Uncle Mott's cheeks as he told us all good-bye and hugged my mama and me at the door before he left. That was the last time we saw Uncle Mott.

After all of Grandma Lou's possessions were cleared from her little home in Cardin, Oklahoma, and all of her keepsakes were divided up, a large cardboard barrel with metal ends on it that contained Grandma Lou's belongings was sent to us. I remember that the barrel had a lot of bedding and towels and such, but in between those items were the breakable things. There was a wall hanging of an Indian on a horse that was made of plaster of Paris and finished in bronze paint. My mama told me that the picture was that of my Grandpa George Paden, but we both knew she was just kidding. I later carried that picture with us each time we moved, and even glued it together at one point, until it became damaged beyond repair, which saddened me a great deal.

There were also some family pictures in that barrel, mostly of daddy and "Little" Mott when they were young. These pictures stayed with us also for many years until the day our basement flooded and most of the pictures were ruined. One thing I still have is Grandma Lou's old "blown glass" paperweight. It is very beautiful, with many pieces of colored glass, and has a large five-petal blue flower in the middle. When we would visit Grandma Lou when I was very young, I remember sitting on the floor rolling it around along with another one that had been Grandpa Stanley's. It had something to do with Grandpa Stanley's "Odd Fellows Lodge" and had three rings connected in the middle of it, like a chain. Someone else must have been given that one. I've often wondered who that lucky person was.

I don't recall Aunt Doris coming back to Oklahoma for her Mother Lou's funeral. She was someone who did hold grudges and she was not a person that offered much forgiveness on many issues, so it is possible that she still had her feelings hurt over the "Wallace the Cat" incident.

Grandma Edna stayed with us for a short while after attending Grandma Lou's funeral. I guess death and burials were on her mind at the time, because, for the sum of $35, she purchased a burial plot in the South Heights Cemetery in Sapulpa, Oklahoma, on June 8, 1955 — less than 10 days after the death of Grandma Lou. Her name at this time was Edna Potter, and her address was listed as 761 Turk Street, in San Francisco, California. I had thought that she had always lived on Market Street when she lived in San Francisco — but then again, when did Edna ever use her real address? In addition to the location of the burial plot, various legal agreements, and so forth, the deed stated that:

"This Cemetery shall be maintained for the interment of persons of the white race only."

That legal agreement was only just noticed while digging through old files a while back. I don't recall ever seeing anything like that on a cemetery deed before, but that may have been very common in Oklahoma in the 1950s.

Chapter 61: Preston Paden Passes Away — 1957

I think it had been a year or more since we had seen Grandma Edna when her trunk next showed up during the summer of 1957. She hadn't changed much as far as I could tell — still drinking beer, puffing away on cigarettes and telling stories. Mama had been spending nearly every day and night at the hospital with daddy. He was a "county patient," which meant that the county was responsible for the bill. It was obvious that the "county patients" didn't get as good of care as those patients whose families could afford to pay for their own hospital bills. Sometimes it seemed as though the hospital management was wishing for "county patients" to die, and die quickly, in hopes that the next admitted patient(s) would be a private payer(s) which would bring in additional revenue for the hospital. On more than one occasion, mama had come into daddy's room and found his skin color already blue, because someone had turned his oxygen level down too low. It is no wonder that she was afraid to leave him alone in that hospital for very long.

I was very happy when Grandma Edna showed up for this visit. I had spent some nights alone and afraid, and some nights with neighbors where I didn't feel at home. At least I was able to stay in our own apartment when grandma visited us. Mama must have written or called grandma to tell her that daddy didn't have much time left to live. I don't remember how long Grandma Edna was in Sapulpa on this trip but I do know that we went to visit her close friend, Ruth McEwen, and later, we went to visit Uncle Ginney. I snuck into the hospital a few times to see daddy, in violation of rules that stated that all visitors had to be at least 12 years old to visit someone in this hospital. Daddy was just lying there, asleep as far as I could tell. I missed him a lot. I wished that he would wake up and say something to me.

I remember one day when my mama took a taxi home from the hospital. She came in and said that daddy was resting well, and she needed to take a shower and clean up. She gave me a hug and asked me if Grandma Edna and I had eaten breakfast yet. "Yeah," I said, "I had some ice cream and grandma had beer."

"You weren't supposed to tell," Grandma Edna growled at me. I could tell by the way she growled that I had messed up again, and also by the way that my mama looked at Grandma Edna. I didn't remember that I wasn't supposed to tell anybody that grandma said it was okay if I ate ice cream for breakfast, but she always had beer for breakfast, and that seemed normal for her. I told my grandma that I was sorry, but she acted as if she was a little angry at me for the next couple of days.

For the most part, Grandma Edna and I got along very well. I was so happy that she was staying there with me that I was probably a real pest, always seeming to follow just a few steps behind her wherever she went. And I loved her stories, and would sit wide-eyed for as long as she would talk — just soaking it all in. Grandma Edna also enjoyed the attention and the appreciation of somebody listening to her, so we made a good pair.

I was a little confused about the activities that she had been involved in and the stories she told about some other gangsters. Grandma Edna talked about "Blanche" a lot. I knew that they must have been very good friends. She also told stories about a couple of people named Bonnie and Clyde. I didn't have the foggiest notion of who Bonnie Parker and Clyde Barrow were, just that they were some of her friends judging from the way that

482

she described them, and Grandma Edna talked like they were people that she knew very well. For years I thought they were just some more people of grandma's gang that she ran around with. Later the movie, "Bonnie and Clyde," premiered in New York City on August 13, 1967, — just nine days before my 21st birthday. At the time, I told all of my friends that my grandma ran around with them.

Edna Murray and Blanche Barrow -- Exchanging stories at the Women's Farm 1 at the Missouri State Women's Penitentiary. "Courtesy of the Collection of Debbie Moss"

Edna Murray on the left, Blanche Barrow on the right – 1937 – at the Missouri State Women's Penitentiary, Jefferson City, Missouri. "Courtesy of the Collection of Debbie Moss"

Blanche Barrow – Edna Murray – "Pen Pals" at the Missouri State Women's Penitentiary. "Courtesy of the Collection of Debbie Moss"

Taken in 1937, Edna is on the left, Blanche Barrow is the 3rd from left "Courtesy of the Collection of Debbie Moss"

Edna Murray - posing for a picture for the story that she wrote for a Detective Magazine while in prison.

Research has set me straight on a lot of my misconceptions, and I now know why Grandma Edna was so knowledgeable about Bonnie and Clyde. Edna Murray and Blanche Barrow (the sister-in-law of Clyde Barrow) were "pen pals" in the Women's Section of the Missouri State Penitentiary at Jefferson City, Missouri, from February of 1935 until Blanche was released on March 23, 1939.

Not only did they share their stories about their criminal careers with each other, but both women wrote their own memoirs while in prison. Edna sold her stories to a detective magazine for $25. Blanche Barrow's memoirs were later turned over to John Neal Phillips who wrote the wonderful book, *"My Life with Bonnie and Clyde."*

Blanche Barrow on the left – Edna Murray on the right at Farm 1, Missouri State Women's Penitentiary, Jefferson City, Missouri. "Courtesy of the Collection of Debbie Moss"

On June 13, 1957, on an incredibly hot summer day in Oklahoma, my mama came home and told me that my daddy — my daddy who was only 41 years old — was no longer with us. "He died, baby," she said to me, "but he won't suffer any more." I couldn't understand why she wasn't crying. Mama just spoke those words in such a matter-of-fact manner, and then she sat down and proceeded to wipe perspiration from her brow and looked very exhausted. It was almost as if she had completed a very long and hard journey, and was in the process of regaining her composure before setting out on another difficult journey.

I ran into the bathroom, wrapped myself up in the shower curtain, and stood in the shower and sobbed and cried for what seemed to be about 30 minutes. It was only after I realized that the act of standing there — stuck to the plastic curtain by tears and sweat — was not going to bring my daddy back, that I finally settled down and faced reality. I knew that he was better off now since he didn't suffer any more — but it still hurt and it hurt really badly! It seemed as if every time I thought about my daddy — which was about every 15 minutes — I would get this awful churning feeling in my stomach that made me feel like I was going to throw up.

I was 10 years old when my daddy died. I had grown a lot taller in the past year and none of my summer clothes fit me anymore. Besides that, I never had anything "dressy" enough to wear to a funeral — in the way of summer clothes. It was hard enough to afford school clothes, let alone funeral clothes. Summer clothes were just anything that you could find that was clean, lightweight, and cool. Somehow it was decided that grandma would take me shopping for a dress to wear to daddy's funeral. It was hot and muggy, and Grandma Edna didn't seem to be in the mood for shopping — I could just tell that from the very beginning of our shopping trip. Then she had me trying on dresses that weren't even my size. I didn't want to wear a dress in the first place, let alone one that I didn't even like the looks of. Grandma Edna was getting a little "put out" with me for not liking anything she picked out, and I was getting a little "put out" with her choices of dresses for me to wear. Finally she came up with yet another blue dress — this time "baby blue," no less. But, at least, it did fit. So even though I didn't like the dress because it was "baby blue," just to please her — and to get her out of that awful mood she was in — I said I liked it, and she bought the dress, and then we headed straight for Clarence's place so she could get a cold beer.

Funerals are not fun! I can't say that I ever enjoyed going to a funeral, but a funeral really sucks when you're just a kid, and it's your daddy that they're having the funeral for. Daddy had been sick for a very long time, and was unable to get out and socialize, as he formerly did. Add to that, the fact that he was in a crappy nursing home for quite a while, followed by a hospital stay in an oxygen tent for 11 months. It wasn't as if he still had a lot of friends that he spent time with in his final days. I suppose that a lot of his older friends had either died or had just forgotten about him. Except for Grandma Edna, mama, and me, several of my mama's family, Uncle Ginney's family, and a handful of friends, there wasn't much of a crowd at my daddy's funeral. I felt so sorry for him — not solely because he was gone, since I had resolved myself to being glad that he wasn't suffering anymore — but also, because he had missed out on so much in life even while he was still alive. And at the time of his death, I hadn't even known about the time he had spent in prison, decades before.

My daddy, Preston LeRoy Paden, was born on December 27, 1915, and passed away at the age of 41, on June 13, 1957. He was in the Bartlett Memorial Hospital in Sapulpa, Oklahoma, at the time of his death. The attending physician, Dr. Thomas D. Burnett, attributed his death to congestive heart failure that had occurred during the last few days preceding his death, and also due to pulmonary emphysema that he stated that Preston had for the previous six years.

Daddy's funeral service was at the Buffington Funeral Home in Sapulpa, on June 15, 1957.

My mama's family had come to Sapulpa for daddy's funeral, and afterwards, I traveled back to Kansas with my aunts and uncles and cousins, leaving mama in Sapulpa to wrap up the loose ends and to follow us shortly later.

Grandma Edna left to go home to San Francisco.

I know it has to be hard to lose your only son, especially him being still a young man, but I don't remember grandma ever letting on that she was hurting. Maybe she just didn't let it show. Edna was different than most folks when it came to showing feelings — and I suppose her personal history had left some calluses. You didn't see her express certain emotions when you thought she would, and "… all hell would break loose" when you least expected it.

Edna did do one last touching thing for her son and it rather surprised my mama. Edna insisted on providing her son's burial plot. It had been purchased two years before when she was in Sapulpa, right after Grandma Lou's funeral. She always had certain etiquette about proper and dignified burials. Daddy is buried very close to Uncle Ginney and his wife, Aunt Jewel, in the South Heights Cemetery, in Sapulpa, Oklahoma. I was glad that he was buried next to his relatives. Uncle Ginney was alive when daddy died, but Aunt Jewel was already buried there.

Preston L. Paden (Born on 12-27-15 and Died on – 6-13-57) "Courtesy of Bill Stanley"

Chapter 62: Living In Kansas

After my daddy died, but before my mama moved to Kansas, I stayed with my Aunt Zelma and Uncle Dale Dungan, just outside of Columbus, Kansas. They had three young girls by then, and the oldest girl, Dixie, was just one year older than I was. I thought this was great since I unfortunately didn't have any other brothers and sisters, and I was used to being in the company of adults. Also, except for a brief stay with Grandma and Grandpa Keith when I was very young, I had never lived in the country before.

The Dungans spent just about every weekend during the summer down on the Neosho River. When Uncle Dale heard that I didn't know how to swim, he said I needed to take swimming lessons as soon as possible, and well before they took me to the river for camping and fishing. Well, right off the bat, I got a third degree sunburn from sitting around the edge of the pool while listening to the instructor. I spent a week going half naked and wearing some really stinky salve that made me smell like a fish, and the smell alone kept the other kids as far away as possible from me. I ruined my uncle's undershirts, which were the only thing I could wear, because of the smelly oil that refused to ever wash out. To make matters worse, I had to sit at the far, far, end of the supper table when we ate. My favorite trick was to see just how close I could sneak up to somebody before they could smell me.

By the time mama arrived in Kansas, her little "city girl" had turned into a first-class tomboy. Here I was, suntanned, brown as a bean, skinned knees and elbows from learning to ride a bike and do tricks on the monkey bars, and very proud of the fact that, "I can swim," which I yelled to my mama when she first arrived. The other kids found more enjoyment in telling my mama how I had smelled like a dead "carp fish" for over a week, and how I had gotten at least a million chiggers from picking blackberries — that made me swell up like a balloon.

My summer as a country girl was full of learning experiences, to say the least.

Shortly after my 11th birthday, I started attending Central Junior High School in Columbus, Kansas. Mama and I had a nice little apartment, and daddy's monthly Social Security check was enough for us to get by on and we didn't seem to have the same degree of money problems as before. I got my very first bicycle, and how I loved that thing! I literally rode the wheels off of it.

I met my first, and very best friend, Carolyn Cooper, in Junior High School on the very first day of class — and, as a bonus, she wore the same size shoes as I did. So, finding that we had "twin feet," we traded shoes. She was the daughter of the Superintendent of Schools, and of course, the orneriest girl in class. We ran together all through our three years of Junior High School and all four years of High School. Carolyn was a good friend and confidant. What one of us didn't think of, the other one did.

My teenage years were basically good ones, with the usual ups and downs that kids have to deal with. I liked school and I made good grades, but I also liked to clown around and make everyone laugh, which sometimes got me in trouble with my teachers.

490

I never had any difficulty in making friends, but sometimes being friends "creates" trouble — especially when you are a teenager and every little thing is thought to be huge. Once, I remember, Carolyn was angry with me for a whole month because I made the cheerleader squad and she didn't. The next year, she made the cheerleader squad and I didn't. You're darn right I was jealous. And I pouted for a few days and felt sorry for myself, but that wasn't any fun, so I got over it.

When my mama first started having a gentleman caller at the house, I resented him because he wasn't my daddy. But he was nice to me, and a fun sort of guy, so it wasn't long before we were getting along just fine. I was glad that my mama had a companion, because I was spending more and more time with my friends. I wasn't real surprised when he, Bob Silcott, and mama got married, but I was surprised when I found out that they were expecting a child. I was worried, too, because I knew mama wasn't supposed to have any more children due to her medical condition.

I was 12 years old when my little sister, Lisa Gail Silcott, was born. They had a really tough time of it. Mama had a heart attack during childbirth. And little Lisa had to be delivered with instruments. Although they came home from the hospital together, it wasn't long before mama had to go back. She had suffered another heart attack, and it was "touch and go" for several weeks before she was able to return home. She did pull through the ordeal reasonably well, and she never let on that she didn't feel well.

Our freshman class, the first of the "baby boomer" generation — most of us were born in 1946 — was the largest class up to that point in time to attend Cherokee County Rural High School in Columbus, Kansas. I don't think that our class will ever be forgotten. It might have had something to do with our daddies being in the war, because we were as ornery a bunch of little rebels as there ever was.

I enjoyed my high school years, as well as my friends, the school trips, summer vacations, county fairs, and boyfriends — along with wearing their class rings with a half roll of tape stuffed under them, and their letter jackets that had sleeves way past my hands and hung at the bottom down below my knees. But there was one thing that was always in the back of my mind and spoiled a lot of the good times. My mama's health was failing. She made several more trips to the hospital over the years, each one becoming more difficult to recover from. I could see the downhill spiral just like when my daddy's health was failing. And I prayed again, as I had for my daddy, that she would get better and be able to enjoy life again.

Chapter 63: My First Car — "Old Cancer"

Mama had never wished to drive, which I think had something to do with her heart condition; and she also feared that, with her medical problems, she would risk being the cause of an accident that would bring harm to someone. My stepdad, Bob Silcott, purchased a car for me once I received my driver's permit, which guaranteed that mama and I would have transportation when he was away from home. Bob did construction work — such as building bridges — and was usually only home on the weekends.

The car he bought me was a two door, white over red, 1958 Chrysler hardtop, that didn't look half bad when we bought it. After about 5,000 times of "dragging Main Street," (cruising the main streets in town by car) carrying 10 or more teenagers at a time, a few trips out of town, and 40 flat tires later, the car was starting to look pretty bad. But it was the car's onset of rusting around its wheel wells that earned it the nickname of "Old Cancer." One day Old Cancer decided to drop her left quarter panel right in the middle of downtown Main Street, which was the first of her many catastrophes. Then the solenoid switch went out on Old Cancer and the only way we were then able to start her was to open her hood and "short across" with a screwdriver. If we melted one, we melted 100 screwdrivers down to mere nubs. I could have bought 20 solenoids with what I had invested in screwdrivers.

Our gang traveled on a tight budget though, and sometimes it was rough just to come up with the nickel for gas that the passengers had to put in the beanbag ashtray on the dashboard before riding in Old Cancer. She probably didn't get the best gas mileage, but gasoline was only $0.22 a gallon in those days. And for another $0.25 a pack, we could puff on cigarettes, looking really cool, while we "dragged Main Street."

I was about the only girl in my class that had transportation, so I felt that I had to provide rides for all of my girlfriends, and sometimes for some of the boys, too. However, when it started getting close to curfew time, it wasn't always easy to deliver everyone to their homes on time. Once, I remember getting home rather late, and mama wasn't happy. I can't remember everything she had to say to me, but I do remember her saying, "You start acting like Martha Edna, staying out all night, and you won't go anyplace." I knew I had upset my mama for sure when she insinuated that I was acting like Grandma Edna.

Mama enjoyed my friends, and she always laughed and got a real kick out of our stories. We could tell her anything and probably told her too much at times although she would never rat on us. Since she spent her teenage years in the Kansas State Tuberculosis Sanatorium in Norton, Kansas, she was all the more happy that I could enjoy my teenage years, and in a way, she was perhaps, living her teenage years vicariously, through me.

My American History teacher, who also taught an Auto Mechanics class, was always so amused at my method of getting Old Cancer running that he would let me out of class a few minutes early before lunch hour, so that she would be running and I would have half a chance of getting out of the parking lot in time to make the Dairy Belle for lunch — which was at the other end of town. I suspected that he had some sort of an

494

arrangement with the teacher we had immediately after lunch, because if I was late getting back from lunch, so were three quarters of her class who piled in on top of each other to ride with me. We held the record for getting more people in one car than our biology teacher did for swallowing gold fish in college. My biology teacher always told that story in my first class of the day, immediately following breakfast.

One day after school we thought Old Cancer's injuries would prove to be fatal. She broke a U-joint, and before I could get her shut down, my good friend, Connie Taylor, the mayor's daughter, who was sitting on the hump on the back floor, thought the injuries to her butt would also be fatal. Every time the drive shaft hit up under her, her head would hit the roof of the car and would knock her back down on the hump just in time to receive another blow to her butt.

Our Auto Mechanics teacher volunteered to take Old Cancer as a class project and repair her U-joint if I would promise to quit threatening to instigate a walkout because girls weren't allowed to take the Auto Mechanics class. I always suspected that the real reason he volunteered was because secretly he wanted to see what Old Cancer was made of that allowed her to take so much punishment. Old Cancer was soon on the road again with her newly installed U-joint.

Another little mistake I made, and I clearly remember it, just about got me "grounded for life." After coming home from school one day, I had just parked the car under the carport, had both of my arms full of books and gym clothes, and I bailed out of Old Cancer with a cigarette gripped between my lips when mama was looking out of the back door.

"Well, if you don't look just like Martha Edna Junior with that damn cigarette hanging out of your mouth — and there followed another 15 minute dissertation from my mama about the stupidity of smoking. I knew she was right, and that I had let peer pressure get me hooked on cigarettes. It was a long time before I broke that silly habit too.

In the days to pass, Old Cancer's gear shift mechanism — consisting of a box full of pushbuttons — threw a rod, and whenever I pushed in the drive button, the reverse button would fly out and land in the back seat, if it didn't first hit someone in the head. We usually had to search around 6 to 8 pairs of feet to find the button, locate a screwdriver that didn't have the tip burned off, borrow somebody's electrical tape, and perform a "major repair job" to the shifter box before we could back the car up again. Next to go were the lever type door handles, not unlike those found on the early models of refrigerators. One cold winter day, a door handle just seemed to fall off in the hand of one of my passengers. A few days later, the other one fell off in my hand. We soon located what function the levers served and found we could duplicate the function with a thumb in a reasonable length of time in the daylight, and in less than four or five minutes in the dark. One night when we were "dragging Main Street," the center of Old Cancer's steering wheel just seemed to explode. From that point on, the only way to honk her horn was to touch two wires together. Her rear view mirror soon found a new resting place on the dashboard, her ignition key wore so thin that it took the art of holding your mouth just exactly right in order to get it to turn, and her brakes failed so often that we had to add a beanbag ashtray, labeled "brake fluid," beside the one labeled "gas." I had some pretty strong leg muscles from bleeding the brake lines on Old Cancer, and driving her had truly become an art.

One night an over-loaded carload of us were dragging the main street of a nearby town — Pittsburg, Kansas — when someone, who had obviously indulged in too many alcoholic beverages, backed out of a parking place and right into the side of our car. It looked like someone had taken a huge can opener to her right side, and we felt sure that Old Cancer was finally doomed. I stomped around the street for quite some time, picking up pieces, and informing the intoxicated gentleman who had backed into Old Cancer, that he had absolutely ruined a perfectly good automobile.

I remember well the day the insurance adjuster came to inspect Old Cancer. As he examined the left side of the car with a frown on his face, I explained that with just a little old quarter panel "transplant" she would be fine. Wishing to gain entry to the car, he stared blankly at the location where the handle should have been. I managed to open the door in record time and explained that a five minute weld job would put the handle — kept in the glove box — right back where it should be. He just wasn't holding his mouth right when he attempted to turn on the ignition, and Lord only knows how he happened to get his chin on the wires that were meant only for honking the horn. I think he had the most incredible look of all on his face when I threw open the hood and volunteered to start it for him with my trusty "burnt to a nub" screwdriver in hand. Of course he would have to hear her lovely engine purr, but when he decided to back out of the driveway, and buttons started flying into the back seat, that was the last straw. He just sat there looking rather oddly at the peculiar position of the rearview mirror on the dash, and at the beanbag ashtrays, holding a few nickels each, labeled "gas" and "brake fluid." But before he left, he said he did have to agree with me that Old Cancer was the most remarkable vehicle he had ever seen.

I almost cried when they hauled Old Cancer away. There would never be another automobile like her.

With the insurance money in hand from Old Cancer, and a little extra to boot, my stepdad, Bob, bought us a white 1959 Ford that we called "The White Ghost." It would never hold a candle to Old Cancer, but it was good transportation.

I think that my memories of the days of Old Cancer are so dear and important to me because those were the days that truly tested the morals that my parents had taught me. These were the days of my teenage years when I could have taken after my Grandma Edna's behavior and gone astray. I know for a fact that my mother worried each and every day that I might take after my Grandma Martha Edna, who at that same age, made decisions that haunted her for the rest of her life.

Not before putting limburger cheese in the boilers and packing the front entrance of the school with snow — both events halting classes for some time — and leaving a "history of firsts" for events that took place at the Cherokee County Rural High School (CCRHS) in Columbus, Kansas, the Class of 1964 graduated and moved on to our individual journeys in life.

Cherokee County Rural High School – CCRHS, Columbus, Kansas, where we spent a good deal of time one night standing on each others shoulders packing the big front doors with snow. "Courtesy of Bill Stoskopf"

CCRHS Janitors ready to tackle the "snow removal" project.

Chapter 64: Naomi Passes Away — 1964

One of my very best friends, Diane Gust, and I were scheduled to take a Civil Service Test at the nearby Parsons Junior College in Parsons, Kansas, on Saturday, June 13, 1964.

Upon awakening that morning, I had never seen it rain so hard before in my life. My shuffling around in an attempt to get ready had awakened my mama, and I talked with her before leaving the house to pick up Diane. Mama asked me what day it was, and I said it was Saturday. She said, "No, I mean what is today's date?" I told her that it was June 13th. After I had said that, I realized that it was the 7th anniversary of my daddy's death. I'm positive that my mama also knew that, but neither of us mentioned it, or wanted to mention it, or even wanted to dwell on that sad day. I kissed her good-bye and left the house.

After Diane and I made the trip to Parsons, Kansas, and completed our exams, we started back for home. Upon reaching the edge of town, we discovered that the high waters from the rain had closed the roads so we pulled into the parking lot of a restaurant. We stayed inside there for hours, waiting for the water to subside. I remember having an unusually antsy feeling that I should be home. I didn't know why I felt this way because my stepfather's mother, Grandma Silcott, was at home with mama and my little sister, Lisa, and Grandma Silcott was very capable of taking care of things.

Several Kansas State Highway Patrolmen had also gathered at the restaurant where we were waiting, and I noticed that they were paying particular attention to us. A couple of the patrolmen approached us and inquired as to our identity. We explained where we had been and where we were going. For some reason, we were told that we could follow the patrolman that was headed in the same direction that we were. So we took his advice and here we were — the only cars on the highway that I could see — following the patrolman in the lead car, carefully treading water right down the middle of the center line of the highway.

Upon arriving back home in Columbus, Kansas, I soon discovered the reason for the personal escort home, and also why I had experienced the previous uneasy feeling. My mama had passed away on the exact date that my daddy had died, 7 years previously.

After my mama's funeral and burial, it was still weeks — maybe even months — before the realization set in that she was gone. I was 17 years old at the time and I wasn't ready for my mama to die. I still needed her. I was angry. I was very, very angry. I had been praying to God for so many years. Why would he take my daddy and now my mama, and leave me and my little 5 year old sister without a mama?

I was very angry with God.

Chapter 65: My Last Visit With Grandma Edna

The year was 1964 and I was living in Columbus, Kansas, with my little sister, Lisa, and my stepdad's (Bob Silcott) mother, Grandma Silcott. While I had been out one afternoon, Grandma Edna had left a message for me that she was visiting in Sapulpa, Oklahoma, and would like for me to join her there. I was really excited to be seeing her again, for it had been over 7 years since the last time we were together. I asked a couple of my girlfriends to take me to the bus depot in Joplin, Missouri. Grandma Edna had said that she would be at Ruth's place — her friend, Ruth McEwen — and I knew that it wasn't far from the bus station in Sapulpa.

I remember the visit well. I planned my wardrobe, dressed in my favorite skirt and sailor-style blouse with a blue tie at the neck. I was sure my grandma would like it because I remembered her often wearing blouses with big collars and ties at the neck. I dressed in pointy-toed, high heel shoes that, although they weren't the most comfortable of shoes, perfectly matched my navy blue, straight skirt. The night before I traveled, I slept with rollers in my hair, and even though the rollers kept me from sleeping well that night, I felt assured that my hair looked just right for my upcoming visit with Grandma Edna.

I was carrying my new bright red luggage that was given to me as a gift from my mama for my high school graduation. It was the last gift she ever gave me — a three-piece set of Samsonite luggage, that included what mama referred to as a little "train case." To me it was the most beautiful luggage that I ever saw, complete with its bright yellow and orange patterned lining. I suppose that mama knew that I was going to travel a lot in the future. I loved that set of luggage and I was "walking proud."

I couldn't sit still as the bus pulled into the Sapulpa Bus Terminal since it had been so long since I had seen Grandma Edna and my old hometown. I was fidgeting and walking up and down the sidewalk as the bus driver was retrieving my luggage out of the luggage compartment underneath the bus. I noticed that Sapulpa hadn't changed much as I walked towards the rooming house that Ruth managed in the Unit Block on East Dewey. It took a minute or so for my eyes to adjust from the bright sun outside to the dimly lit stairway just beyond the entrance of the rooming house. Sure enough, there was the same old screen door leading out into the hall that I had run in and out of so many times as a youngster. I could hear Grandma Edna and Ruth talking in the sitting room. Gently knocking on the screen door, I could feel my heart pounding with anticipation. Ruth jumped up and ran to let me in the door, and gave me a big hug. Grandma Edna remained seated, a beer in one hand and a cigarette in the other hand. She looked me up and down for a few seconds and then said, "My God, you're tall and skinny, just like your mama. I thought you'd be stacked up like me." (I don't know if Grandma Edna ever heard about it, but Bessie Green once described Edna as: "… built like a tent, with a big mouth full of gold teeth"). I wasn't sure how to respond to grandma's remark, so I just stood there with a silly grin on my face. Ruth jumped in with, "Edna, what do you mean? Your granddaughter looks like a model." Grandma Edna said, "Well, she needs some meat on her bones." And, finally, she made some motion for me to come over to her and said something about a hug. Then she said something about my mama's

504

recent death — "Sorry to hear about your mama." Grandma Silcott had told her about mama passing when Grandma Edna had called. I told Grandma Edna that she hadn't changed a bit. That was the truth — a cigarette in one hand and a beer in the other hand, open toed sandals with wedge heels, even the same hairdo — that was, indeed, the same Grandma Edna that I had always remembered.

Grandma Edna asked me about what happened to my mama. I told her that she always had a bad valve in her heart and the years of strain put on it from pumping blood through her terribly scared lungs had finally taken its toll. "Yeah, she was always sickly," was grandma's reply — said in a tone that went against my grain. I gave it my best to put on a smile, and I quickly changed the subject.

I asked Ruth about Clarence. I always liked Clarence and he was good to me and would always boost me up on a big, tall stool and give me a "sarsaparilla," he called it. I assumed that he was still running the cigar store and beer joint downstairs around the corner. Ruth pointed to the rooms across the hall where Clarence slept and said he spent most of his time right there nowadays. I turned to Grandma Edna, seeking an explanation. She just said, "He's not good, he's real bad." Later, when we went across the hall to get something out of the kitchen, I could see Clarence in bed in the other room and could hear his snoring. There was also a strong smell of alcohol coming from that direction which led me to believe Clarence was in his final stages of chronic alcohol abuse.

We later went to Uncle Ginney's house, where we spent the next few days. Uncle Ginney was grandma's baby brother and now the only one of her brothers that was still alive. I also was able to see all of daddy's cousins again. One of them, Vicki Lynn, was younger than I was by a year or so, and we had been very close when I had lived there. As teenagers are wont to do, we ran around town, "dragged Main," and went to the local teenagers' hangouts. We got caught sneaking in past curfew one night and received a lecture from Uncle Ginney. He wasn't real mad at us though. I fixed him some sunny-side up eggs, with bacon; for breakfast and he thought I was a pretty good kid, after all. Grandma Edna was still having beer for breakfast and, I swear, was still telling the same stories. I wish I would have paid more attention and taken notes. The one thing I had always remembered her talking about was that Doris was responsible for getting everyone in trouble. Since she had always said that, I didn't really listen. I don't think Uncle Ginney was paying much attention to her, either.

I do remember thinking that Grandma Edna was looking older. And I now know that what I was seeing was the telltale signs of all of her smoking and drinking over the years. Her skin seemed dull — not just her face — but all over. And her ankles, although they had never been skinny, they were now quite swollen. Her breathing seemed a little labored, and she lifted her shoulders to assist her in taking a breath, just like I had seen my daddy do in his later days.

We all hugged and said our good-byes to each other before I got on the bus to head back home to Columbus, Kansas.

I didn't know it at the time, but this visit would be the last time that I would ever see my Grandma Edna.

Epilogue

1. Dora Vinita "Doris" Stanley McCormick (July 20, 1900 – December 6, 1982)

Aunt Doris lived her last years in what would be considered to be a normal life style. She was a good wife to her husband, Jay, and he was always crazy about her. Her son, Mott Farrell, had always been a law-abiding citizen and was quite prosperous in his insurance business. He bought Doris and Jay a new home in the Los Angeles area, and was every bit the son that a mother could hope for.

Aunt Doris was very proud of her home and she used to send us pictures of their yard and house, both the inside and outside of it. I remember that all of her kitchen appliances were red — red refrigerator, red stove, everything was red. And because they didn't want to have to mow the lawn, their back yard was concreted in green which I always thought was funny. Aunt Doris also sent us pictures of Wallace, their cat. She seemed happy, and I believe that her final years were good ones.

The one thing that Aunt Doris had a hard time with was her aging process. She really hated the fact that she was getting older. Earlier in life, she had lied about her age in order to get married, and she said that she was 18 years old when, in fact, she was only 15 years old at the time. Well, she changed her mind about wanting to be older than she really was, and, as the years went by, she eventually said that she was younger than she really was. Her Social Security records showed that she was born in 1906, when in fact, she was born in 1900.

Uncle Jay McCormick preceded my Aunt Doris in death by a year or so — passing away in 1980 or 1981. At the time of her death at age 82, Aunt Doris was living with her son, "Little" Mott, at 4001 W. 232nd Street, in Torrance, California.

When she passed away, at the Little Company of Mary Hospital in Torrance, Doris was suffering from a urinary bladder infection, kidney failure with chronic obstructive disease, and finally, cardiac arrest. She was buried on December 9, 1982, at Green Hills Memorial Park in San Pedro, California.

And yes, I believe that my daddy's Aunt Doris suffered from a guilty conscience because she introduced him to the criminal activities of her world, and later, she let him take the fall for her. On the other hand, she was always someone that daddy and I looked up to, and we felt that we were supported and loved by her. I will always remember her smile, her laugh, and her air of confidence.

Doris was a proud lady — very smart — and also very vane. One of my daddy's cousins told me about the time he took his family out to California on vacation, and had hoped to see some of the relatives while they were there. Aunt Helen (Uncle Mott's widow), came down from Los Angeles to meet them, and they were driving through Torrance to see "Little" Mott, Ruth Evelyn, and Doris and Jay. They had called ahead and talked to Doris, telling her when they would be arriving. When they arrived at the address that Doris had given them, there didn't seem to be anyone home. The drapes were all drawn and nobody answered the door. Thinking that they might have gone to the wrong house, they talked to the neighbors next door. The neighbors said, "Oh, yes, that's where Doris and Jay McCormick live, and we saw them out in the yard just a little while ago." Well, after knocking on the door one last time, they finally gave up.

Daddy's cousin said to me, "I don't know if you know it or not, but the Stanley family was a strange bunch." We both got a big laugh out of that statement. I said that from what I knew and could remember of Aunt Doris, she probably needed her hair done, or something like that, and wasn't comfortable with her relatives seeing her at that time. But only my Aunt Doris would know the real reason why.

Rest in peace, Aunt Dode.

2. Jess Doyle (1900 – March 12, 1942 or 1947)

Jess Doyle was turned over to the State of Nebraska where he was tried and convicted of robbing the First National Bank in Fairbury, Nebraska, on April 4, 1933. This robbery was of a reported $151,350 — $25,650 in cash and $125,700 in bonds. One of the robbers, Earl Christman, lost his life from a gunshot wound he received in this robbery. Jess got off a little easier — he was sentenced to 10 years in the Nebraska State Penitentiary.

As inmate number 11261, Jess had been in the Oklahoma State Penitentiary at McAlester. As inmate number 9845, he served time in the State Penitentiary at Lansing, Kansas, and as inmate number 12369, he served time in the State Penitentiary in Lincoln, Nebraska.

That wasn't the end of Jess Doyle's obligations though, as he was committed to the United States Penitentiary in Atlanta, Georgia, as register number 51004-A, on May 14, 1937, for assault and robbery of the United States mail. He was given a sentence of 25 years, but he died in jail well before he even served half of his whole sentence.

Rest in peace, Jess Doyle.

3. Gloyd Augusta "Ginney" Stanley (December 17, 1904 – September 14, 1970)

Uncle Ginney was my favorite of all of Grandma Edna's brothers. I guess it's because I knew him the best and he was a big part of my life. Uncle Ginney was always good to his wife, Jewel, and to me, my daddy, my mama and all of his kids and grandkids. His youngest daughter, Vicki Lynn, was a year or so younger than I was, and we were the best of friends.

When his wife, Aunt Jewel, was very ill with cancer of the kidneys, Uncle Ginney did everything he could do to make her last days as pleasant as possible. Once, when Aunt Jewel was in the hospital, she asked for some watermelon. Even though it was not watermelon season at the time, Uncle Ginney had a watermelon shipped from California so that she could have her wish. I remember that there was a lot of controversy among family members about how foolish it was to spend so much money to have a watermelon shipped from California. My daddy said that it was Uncle Ginney's business how he spent his money, and it shouldn't be of any concern to anyone else.

Uncle Ginney worked as an engineer for the Frisco Railway for many years.

Frisco Railway Station, Sapulpa, Okla.

He had an unfortunate accident that abruptly ended his life on September 14, 1970, at the age of 65.

Ginney Stanley was helping his friend, Joe Naifeh, of Naifeh Brothers Foods, push his Model T Ford onto the street in Sapulpa, Oklahoma. An insensitive and reckless teenager came speeding around the corner in his car and struck Ginney, killing him there on the spot.

Gloyd Augusta "Ginney" Stanley was laid to rest, next to his wife, Jewel, at the South Heights Cemetery in Sapulpa, Oklahoma. Their nephew, my daddy, Preston Paden, is in the grave next to them.

I was not aware of this accident until several years later. I was terribly saddened to hear of my Uncle Ginney's death. He was always one of my fondest relatives.

Rest in Peace, Uncle "Ginney."

4. Harry Clinton Stanley (August 25, 1890 – 1940s)

Uncle Harry Clinton Stanley, the eldest of the Stanley siblings, had fought in World War I and was one of the prisoners of war (POWs) who experienced an attack of mustard gas.

When Harry returned home from the war, he was very ill and was suffering from symptoms of a a tubercular type of lung disease, due to the gasses that he had previously been exposed to. After spending some time in the infirmary, he was released to go home.

During Prohibition, Harry and his brother, Mott Stanley, ran a bootlegging operation out of Commerce, Oklahoma. He served 6 months in the Sedgwick County Jail in Wichita, Kansas, and was fined $1,000 for harboring his sister, Edna "The Kissing Bandit" Murray. His wife, Mary ("Sybil"), was also convicted and given a 5 year suspended sentence.

I think they got a raw deal. After all, letting your sister spend the night isn't exactly something that every other person in the world wouldn't also do.

Harry and his wife, Mary ("Sybil"), had two boys, whose names, I believe, were Marcey and Marion — and one girl, who I believe was named Dorothy. The last information I had was that their children were living in Bakersfield, California.

Harry did not live a long life, and died from complications of his service-related lung disease he acquired in World War I.

Rest in Peace, Uncle Harry.

5. Mott Clinton ("Little" Mott) Farrell (April 19, 1918 – May 9, 2008)

"Just like brothers" — that's what my daddy and "Little" Mott both said of each other. They were raised together, without their parents, by their Grandmother and Grandfather Stanley in Cardin, Oklahoma.

"Little" Mott was very sad to hear that Preston, his big brother and childhood protector, had passed away. But "Little" Mott had his own life to live and, although he was a prosperous man in his insurance business, he also had his sorrows to contend with. He was a good son, and looked after his mother, Doris — even buying her a new home and making sure she didn't want for anything.

A couple of years after "Little" Mott lost his stepdad, Jay McCormick, his mother, Doris, who had been living with him at the time, passed away. Then his childhood sweetheart and wife of many years, Ruth Evelyn, began to suffer from Alzheimer's disease. They never had any children and he was the only one remaining to assist her with her illness. He hired a caretaker to be her nurse — a very nice woman from the Philippines. Aunt Ruth Evelyn Farrell passed away on October 10, 2001. She was about 80 years old at the time of her death.

"Uncle" Mott (he was also my "Uncle" because it seemed like he was my daddy's brother), was getting on in years himself, and did not want to live alone, so he decided to marry Ruth Evelyn's nurse, Eden, after his wife's death. I believe Mott and Eden loved each other very much.

We corresponded right up until the end, with "Little" Mott telling me what he could recall from his days growing up with my daddy in Cardin, Oklahoma. And "Little" Mott sure did love his Grandma Louie Stanley, just as my daddy did.

Eden seemed to be a very kind person who cared very much for Mott. She called me when he passed away, not long after his 90th birthday. She said that on his recent 90th birthday was the first day that he had not gotten out of bed and dressed himself. She said that he had always been very particular about his appearance and always dressed very professionally.

"Little" Mott Farrell was 90 years old on April 19, 2008, and passed away from kidney cancer a few weeks later, on May 9, 2008.

Rest in Peace, "Little" Mott.

6. Earl Charles Stuchlik (June 5, 1895 – Unknown)

Before Earl Stuchlik was incarcerated for passing counterfeit money with my Aunt Doris, he was once again arrested for counterfeiting in March of 1933. He finally made probation on December 2, 1933. However, his probation was revoked on May 22, 1935, when he was sent back to Leavenworth for another 18 months — again, for counterfeiting.

After his conditional release from the United States Federal Penitentiary in Leavenworth, Kansas, on August 5, 1936, Earl Stuchlik stayed away from behind bars for only a short while.

On December 29, 1938, his probation again was revoked due to an episode which occurred at Hill City, Kansas, at an American Legion meeting. It seems as though Earl broke up a craps game by firing a gun which wounded four men — some being injured seriously. But Earl said he was just a victim of circumstances in this instance. He said he had been gambling in Kansas City prior to the alleged violation and claimed that he had obtained some counterfeit money in a gambling house there. He denied that he knew the money was counterfeit, but did plead guilty to being in a place where he shouldn't be in, and drinking beer, although he said he was never intoxicated. He also admitted to having engaged in questionable activities over the years as the means of his livelihood.

On January 4, 1939, Earl Stuchlik was received at South Kansas City Police Headquarters in Kansas City, Missouri, on charges of counterfeiting. Poor Earl just couldn't stop printing that dough. After being denied parole in August of 1940, he was given a conditional release on September 4, 1942, based on a clean record for "good time" served.

The Associate Warden's report on Earl stated that he may be regarded as a confirmed offender — but he did not appear to be a vicious type, and was intelligent enough to realize the advantages of an adequate adjustment to confinement. He could be expected, however, to present some disciplinary problems as a result of conniving and possibly gambling. His conduct in his previous terms at Leavenworth was considered satisfactory. He had no reports for violations of institutional rules during the period of time comprising his three work assignments and four cell assignments. His last assignment was working as an attendant in Annex No. 3 of the prison hospital. The reports of the officers under whom he worked, rated his work consistently as "good."

Earl Charles Stuchlik, inmate number 46943, along with one or more other Leavenworth inmates, was not allowed to correspond with Hall C. Davis, an attorney out of Topeka, Kansas, because they had attempted to solicit legal business for Mr. Davis among the inmates of that institution. That order was signed by Warden F. G. Zerbst.

The medical report for Earl Stuchlik stated that he had enjoyed good health since his incarceration, that he had been hospitalized on two occasions — once for a diagnostic lumbar puncture, which was negative — and once for treatment of defective vision. He was given a stamp of "discharged — improved" on each occasion. He stated that he had a previous case of syphilis, but with adequate treatment, his disease had been declared to be non-communicable. His blood tests proved to be "negative" of having any disease as of May, 1941. His IQ was 93 and he was believed to be of normal intelligence.

It is doubtful that Earl had any further contact with Doris, or any of the Stanley family, after his release from prison on September 4, 1942. Most probably, he returned to Hill City, Kansas, to assist his ailing father who had been pleading for his release through Social Services dating back to March of 1941.

Rest in peace, Earl.

7. Fred Stanley (October, 1891 – October 9, 1949)

Not long after we had moved to Sapulpa, Uncle Ginney told daddy that his Uncle Fred Stanley had died. He had been an oil-field worker in western Kansas, and was living by himself at the time of his death. We were told that his wife, Lucille, and their children were living in Bakersfield, California.

The newspaper story said that Marshal Dave Break followed a known drunk (Fred Stanley) home, since the suspect appeared to be driving while intoxicated. Marshal Break pulled into Stanley's driveway, proceeded to Mr. Stanley's car, and found a pint of whiskey inside the car. Fred Stanley then shot Marshal Break three times — killing him. A neighbor fired at Fred Stanley and the fire was returned. Stanley, when cornered in his house by the local sheriff and a posse, decided to kill himself. This had occurred in Florence, Kansas, on October 9, 1949. Fred Stanley,

516

who was born in October of 1891, was about 58 years old at the time of his death.

Daddy was saddened to hear this, but he said that his Uncle Fred had always been sort of the black sheep of the family.

Rest in peace, "Uncle Fred."

8. Mott Stanley (May, 1896 – 1955)

I remember when daddy's Uncle Mott Stanley died. I can't remember exactly when he died, but I remember when we received the news. It was sometime in 1955 and he was about 59 years old at the time of his death. Daddy and I were both very saddened, since we both loved him so much. Although he and his wife, Aunt Helen, could never have any children of their own, they nevertheless, loved children. We used to visit them when we lived in California, and I remember that they had a huge orange orchard next to their house. Uncle Mott would take me out to the orchard while carrying me on his shoulders, and let me pick the prettiest, ripest oranges on the tree.

Aunt Helen was also a very sweet person. She was from Cardin, Oklahoma, and had a brother named John — John Hemphill. John, in turn, had a daughter named Judy, a little older than I was, that I used to play with when our families visited each other.

The day that Uncle Mott passed away, Uncle Ginney came to our house and told us about it. Uncle Mott, just like his father, Nicholas Drew "Charles" Stanley, had suffered a cerebral hemorrhage and passed away at his home. Aunt Helen had found him early in the morning in the bathroom. There was some joking about whether he had his hat on at the time of his death. Aunt

Helen used to say that Mott put on his underwear, his socks, and his hat, in that order. I don't know if that is exactly the truth, but I hardly ever remember seeing him without his fedora hat. He was a good man. He did his fair share of bootlegging — just like many folks did during Prohibition. I can't say that I blame him for that. You can't just take away what people are used to and not expect retaliation.

Rest in Peace, "Uncle Mott Stanley."

9. Volney Davis (January 29, 1902 – July 20, 1979)

On June 3, 1935, Volney Davis was charged with conspiracy to kidnap, and conspiracy to transport a kidnapped person across state lines. On June 7, 1935, he was sentenced to life imprisonment in the United States Federal Penitentiary at Leavenworth, Kansas. Volney was later received at Leavenworth as inmate number 47101, on June 14, 1935. He was later transferred to the United States Penitentiary at Alcatraz Island, California.

Volney, by this time, was tired of being on the lam, tired of the fear of being caught, and tired of running. He wished he hadn't joined the outlaw gang of hoodlums in Tulsa, Oklahoma, when he was a kid, and wished he could have taken it all back. After his capture, he outwardly became penitent and full of remorse. While he awaited sentencing, he wrote the following letter to his family:

June, 3, 1935

My dear Mother, Father and Sisters,

At last I am in a position where I can write to you all again. And I am sure glad that I can for it has been awful to be running

518

around over the country and not being able to write to the only ones in this world that really love me. I am here in Jail and have entered a plea of guilty to conspiracy in this case, I guess you have read about it in the papers. I will be sentenced on Friday this week. I don't know what I will get but I expect it will be a life sentence. I guess I will be sent to the government prison out in California, but before I go there I will be held for thirty days in some prison here. But I won't be here long enough time for you to come to see me. But just as soon as I am where you can have time to come to see me I will let you know when and where to come. I have some property and some money I want to turn over to you but if you can I want you to bring Ruby with you as there will be quite a bit of running around and she can do it better than you.

I would like to see all of you before I go away for good but it may be impossible as it will cost too much. Tell all the kids hello for me and tell the boys to take a lesson from my experience and never touch anything that don't belong to them. For a man can get more enjoyment out of ten dollars he has earned honestly than he can a thousand got dishonestly. I know from sad experience. I am telling you this to tell them because it may do some good and I know my life has been spared for some reason in this world and if I can keep some young boys from going wrong I have accomplished something in this world. I would give anything if I could start over again, for I know I could be successful in business if I was free for I have been fairly successful in business transactions while I have been dodging the law and I know if I had been free to have taken care of them like any other citizen I could have done much better.

Papa and Mamma I don't want you all to feel too bad about this for after all you will know where I am at night when you go

519

to sleep and I won't be in danger of being killed any moment. And I promise if such a thing should happen as I am ever a free man again I will make an honest living regardless of how little I can earn. And I will be a model prisoner where ever I go and for whatever length of time I get. I have been treated good here and am well in body. I hope wherever I go that I get work that won't be injurious to my health. Well, I don't know much more to write but I will sure write every time I get a chance and try to make up for the lost time.

Tell Uncle Newt hello and I sure would like to see him.

I am going to write a letter to Bertha soon and Irene. I think I know their address, but in case I don't, tell them you heard from me.

Be sure to tell me how Buelah is and when you saw her last. I sure do hope she gets well.

Guess Mildred is O.K. I hope so. Well, I will close. With all my love to you all, as ever,

Volney Davis

Volney Davis was received at Alcatraz, as inmate number 271, on October 26, 1935, where he would remain until April 2, 1947, when he was returned to Leavenworth, Kansas. Paranoia was part of Volney's personality and he thought somebody was out to get him. After he had testified in St. Paul, Minnesota, he figured somebody would surely "rub him out" at Alcatraz.

Volney Davis had been in Alcatraz for about 9 months when he received word that Alvin Karpis would be arriving there soon.

He just knew that Karpis had it in for him and would kill him if he got the chance. It had been a long time since Volney had fought in the ring in McAlester, Oklahoma. He thought that this was a good time to get back into fighting shape.

Volney played handball in the recreation yard every chance he had, giving it his all. The rumor around the prison was that he was planning to escape, and was getting in shape for a long swim.

Volney tried to befriend Karpis when the latter arrived at "The Rock." After all, they had some pretty big "scores" together in the past. Alvin Karpis was probably even more paranoid than Volney was, and Alvin felt sure that Volney was trying to get information out of him for the G-men. When he accused Volney of snitching, saying, *"Look Volney, the Touhy Gang wound up being wanted for that Hamm caper, and were even tried for it, but you know we did it. You know something? I'm still trying to figure out just how the hell the government finally figured out that it was us guys that took Hamm. I wasn't even indicted until April, 1936, and that was after you guys "took the fall" on the Bremer thing."* Volney knew that there wouldn't be any good relationship with "Ray" (as the boys in the joint all referred to Karpis). Volney, as early as January of 1937, thought that the next move would have to be his.

Karpis and Volney didn't even speak to each other for some time. Then, in June of 1937, Volney had worked himself into a frenzy, spending his free time on the hand ball court, and waiting for Karpis to "get him." He was out there on the court, giving it hell, when he saw Karpis come to the bottom of the steps. Volney motioned for "Ray" to come over to him. Karpis thought

521

that was strange since they hadn't even spoken to each other for months.

"Yeah, Volney, what is It?" Karpis could see that Volney was tense.

"I want to ask you something," said Volney.

"Go ahead," answered Karpis.

"What's the matter? Don't you want to talk to me or have anything to do with me," asked Volney.

Before Karpis even had a chance to reply, Volney said, "If you don't wanna talk, I don't care, 'cause I never did like you anyhow, and now I like you even less, and if you don't like what I'm saying, just open your mouth and I'll beat the piss out of you right here and now."

Karpis said he figured there was only one thing to do, so he swung at Volney and grazed the bridge of his nose, tearing the flesh a little. In a very short time, Volney gave him two right hooks and a left to the head. Karpis was trying to figure out who he was, where he was, and why he was lying on the ground in the yard. As a boot caught him in his rib cage, Karpis was gasping for air and trying to catch his breath when someone started yelling at Volney — "You bastard, don't you be kickin' that guy, he's no cat!" It was "Boxhead" Brown (inmate number 131), one of Karpis' friends. "Fightin's one thing, but kickin' is another," Boxhead screamed.

"Goddamn it! I gave him the first punch," Volney screamed angrily. The cell house screw quickly appeared and broke up the fight.

According to Karpis, he wouldn't say what happened and said that whatever Davis said was all right with him. He also stated later in his book, *"On The Rock,"* that he was up against a guy in perfect condition with hard muscles and excellent coordination, and one who had fought in the ring at McAlester, Oklahoma. (Davis was a slender man, only 5'9½" and weighed 142 pounds. Upon entering Alcatraz, it was documented that his physical examination found him to be in good condition except for an enlarged thyroid gland. His intelligence test found him to be about average and it was stated that he had a 6th grade education. He drank liquor but never used drugs).

The San Francisco Examiner ran an article headed, "Karpis knocked down and stomped by Davis."

Alvin Karpis and Volney Davis both had to spend time in the hole for fighting. According to Karpis, Volney filled out a "cop-out" slip and got out of the hole, but Karpis got out of the hole without the "cop-out" slip.

Another side of this story was told by William "Willie" Radkay, Alcatraz inmate number 666, during one of the documentaries he made concerning his incarceration in Alcatraz.

In his discussion about Alvin "Creepy" Karpis, Willie made the following comments: *When a guy got a visit from an FBI officer, he would come back to his cell and talk loudly — letting the other prisoners know what went on, everything that was said, and why they made the visit. When Karpis started talking about getting out on parole, the other guys laughed at him — thinking there was no way that he was going to get out on parole. So one day Karpis had a visit from two guys, and came back to his cell and said they were his lawyers. Another convict, who was mopping the corridor, yelled out that he saw the two guys check in their guns — meaning that the two visitors were FBI agents, not lawyers. When Volney Davis heard this, he waited to get Karpis out in the yard, and he beat the shit out of him — smashing his head into the concrete. Machine Gun Kelly and all the other guys hated Karpis because he had lied, and they knew he had snitched on someone. After Karpis did get out on parole — and later on, the story was that he committed suicide — the guys at Alcatraz knew he was tracked down and killed for snitching. They thought the assassination was pulled off by two brothers out of Michigan."*

Willie didn't mention the names of the assassination team.

Volney Davis carried out his promise to his parents and — other than the fight with Alvin Karpis — was a model prisoner during his time in prison at Alcatraz. Volney, slim and white haired at age 52, appealed his sentence in July of 1954, claiming he did not know his constitutional rights when he pled guilty. He lost that appeal. However, on September 2, 1957, the Governor of Oklahoma paroled Volney Davis from his 1923 murder conviction which, in effect, transferred him to custody of the United States Federal Penitentiary at Leavenworth, Kansas, where he served out his life sentence for the Bremer kidnapping.

Then on August 4, 1959, Volney Davis was finally released on parole to go to work for Mr. Ed Galley, owner of a printing shop named El Sobrante, located at 3575 San Pablo Dam Road, El Sobrante, California.

In keeping with his promise to his family after his guilty verdict in 1935, Volney Davis would now make a living at an honest job.

Then, on June 9, 1966, Volney Davis received a pardon from President Lyndon Johnson.

It was January 14, 1969, before Volney's old buddy, Alvin Karpis, was paroled and deported to Canada. He had served nearly 33 years for his role in the Hamm kidnapping.

Author's note:

I corresponded with a lady by the name of Melissa A. Kendrick, who was Volney Davis' nurse in his later years when he was a patient at the Sebastopol Convalescent Hospital, located at 477 Petaluma Avenue in Sebastopol, California, which was about 52 miles north of San Francisco, California.

Melissa said that Volney seemed to be a nice old guy and she really liked him. She said he told her that he used to be a member of the Ma Barker Gang and that he had "narced" (telling someone in authority about a wrongdoing) on them when he was sent to prison. He was afraid that the gang was going to find him. She said that she had never heard of this gang, but that Volney was very afraid of them, and that the staff there tried to calm him down and tried to lessen his fears.

Melissa also said that he wasn't there a very long time, but she could remember him well. He was in the bed by the window in room 11, in the center hall. He was rather tall and very thin, and he was lonely and

> *scared. She said that one day they were in the room alone and she told him that she wouldn't let anyone come in to harm him.*
>
> *Melissa couldn't remember if Volney passed away while at the nursing home or if he died after he was moved to a hospital. She only remembered that he was there in the late 1970s which would have been shortly before his death.*

On August 26, 1979, Volney Davis' old buddy, Alvin Karpis, died from an apparent heart attack at his last home, in Torremolinos, Spain. It was first believed he had taken an overdose of his prescribed sleeping pills. Alvin also must have had demons that kept him from being able to sleep well.

From corresponding with a couple of Volney Davis' nephews over the years, I have learned a few additional things about him. In the mid 1960s, after he had been released from prison and pardoned by President Johnson, Volney was living in the Sonoma - Napa area. He was living with a very interesting woman who was an artist that painted mostly nudes. She and Volney lived on the river, and Volney shared some stories with his nephew about hanging out on the river with some hippies who were high on acid and ran around naked. Volney's nephew said that Volney was "quite a character."

At the time of Volney's death he had worked in maintenance and repair for about 5 years for a company known as "Bohemian Grove." He had resided at 6980 Mirabel Road, in Forestville, California, which is located in Sonoma County. The person who contributed this information, which was included on the death certificate, was James Ervin. He referred to himself as Volney's stepson, and, at the time, was residing at 17 Echo Drive, Corte Madera, California.

Volney's doctor stated on his death certificate that Volney had suffered from acute pneumonia for one day, and had suffered from extreme atherosclerosis for years. He also stated that Volney suffered from multiple premature senile processes.

Volney Everett Davis was laid to rest on July 23, 1979, at Sebastopol Evergreen Lawn, in Sebastopol, California.

Rest in Peace, "Curly."

10. Edna Murray "Potter" (May 26, 1898 – April 13, 1966)

It was August of 1969 when my husband, Casey Tippet, and I had just become parents of our daughter, Stacy Tonette Tippet, and I wanted to tell everyone about her arrival. I tried to call the phone number that I had in my address book for Grandma Edna, on Market Street, in San Francisco, California. It was disappointing and a bit worrisome to find out that the phone number had been disconnected. Next I called Aunt Doris. Aunt Doris was so happy to hear from me. She wanted to know all about what I had been doing, how my life was going, where we lived, what my husband did, what we liked to do, what we named our daughter, and just fired question after question at me. I was finally able to tell her that I had tried to contact Grandma Edna, and found that her phone number was no longer in service. "Oh Honey," Aunt Doris said, "your grandma died."

"She died!" I exclaimed. "When did she die?"

"Oh, I don't know, it was several years ago," Aunt Doris told me.

I asked, "What was the matter with her?"

"Well, she was old," aunt Doris responded. "She was in her seventies, I think."

"Well, nobody told me," I said.

"Oh honey," Aunt Doris said, "we (Edna and Doris) hadn't talked for years. She left me a life insurance policy and I just told them to keep it! I didn't want anything from her, and I didn't want anything to do with her funeral."

I couldn't believe my ears. "Why, Aunt 'Dode'? She was your sister."

"She tried to destroy me!" Doris responded. "She told Jay's mother everything she could think of to hurt our relationship."

At that point, I didn't know what to say. Doris didn't remember and didn't care when Grandma Edna had died, where she was buried, or anything about her. I couldn't believe that they had become so distanced from each other. Aunt Dode and I kept in touch for a few years after that and I always enjoyed corresponding with her, but I could never understand her relationship with my Grandma Edna.

I also felt pretty badly about not having stayed in contact with Grandma Edna. I worried that maybe there wasn't anyone to coordinate her final arrangements — maybe the county had just put her in a wooden box and buried her in an unmarked grave. I grieved about Grandma Edna's death for a long time.

Uncle Mott, ("Little" Mott) wouldn't say much about why Doris and Edna were such enemies either, but he mentioned one time that he thought that his mother, Aunt Dode, didn't care for the man Edna was married to. I know that wouldn't have stopped Doris from talking to her sister if she had wanted to. I believe that after the smoke had cleared and Doris had started a new life with her husband, Jay, she didn't want her current mother-in-law to be informed by Edna of her wilder days. And Edna, still reminiscing about her wild days, may have easily "let the cat out of the bag."

It was in the year 2006 when my genealogy friend, Vicki Walker Cooper, called me early one morning with the news that — after staying up all night — she had found out when Grandma Edna had passed away, and where she was buried. You just had to know how important it was to Edna to have a proper funeral service and a dignified burial in a respectable cemetery in order to understand how totally elated I was to receive this information. And to this day, it is just the most amazing thing to me.

Edna's last marriage was to Henry Alexander Potter, Technician 5th Grade, United States Army. This marriage entitled her to a burial plot in the Golden Gate National Cemetery, in San Mateo County, in San Bruno, California.

Martha Edna Potter, had passed away on April 13, 1966, at the age of 67. She was buried on April 15, 1966, in Plot Number 2c2744 in the Golden Gate National Cemetery, 1300 Sneath Lane, in San Bruno, California. The cemetery was dedicated on Decoration Day (later named Memorial Day), May 30, 1942, and is now closed to new entries. I am pleased to know that Grandma Edna must surely have been comforted by knowing that this plot was reserved for her. Although closed to new internments, it remains an absolutely beautiful cemetery, groomed to perfection, and decorated on every appropriate occasion.

A small obituary in the San Francisco newspaper read:

Potter, Martha E. 4-13-1966, Devoted wife of Henry Potter, loving sister of Giney (should say Ginney) Stanley and Doris McCormick. Services, Friday afternoon 12:15 o'clock at Halstead and Co., 1123 Sutter St. Interment, Golden Gate National Cemetery.

I find it humorously ironic to recall how one of Edna's greatest fears was dispelled — that of being buried in potter's field, where the poor and unidentified are buried at public expense. In the end, it was a man named "Potter" — U. S. Army Technician, Henry Potter, her 6th and final husband — who made it possible for her, through marriage, to be given a dignified burial, with honor and respect, in a U. S. National Cemetery — and NOT in potter's field.

Edna and her husband, Henry, a service station attendant, were living at 1657 Market Street, in San Francisco. On or about April 3, 1966, she was taken to Children's Hospital at 3700 California Street (later renamed as "The California Pacific Medical Center"). She had surgery on April 5th for intestinal ulceration and constriction. On April 9th, she had another surgery due to post operative blood clots and bilateral leg gangrene. In addition to these ailments, at the time of her death at 10:35 a.m. on April 13, 1966, she also suffered from hypertension, osteoporosis and emphysema.

I feel sad when I think of my Grandma Edna's life. Although she never seemed to regret any of her past, and appeared to enjoy reminiscing about it, I can't help but believe that she regretted not having much to show for it. I can't remember that she had any hobbies or activities that she enjoyed doing. I don't believe that she ever had any collections or keepsakes that were dear to her. Edna never possessed any valuables that I was aware of. Besides the magnificent string of pearls that she told me about having at one time, she never talked about having anything of value. Maybe all those many years on the lam, running and hiding and living out of a suitcase, had something to do with it. As far as I know, she had always resided in small modest apartments and had lived a simple life. I think she was happy as long as she had her beer and cigarettes — especially if she had someone to listen to her stories.

Edna and Doris grew up together, fighting like sisters do, and lived together and covered for each other throughout their criminal careers, up into their mid-thirties. It was long after they had changed their ways of life that they started blaming each other for their past lives and became estranged. But even though Doris wouldn't speak to her, Edna made one final attempt for forgiveness by leaving her the only thing of value she had — a small $1,000 life insurance policy. But Doris, undoubtedly the more stubborn of the two, wouldn't accept it — even after her sister's death.

Probably, if she had lived in today's world, and was afforded treatment by medical professionals, Edna would have been diagnosed as bi-polar, and maybe with attention deficit disorder (ADD). There is no doubt in my mind that she had a chemical imbalance and lived most of her life treating herself with whatever remedy she could find — mostly with alcohol.

Edna wasn't a bad person. She got caught up in the excitement of the outlaw life, and eventually with a gang of people

531

that not only did she not trust, but she feared would kill her at the drop of a hat. Even Volney Davis, whom she loved more than anyone, wasn't someone that she could trust not to turn on her. Edna would never have testified against Volney had he not been the one to "cave in" first. And Jess Doyle was telling his story long before Edna told anything.

She wasn't stupid — and she knew the rules. She was "street smart" and never gave up anything that she didn't have to — not to the "laws" anyway. And even though she told a lot of stories, Edna took many secrets with her to her grave.

Rest in peace, "Grandma Rabbit."

Martha Edna Stanley Potter's final resting place

Acknowledgments

Larry Alloway

Mary Jane Alloway

Tom Armour

Robert (Bob) Bates

Jill Beardsley

Lisa Canaday

Mickey Canaday

Vicki Walker Cooper

Estella Cox

Ronald Davis

Tom Donahue

Stephan Dumire

Robert (Bob) Ernst

Verla Geller

Mario Gomes

Al Grooms

Jeffrey Gusfield

William J. (Bill) Helmer

Ken Holmes

Sandy Jones

Mike "Spanky" Koch

Robert (Bob) Livesey

Paul Maccabee

Linda Mattix

Rick Mattix

Shelley Mitchell

Naomi Morgan

R. D. (Ron) Morgan

Debbie Moss

Bridget Nielson

Patti Tippet Nutt

Naomi Keith Paden

Preston LeRoy Paden

Fred Mark Palmer

Colleen Pecora

John Neal Phillips

Sheriff Johnny Philpot

Martha Edna Stanley Potter

Ellen Poulsen

Karron Prince

Ted Prince

Robert Raines

Jim Redstone

Bick Smith

Cynthia Schreiner Smith

Lucy Smith

Robert "Buffalo Bob" Smith

Melissa Spawn

Jim Spawn

Louise Stanley

Mike Stanley

William James (Bill) Stanley

Amy Stovall

Patty Terry

Casey C. Tippet

David C. Tippet

Michael Webb

Buddy Barrow Williams

Christie Williams

Robert (Bob) Winter

Special Thanks

Hours of writing letters, hours of phone conversations and taking notes, reading thousands of pages of history, diggin' up bones and weeding out the myths, formed the backbone that this book was built on.

From my list of folks that helped me along this book-writing journey, I would like to give special thanks to the following people:

Al Grooms – Al definitely brightened my day when he provided me with the FBI files that he had found on my family. I was in awe with my nose glued to those files for days. I remember Al once told me that the FBI probably had a file on me too.

Thank You very much, Mr. Grooms.

Jeffrey C. Gusfield – Jeff is a wonderful person to have as a friend. He always has something kind to say. Even when he was working on his book, *"Deadly Valentines,"* Jeff took time away from his own writing project to help me. He once spent many hours going through my manuscript and setting up "The Table of Contents" for me.

Thank You very much, Mr. Gusfield.

William J. (Bill) Helmer – Bill co-authored some excellent True Crime genre books with Rick Mattix and has a beautiful and fluid writing style that will never be matched. He also shared many facts and insights with me that he believed would help me to better know and understand my family history for my book. In addition, he was very helpful in assisting me in determining the actual title of this book. I will always be grateful to Bill, for his help and, most of all, for his friendship.

Thank You very much, Mr. Helmer.

Rick Mattix – Rick's collection of Gangster Era history and files were like none other. Researching the Gangster Era had been his passion for most of his life. Rick was always willing to share his research with me, and for that act of kindness, I will be forever grateful. Rick Mattix passed away before I could finish my book, and although I was very saddened, not only to lose a friend, but, also I then knew that he would never see my finished product. This made me even more determined to "get the facts" the way Rick would have wanted.

Thank You very much, Mr. Mattix.

Shelley Mitchell – Shelley, a gangster historian in her own right, has a great knack for spotting grammatical errors, misspelled words, and poor punctuation. I was so thankful when she agreed to this tedious job of helping me with the first edit.

Thank You very much, Ms. Mitchell.

Debbie Moss – From the time that Rick Mattix introduced me to Debbie Moss, who is a cousin of Blanche Barrow, we have definitely been "comrades in crime." I was so excited when Debbie shared with me the photos she had of her cousin, Blanche Barrow,

538

and my Grandma Edna Murray when they were "pen pals" at the Women's State Penitentiary in Jefferson City, Missouri, from February, 1935, until March of 1939. Debbie has also helped me many times with her expertise in graphics design, doing the artwork for my website, www.pamtippet.com, and assisting me with the cleaning and preparation of pictures for my book. In addition to her professional talents, Debbie has become a personal friend of mine with whom I have spent many pleasurable hours of fun, laughter, and the best of times.

Thank You very much, Ms. Moss.

Ellen Poulsen – Author of *"Don't Call Us Molls: Women of the John Dillinger Gang,"* Ellen gave us the most information that had ever been uncovered on the paramours of the 1930s gangsters. This was the first book I purchased while researching for my story. I felt very blessed that it was Rick Mattix who had first introduced Ellen to me, and while we were both devastated by Rick's death, Ellen knew of my additional grief – that I had also lost my best supporter. She said she would help me in any way that she could – and little did I know just how much help she would be!

Thank You very much, Ms. Poulsen.

Robert "Buffalo Bob" Smith – I had written my story – pretty much had said everything I wanted to say – and was in somewhat of a slump when our mutual friend, Bill Helmer, introduced Bob to me. Bill said "… Bob's a mathematical genius, a great fact-checker, knows a lot about some useful stuff, including proof-reading, and especially, indexing." Bob also assisted in researching, verifying, and expanding on some important events in this book. Bill was right, and Bob has been my right and left hand on this project, as well as becoming a great friend.

Thank You very much, Mr. Smith.

Robert (Bob) Winter – Bob is another very knowledgeable historian who has researched the history of the Barker-Karpis Gang for many a year. He even wrote his own book about them, *"Mean Men – The Sons of Ma Barker."* Bob very graciously shared with me all he had learned about my family, and he certainly opened my eyes to several things. We became very good friends and corresponded frequently until he passed away on September 11, 2012. Bob told me that I was the only relative of a gangster or outlaw that he ever corresponded with.

Thank You very much, Mr. Winter, and may you rest in peace.

In Memory of Rick "Mad Dog" Mattix
(September 21, 1953 – October 27, 2010)

After the death of a true friend, Rick Mattix, his wife Linda said to me, "Rick was really excited — well, as excited as Rick ever got — about you writing a book about your Grandma." Linda went on to say that Rick believed the story of Edna Murray was a story that needed to be told, and who else would know her better than her granddaughter.

Rick Mattix was the first historian to send me information and pictures concerning my Grandma Edna's criminal career. And if you knew anything about Rick "Mad Dog" Mattix, you knew that his gangster era collection is huge. Rick helped me so much — more than anyone else ever could have — I am sure. I feel so fortunate to have known him, to have been able to "pick his brain," to have had him as a friend and to have enjoyed many fun times with him and Linda.

As many of us "Gangsterologists" do, I too, miss Rick very much. Hardly a day goes by, especially when working on my book, that I don't have a question for him, or want to discuss something with him, or run across something I think he would enjoy seeing or reading. It's for certain that I will always remember Rick and the book that he and his good friend, Bill Helmer, wrote, *"The Complete Public Enemy Almanac."*

This book will always have a permanent spot on my desk.

Rest in peace, "Mad Dog."

541

Sources – Documents

American Merchant Marine at War, www.usmm.org

Archival Records Operations Unit, NARA Pacific Region, San Francisco, CA

California Death Records Index, Golden Gate National Cemetery, San Bruno, CA

Carthage, Missouri, Public Library

County of San Francisco Vital Records, San Francisco, CA

Emporia Gazette (January 14, 1935), Emporia, KS

Federal Bureau of Investigation, Washington, DC

Files from the Federal Bureau of Investigation

Gangster Museum of America, Hot Springs, AR

Gangsterologists Group

Hutchinson Correctional Facility, Hutchinson, Kansas

Jefferson City Post-Tribune, Jefferson City, MO

Joplin, Missouri, Library

Joplin Globe, Joplin, MO

Joplin News Herald, Joplin, MO

Kansas State Historical Society

Little Rock Library, Little Rock, AR

Lubbock Morning Avalanche (August 24, 1934), Lubbock, TX

Lyons Daily News (1936), Lyons, KS

Lyons Public Library, Lyons, KS

Miami Public Library, Miami, OK

Milwaukee Journal Sentinel (September 11, 2009), Milwaukee, WI

Minneapolis Star Tribune (Feb. 14, 2009), Minneapolis, MN

Missouri Dept. of Corrections, Jefferson City, MO

Missouri State Archives, Jefferson City, MO

Norton County News Files, Norton, KS

Oakland Tribune (August 24, 1934), Oakland, CA

Office of Vital Records, Sacramento, CA

Oklahombres Association

Ottawa County School Census (1916-1918), Ottawa County, OK

Parsons Public Library, Parsons, KS

PIC (Partners in Crime)

Pittsburg Public Library, Pittsburg, KS

Rice County Court Records, Lyons, KS

San Mateo Times (August 24, 1934), San Mateo, CA

Sapulpa, Oklahoma, Historical Society

Sapulpa Daily Herald, Sapulpa, OK

St. Paul, MN Gangster Tour

St. Paul, MN Pioneer Press (1936)

The Daily Oklahoman (Feb. 12, 1935)

True Detective Magazine

U. S. Bureau of Investigation Files

U. S. Census Records (1860-1920)

U. S. Department of Justice, Washington, DC

Vinita Public Library, Vinita, OK

Sources – Books

A Devil Incarnate – William Radkay, as told to Patty Terry, 2005

A Murder in Tulsa – Michael Koch, 2009

Bloodletters and Badmen – Jay Robert Nash, 1973

Dillinger: The Untold Story – G. Russell Girardin, William J. Helmer, Rick Mattix, 2005

Don't Call Us Molls – Ellen Poulsen, 2007

Here's to Crime – Courtney Ryley Cooper, 1937

In Prison – Kate Richards O'Hare, 1920

Irish O'Malley & the Ozark Mountain Boys – R. D. Morgan, 2011

J. Edgar Hoover & His G-men – William B. Breuer, 1995

Lawmen Crimebusters and Champions of Justice – John Slate, R. U. Steinburg, 1991

"Ma" – The Life and Times of Ma Barker & Her Boys – John Koblas, 2007

Mean Men – The Sons of Ma Barker – Robert Winter, 2000

My Life with Bonnie & Clyde – Blanche Caldwell Barrow, John Neal Phillips, 2005

On the Rock (Special Edition) – Alvin Karpis, as told to Robert Livesey, 1980

Outlaws Mobsters and Murderers – Diana Claitor, 1991

Prison Labor for Private Profit – Kate Richards O'Hare, 1925

Robbin' Banks & Killin' Cops – Robert R. Ernst, 2009

Taming the Sooner State – R. D. Morgan, 2007

The Complete Public Enemy Almanac – William J. Helmer & Rick Mattix, 2007

The Dillinger Days – John Toland, 1995

The FBI in Peace and War – Frederick Lewis Collins, Lester December, 1962

The FBI Story – Don Whitehead, 1956

"Friends & Fun"

Along my researching and book writing journey are some of my best memories. Here are a few that I would like to share with my readers.

Shelley Mitchell, Buddy Barrow, Pam Paden Tippet, Fred Mark Palmer, Robert Raines, Christie Barrow and Debbie Moss – Hangin' out at the Gangster Museum of America, Hot Springs, Arkansas.

Mike "Spanky" Koch, Ken Holmes, Pam Paden Tippet, Jill Beardsley, Debbie Moss, Buddy Barrow and Christie Barrow – "Grave 'Stompin'" in Madill, Oklahoma.

Rick "Mad Dog" Mattix, Mike "Spanky" Koch, R. D. "Ron" Morgan, James Knight and Pam Paden Tippet – spending a little quality time at the Bonnie & Clyde apartment in Joplin, Missouri.

Pam Paden Tippet and Ryan McArdle (aka "Baby Face" Nelson) – at the Wabasha Caves Gangsters Tour in St. Paul, Minnesota.

Mr. Robert "Bob" Winter, author of *"Mean Men: The Sons of Ma Barker"* – Bob was a great friend, and I enjoyed corresponding with him for several years.

Robert A. "Buffalo Bob" Smith (Indexer Deluxe), and author Pam Paden Tippet share a laugh concerning, "... surely we could find just a few more aliases to put in this index!"

Dennis Lippe, Jill Beardsley, Karen Lippe, Debbie Moss, Pam Paden Tippet, Christie Barrow, Mike "Spanky" Koch, Naomi Morgan, R. D. "Ron" Morgan and Buddy Barrow – Hangin' out in Claremore, Oklahoma, at the Oklahombres Rendezvous.

Debbie Moss of DebeZ Graphics – our "website, book covers, and all that" girl – and the notorious, one and only, William J. "Bill" Helmer – author of so many gangster books that we have lost count.

Edna Murray's granddaughter, Pam Paden Tippet, with none other than Grandma Edna Murray – Played by Cynthia Schreiner Smith, Gangster Tour Guide, at the Wabasha Caves in St. Paul, Minnesota.

Freda Dillard, Boots Hinton, and Ken Holmes behind the counter at the "Bonnie & Clyde Ambush Museum" in Gibsland, Louisiana.

Hangin' Judge Parker (aka Dennis Lippe), Edna "Rabbit" Murray (aka Pam Paden Tippet), Rose of Cimarron (aka Naomi Morgan), and Belle Starr (aka Karen Lippe) – Oklahombres Rendezvous in Claremore, Oklahoma.

Sequoyah County Oklahoma Sheriff Johnny Philpot takes Pretty Boy Floyd's Tommygun away from Edna "The Kissing Bandit" Murray (aka Pam Paden Tippet). Edna is asking, "How 'bout a kiss and you let me keep the Tommy?"

We meet again – At the Wabasha Caves Gangster Tour, Brett Williams (aka "John Dillinger") and "The Kissing Bandit's" granddaughter, Pam Paden Tippet.

Lunch at "Fred & Red Chili" in Joplin, Missouri, before going to the book signing at "Always Buying Books," 5357 N. Main St., Joplin - Debbie Moss, Naomi Morgan, R. D. "Ron" Morgan, Pam Paden Tippet, and Mike "Spanky" Koch.

Dave Otis and the "Kissing Bandit's" granddaughter, Pam Paden Tippet, standing in front of Buddy Barrow's exact replica of the 1934 "Bonnie & Clyde" death car.

Buddy Barrow, nephew of Clyde Barrow, is shown under the gun of the granddaughter of Edna "The Kissing Bandit" (aka "Rabbit") Murray. Rabbit borrowed the colt .45 from Frank West after he shot Sam Starr.

In Sallisaw, Oklahoma, "The boys are inside – They have some pretty good bread here, but we're after the dough."

Pam Paden "Rabbit" Tippet and Rick "Mad Dog" Mattix – who says a rabbit and a dog can't be buddies?

Verla Geller, Great Niece of Arrie "Kate" Barker, R. D. "Ron" Morgan, Rick "Mad Dog" Mattix and Pam Paden Tippet – at a Joplin, Missouri, book signing on 12-08-07.

Whenever we go to the Akins Cemetery just outside of Sallisaw, Oklahoma, we always stop and pay a tribute to Charles A. "Pretty Boy" Floyd. If at all possible, we pour him a beer and drink a toast. This was on October 15, 2010. Rest in Peace, Charlie.

Pam Paden "Rabbit" Tippet with a Tommygun – gets the story while sitting on Al Capone's lap – at the Gangster Museum of America, Hot Springs, Arkansas.

At the Halloween Gangster Party – "Comrades in Crime" for over 48 years – Pam and Casey Tippet

INDEX

558

M

S